Schooldays in Imperial Japan

SCHOOLDAYS IN IMPERIAL JAPAN

A Study in the Culture of a Student Elite

Donald Roden

University of California Press

Berkeley / Los Angeles / London

University of California Press
Berkeley and Los Angeles, California
University of California Press, Ltd.
London, England
© 1980 by The Regents of the University of California
Printed in the United States of America

1 2 3 4 5 6 7 8 9

Library of Congress Cataloging in Publication Data

Roden, Donald T
   Schooldays in Imperial Japan. A study in the
culture of a student elite

   Originally presented as the author's thesis,
University of Wisconsin, 1975.
   "Published under the auspices of the Center for
Japanese and Korean Studies, University of California,
Berkeley."
   Bibliography: p.
   Includes index.
   1. Education—Japan—History. 2. Students—
Japan—History. 3. Elite (Social sciences)—Japan—
History. I. California. University. Center for
Japanese and Korean Studies. II. Title.
LA1311.R62   1980   370'.952   79-64477
ISBN 0-520-03910-6 .

For Chie

Contents

Abbreviations   ix
Preface   xi
Introduction   1

ONE/Toward the Foundation of the Higher Schools   13

TWO/Between Nation and Campus: The Making
of the Higher School Gentleman   42

THREE/Seclusion and Self-Government   71

FOUR/The Culture of Ceremony   95

FIVE/Public Tyranny   133

SIX/The Higher School Catharsis   154

SEVEN/From Meiji to Taishō: Broadening Perspectives
and Enduring Traditions   192

EIGHT/The Higher Schools and Japanese Society   230

Appendixes   255
Glossary   261
Bibliography   269
Index   289

Abbreviations

DIKGKZ	*Dai Ichi Kōtō Gakkō Kōyūkai zasshi*
Gokō gojūnenshi	Dai Go Kōtō Gakkō Kaikō Gakujūnen Kinenkai, ed., *Gokō gojūnenshi* (Kumamoto, 1939)
"Jiyūryōshi"	Dai San Kōtō Gakkō Kishukusha Ryōshi Henshūbu, ed., "Jiyūryōshi" (unpublished manuscript)
KKGK	*Kyūsei kōtō gakkōshi kenkyū*
Kōryōshi	Dai Ichi Kōtō Gakkō Kishukuryō, ed., *Kōryōshi* (Tokyo, 1925)
Rokujūnenshi	Dai Ichi Kōtō Gakkō, ed., *Dai Ichi Kōtō Gakkō rokujūnenshi* (Tokyo, 1939)
Shūgakuryōshi	Shūgakuryōshi Hensanbu, ed., *Shūgakuryōshi* (Kumamoto, 1938)

Preface

Some years ago Frederick Rudolph expressed concern over the institutional approach to the history of education, an approach that dwelled on curriculum, administration, and endowments, but neglected student culture as a "historical tradition." [1] A recent surge of books, stimulated in part by campus uprisings in the late 1960s, indicates that the student is no longer the object of historiographic neglect. Still, research tends to focus on sporadic decades when students have made a conspicuous entrance on history's public stage. Comparatively little is written about the inner-life of the school, the daily customs of the students, and the private interactions between teacher and pupil.

This book attempts to probe the behavioral changes and continuities within one institution—the Japanese higher school—from the late-nineteenth century to the outbreak of World War II. Because the higher schools admitted a mere fraction of 1 percent of late-adolescent cohorts in any given year, the book does not constitute a history of modern Japanese youth; rather, it is a history of the values and mores of a tiny community of students and teachers, which assumed a major role in defining social status and high culture in prewar Japan. Attention centers, therefore, on the higher school lifestyle as the cultural ideology of an academic elite. I hope that the book will contribute to an understanding not only of Japanese education but of socialization for leadership in a newly industrialized society. The higher schools flourished in that wider historical arena, which they shared with the British public school, the German Gymnasium, and the New England liberal arts college.

From the emergence of *Schooldays in Imperial Japan* as a Uni-

1. Frederick Rudolph, "Neglect of Students as a Historical Tradition," in Lawrence Dennis and Joseph Kauffman, eds., *The College and the Student* (Washington, D.C., 1966), pp. 47–58.

versity of Wisconsin dissertation, I have accumulated numerous debts. First, I am grateful to John Dower and Harry Harootunian. The dissertation could never have been completed in the fall of 1975 without Professor Dower's encouragement, incisive criticism, and generous willingness to peruse chapters at the busiest of times. My debts to Professor Harootunian span nearly a decade. He has stimulated my interest in social history, offered helpful suggestions for revising the manuscript, and given generously of his time and hospitality. Professor Harootunian's perspective on the pervasive tensions between politics and culture—the public and private spheres of action in prewar Japan—has been a guiding light through all phases of this project. Special thanks must also go to Henry D. Smith and Earl Kinmonth. Before I commenced the dissertation, Professor Smith shared information about sources and research institutes in Japan and introduced me to the special role of the higher schools in shaping prewar thought. As a friend and colleague, Professor Kinmonth has offered me numerous insights into the general temperament of Meiji youth.

In Japan my debts are equally great. Toita Tomoyoshi and Terasaki Masao advised me and lent valuable materials from their personal collections. Professor Terasaki has continued to offer suggestions through the final stages of revision. I have benefited as well from younger colleagues and friends, especially Matsuda Takeshi, Ishikawa Taneo, and Hashimoto Mitsuru. To numerous higher school alumni who generously shared their memories and memorabilia with me, I owe a special debt of gratitude. They have provided abundant material for me both to praise and blame the school that so deeply affected their personal lives. I wish especially to thank Takahashi Samon, Yamauchi Naosuke, and Komatsu Michio for helping me to acquire photographs from the albums of Hirosaki and First Higher. Unless otherwise stated, the photographs were taken during the 1920s or 1930s.

In addition, the following persons have read all or parts of the manuscript at various stages: Rudolph Bell, Paul Clemens, Martin Collcutt, Marius Jansen, Solomon Levine, Maurice Meisner, and Deirdre Roden. Professor Ardath Burks read the entire penultimate draft with great care; and the staff at University of California Press, notably Gladys Castor and Susan Peters, deserve my special thanks. For everyone's suggestions I am most grateful, although the author alone bears responsibility for existing errors.

In the interest of uniformity, I have adhered to several stylistic conventions. Although they were technically called "higher middle schools" until 1894, I use the simpler and more widely understood term "higher school" throughout the narrative. Further, I have chosen the title "headmaster" over "principal" for chief administrators who, on several occasions, identified themselves with their counterparts at Rugby and Eton. "Schooldays" appears as one word, which is in accordance with *The Oxford English Dictionary*. I also take this opportunity to acknowledge assistance from Patrick McCarthy's *Matthew Arnold and the Three Classes* (New York, 1964), John Gillis's *Youth and History* (New York, 1974), David Newsome's *Godliness and Good Learning* (London, 1961), and S. N. Eisenstadt's *From Generation to Generation* (New York, 1964) in selecting epigraphs from the works of Thomas Arnold, Edward Thring, and Elie Halévy.

Finally, an expression of gratitude to my family, and most especially to my wife, Chie, whose unending help and encouragement has made this book a reality.

Introduction

The flowers of literature are blooming
And the great tide of ideas gushes forth.
How joyful we are to be here in the capital
As students of the First Higher School
Where myriad volumes are stored
And where the autumnal sunset over Musashino
Entices us to sing.

The lead stanza of a school song may have run through the mind of a seventeen-year-old student as he waited at Utsunomiya Station for the evening express that would carry him from the home of his parents, a provincial town in Tochigi prefecture, to the home of his spirit, the First Higher School in Tokyo.[1] It was 1920, the year when the World War I boom in Japan's industrial economy suddenly collapsed. Hara Kei was serving his third year as the first untitled prime minister, and the question of universal suffrage was before the Forty-second Diet. It was also the year when the first May Day celebration was staged by labor unions in Ueno Park; when the popular magazine *The Housewife's Friend* entered its third year of circulation; and when young shoppers on the Ginza in Tokyo hummed the latest hit song, "Soap Bubbles." But all of this was of little concern to the student, who was dressed in an old, worn-out uniform, stood on battered wooden clogs, and boasted that "historical events" had no influence on his "inner

1. The scene is based largely on Tezuka Tomio's recollections in *Ichi seinen no shisō no ayumi* (Tokyo, 1966), esp. pp. 43–44. I have taken liberties in pinpointing the date (although 1920 is the year Tezuka entered the First Higher School) and providing additional historical background in order to place the author's nostalgic recollections in a broader social context.

heart."[2] The train screeched to a halt, and the student boarded a stuffy, malodorous car filled with exhausted passengers slumped over in their seats and oblivious of their own stench. Jolted from his reverie by the visceral realities of commuting, the student glared briefly at the "ignorant crowd" (*shūgu*). Then, with his head in the air, he clumped loudly down the aisle to a vacant seat, sat down, closed his eyes, and struggled to refocus his thoughts on "the greatest problems of existence."

Who is this student who sways on high wooden clogs when society wears shoes, who invokes philosophy when society talks of serialized romance, who contemplates the existence of an inner soul when society struggles for bodily sustenance? Such audacious posturing is often associated with aristocracy in decline or with bohemian counterculture; but this student is neither scion of a faltering noble house nor avant-garde artist. He comes from a rural middle-class household of modest means, prodigious energy, and total ignorance of "sweetness and light." The cultural style he affects is a recent acquisition, bestowed by an educational experience that seems singularly out of touch with the technological and economic demands of a mass, industrial society. He is a "cultivated man," who stands in bold defiance of the "specialized expert" and the norms of rational performance.[3] How such a student could make so conspicuous an appearance on the social landscape of prewar Japan, and why his appearance is important to perceptions of class, culture, and personality, are questions that strike at the core of this study.

Education and Social Structure in the Modernization of Japan

During the Meiji period (1868–1912), Japan experienced what R. R. Palmer has called "the most remarkable transformation ever undergone by any people in so short a time."[4] What ap-

2. Ibid., p. 24.
3. The tensions between the "cultivated man" and the "expert" are discussed in Max Weber, *From Max Weber: Essays in Sociology*, trans. Hans Gerth and C. Wright Mills (New York, 1958), pp. 235–244, 426–438.
4. R. R. Palmer and Joel Colton, *A History of the Modern World* (New York, 1978), p. 541. The statement first drew my attention from reading Kenneth Pyle, *The New Generation in Meiji Japan* (Stanford, Calif., 1969), p. 3. Pyle used an earlier edition of Palmer's textbook, which, despite successive revisions, has not changed its lofty estimate of Japan's transformation.

peared in the early 1800s to be a retrogressive network of agrarian-feudal domains, fossilized from within and secluded from without, emerged in the early twentieth century as a rapidly industrializing nation-state and world power. Critical to this metamorphosis was the Meiji Restoration, a conjuncture of social disruptions and political reforms spanning four decades (ca. 1840–1880). The Restoration culminated in the overthrow of the Tokugawa Bakufu and the installation of a bold, new leadership of young samurai and court reformers who served as national spokesmen under the unifying aegis of the revitalized Imperial house. Notable actions taken by the young Meiji leaders included the abolition of hereditary class distinctions among samurai, peasants, and merchants; the consolidation of the former feudal domains into a single political unit, the viability of which would be guaranteed by a legal-rational constitution and a vast civil bureaucracy; the establishment of a universal tax base for the development of industry and communications; and the organization of a national school system for the transmission of Western learning. The reforms were instrumental in the emergence of Japan as a highly differentiated, urban-industrial power by 1920.

Yet, for all the drama of Japan as the first non-Western civilization to industrialize and to join the family of imperialist nations, historians on both sides of the Pacific and of all theoretical persuasions have great difficulty attaching an unambiguously revolutionary label to the nation's late-nineteenth-century transformation. The dilemma of choosing appropriate categories of analysis was already apparent between 1925 and 1935, when Japanese historians debated whether the Meiji Restoration was the harbinger of bourgeois-democratic revolution or a more elaborate, though still undisguisable, form of feudal absolutism.[5] Striving for a new synthesis before the outbreak of the Pacific War, E. H. Norman viewed the Restoration as a partial revolution: "a political revolution carried out from above which was not permitted to become a social revolution."[6] Subsequent historians have culled evidence from the Tokugawa

---

5. For brief discussions of the debate, see John W. Dower, ed., *Origins of the Modern Japanese State: Selected Writings of E. H. Norman* (New York, 1975), pp. 35–37; George M. Beckman, "Japanese Adaptations of Marx-Leninism," *Asia Cultural Studies* 3, International Christian University, Tokyo, October 1962, pp. 103–114; H. D. Harootunian, *Toward Restoration* (Berkeley, 1970), pp. ix–x.

6. Quoted in Dower, p. 20.

past which suggests that many changes formerly attributed to the Meiji period were actually set in motion long before.[7] The current consensus is to resist any theory, whether developmental or Marxist, that attempts to break Japanese history into clearly demarcated stages of growth. As Tetsuo Najita has observed, "the history of modern Japan is not a unilinear achievement of higher levels of rationality."[8]

The tug and pull between bold iconoclasm and traditionalistic conservatism was perhaps most apparent in the educational system that developed in the wake of the Restoration. Ostensibly, the early Meiji school system was geared toward the dissemination of useful knowledge purged of Confucian pieties and moral abstractions. At the university level, the commitment to science and technical learning was particularly pronounced and has been credited by James Bartholomew as "absolutely essential to Japan's entire modernization process."[9] Education was not only secular but also available in theory to all persons regardless of heritage or place of birth. Replacing family background, performance on impartial entrance examinations determined matriculation beyond the universal and compulsory primary school. The promise of social mobility through the national educational system is often cited as an effective measure by which the Meiji leadership liquidated arbitrary class privileges.[10]

Nonetheless, the development of education in the Meiji period cannot be reduced to a paradigm of expanding secularization and social mobilization. The strictly utilitarian and materialistic definitions of knowledge of the 1870s endured only a decade as schools below the university level gave increasing attention to traditionalistic ethics and civic rituals. More significantly, the educational furor (kyōikukyō) which the egalitarian promise of social mobility had aroused in early Meiji dissipated by World War I with the realization that achievement had in fact

7. The explorations of American scholars into Tokugawa institutional history during the 1950s and 1960s are best summarized in John W. Hall and Marius B. Jansen, eds., *Studies in the Institutional History of Early Modern Japan* (Princeton, 1968).

8. Tetsuo Najita, *Japan* (Englewood Cliffs, N.J., 1974), p. 15.

9. James R. Bartholomew, "Japanese Modernization and the Imperial Universities, 1876–1920," *Journal of Asian Studies* 31, no. 2 (February 1978):252.

10. Herbert Passin, *Society and Education in Japan* (New York, 1965), chap. 6; Ronald P. Dore, "Education: Japan," in Robert Ward and Dankwart A. Rustow, eds., *Political Modernization in Japan and Turkey* (Princeton, 1964); Asō Makoto, ed., *Erīto* (Gendai no esupuri, no. 95), Tokyo, June 1975, pp. 151–166. I am indebted to Passin for the metaphorical characterization of the school system as a "ladder."

been a disguise for status. Kamishima Jirō has argued that, although Japanese modernization was predicated on "the destruction of the barriers of feudal status" through education, the actual result was a "resurrection of status discrimination," which was in some ways as pervasive as the feudal statuses of the Tokugawa period.[11] Concurring with Kamishima, a number of postwar scholars in Japan have insisted that the government's promotion of the achievement ethic was an ideological device to support what Nambara Shigeru once called "a narrow class-discriminating assortment of schools."[12]

Just as contemporary American and Japanese scholars disagree over the evolving relationship between education and social structure in post-Restoration Japan, so were Meiji educators torn between the conflicting needs for aristocracy and equality.[13] In an attempt to resolve this dilemma, they crafted a school system which, by the turn of the century, allowed for limited social mobility while reaffirming the legitimacy of stratified society. To simplify drastically: rational standards of performance regulated admissions to each ascending level of the school system, provided that the applicant was male and came from a family that could cover the nominal costs of tuition and board. (Women and working-class poor were thereby disqualified on the basis of ascribed status from entering the competition for academic laurels.) Yet, as ambitious young men climbed the academic ladder, from the universal primary school to the progressively more selective middle, higher, and university levels, they acquired certain traits peculiar to their newly achieved status. These manners and attitudes constituted the behavioral norm of the educated man in prewar Japan, a norm that was clearly distinct from the tight-lipped, flag-saluting standard imposed on the student masses in the primary and normal schools. While compulsory education was producing children for the family state, higher education nurtured the values of honor and loyalty among prospective leaders. Such behavioral criteria for distinguishing the social worth of a university graduate from a primary or normal-school graduate were inherently

11. Quoted in Kadowaki Atsushi, "Risshin shusse no shakaigaku," in Kadowaki Atsushi, ed., *Risshin shusse* (Gendai no esupuri, no. 118), Tokyo, May 1977, p. 18.

12. Kaigo Tokiomi and Terasaki Masao, *Daigaku kyōiku*, Sengo Nihon no kyōiku kaikaku, vol. 9 (Tokyo, 1972), p. 132.

13. This tension is discussed in a broad context in Seymour Lipset and Hans Zetterberg, "A Theory of Social Mobility," in Reinhard Bendix and Seymour Lipset, eds., *Class, Status and Power* (New York, 1966), p. 579.

ascriptive—that is, they were assigned to, or at least expected of, a student in a given institution and had little to do with innate abilities.[14]

By combining norms of achievement with norms of ascription, the educational system controlled the pace of social change during the technological and industrial transformation of Japan. The schools eased the transition from government by hereditary feudal social class to government by a new middle-class status group of academic achievers. The change was significant but not revolutionary. Even though commoners slowly replaced the progeny of the samurai class in the university,[15] the new educated elite of the early twentieth century retained many of the attitudes of their Tokugawa predecessors toward manliness, honor, and public service. The institution that was instrumental in this conservative transformation from social class to status group—that, according to Inoue Tetsujirō,[16] preserved the "samurai spirit" as Japan entered the industrial age, and that encouraged selected youth in the 1920s to board trains with heads raised and minds fixed on Kant—was the higher school.

A Case Study in Elite Socialization

Comparable to the upper-level Gymnasium in Germany and to the public schools in England, the higher schools were national academies, which prepared an exclusive group of students for the Imperial University. Historically, they flourished from 1886 to 1949, during which time the number of national higher

14. The distinction here between achievement and ascription is important. Whereas achievement prescribes that an individual be judged by performance, at any time and in any situation, ascription prescribes that he be judged by attributes he already possesses, which may include age, sex, or ethnic heritage, but also "collectivity memberships" and places of residence. (Talcott Parsons, *Toward a General Theory of Social Action* [Cambridge, Mass., 1951], pp. 82–83, 207–208; *The Social System* [Glencoe, Ill., 1951], pp. 170–173.) Furthermore, as Theodorson notes, ascriptive norms are often attached to previously achieved positions, as was the case in Japan. (George A. and Achilles G. Theodorson, *A Modern Dictionary of Sociology* [New York, 1969], p. 17.) The seemingly paradoxical insinuation of ascriptive norms into the structure of an achieving society is analyzed further by Leon Mayhew, "Ascription in Modern Societies," in Edward O. Laumann, et al., eds., *The Logic of Social Hierarchies* (Chicago, 1970), pp. 308–321.

15. There is no in-depth statistical study of the social backgrounds of university students in Japan before World War II. Scattered information on the declining proportion of students of samurai origin can be found in Shimizu Yoshirō, *Shiken* (Tokyo, 1957), pp. 108–110; Passin, pp. 120–121.

16. Inoue Tetsujirō, "Meiji shōnen no gakusei kishitsu oyobi kongo no kibō," *Risō* 83 (March 1938):62–63.

schools rose from five to twenty-five.[17] Despite a gradual increase in enrollment, the schools never admitted more than one percent of the male population between the ages of sixteen and nineteen. Admission to the higher schools, on the other hand, virtually guaranteed passage to the university and, in many cases, positions of leadership in adult society.

To the historian of institutions, the higher school is significant as a bridge to the university and has been treated as such in the standard surveys of Japanese education.[18] This view, however, overlooks the cultural and social ramifications of boarding-school life. As more than a structural appendage to the universities, the higher schools provide a unique opportunity to examine the developing psychology of a young elite that was assembling for the first time under one roof. C. Wright Mills has argued that because of its "face to face milieu" the "proper secondary school" assumes even greater importance than the family in the study of elites;[19] and this view is especially valid for Imperial Japan where the preadolescent upbringing of middle-class children was incongruent with the social and philosophic claims of the governing elite. The higher schools were responsible for the resocialization of these youths during late adolescence.

While historians have yet to penetrate the depths of the higher school experience, there is today a bustling popular market for memoirs, novels, movies, and comic books depicting the schooldays of Japan's prewar elite.[20] As a consequence, thirty years after the abolition of the all-male boarding academies, the image of the higher school student—standing tall on his elevated clogs, the black cape of his uniform flowing proudly in the wind, battered copies of Roland's *Jean Christophe* and *San-*

17. In addition there were, by 1930, four private and three municipal academies, bringing the total to thirty-two. These latter institutions carried far less prestige.

18. For example, Nakajima Tarō, *Kindai Nihon kyōiku seidoshi* (Tokyo, 1969); Naka Arata, *Meiji no kyōiku* (Tokyo, 1967); Kurasawa Tsuyoshi, *Gakkōrei no kenkyū* (Tokyo, 1978); Passin, *Society and Education in Japan*; Monbushō, ed., *Gakusei hachijūnenshi* (Tokyo, 1954). Each of these works takes an institutional approach and says little about life within the schools. In the head note for the Bibliography, I discuss more specialized works that examine the higher schools, again largely from an institutional perspective.

19. C. Wright Mills, *The Power Elite* (New York, 1959), p. 15.

20. Examples of popular novels and memoirs dealing with higher school life include: Kita Morio, *Dokutoru Manbō seishunki* (Tokyo, 1967); Ōgiya Shōzō, *Aa gyokuhai ni hana ukete* (Tokyo, 1967); Nōberu Shobō Henshūbu, ed., *Aa seishun dekansho* (Tokyo, 1969); Yamamoto Kazuya, ed., *Waga seishun kyūsei kōkō* (Tokyo, 1968); Kimijima Ichirō, *Daryō ichibanshitsu: Tanizaki Jun'ichirō to Ichikō ryōyū-tachi to* (Tokyo, 1967); Togawa Yukio, *Hikari hokuchi ni* (Tokyo, 1973).

tarō no nikki tucked firmly under his arm—is still imprinted in the mind of a large segment of the reading public. Needless to say, the "old higher school" (*kyūsei kōkō*) mystique would not endure to the present without the active assistance of "old boys" who attended the schools. The writing of popular novels and picture books, the financing of monuments and museums, the staging of "dormitory song festivals" each year at the Kōdō-kan in Tokyo and the Nakanoshima Auditorium in Osaka— these represent the highly visible and well-publicized activities of the most energetic and fiercely loyal alumni in the country and perhaps, in all seriousness, in the world. The institutional loyalty of the British public school graduates, says Richard Storry, is "a pale, unimportant phenomenon by comparison with the higher school old boy network."[21] The unmitigated devotion of the alumni may be the most telling evidence that the meaning of the higher school experience transcends a strictly empirical analysis of interlocking institutions. For those who attended the higher schools also enrolled at the Imperial universities; yet conspicuous displays of affection for the former have contrasted with a conspicuous absence of affection for the latter.

The reason behind this apparent anomaly was sought in a series of interviews with past graduates, who almost invariably responded that the higher schools were unique in instilling a spirit that transcended the life of the institution.[22] While Japan's rapid industrialization transformed institutions, including the university, into hollow shells, the old higher school, according to these graduates, stood alone as both a spiritual and a physical entity. Whether or not one accepts the Hegelian proposition that institutions may have "souls," the tendency of alumni to view their alma mater in idealistic terms hints at the broader influence of the higher school experience on the graduates' world view. The significance of the higher school lies in shaping con-

21. Storry's remark is found in his annotations to Kurt Singer's *Mirror, Sword and Jewel* (New York, 1973), p. 83.

22. Over the course of doing research for this study, I interviewed a number of prominent higher school alumni in business, government, and academia, including Tsuneizumi Kōichi (Feb. 5, 1971), Ishida Shōken (Feb. 8, 1971), Uchiyama Natsuo (Feb. 8, 1971), Takahashi Seiji (Feb. 11, 1971), Kōzu Yasuo (Feb. 15, 1971), Wada Heishirō (Dec. 25, 1970), Shirayama Keizō (April 3, 1971), Kamishima Jirō (June 25, 1971), Kuwabara Takeo (June 2, 1971), Inoue Kiyoshi (July 8, 1971), Funayama Shin'ichi (July 1, 1971), Niizeki Takeo (Oct. 5, 1971), Amano Teiyū (October 12, 1971), and Maruyama Masao (May 3, 1976).

sciousness and imbuing social attitudes among students who later became prominent in prewar and postwar society.

Schooldays in Imperial Japan focuses on the role of the higher schools in the diffusion of specific intellectual attitudes and behavioral norms that defined status and honor. Although emphasis is on the political and cultural socialization of a young elite and on the attendant reproduction of certain values and behavior patterns over time, the history of the higher schools is neither uneventful nor static. "An idea changes in its persistence as well as in its rejection," Joseph Levenson once noted; and adherence to a traditional notion of honor or loyalty may have a quite different connotation in the bourgeois-industrial world than in agrarian-feudal society. Like the late-Victorian strain of "muscular Christianity," the doctrine of reified *bushidō* in the Meiji higher schools blended, almost indistinguishably, into the modern currents of Social Darwinism. Furthermore, the paradox of gentlemanly cultivation in a technocratic age created as much tension in the Meiji higher school as it did in the Edwardian public school or Wilhelmian Gymnasium. The tension, as we shall see, was symptomatic of the intellectual and psychological growth of the student. Despite continuing pedagogical concern for moral education, the higher school graduate of the 1930s differed significantly from the graduate of the 1890s. Whereas the character of the earlier graduate was defined largely by the teacher, the personality of later students was often graced by a philosophic perception of self.[23]

The growth of the higher school student from a wooden character into a complex personality was paralleled by dynamic interactions between teacher and student and between student and student. This study treats both the pedagogical ideals of the teachers and the internal configurations of the student culture. The two perspectives are essential, for students do not act in complete isolation from their teachers. Nor do the policies enunciated by headmasters always dictate the behavioral norms of pupils. Yet, contrary to theories of generational conflict and of youth as an independent agent of social change, higher school students and faculty were united on most issues of substance, especially those pertaining to the relationship be-

23. On the distinctions between character and personality in the rise of political elites, I have benefited greatly from conversations with my colleague in the Rutgers College History Department, Richard L. McCormick.

tween school and society. They stood together because they had a common ideological stake in the institution's strength and in the cultural ideal symbolized by status. For higher school students, the undifferentiated mass of cohorts was never the object of their "fidelity," which was restricted to the inner circle of peers and teachers within the academies.[24] The absence in modern Japan of any class-bridging generational youth movement, comparable to the May Fourth Movement in China, could be attributed in part to the enduring particularistic loyalties of the student elite to their alma mater and to the consciousness they shared with their teachers.

The Unfolding Story

The sequence of chapters reflects the chronological development of the higher school as it becomes an increasingly diversified psychological and cultural institution. In an unsettled age of conflicting social values, the higher schools emerged in the 1880s under the tutelage of educators who were determined to remold unruly students into self-abnegating gentlemen capable of leading the nation in the face of international hostilities. The first two chapters discuss the foundation of the all-male academies, with particular attention to developments in Tokyo's First Higher School, the most prestigious of the preparatory schools and the focus of examination throughout the book.

In the 1890s, higher school headmasters abandoned their ideal of cultivation through coercive regulation and gave students increasing authority in the management of residence halls. Chapters 3 through 6 examine the sequential response of students to slackening faculty control. Here we will consider the initial consensus to seek security and identity in fraternal rituals, athletics, and the unquestioning bondage to peer group; the subsequent rebellion by a few intellectuals against the tyranny of their peers; the ultimate reconciliation between campus Philistines and intellectuals under a synthesized "school spirit" (kōfū) and a new perception of "adolescence" (seishun) as a period for philosophic and personal explorations.

With expanded opportunities for self-expression, higher school students participated creatively in the cultural and intellectual currents of the 1920s, but always as privileged youth

24. Erik H. Erikson, "Youth: Fidelity and Diversity," in Erik H. Erikson, ed., *The Challenge of Youth* (Garden City, N.Y., 1965), pp. 1–28.

whose personal freedom was a prerogative of status. Chapter 7 discusses the changing perspectives and enduring traditions of higher school life after World War I, and chapter 8 gauges the broader impact of the higher school experience on the political and social behavior of the alumni.

In some ways, the story that follows may seem old-fashioned; tradition supersedes revolution; elites supersede masses; character supersedes typology; and literature supersedes statistical models and graphs. The latter priority is of importance because diaries, memoirs, dormitory annals, and schoolboy romance record the joys and sorrows of growing up in Imperial Japan. This is a history we must feel to understand, and that will require some attempt to depict the substance of student life. What was it like to jump into a bathtub with twenty friends or to relieve oneself through the dormitory window while reciting from *Demian*?

Still, the study is neither an exploration of the esoteric nor an exercise in *la petite histoire*. Student customs in Japan often had counterparts in the obscure, "subterranean traditions" of educated elites in the West.[25] Despite occasional idiosyncrasies, the higher school subculture is open to comparative analysis. More important, the songs, slogans, games, and toilet habits of students were symbolic representations of status. They extended Nietzsche's "pathos of distance" between society and an emerging middle-class elite who became leading figures in politics and culture from World War I to the present.

25. David Matza, "Subterranean Traditions of Youth," *Annals of the American Academy of Political and Social Science* 338 (November 1961): 102–118. Attention was drawn to this article from reading John R. Gillis, *Youth and History* (New York, 1974).

CHAPTER ONE

Toward the Foundation of the Higher Schools

The strongest nation is that in which the individual man is most helpful and most independent. The best school is that which exists for the individual student. . . . The basal idea of higher education is that each student should devote his time and strength to what is best for him; that no force of tradition, no rule of restraint . . . should swerve any one from his best educational path.

DAVID S. JORDON, "THE UNIVERSITY
AND THE COMMON MAN" (1898)

There is no earthly thing more mean and despicable in my mind than an English gentleman destitute of all sense of his responsibilities and opportunities, and only revelling in the luxuries of our high civilization, and thinking himself a great person.

THOMAS ARNOLD, LETTER TO J. P. GELL (1840)

The story of the Japanese higher schools does not begin with their formal organization in 1886. Like the elite boarding schools in the West, the higher schools were not the pedagogical invention of a single educator; rather they embodied a complex of ideals, which originated in the eighteenth century, were reacted against during and immediately after the Meiji Restoration, and were resynthesized in the 1880s. The higher schools of the middle Meiji period represented the product of nearly a century of heated discourse among educators over the proper use of advanced education in the socialization of the prospective elite. The dispute focused on tensions between humanism and vocationalism, between bureaucratism (the ethic of responsibility) and idealism (the ethic of ultimate ends), and between pedagogical demands for discipline and student needs for freedom and self-expression.

The most important issue was the interrelationship of education, social structure, and national strength. Should education reaffirm social class distinctions and values, as had been the case during most of the Tokugawa period? Or should it break down these distinctions by functioning as an egalitarian agency for self-improvement? In the aftermath of the Meiji Restoration, many influential educators spoke enthusiastically of egalitarianism and self-help in education. Yet, contrary to the putative logic of modernization that dictates inexorable movement toward meritocracy, the backdrop to the foundation of the higher schools in the 1880s featured a group of educators who were already disenchanted with the ethic of self-improvement for its presumed contribution to the moral corruption of educated youth. These educators sought to reconcile social mobility with the traditional concept of a cultivated elite. Ultimately, the higher school would play a key role in the resolution of this dilemma.

Schools for the Gentleman Warrior

Alumni historians for local higher schools often look back to the Tokugawa domain school (*hankō*) as the historical antecedent of their alma maters.[1] Usually the claim for this lineage is based on geographical location. A number of the schools were actually founded on or near the sites of former domain academies; in some instances, the name of the old domain school was retained as a nickname for the higher school. The higher schools were also influenced by the general philosophy of the domain schools, which provided a clearly articulated precedent for the moral education of the young elite.

By the end of the Tokugawa period nearly every feudal principality in Japan had a domain school for the education of the samurai elite. At the time of the Meiji Restoration, there were approximately three hundred samurai academies, which represented the first successful attempt by governing officials to systematize the transmission of knowledge for a significant seg-

---

1. See, for example, the essays in Dai Shichi Kōtō Gakkō Zōshikan Dōsōkai, ed., *Shichikō omoideshū* (Kagoshima, 1963), which make frequent reference to the domain school heritage of the Seventh Higher School; see also Tomatsu Nobuyasu, ed., *Shikō hachijūnenshi* (Kanazawa, 1967), p. 42.

ment of the population. Even though the purposes and curriculum in the schools conformed to a general model, the institutions were never integrated into a centrally controlled network and existed at the mercy of local feudal lords who underwrote their expenses. Fukuzawa Yukichi noted that education in the domain schools was "learning appropriate to the world of rulers."[2] On one level, this meant equipping young samurai with the literary and martial skills they needed in order to function effectively in their incongruous role as salaried bureaucrat and feudal warrior. Yet, despite declamations on the value of practical learning (*jitsugaku*) and on the importance of talent (*jinzai*) in the operations of government, the fundamental thrust of education remained moral, for the ideal product of the domain school was the man of cultivation, the samurai gentleman. In accordance with Confucian canon, Tokugawa educators believed that the effectiveness of government depended on the moral development of leaders; as stated in *The Doctrine of the Mean*, "When righteous men are available, government will prosper, and when righteous men are lacking, government will collapse." To become a righteous man, one had to nurture the inborn proclivity for virtue, honor, and exemplary public service and reject worldly gratification. Righteousness was not the product of commercial enterprise or manual work; it was cultivated, rather, through concentrated study of the great philosophers and their commentators. The commitment of the feudal lords to the domain schools rested ultimately on the Confucian faith in education as the supreme "socializing force" in the formation of a select group of superior men to run the government.[3]

As with most traditional philosophies of education, the Confucian ideals that underlay the Tokugawa domain schools were unapologetically elitist. The Confucian definition of the gentleman was predicated on the inferiority of common man: "The gentleman reaches upward, the inferior man reaches downward; the gentleman understands what is right, the inferior man understands what is profitable; the gentleman cherishes virtue, the inferior man cherishes possessions."[4] The worlds both of man and of nature were unequal; and thus, in accor-

2. Ronald Dore, "Education: Japan," in Robert E. Ward and Dankwart A. Rustow, eds., *Political Modernization in Japan and Turkey* (Princeton, 1964), p. 179.
3. Joseph R. Levenson and Franz Schurmann, *China: An Interpretive History* (Berkeley, Calif., 1969), p. 64.
4. Wm. Theodore de Bary, ed., *Sources of Chinese Tradition* (New York, 1960), p. 33.

dance with the doctrine of the righteousness of status (*taigi mei-bun*), it was assumed that the small educated elite were inherently obligated to give moral guidance to an illiterate populace. This assumption was valid for the Chinese ideal, in which gentlemen attained status through educational achievement, and for the original Tokugawa domain schools, where education reaffirmed the status distinction of the hereditary elite.[5]

In most domain schools, educators subscribed to Weber's "pedagogy of cultivation" over specialized studies for "expertness" or child-centered development.[6] Gentlemanly cultivation required disciplined training in the form of a balanced curriculum of Confucian philosophy (*bun*) and martial arts (*bu*). For younger samurai students, the typical school day was an agonizing routine of rote memorization and forced habituation backed up by the threat of punishment. Ronald Dore has described the scholastic side of the curriculum as "plainly dull" and "almost meaningless":[7] the pièce de résistance consisted of recitations from Confucian classics in an esoteric tongue as tedious to the student as Greek or Latin drills in the West. Beyond the recitations, domain school students underwent formalized training in the martial arts and participated in religious ceremonies at the school shrine. In every endeavor, whether receiving a meal or exiting for the lavatory, the student was required to uphold the "niceties of rank and status" within the samurai class.[8]

More important than the actual content of learning was the social ambience in which that learning took place. Dewey once defined character training as "a literal building into the mind from without," and environment was certainly an essential component in the cultivation of the samurai gentleman. The Tokugawa domain school was a world unto itself, according to Dore, "an island of privilege,"[9] where the choreography of daily rituals cushioned the shock of unpredictable departures from social etiquette. As a social unit, the schools have been likened to a family, with the teachers in the role of authoritarian father figures reigning over surrogate sons, who were seated and accorded respect on the basis of age and hereditary rank

5. R. P. Dore, *Education in Tokugawa Japan* (Berkeley, 1965), p. 152.
6. Max Weber, *From Max Weber*, pp. 426–427.
7. Dore, *Education in Tokugawa Japan*, p. 152.
8. Ibid.
9. Ronald P. Dore, "The Thought of Men: The Thought of Society," in *Asian Cultural Studies* 3 (October 1962): 79.

The Foundation of the Higher Schools   17

within the samurai class. The ascriptive, familial nature of the closed school community was especially pronounced among students who lived in dormitories under the constant supervision of teachers or older peers. The setting was further characterized by simplicity, piety, and puritanical self-restraint. Students had to contend with coarse clothing and poor food (*soi soshoku*) as necessary penance toward the perfection of moral faculties and as defense against the lure of wealth and luxury, which could destroy the status honor of the samurai gentleman.[10]

Traditional education, conducted in an atmosphere of rigid discipline and forced recitations of nonvernacular literature, hinders the development of an autonomous youth culture.[11] Ronald Dore's observation that domain school students lacked the "team spirit" of British public school students is, therefore, not surprising.[12] Yet, beneath the façade of rigid formality, there were opportunities for fraternal camaraderie. Informal histories of the domain schools have revealed sporadic outbursts of rowdiness among students and awesome rites of passage, which took place surreptitiously when educators were not present.[13] Indeed, at the Zōshikan in southern Kyūshū, students were encouraged to join a fraternal association that cultivated esprit de corps in an assortment of strenuous and often daring outdoor activities.[14] (Such displays of camaraderie and rugged independence among young Kyūshū samurai were leg-

10. Karasawa Tomitarō, *Gakusei no rekishi* (Tokyo, 1968), pp. 12–13.
11. This question is addressed in W. J. Ong, "Latin Language Study as a Renaissance Puberty Rite," in P. W. Musgrave, ed., *Sociology, History and Education* (London, 1970), pp. 232–248.
12. Dore, *Education in Tokugawa Japan*, p. 313.
13. Karasawa has stressed that beneath the strict etiquette and civility (*reigi sahō*) on the surface, there was a rough and almost untamable young spirit (*Gakusei no rekishi*, pp. 4–5). While the descriptions of domain school life are generally placid, Wada Heishirō, the librarian at Nara Prefectural Library, has stressed that no school was able to prevent its students from occasionally going on a rampage in a sudden uncontrolled "break in etiquette" (*bureikō*). These eruptions, Wada contends, were the precursor to the higher school "storm" that will be discussed in chapter 4 (interview, Dec. 25, 1970). Saitō Tokutarō, in a book that otherwise emphasizes the orderly aspects of domain school life, does talk about the collective rituals of student groups in Kyūshū that tested the courage of the participants. One such game was called "the last cast" (*undameshi*), in which participants sat in a circle around a loaded rifle that twirled dangerously on a rope. Saitō Tokutarō, *Nijūroku daihan no hangaku to shifū* (Osaka, 1944), pp. 33–34.
14. Along with their scholastic regimen in the Zōshikan, the members of the Satsuma youth association (*gōjū*), according to Ivan Hall, "climbed mountains, swam rivers, and vaulted ditches with imaginary invaders in mind." The fraternal intimacy of the *gōjū* members, combined with their "minimal association with outsiders" and "puritanistic self-restraint," is suggestive of the early subcultural ethos of the higher school. Ivan Hall, *Mori Arinori* (Cambridge, Mass., 1973), pp. 32–46.

endary in the Meiji period and, as we shall see, inspired provincial higher school students to proclaim the rustic warrior as their heroic ideal.) Undoubtedly, the urge to demonstrate manliness in unrestrained feats of courage was fairly widespread among samurai youth, especially during the late Tokugawa period when rowdiness and outright protests became a serious problem in many of the schools.[15] Ironically, as administrators made bold innovations in the curriculum and established new standards of rewards on the basis of performance rather than hereditary rank, the domain academies began to lose control over their students, who increasingly in the 1850s and 1860s enrolled in the private academies that were sprouting up across the country.

The assertions of independence and displays of rebelliousness by samurai youth cannot be separated from the broad political and social dislocations of late Tokugawa. The inability of the *baku-han* bureaucracy to deal effectively with either the internal fiscal crisis or the external threat of colonial incursion triggered a ground swell of dissatisfaction with existing administrative structures and entrenched bureaucratic personnel. Thus the stage was set for a group of new historical actors, the men of noble purpose (*shishi*); these young samurai renounced the incompetence and hypocrisy of their elders and embarked on an independent quest for responsible public positions. It was these discontented youth who gathered in the heretical academies of Yoshida Shōin and Mazaki Sorō to nurture their personal ambitions and political aspirations in a pedagogical atmosphere free of hierarchical ranking and arid discussions of propriety.[16] Studies by H. D. Harootunian and Kamishima Jirō

15. Karasawa, *Gakusei no rekishi*, p. 6; Saitō Tokutarō, p. 559; Kokubo Akihiro, "Kindai gakkō hōshiki no dōnyū," in *Kindai kyōikushi*, Kyōikugaku zenshū, vol. 3 (Tokyo, 1970).

16. Yoshida Shōin's Shōka Village School was one of the innovative and influential private academies. Both Tokutomi Sohō and Hirose Yutaka have called Yoshida "Japan's Pestalozzi" in deference to his humanism and concern for the personal development of his students as "kindred souls." Like other private schools, the Shōka Village School was marked by a friendly ambience for building a "spiritual union through close personal contact between pupil and teacher." See Yamaguchiken Kyōikukai, ed., *Yoshida Shōin zenshū*, vol. 4 (Tokyo, 1938–1940), p. 178; Hirose Yutaka, *Yoshida Shōin no kenkyū* (Tokyo, 1943), pp. 370ff; Tokutomi Sohō, *Yoshida Shōin* (Tokyo, 1942), p. 212. For a delightful description of student life in one of the bakumatsu private schools for Western studies, see Fukuzawa Yukichi's discussion of his "rough and tumble" days at the Ogata School in Osaka during the late 1850s, in *The Autobiography of Fukuzawa Yukichi* (New York, 1966), chap. 4. The peer-group camaraderie in Ogata's School and the Shōka Village School would suggest the emergence of an independent youth culture.

have suggested that a modern "youth culture" (*seinen bunka*) originated in the Restoration academies, which granted rebellious students a moratorium for establishing horizontal friendships and for achieving a new sense of identity as leaders of an emerging nation.[17]

State and Education in Early Meiji Japan

The young samurai who led the final drive to overthrow the Bakufu and who assumed prominent positions in the new Meiji state were the products of domain academies and iconoclastic private schools. Still, the school system they fashioned in the 1870s bore little resemblance to either precedent. There were, of course, lessons to be learned from the Tokugawa experience. The domain school presented a model of education that was functionally linked to the ruling bureaucracy; but the gradual loosening of ascriptive criteria before the Restoration did not dispel the school's long-standing image as a bastion of hereditary privilege and an obstacle to the fulfillment of personal ambition. In contrast, much of the appeal of the private academy derived from the expectation that personal fulfillment would be more easily achieved outside the framework of official education; this held true for young samurai, who were disqualified from high office because of age, as well as for the sons of merchants or wealthy peasants, who were disqualified because of class background. Thus, the persisting dilemma for the early Meiji leadership was the construction of a school system that was tightly integrated into the sociopolitical order while upholding the legitimacy of individual achievement, regardless of age or heredity.

Of more immediate concern was the expeditious and widespread dissemination of Western learning. Japan's geopolitical position during the Restoration was perilous. As a result of the unequal treaties negotiated with the Tokugawa Bakufu in the 1850s, the Western powers had established semicolonial communities with preferential trading privileges and extraterritorial authority in six coastal ports; Restoration leaders feared that unless emergency reforms were undertaken, Japan would be-

---

17. H. D. Harootunian has suggested this in *Toward Restoration*, esp. pp. 229–236 and 403–410. See Kamishima Jirō, *Kindai Nihon no seishin kōzō* (Tokyo, 1974), p. 74; see also Albert Craig, "Kido Kōin and Ōkubo Toshimichi," in Albert Craig and Donald Shively, eds., *Personality in Japanese History* (Berkeley, 1970), pp. 275–277; and Okawada Tsunetada, "Seinenron to sedairon," in *Shisō*, no. 514 (April 1967), pp. 445–448.

come like China, "a country of impaired sovereignty." [18] They gave high priority to the establishment of a school system based on Western models, as evidenced in Kido Kōin's 1868 "Petition for the Urgent Promotion of General Education." [19] Elsewhere, Kido ranked the systematic dispersal of learning with the development of the military as the twin pillars of the imperial state. [20]

The attitude toward education during the nervous first decade of the Meiji state has often been described as "utilitarian" and as influenced by the philosophies of Fukuzawa Yukichi, Nishi Amane, Uchida Masao, and other official advocates of Western learning. For these scholars, knowledge was an empirical entity, separable from the realm of ethics, subject to rational, inductive investigation, and instrumental to the economic well-being or happiness of the individual. In 1871 Fukuzawa Yukichi stated that the purpose of education was "a mastery of things and events," which enabled the student to lead a self-sufficient and dignified life. [21] Since Fukuzawa and Nishi were familiar with the ideas of Compte, Mill, and Bentham, they may have resynthesized Japanese educational philosophy by drawing on Western positivism and on materialism in Neo-Confucian thought. Yet, the theoretical attempt to strip knowledge of its moral embellishments was only one aspect of the utilitarianism of early Meiji education. More remarkable was the functional posture of government officials who transplanted the structures, curriculum, and some of the theoreticians of "civilized learning" from Europe and America to Japan. In the post-Restoration years, huge sums were allocated to send Japanese students abroad, hire foreign teachers and advisers, duplicate the French district system, and purchase classroom paraphernalia that would reproduce the ambience of the Boston primary school—complete with desks, blackboards, and Marcius Wilson's *Fifth Reader*—in downtown Tokyo. [22] The underlying supposition was that Western models must be scrupulously adopted; and the speed with which this transplantation took place suggests that intellectual change could barely keep pace with institutional change.

The emulation of Western models was accompanied by ver-

18. Dower, ed., *Origins of the Modern Japanese State*, p. 150.
19. Motoyama Yukihiko, ed., *Meiji kyōiku seron no kenkyū*, vol. 1 (Tokyo, 1972), p. 11.
20. Tōyama Shigeki, *Meiji ishin* (Tokyo, 1967), p. 289.
21. David A. Dilworth and Hirano Umeyo, *Fukuzawa Yukichi's An Encouragement of Learning* (Tokyo, 1969), p. 1.
22. Herbert Passin, *Society and Education in Japan*, p. 71.

bal assaults on the Tokugawa pedagogy of cultivation. Fukuzawa and other advocates of "civilization and enlightenment" sympathized with the declassed feudal aristocracy but objected to the scholastic regimen in the domain schools.[23] "Learning does not mean useless accomplishments, such as knowing strange words, or reading old and difficult texts, or enjoying and writing poetry," Fukuzawa contended. ". . . this kind of unpractical learning should be left to other days, and one's best efforts should be given to practical learning that is close to everyday needs—the forty-seven letters of the alphabet, the composition of letters, bookkeeping, the abacus and the use of scales."[24] Fukuzawa's view was echoed in the preamble to the Educational Code of 1872, the proclamation that shaped the early Meiji school system: "They [the samurai] indulged in poetry, empty reasoning, and idle discussions, and their dissertations, while not lacking in elegance, were seldom applicable to life."[25] Criticism of the idleness and impracticality of the former elite was combined with an attack on the notion of education as a hereditary privilege. According to the Code, "The evil tradition which looked upon learning as the privilege of the samurai" had to be abolished in favor of an open system of education in which each individual would compete for academic laurels (and concomitant social status) in accordance with ability and determination. Education was not the prerogative of those who, by birth, were at the top of society; education was "the capital to rise in the world" (mi o tateru no zaihon). The Code assumed that education would stimulate the individual to improve his economic welfare and position in society. Those who did not struggle to make the best of their opportunity to rise up in the world deserved to languish at the bottom of the social order. Simultaneously, the individual's initiative in acquiring academic skills and advancing in the world was a definite boon to the nation. As Fukuzawa argued, personal and national independence were inseparable.[26]

The administrative structure and organization of schools which supported the materialistic ethic of self-improvement

23. For a revisionist view of Fukuzawa, see Earl H. Kinmonth "Fukuzawa Reconsidered: *Gakumon no susume* and Its Audience," *Journal of Asian Studies* 37 (August 1978):677–696.

24. Quoted in Passin, pp. 206–207.

25. Ibid., p. 211.

26. Carmen Blacker, *The Japanese Enlightenment* (Cambridge, England, 1964), pp. 67–68.

(*risshin shusse*) was outlined in the specific articles of the Educational Code of 1872. The Code presented plans for a national school system under the centralized control of a Ministry of Education in Tokyo. The projected structure resembled a pyramid with all school-age children attending primary school and then progressing, in steadily decreasing numbers, through the middle schools to the university. Competitive entrance examinations would determine admissions beyond the compulsory primary school. Specifically, the plan called for 53,760 primary schools, 256 middle schools, and 8 universities—targets that soon proved to be unrealistic.[27]

The Educational Code created as many problems as it attempted to resolve at all levels of the school system.[28] Concerning higher education, the tripartite division of schools was oversimplified and could not accommodate the needs or expectations of ambitious youth. It was dubious to assume, for example, that every primary school would prepare students equally for middle school or that every middle school would, in turn, prepare students equally for the university. Moreover, until 1897 there was only Tokyo University, called the Kaisei Gakkō before 1877. With an enrollment of 340 students in the departments of law, science, literature, and medicine in 1880, the university was hardly equipped to meet the national demand for higher education.[29] Part of the slack was assumed by private schools, which emerged haphazardly during early Meiji and served primarily as technical institutions in commerce and law. These included the precursors to Keiō, Waseda, Hosei, and Meiji universities, along with a host of foreign-language preparatory academies. Although the private colleges helped to satisfy the demand for higher education, their status was clearly inferior to Tokyo University, the only guarantor of public office.

The inadequacies in the structure of higher education were compounded in the realm of pedagogy. By rejecting the ideals of gentlemanly cultivation, the architects of the early Meiji school system reduced education to a business exercise, with the school functioning as, in Nitobe Inazō's words, a "mart

27. Passin, p. 73.
28. Popular resentment against the primary schools is discussed in Tamaki Hajime, *Nihon kyōiku hattatsushi* (Tokyo, 1954), pp. 23–26.
29. Konishi Shirō et al., eds., *Nihon gakusei no rekishi* (Tokyo, 1970), p. 94.

of information."[30] The faculty of the public university and private colleges was predominantly American and European and scarcely interested in the spiritual welfare of the students. After all, they were paid to transmit useful knowledge, not to act as moral guardians. To say that the mainstream of educators in the 1870s had no conception of ethics is an overstatement. Fukuzawa Yukichi was more concerned with the moral demeanor of his students at Keiō than were his colleagues at Tokyo University; however, even he viewed morality as a function of material progress rather than a product of education.[31] A nation's advances through the Spencerian stages of "barbarism" and "semibarbarism" to the plateau of "civilization," according to Fukuzawa, ennobled the human spirit.[32] This optimistic faith in the righteousness of progress sanctioned the view of knowledge as "capital" in the quest for wealth and status, and was anathema to late-nineteenth-century educators who divorced moral development from material civilization.

Cultural Dislocation and the Early Meiji Student

The Educational Code's promise of social mobility through academic achievement was bound to affect the disposition of youth in the early Meiji period. The generation of unattached idealists, who had appeared before and just after the Restoration, was challenged by the government to reorient their quest for personal fulfillment from a struggle against established authority to a struggle for wealth and rank within the institution of the new state. In effect, the government had appropriated one of the great psychological forces that ignited the movement for Imperial Restoration—the quest for self-definition in public affairs—to which it gave universal legitimacy within the framework of a national educational system; the school became the public battleground for the ideology of achievement. Unless Meiji youth sought their fortunes in accordance with the accepted rules of academic competition, they would constitute a potentially destabilizing political force. By recognizing the personal ambitions of youth within the school system, the Meiji

30. Nitobe Inazō, *Japan: Some Phases of Her Problems and Development* (London, 1931), p. 232.
31. Blacker, chap. 5; Kenneth Pyle, *The New Generation in Meiji Japan*, p. 34.
32. Alan Stone, "The Japanese Muckrakers," *Journal of Japanese Studies* 1 (Spring 1975):400–401.

leadership surmised that individual achievement could gain respectability as the new ideology for maintaining national order.

The initial response to the new ideology of self-improvement must have gratified the post-Restoration leadership. The zeal with which educated youth of mostly samurai and wealthy peasant lineage became engrossed in translations of Smiles's *Self Help* and Fukuzawa's *Encouragement of Learning,* or in new popular magazines (which featured the personal dreams and expectations of young men for the future) suggests that the idea of unrestricted achievement had considerable appeal.[33] Moreover, the exodus of many provincial youth who sought admittance to preparatory schools in Tokyo indicates acceptance of the official notion that learning, rather than rebellion, was the key to self-improvement. To be sure, there were a few who refused to accommodate the quest for personal identity within the guidelines of the Educational Code. These were Irokawa's "wandering truthseekers," whose persistent Restoration idealism distinguished them from the mainstream of educated youth and led them inexorably into the role of grass-roots activists in the agrarian phase of the "people's rights movement."[34] Their numbers were miniscule, however, in comparison with the new generation's majority, whose ambitions focused on government careers. In the 1870s both the Tokugawa gentleman and the Restoration idealist had become anachronisms in a landscape increasingly dominated by urban students, their self-seeking pragmatism mirroring the accepted ideals of the day.

In establishing a politically safe framework for youth's struggle for wealth and status, at least until the early 1880s, the government created a potentially more serious problem of cultural and psychological dislocation. Despite long-range plans for regional universities, higher education in the 1870s was centered in Tokyo, the urban "showcase," as Henry D. Smith puts it, for "civilization and enlightenment."[35] Ascent of the academic ladder required youth to leave their families and venture to the capital, remembered by Tokutomi Roka as "our promised land" and the source of "inexhaustible fascination."[36] When the sons

33. The popular literature on self-improvement and the quest for success in Meiji Japan is analyzed by Earl Kinmonth in "The Self-Made Man in Meiji Japanese Thought," Ph.D. dissertation, University of Wisconsin, Madison, 1974.

34. Irokawa Daikichi, *Meiji no bunka* (Tokyo, 1970), chap. 3.

35. Henry D. Smith, "Tokyo as an Idea: An Exploration of Japanese Urban Thought Until 1945," *Journal of Japanese Studies* 4 (Winter 1978):53.

36. Tokutomi Kenjirō, *Footprints in the Snow,* translated by Kenneth Strong (New York, 1970), p. 107.

of declassed samurai or wealthy peasants finally arrived in the "Paris of the Far East," their enthusiasm often overflowed into frenetic posturing.[37] The early Meiji students were unruly and free-wheeling. They delighted in swaggering down congested streets, often in tattered kimonos and with swords at their sides, boasting of themselves as prospective leaders of the nation.

The Kaisei Gakkō and assorted private schools were unprepared for the influx of energetic samurai youth from the provinces. The first foreign teachers in the advanced schools were described by an American observer as "graduates of the dry-counter, the forecastle, the camp, and the shambles" who brought "the graces, the language, and the manners" of the "gambling saloon" to the Japanese classroom.[38] Fortunately, the quality of the faculty improved markedly after 1872, when the government began to recruit beyond the treaty ports. Still, communication between foreign professors and their students remained, with few exceptions, at a low ebb throughout early Meiji. An equally serious problem was the lack of facilities for provincial students. Classrooms were crowded, on-campus housing was inadequate, and extracurricular activities were nonexistent. From his days at the medical college connected to the Kaisei Gakkō in the early 1870s, Koganei Ryosei remembered the indiscriminate herding of students into a tenant house that had been formerly occupied by the servants of a Tokugawa overlord. "Since the boarders ranged from children like me (and I had not yet reached thirteen) to fathers who had grown children of their own, it was really quite a hodgepodge."[39] And so it was in most of the colleges and preparatory schools, which admitted students strictly on the basis of their relative intellectual skills regardless of age.[40]

With the fluctuating structure of public schools, the transient existence of private schools, the confusion and turnover of foreign faculty, and the lack of institutional symbols (uniforms, badges, extracurricular clubs), early Meiji students were compelled to fend for themselves. At the Kaisei Gakkō, students re-

---

37. Karasawa, *Gakusei no rekishi*, p. 29.
38. Quoted in Edward R. Beauchamp, *An American Teacher in Early Meiji Japan* (Honolulu, 1976), p. 86.
39. Ōmuro Teiichirō, *Daigaku oyobi daigakusei* (Tokyo, 1941), p. 7.
40. The clear exceptions to this generalization are the special "tributary students" (*kōshinsei*) who were selected on the basis of age as well as academic promise. See Karasawa Tomitarō, *Kōshinsei* (Tokyo, 1974), p. 9.

sponded to the vacuum of institutional authority by establishing a primitive, undocumented structure of "self-government" whereby older and rougher students took command over their much younger underlings. Reports of "clenched-fist punishments" (*tekken seisai*) inflicted on delinquent peers accused of dishonesty or "flattery" (*tenyu*) indicate that the older roughnecks took their unintended responsibility in earnest.[41] Inoue Tetsujirō, who attended the school between 1875 and 1880, believed that the rugged self-reliance of older students was a vestige of the late Tokugawa "samurai spirit" as manifested in the headstrong behavior of young warriors from the outlying domains.[42] If this was true, a transformation of historical space imbued originally heroic actions of defiance in the 1860s with a desperate, pathetic hue a decade later.

By the early 1880s, the bold, swashbuckling student was being overshadowed by the more refined hard-worker, whose pragmatic schemes for rising in the world precluded swaggering down city streets. Suddenly, college faculty were concerned less about the effrontery of student roughnecks and more about the "narrow intellectualism" of the emerging majority.[43] "They just sit at their desks absorbed in their studies," complained Hirai Nobuo in 1881, "failing to realize that their brains might expire with the oil in their lamp."[44] The under-exercised, sometimes consumptive, and single-mindedly devoted student was joined by a third group who were neither provincial roughnecks nor serious achievers but a distinct minority of unabashed playboys. For these students, many with literary predilections, the excitement of city life was so irresistible that noble dreams of the future were temporarily discarded for hedonistic recreation.

The roughnecks, the serious achievers, and the dandies are all represented in Tsubouchi Shōyō's pioneer novel, *The Temperament of Present-Day Students*, published in serial from between 1885 and 1886. The book is a vivid testimony of the dislocation and confusion of student life in early Meiji. In this novel, Shōyō categorizes students by their reaction to the urban environment. At one extreme are the fun-loving youth who regularly patronize the amusement quarters and indulge in bil-

41. Ōmuro, *Daigaku oyobi daigakusei*, p. 19.
42. Inoue Tetsujirō, p. 62.
43. William G. Dixon, *The Land of the Morning* (Edinburgh, 1882), pp. 364–368.
44. Quoted in Imamura Yoshio, *Nihon taiikushi* (Tokyo, 1951), p. 103.

lowing silk kimonos, white socks, colorfully banded sailors, and parasols. (They are called "the soft faction" [*nanpa*] in Mori Ōgai's autobiographical novel about the same period.)[45] With their dandyish fascination with clothes and accessories and their frequent visits to local brothels, the young philanderers are hard pressed for money. Shōyō details the devious ways whereby students manipulate their parents into sending funds for pleasurable activities. He also relates that students who had incurred the largest debts were assigned the mock titles of a sumo champion or rewarded a degree of "doctor of profligacy" (*intōgaku no hakushi*).[46]

At the other end of the spectrum are the members of the "diehard faction" (*gankotō*) or Ōgai's "rough faction" (*kōha*). The lonely representative of this group is Kiriyama Benroku, a country boy from Kyūshū who, besieged by worldly temptations in the alien urban environment, clings desperately to the customs of his boyhood. Shōyō describes Kiriyama's room as a rustic sanctuary from "civilization and enlightenment": the splintered wall-paneling and shredded floor-mats evidence countless judo and kendo matches. His kimono of coarse duck-cloth reeks of accumulated dirt and perspiration. His favorite book is a well-worn copy of *The Tales of Sangorō*, that mighty adolescent warrior from Kyūshū who never winced at an opponent's sword or lost his heart to a woman. When his dandyish friend Sugawa suggests that he use a knife to cut open a watermelon, Kiriyama responds defiantly by smashing the fruit in half with his fist and then utters this proclamation:

> It's no good the way all of you are carried away by luxuries. Why, back home, we used to catch rabbits in the mountains, skin them, boil them, and eat them up. How shameful that guys around Tokyo are so effeminate. They are almost like women, what with the way they eat and dress. . . . I guess they think it's their manly duty to primp themselves up in fluffy gowns.[47]

As an unflinching diehard, Kiriyama stands against the puerile attractions of city life. He refuses to wear fancy clothes, consume Western delicacies, or ride in rickshaws. But his stance

45. The term Ōgai uses is *nanpa*, which may be translated as "soft faction." See Mori Ōgai, *Ita Sekusuarisu*, in Chūō Kōronsha, ed., *Nihon no bungaku* 2 (Tokyo, 1970), p. 108. This book has been translated by Kazuji Ninomiya and Sanford Goldstein, *Vita Sexualis* (Rutland, Vermont, 1972).

46. Tsubouchi Shōyō, *Tōsei shosei katagi*, in *Nihon no bungaku*, vol. 1 (Tokyo, 1971), p. 79.

47. Ibid., p. 74.

entails more than the favoring of a fist over a knife to sever a watermelon. At issue are his identity and the extent to which self-definition is determined by feminine or masculine influences. Kiriyama resists dandyism and champions *machismo*, an exaggerated masculinity arising from a deep-seated fear of the dainty, the soft, or the delicate. The greatest evil, in his view, is submission to women, an act which sends the innocent student tumbling into a life of degeneracy and financial ruin. He advises fellow students to develop their "will-power" and "to behave in such a way that [they] will be hated by women." [48] Translated into action, this means wearing tattered clothing, walking down the street with fists tightly clenched, and focusing stray sexual fantasies on members of the same sex. "Better to indulge in the pleasure of men than the pleasure of women," Kiriyama states bluntly. [49] In his unhesitating disdain for women, Kiriyama is said to reflect the values of his native Kyūshū, where, according to Tokutomi Roka, young men were known to avoid contact with the opposite sex by strutting around with their "chests stuck out and elbows folded square." [50]

Between the "rough faction" and the "soft faction," Shōyō and Ōgai portray an array of students who fluctuate, depending on the color of their socks (white socks attract courtesans, blue socks apparently repel them), the quality of their kimonos, their use of perfumed hair-cream, or their way of walking down the street. [51] The disparate tastes and habits of the early Meiji students reflected profound socio-psychological tensions between city and rural values, conceptions of masculinity and femininity, and the new ideology of self-improvement and the pre-Restoration tradition of puritanical self-restraint. Further, the confusion and conflict over cultural identity constituted only one of the forces that fragmented student culture. The students were also divided over the highly volatile political issues of the "people's rights movement." Between 1878 and 1883, the campuses were centers for heated debates over the establishment of parliamentary government. [52] While few of the "politi-

48. Ibid., p. 75.
49. Ibid., p. 76.
50. Tokutomi Kenjirō, p. 104.
51. These distinctions are discussed in Kawatake Shigetoshi, *Tsubouchi Shōyō* (Tokyo, 1939), pp. 86–97; Mori Ōgai, *Vita Sexualis* (Rutland, Vermont, 1972), pp. 61–63 and 85; Karasawa, *Gakusei no rekishi*, pp. 51–58.
52. Student political activity during the "people's rights movement" is discussed in Tamaki Motoi, *Nihon gakuseishi*, pp. 39–52; Karasawa, *Gakusei no rekishi*, pp. 31–38; Kawatake, pp. 115–116; Okawada, pp. 448–452.

cal youth" (*seiji seinen*) actually joined the more radical people's rights societies that were organizing in rural areas, many did become outspoken critics of the government and clashed openly with contemporaries who steadfastly supported the Meiji leadership.

The kaleidoscopic strains of dandyism, stoicism, materialism, and political activism among students in the late 1870s and early 1880s were not welcomed by government officials and educators. Whereas the "rough faction" elicited more sympathy than the "softies" or the political activists, all students were criticized for lacking moral character and neglecting the national interest. Though largely sons of former samurai, the students behaved like a class of parvenus, ignorant of honor and loyalty and victimized by what Shōyō described as a cult of "exhibitionism" (*miebōshugi*). Experience contradicted the apostles of "civilization and enlightenment" who had argued that character could be abandoned to the vagaries of material progress; therefore, institutions would have to assume greater responsibility for the behavior of students outside the classroom. As a remedial first step in this direction, the government resorted to stringent measures, beginning with the issuance of the Law on Public Meetings in April 1880, restricting political gatherings and debates. When a few students continued to hold meetings in the early 1880s, police were dispatched to maintain order.[53] But threat of forceful intervention on the campuses was not the ideal means for calling attention to the "duties of studenthood" (*shosei no honbun*). Instilling in the prospective elite a common ethic of responsibility and high moral standards required, instead, a modification of the ideology of achievement and a sophisticated revamping of educational policy.

The Call for Reform

By the early 1880s it was apparent that the concept of education as the "capital" for personal advancement did not provide an adequate ethical framework from which to launch bureaucratic or political careers. Reluctantly, educators concluded that the disparate strains of political and dandyish youth were partially the fault of an educational system which had, as Nitobe Inazō later commented, "*deviated* from character building, or the

---

53. Tamaki Motoi, pp. 44–52.

training of the gentleman, to the acquisition of knowledge and utilitarian purpose" at the expense of the "higher attributes of manhood."[54]

There were many who criticized the general trend of schooling during the 1870s and thus stood at the forefront of what some historians call the "conservative counterattack" or "countertrend" in the modern history of Japanese education.[55] One of the most illustrious was Motoda Eifū, private tutor for the Meiji Emperor, who believed that the learning process had degenerated into an "outward show," a veneer of technical expertise coating a vacuum of moral integrity.[56] Joining Motoda in the attack on utilitarian excesses was Nishimura Shigeki, a fellow Confucian scholar who headed the Compilation Board of the Ministry of Education. In a series of speeches delivered at Tokyo University in 1886, Nishimura called upon students and faculty to help in rebuilding the battered foundation of national morality. Nishimura urged that constraints be imposed on materialism and extravagance in the cities and that attention be refocused on the virtues of "diligence," "stoic resilience," and "perseverance."[57] Nishimura's insistence that higher education also allow time for character development compelled him in later years to lament the passing of the domain school and the fading of the gentlemanly ideal. "If we had not lost the spirit of the education of the domain samurai when the domains were abolished," he said in 1890, "but had carried them over into the national education, we should not have lost the virtues of loyalty, filial piety, honor, and duty, which had been cultivated for several centuries, nor would educated men today need to deplore that morality has fallen to the ground. . . . If today we want to develop moral education on national principles, we should take the former education as our model."[58]

While the legacy of the domain schools considerably influenced the restructuring of higher education in the late nineteenth century, few educators agreed with Nishimura that a

54. Nitobe Inazō, *Japan: Some Phases of Her Problems and Development*, p. 232; also Nitobe, *Japanese Nation* (New York, 1912), pp. 192–193.

55. Ivan Hall, p. 342; Passin, pp. 81–86.

56. Donald Shively, "Motoda Eifū: Confucian Lecturer to the Meiji Emperor," in David Nivison and Arthur Wrights, eds., *Confucianism in Action* (Stanford, 1959), p. 315; also Passin, pp. 226–228.

57. Yoshida Kumaji, ed., *Nihon dōtokuron* (Tokyo, 1935), esp. pp. 88–97 for discussions of the manly virtues.

58. Quoted from Donald Shively, "Nishimura Shigeki: A Confucian View of Modernization," in Marius Jansen, ed., *Changing Japanese Attitudes Toward Modernization* (Princeton, 1965), p. 212.

samurai academy should be resurrected in toto as a pedagogical model. On the other hand, prominent intellectuals in the 1880s shared Nishimura's concern for the declining morals of youth. For example, Tokutomi Sohō, an avowed proponent of Spencer's theory of evolution, was as alarmed as Nishimura and Motoda by the school's failure to meet spiritual needs. In his oft-quoted book of 1886, *Youth of the New Japan*, Tokutomi attacked the "knowledge only" educators who cared little that their students were moral invalids.[59] According to Tokutomi, youth of the day had been taught to equate "fortitude" (*gōki*) with barbarism and "flattery" (*biga*) with elegance. As experts in "the field of kowtowing" (*kōtōgaku*), they were reduced to "prostitutes who peddle blandishments and love."[60] Against this vulgar trend, Tokutomi projected his image of the ideal young man as a patriot (*kokushi*), a youth who was strong in mind, parsimonious in words, determined in action, and schooled in Spencerian ethics. The patriot reviled the temptations of money or sex, seeking inspiration in the masculine ideals of the countryside. He was a "country gentleman" (*inaka no shinshi*) whose courage, perseverance, diligence, and selfless desire to serve the state placed him in the best traditions of his Victorian counterpart.

Miyake Setsurei, Inoue Tetsujirō, Yamaji Aizan, and other writers and critics in the 1880s joined the attack on the early Meiji educational system. Despite differences among observers on reforming the schools, there was a general consensus that utilitarianism and achievement had been overemphasized, that morality had been neglected, and that the nation would suffer unless the spiritual foundation of the school system was strengthened. Students attending institutions of higher learning were more than specialists or experts; they were men of character, reflecting the qualities outlined by Tokutomi and Nishimura.

Not even the most ardent utilitarian could deny the need for a moral elite. The problem stemmed from the assumption that virtue was a by-product of an education centered on "the mastery of things and events." Reformers wanted moral training (*tokuiku* or *shūyō*) restored as a fundamental component of the

59. Tokutomi Sohō, *Shin Nihon no seinen*, in *Nihon gendai bungaku zenshū*, vol. 2 (Tokyo, 1967), p. 264.
60. Ibid., p. 247; I have also used the discussions of this essay in Pyle, *The New Generation in Meiji Japan*, pp. 32–36, and Irwin Scheiner, *Christian Converts and Social Protest in Meiji Japan* (Berkeley, 1970), pp. 216–217.

curriculum. It was one thing, of course, to theorize about the kind of person who should emerge from the school system or to demand that more attention be given to character building; it was quite another to reshape the schools so that these goals were carried out.

The New Look at Preparatory Education: Orita Hikoichi at the Osaka Middle School

Educators who were most concerned with the behavior of the young elite focused their attention less on the university, where students were older and too close to their adult careers to be bothered with ethics, and more on the secondary schools. Many assumed that the best hope for curbing the spread of careerist-pragmatism, exhibitionism, and materialism lay in the development of character long before students entered the university. But secondary education during the early Meiji period constituted a very weak institutional base for the character-building program of educational reformers.

The Educational Code of 1872 had envisioned two different purposes for secondary education: to advance the level of general knowledge among a large segment of the populace, and to prepare selected students for admission to the national university. While the government encouraged local school districts to establish middle schools, officials quickly changed their policy when they realized that the maintenance of equal standards for university preparation in middle schools across the country was impossible. Since most university courses were presented in English or German, the quality of secondary education depended on foreign language instruction, and the number of trained foreign language teachers was severely limited. Consequently, in 1873 the Ministry of Education announced that it would provide public funds to a select number of specially designated middle schools, henceforth designated as "government foreign language schools" (kanritsu gaikokugo gakkō); the remaining middle schools would have to rely on their own resources.[61] This action destroyed any hope for popular secondary education and distressed the families of former feudal lords, who had to assume full responsibility for financing local middle schools or witness their extinction along with the memory of the do-

61. Motoyama Yukihiko, ed., Meiji zenki gakkō seiritsushi (Tokyo, 1965), pp. 22–23.

main schools.[62] Between 1873 and 1875 seven institutions were elevated to the rank of "government foreign language school" on the basis of existing faculty or proximity to foreign settlements, regardless of earlier academic tradition. During the following decade, these schools underwent continual changes in structure and nomenclature; two institutions emerged as the primary targets of government funding: the Tokyo English Academy (renamed the Tokyo University Preparatory School in 1877) and the Osaka English Academy (renamed the Osaka Middle School in 1880).

Not only was the structure of secondary education unstable, but the philosophy of instruction was oblivious to character development. The guiding principle in all classroom endeavors was the efficient raising of the student's competence in spoken and written English or German. This pedagogy of expedience compelled the administration of the Tokyo English Academy to issue the following statement in 1875: "What the student desires most is to graduate as quickly as possible so that he may move on to the various technical fields in the university. Hence, this school should assume the role of a preparatory institution for technical students or an institution for preprofessional students to encourage and advance career ambitions."[63] The statement mirrors the utilitarian ideals of "civilization and enlightenment" and illustrates the pedagogical disposition to narrow the scope of language training in order to meet the professional requirements of the university.

Called the "regular system" (*seisoku seido*), the Ministry of Education's prescribed language program emphasized oral drills and reading exercises from practical texts in geography and the sciences and required the perseverance of a foreign teaching staff who served as mechanical voice-boxes for the students to imitate.[64] Native instructors were rarely visible in the daily classroom activities, and not surprisingly, few students from this period have fond memories of their schooling. Miyake Setsurei, who studied at the foreign language school in Nagoya before moving to the Tokyo University Preparatory School, remembered: "At Nagoya there were many American instructors; in the case of geography, for instance, we had to memorize the

62. Ibid., p. 26.
63. *Rokujūnenshi*, p. 10.
64. Kubota Shōzō, "Kōtō chūgakkō ni okeru gaikokugo kyōiku no ichi," in *KKGK*, no. 7 (January 1976), pp. 17–23.

mountains, rivers, and cities of each state in the United States.
. . . When I transferred to the school in Tokyo, there were even
more foreigners, and they increasingly confused learning with
the study of language."[65]

Miyake's retrospective disdain for the "regular system" of
foreign language instruction was apparently shared by a growing number of school administrators who saw a cause-and-
effect relationship between mechanistic teaching methods and
the diversionary entertainments of students outside the school.
By 1880 the educational community was divided over the issue
of continuing the oral approach to foreign language instruction
or of experimenting with new teaching methods better suited to
the character development of the students. Finally, in July of
1881, the Ministry of Education responded to critics by announcing a new set of regulations for secondary education
(Chūgakkō kyōsoku taikō). According to the revised policy, all
preparatory language schools were now designated as middle
schools with a curriculum divided between lower-level and
higher-level courses.[66] At both levels the Ministry of Education
called for a change of priority from a mechanical focus on foreign language to a more "general curriculum" (futsū kyōka),
which encompassed ethics and literature along with the study
of English. The renewed interest in traditional literature and
philosophy would require additional Japanese staff; and in subsequent communications with individual schools, the Ministry
encouraged the replacement of foreign faculty with native-born
teachers. The implication was clear: Japan, by 1881, had developed sufficiently to break free from "exclusive dependence on
Western teaching methods."[67] Significantly, the new regulations also defined secondary education as "the obligation of
those who are placed above the middle level [of society]"; the
language was manifestly elitist.[68] Thus the Ministry of Education signaled an important departure from the purely utilitarian
ideals of the 1870s and a move toward the restoration of character building for the socialization of a small elite.

The reordering of academic priorities in Tokyo did not result
in immediate changes. Most secondary schools were not prepared to dismiss their staff on one day and rehire a new staff

65. Pyle, p. 59.
66. Kubota Shōzō, p. 15; Motoyama, Meiji zenki gakkō seiritsushi, pp. 32–35.
67. Monbushō, ed., Monbushō dai kyū nenpō (Tokyo, 1966), p. 684.
68. Iwanami kōza gendai kyōikugaku, vol. 16 (Tokyo, 1962), p. 274.

on the next. Nor would they have the financial resources or administrative direction to expand the curriculum. For the next five years secondary education in Japan continued on a "particularly tortuous course," to borrow Ivan Hall's phrase.[69] The passage from compulsory to higher education remained a muddle until the landmark ordinance of 1886, which established the higher school as a clearly demarcated university prep school. Still, the five-year hiatus between 1881 and 1886 was not marred by confusion and indecision in all secondary institutions. At the Osaka Middle School bold reforms foreshadowed educational policies for the higher schools a decade later. The credit for these innovations goes to the young headmaster, Orita Hikoichi, whose eagerness to make the boarding school a source of loyalty and inspiration for its students contributed greatly to the evolution of university preparatory education.

After serving briefly as a supervisor for the government's Physical Training Institute, Orita Hikoichi became principal of the Osaka Middle School in 1880.[70] Having studied at Princeton University, he knew how cohesive a group of students could be in their expressions of loyalty to a school and in their proud isolation from divisive forces in the outer society. In contrast to the orderly world of the Princeton undergraduate, Orita found the Osaka Middle School in virtual chaos. Teachers expended little effort on presentations, unruly students delighted in disrespectful pranks, and administrators stood helplessly in a maze of directives from the Ministry of Education.[71] Aghast at the students' behavior and resolved to add depth to the curriculum, Orita drafted a policy statement in 1881 outlining "urgent needs for the future."

Orita's plan gave direction and purpose to the new government regulations on middle-school instruction. To bring about an "improvement of teaching methods" he demanded that English no longer serve as the medium of classroom instruction

69. Motoyama, *Meiji zenki gakkō seiritsushi*, p. 35. Ivan Hall, p. 416.

70. Orita was born in 1850 in Satsuma, where he received his formative education as a member of a middle-ranking samurai family. He continued his education in Kyoto at the time of the Restoration under the sponsorship of the Iwakura family, which also provided resources for Orita to obtain his master's degree in literature at Princeton University in 1875. Orita remained at the Osaka Middle School (which later became Third Higher) for nearly thirty years. Ofuji Takahiko, "Orita Sensei ni tsuite," *Gakusuikai zasshi*, no. 48 (March 31, 1911), pp. 3–4. Orita's ascetic personality and humanistic pedagogy are discussed in Ishii Kahei and Morita Yoshiaki, eds., *Kurenai moyuru* (Tokyo, 1965), pp. 7–11.

71. The undisciplined and rowdy atmosphere in the school at this time is described in "Jiyūryōshi," pp. vii–viii.

and that the staff, whenever possible, rely on Japanese translations of Western textbooks. With the return to the native tongue and the introduction of new courses in classical Japanese and Chinese literature, Orita terminated the contract of the one remaining American teacher, whose services were no longer needed or appreciated.[72] The release of five foreign instructors between 1879 and 1881 was less a symptom of resurgent nativism than a bold expression of self-reliance. Despite the absence of foreign staff, students continued to spend seven hours a week in English courses, but now the emphasis had shifted from oral drill to literal translation. Concentrating on the formal rather than the spoken language, Japanese teachers were in a better position to cultivate morality among students who had been accustomed to mindless recitation. In retrospect, Orita's view, which became an instructional cornerstone of the later higher school curriculum, had important implications for the sociology of elite education in Japan. Similar to the study of Greek and Latin in Western boarding schools, the concentration on literary English, German, and Chinese created, over the years, a linguistic chasm between the student community and the vernacular society.

A second need was the development of a physical-fitness program. Orita had witnessed the growth of athletics at Princeton, and he was convinced that organized physical activities contributed greatly to the moral well-being of the student. At that time, few schools held classes in physical education, and there was virtually no organized program of extracurricular athletics. University and preparatory students gathered haphazardly for occasional "athletic meetings" (undōkai), which were usually disorderly marathons in which the victors were those who drank the most or courted the most beautiful courtesans.[73] Repelled by the drunken displays in the "athletic meetings," yet determined that an organized physical fitness program be established under the supervision of the school, Orita announced the creation of a required course in calisthenics.[74]

A third area requiring urgent attention was the reform of the

72. Sakakura Tokutarō, ed., Jinryō shōshi (Kyoto, 1939), pp. 87–88.

73. Tsubouchi, pp. 11–12; the early development of extracurricular sports in Japanese schools is discussed in Miyasaka Tetsufumi's "Kagai kyōikushi," in Kagai katsudō no rekishi, Kyōiku bunkashi taikei vol. 1 (Tokyo, 1953); see also Higuchi Ichiyō, "Growing Up," in Donald Keene, ed., Modern Japanese Literature (New York, 1960).

74. Sakakura, pp. 88–89.

student residence system. Previous administrators had ignored the student dormitory, a ramshackle structure, which was over-crowded and chaotic. Sensitive to the possibilities of a well-run dormitory in promoting fraternal camaraderie and institutional loyalty, Orita proposed that students take pride in their place of dwelling. Instead of "temporary quarters" or a random com-plex of "private apartments,"[75] the dormitory should be the center of the school community. As a first step, Orita favored separation of students by age. The pressures for achievement and the emphasis on expedience were no excuse for the ran-dom mixture of twelve-year-olds and twenty-year-olds in the same living quarters. "When younger students live in close proximity to older students," he explained, "they become ac-customed to improper language and activities. Younger stu-dents who have not yet developed their own independence will seldom imitate the best behavior of older students; instead, they will fall victim to improper amusements (*fusei na yūgi*)." These included an "inability to restrict sensual desires."[76] Ori-ta's frank remarks hint at an outbreak of predatory homosex-uality in the Osaka Middle School similar to the "victimization" of preadolescent boys by older roughnecks, which, according to Mori Ōgai, was common in the Tokyo English Academy.[77] To remedy this situation, he urged that a special dormitory be built for the younger students and that stricter discipline be main-tained in all rooms.

The changes Orita Hikoichi instituted at the Osaka Middle School won him notoriety. Nevertheless, he was not alone in his desire to extend the perimeters of preparatory education. The Tokyo University Preparatory School enacted similar re-forms in the early 1880s, including the development of physical education, the abandonment of the regular method of language instruction, and the increase of faculty supervision in the dor-mitory. Thus preparatory education evolved from a narrowly defined program of intensive language training taught by for-eigners to a more expansive liberal arts program taught by Jap-anese scholars. The truncated goals of practical learning were enlarged to include a more general concern for moral growth. Still, with each institution acting on its own, it was unlikely that

75. "Jiyūryōshi," p. 12.
76. Dai San Kōtō Gakkō Dōsōkai, ed., "Kōhon Jinryōshi," unpublished manuscript, p. 526.
77. Mori Ōgai, *Vita Sexualis* (Rutland, Vermont, 1972), pp. 61–72.

preparatory education could be restructured around a uniform set of principles. For this to happen, decisive action by the government was paramount.

Mori Arinori and the Founding of the Higher Schools

The restructuring of secondary education was given a tremendous boost by Mori Arinori, who served as Minister of Education between 1885 and 1889. Mori was one of the most commanding and versatile figures in the Meiji government, serving with distinction as a diplomat before taking over as Minister of Education. His four years in office left an indelible impression on the school system for the duration of the prewar period.

Although Mori never articulated a personal philosophy of education, the reforms instituted under his leadership conformed to one overriding objective: the strengthening of the nation. The relationship between national strength and education was a long-standing article of faith dating back to the pronouncements of Kido Kōin and other Restoration leaders. Nevertheless, Mori feared that this important formula had lost popular appeal, since concern had shifted to the economic and social value of education for the individual and his family. While recognizing that strong individuals build a strong state, he believed that individual achievers should not separate their actions from public duty. Hence, in Komatsu Shūichi's phrase, Mori redirected attention from education for "individual success" (*kojin no risshin*) to education for "national interest" (*kokka no rieki*).[78]

Mori's sense of nationalism and his redefinition of achievement to meet public demands made him a staunch proponent of a differentiated school system in which each level would advance the national interest in different ways. For example, the expectations for primary school students would vary greatly from the expectations for university students. The former were designated by Mori as "citizens" whose "dependent status" prohibited them from attaining more than a rudimentary education. In contrast, students attending the university were recognized as members of "society's upper crust" (*shakai jōryū*), "men of maturity" qualified to pursue advanced studies for

78. Komatsu Shūkichi, "Kokumin kyōiku seido no seiritsu," in *Kindai kyōikushi,* Kyōikugaku zenshū, vol. 3 (Tokyo, 1970), p. 62.

professional careers. Mori's absolute distinction between rudimentary instruction (*kyōiku*) and advanced learning (*gakumon*) indicates that he correlated the conferral of social status with the transmission of knowledge.[79]

In a series of important ordinances issued in the spring of 1886, the Ministry of Education, under Mori's leadership, clarified the purposes of each level of the school system in terms suggesting a hierarchy of social status. The primary schools occupied the lowest level of the hierarchy and were charged "to provide such training as [would] enable the young to understand their duties as Japanese subjects."[80] The emphasis on rudimentary instruction and iron-handed discipline was also foreshadowed in the Normal School Ordinance, which established a separate educational track for the training of primary school teachers. At the other end of the academic ladder, far removed from the regimentation inflicted on students in the normal and primary schools, stood the Imperial University, the unique center for empirical research and advanced study of the tiny academic elite.

Bridging the gap between the masses, who attended the primary schools, and the carefully selected elite in the university were the middle schools. Of the reforms Mori Arinori initiated, none was as far-reaching in its impact on the regulation of social mobility as the Middle School Ordinance of 1886. The Ordinance conferred structure and order upon the most chaotic sector of the school system. After nearly fifteen years of uneven development, the secondary sector was divided into two graduated stages: the first was occupied by a five-year ordinary middle school (*jinjō chūgakkō*) for students aged twelve to seventeen; the second, by a two-year (soon to be three-year) higher middle school (*kōtō chūgakkō*) for students aged seventeen to twenty. (Hereafter I will use the abbreviated term "higher school" (*kōtō gakkō*), which became the official designation in 1894.) Entrance to both institutions would be competitive, although the stipulation of age was a deterrent to precocity.

The Ordinance of 1886 made clear distinctions between the two secondary levels: whereas the ordinary middle schools would receive funds from local prefectures or private foundations, the higher schools were national institutions, financed

79. Ivan Hall, pp. 409–412.
80. Ivan Hall, p. 412.

completely by the central government. Likewise, an indefinite number of middle schools might rise and fall according to local fiscal policy, but the number of higher schools was initially limited to five, thus creating a numerical imbalance, from 8 to 1 in 1890 to nearly 30 to 1 by 1900.[81] The uneven ratio between middle and higher schools was underscored by pedagogical distinctions. In an address at a prefectural conference of school administrators in 1887, Mori lumped the ordinary middle schools with the primary schools as institutions that dispensed an everyday, practical education (*futsū jitsugyō kyōiku*). However, when a student reached the higher school, expectations were "completely different." Mori elaborated:

> Those who study in the higher school may, upon graduation, move immediately into business or pursue a specialized course of study. In either case, they will enter society's upper crust (*shakai jōryū*). Namely, the higher schools should cultivate, among those who are headed for the upper crust [of society], men worthy of directing the thoughts of the masses: be they bureaucrats, then those of the highest echelon, be they businessmen, then those for the top management, be they scholars, then true experts in the various arts and sciences.[82]

Mori set the higher school apart from both the ordinary middle school, where the vast majority of students would move into low-level management positions as clerks or plant foremen, and the university, where students specialized in narrow academic fields. Concomitantly, Mori seemed to reject the idea of the higher school as a mere institutional bridge between lower secondary and higher education. That many successful applicants would eventually climb the academic and social ladders was a foregone conclusion. The real significance of the

81. By the end of 1887, the Ministry of Education had expanded the number of schools from five to seven, although the status of the added academies was somewhat precarious. See chap. 2, n. 62.

Ratio Between Middle and Higher Schools

	1890	1900	1910	1920
Middle Schools	55	194	302	368
	11,620	78,315	122,345	177,201
Higher Schools	7	7	8	15
	4,356	5,684	6,341	8,839

Note: Top figures are for number of schools, and bottom figures represent total student enrollment; Monbushō, ed., *Gakusei hachijūnenshi* (Tokyo, 1953), pp. 1046–1047, 1058–1059.

82. Kyōikushi Hensankai, ed., *Meiji ikō kyōiku seido hattatsushi*, vol. 3 (Tokyo, 1963), p. 153; Komatsu, p. 61; Ivan Hall, p. 417. I have used Hall's translation for the phrase "be they bureaucrats . . . arts and sciences."

schools was their anticipated role in shaping the mind and the entire ethical outlook of the young men destined "to direct the thought of the masses" (*shakai tasū no shisō o sayū suru*). The higher school, he later explained, would be "the wellspring for those who wield the power of future Japan."[83] Hence, the orientation of preparatory education, as prefigured by Orita Hikoichi, was transformed from the middle-school goal of useful learning for the *achievement* of status to training for the *affirmation* of status. The distinction is important, for Mori was charting a special course for the higher schools as an agent of social stratification, which bore distinct similarities both to the Tokugawa domain schools and to elite boarding schools in the West.

83. Ōkubo Toshiaki, ed., *Mori Ainori zenshū*, vol. 1 (Tokyo, 1972), p. 527.

CHAPTER TWO

Between Nation and Campus:
The Making of the Higher School
Gentleman

The first educational task of the communities should be the preservation *of education within the cloister, uncontaminated by the deluge of
barbarism outside.*

T. S. ELIOT, *"MODERN EDUCATION
AND THE CLASSICS,"* (1933)

*In England [the well-bred child] would be the gentleman, a social type
unknown before the nineteenth century, and which a threatened aristocracy would create, thanks to the public schools, to defend itself against the
progress of democracy.*

PHILIPPE ARIÈS, *CENTURIES OF CHILDHOOD* (1962)

The decade that stretched from 1885 to 1895 has been described
as a "major watershed" in the history of modern Japan.[1] The
revolutionary idealism that propelled the overthrow of the
Bakufu and, later, the agrarian phase of the "people's rights
movement" was on the wane at the end of the century as the
Meiji leadership proudly saluted the Restoration as a grand
event (*goisshin*) to be honored (as one honors a historical monument) but not to be relived.[2] Gone, too, was the spirit of bold,
often iconoclastic experimentation that had highlighted the era
of "civilization and enlightenment," when teams of American
and European experts manned the advisory agencies of the
fledgling state. Through the accelerated growth of the tradi-

---

1. Kenneth Pyle, *The New Generation in Meiji Japan*, p. 188.
2. Okawada, p. 447.

tional economy and the establishment of strategic industries, Japan in the 1890s was a strong nation-state capable of humiliating China in armed conflict and of breaking out of the shackles of the unequal treaties. Paralleling these military and diplomatic achievements were the crafting and the consolidation of the permanent fixtures of the imperial-bureaucratic state: the constitution, the civil service, the legal system, the political parties, and the public schools. For each of these institutions, the Japanese leadership adopted a highly discriminating and pluralistic approach that permitted revival of Confucian values and Shinto mythology within the framework of a legal-rational state. Far from being a reactionary turn to the past, the neo-traditional revival confronted the modern challenge of maintaining social integration during industrialization.

The establishment of the higher schools in 1886 provides an interesting perspective on the evolving philosophy of government officials and educators at the end of the century. There were two premises on which the government acted when it restructured the school system. The first of these was the belief that education should be regarded as a moral problem; instruction limited either to the three Rs or to vocational training could result in the rearing of half-educated students whose lack of moral fiber might inhibit Japan's quest for national dignity. Although educators clashed repeatedly over the relative importance of moral versus technical education for years to come, there was general agreement throughout the prewar period that the Educational Code had been rash in promising wealth and fame to the advanced student and had inspired little moral growth within the context of the national community.

In refocusing attention on moral education and national service, the reformers of the late nineteenth century were less concerned with facilitating achievement than with ensuring that the individual student was integrated into a stable social order after the completion of his schooling. Hence, the second premise behind the reforms in the 1880s was that education should play an important role in the socialization of occupational groups and social strata. For the majority of the population, the primary schools assumed all responsibility for anticipatory socialization by preparing students for a "dependent status," according to Mori Arinori, or citizenship within the working classes. Since the percentage of school-age children attending primary schools climbed dramatically from just under 50 percent in 1890 to 95 percent by 1905,[3] rudimentary courses in ethics and civic propriety, centered around daily recitations of the Imperial Rescript on Education, were of increasing sociological importance.

Beyond the universal primary school was a network of academic tracks which had been outlined during Mori Arinori's tenure as Minister of Education and completed in 1903 with the Technical School Ordinance. (See Appendixes I and II for diagrams and enrollment figures for the late Meiji public school system.) The network consisted of distinct lines for teachers' education, vocational training, women's secondary schooling, and advanced learning in the arts and sciences. Another line comprised the private colleges, which, until 1918, were classified by the government, in an unflattering manner, as technical schools (*senmon gakkō*) for wealthy youth who could not enter the public higher schools and university. Admittance to each track was competitive; but once a student had survived the entrance examinations, he or she was assured of training in accordance with a fixed typology of his or her anticipated profession or status. For the normal schools, the ideal type was the hard-driving, tight-lipped instructor; for the vocational schools, it was the efficient, though not particularly imaginative, technician or engineer; for the secondary women's schools, it was the supremely dedicated homemaker; for the private college, it was the innovative and forward-thinking businessman, journalist, or other nongovernmental professional. Behind each typology was the cavalier assumption that the educator, with adequate facilities and resources, could mold the disposition of the student to fit neatly into a demarcated social order.[4]

The problem of anticipatory socialization attained its most conscious and sophisticated level of discourse within the higher schools. More than the university (with its detached empiricist orientation) or the middle school (with its emphasis on achievement), the higher school was concerned with the perfection of human character. The early headmasters viewed the entering higher school students as incomplete persons who, despite remarkable initiative and talent on entrance examinations, were still the products of an undistinguished primary and middle school experience. In order to remold childhood attitudes and

3. Monbushō, ed., *Gakusei hachijūnenshi*, pp. 1036–1037.
4. For a discussion of the "normal school type," see Karasawa Tomitarō, *Kyōshi no rekishi* (Tokyo, 1968), esp. pp. 55–77; the academic tracks are further described in Ivan Hall, pp. 412–437.

habits, the headmasters invented the higher school gentleman, a procrustean model of the ideal human being that was imposed on a group of cloistered students who, initially, were unprotesting recipients.

Mechanisms of Cultivation

Although many of the early higher school headmasters had studied in the West and were aware that Japan had to industrialize in order to survive in a competitive and hostile world, they were distressed by the social and cultural implications of material progress as manifested in undesirable strains of commercialism, hedonism, and utilitarianism. They feared that the transformation of material culture was spawning chaos within the social order, that educated youth, who should be untouched by the corruption of the "vulgar world" (zokukai), had no conception of the "duties of studenthood" (shosei no honbun), and mirrored the worst fashions of the city. Several headmasters attributed the lack of "status and responsibility" (chii to sekinin) among the new generation of educated youth to their parvenu heritage. One explained that loose morals among students were caused by "the abolition of feudalism and the emergence of a new social order,"[5] and another warned against "the customs of lower-class students" (karyū shosei no fugi).[6] Concern over the lowering status of students prompted further speculation in the early issues of higher school magazines: "Why is it that among students today the offspring of merchants and peasants are most likely to ignore moral standards and disrupt the code of respectability?"[7]

Such were the questions that loomed in the minds of those entrusted with shaping educational policy in the new academies. While it is doubtful that the sons of samurai, who still represented the bulk of the student population, acted any differently from the sons of commoners, the perception that this might be the case or that samurai descendants had lost their sense of status honor was significant. It suggested, first, that students desperately needed proper social breeding (shitsuke) to compensate for the lack in either family background or scholastic upbringing, and, second, that despite the inexorable trans-

5. Rokujūnenshi, p. 105.
6. Takahashi Samon, "Kyūsei kōtō gakkō ni okeru kōfū no seiritsu to hatten III," in KKGK, no. 8 (April 1976), p. 12.
7. Yamazaki Nobuki, "Gakufūron," Shōshikai zasshi, no. 18 (Dec. 18, 1896), p. 9.

formation of historical space as Japan faced the twentieth century, the character of future leaders must be located along a spiritual continuum linking past with present, tradition with modernity. The higher school bore a major responsibility in meeting this crisis by establishing a typological model for the young elite and institutional mechanisms that would ensure the systematic cultivation of the ideal type.

Even before the schools were opened or permanently situated, Mori Arinori had made public utterance that the higher school would "cultivate the gentleman" (*shi o yashinau*).[8] The model was more precisely defined by one of Mori's colleagues in the Ministry of Education, Yoshimura Toratarō, who later became the first headmaster of the Second Higher School. Yoshimura envisioned the higher school gentleman as "a man who, regardless of wealth, status, or occupation, elevates his willpower and keeps his thoughts clear and pure." "When standing between heaven and earth, he [the gentleman] never feels ashamed nor allows a speck of filth or ignobility to affect his disposition." The gentleman, according to Yoshimura, was above the lure of money or personal gain, for that might "soil his heart" and undermine his credibility as a "man of purpose."[9]

In detailing the attributes of his educated ideal, Yoshimura would not be diverted by the complexities of terminology or cultural precedent. It made little difference, he explained, whether one referred to the "gentleman" as *shi* (samurai), *kunshi* (Confucian paragon), *shinshi* (the contemporary translation for the Victorian gentleman), or the English *zentorumen*. Variations in nomenclature were trifling, provided students realized that the gentleman embodied the ideal political and social personality for a number of different societies. Whether in China, England, or Japan, he shared a common descent from a class of feudal knights who had, with the passage of time, transformed their social role from primitive warriors to "pillars of society" (*shakai no chūseki*) and "exemplars for the people who occupy society's upper crust" (*shakai no jōryū ni kuraishi hito no gihan*).[10] Emulating the best traditions of the domesticated warrior gentleman, Yoshimura urged his students to become guardians of the social order and dedicated public servants.

Many others, including Tokutomi Sohō and Yamaji Aizan,

8. Dai Yon Kōtō Gakkō Jishūryō Ryōshi Hansan Iinkai, *Dai Yon Kōtō Gakkō Jishūryōshi* (Kanazawa, 1948), p. 1.
9. Toita Tomoyoshi, *Kyūsei kōtō gakkō kyōiku no seiritsu* (Kyoto, 1975), p. 34.
10. Ibid.

called upon higher school students to behave as gentlemen and social exemplars.[11] The real challenge to early school administrators, however, was a problem more of pedagogy than of theory. Almost everyone agreed that a student should be manly, self-restrained, frugal, and pure-minded; but what instructional mechanisms would nurture such an individual? Although specific policies for character building varied slightly from school to school, there were several general assumptions about the best method for cultivating the gentleman which appear to have guided both the Ministry of Education and local school administrators.

The first assumption stipulated that the education of the gentleman proceed by moral training. Educational policy in the early higher schools aimed at molding the personality of the student by placing him in a controlled setting and subjecting him to a fixed instructional regimen. The gentleman-student would be the product of environmental conditioning, or what Herbart (who commanded a sizable following among late-nineteenth-century educators) called the restructuring of the "furniture of the mind" through the use of "presentations." While educators associated with the early higher schools were concerned about the spiritual welfare of the student, they tended to be insensitive to the existence of innate feelings. Instead, they focused on the inculcation of social values through external means, whose application often made the experience of becoming a gentleman as much of an ordeal as it had been in the Tokugawa domain schools.

Exemplifying this attitude was the almost obsessive attention given to geographic setting. In the view of most administrators, the physical surrounding of the school was the most important condition for effective character building. The ideal setting was in the countryside, far removed from the corrupting influence of the city; when pastoral locations were not available, the school would have to be sealed behind high walls and fences. In either case, students were obliged to sever ties with the "vulgar world" and live as if secluded in a monastery. Only then could their demeanor be elevated to a higher moral plane.

In secluding the students physically and socially from the outside world, the architects of the higher schools were adamant about bringing faculty and students together into a close-knit community with pseudo-kinship ties. The idea of a "family

11. *Shūgakuryōshi*, pp. 94–95.

school" was inspired both by the memory of the Tokugawa academies and by the recent recommendations of educators like Orita Hikoichi. Structurally, the community ideal was realized by encouraging students to reside on campus, where they could live as "brothers" under the care of surrogate "fathers" chosen from the faculty. Behind the warm promise to restore the "family school" was an underlying desire to extend faculty control over the daily lives of the students, and to make the school into what Erving Goffman has called a "total institution"—"a place of residence or work where a large number of like-situated individuals, cut off from the wider society for an appreciable period of time, . . . lead an enclosed, formally administered round of life." [12]

It was further hoped that the collective experience of living together under a common roof would generate among the students a strong sense of institutional loyalty that could be transmuted into national loyalty. The early higher school administrators championed institutional idealism and seriously believed that the spirit of the school was organically linked to the national ethos. To strengthen this relationship, they devised an elaborate network of symbols (flags, uniforms, badges, mottoes) and sponsored numerous patriotic celebrations through which the students identified the "spirit of the school" (*kōfū*) with the "spirit of national devotion" (*aikokushin*). The codification of student behavior in civic rituals increased the likelihood of graduates subordinating private claims for the public good: the true mark of a gentleman.

The emphasis on physical environment, nation, and school spirit overshadowed developments in the formal academic curriculum. Since education in the higher schools was a total experience, administrators and faculty were reluctant to view classroom instruction in isolation from the pedagogical goals of building character. This staunchly antivocational attitude, epitomized in the claim by an early higher school pedagogue that "Chinese learning is the only study for building human beings," undoubtedly discomfited government officials. [13] The

12. Erving Goffman, *Asylums* (Garden City, N.Y., 1963), p. xiii; the application of Goffman's theory to the British public schools has been suggested by Ian Weinberg, *The English Public Schools* (New York, 1967), p. 8, and John R. Gillis, *Youth and History* (New York, 1974), p. 109.

13. Orita Mitsuru, "Natsukashii Ichikō jidai no kaiko," in *Ichikō Dōsōkai kaihō*, no. 34 (May 25, 1937), p. 31.

Middle School Ordinance of 1886 specified a division of the higher school curriculum into seven courses: law, medicine, engineering, literature, science, agriculture, and commerce. While supplementary remarks by Mori Arinori on the importance of cultivation for leadership raised questions as to how rigorously these specialized fields should be pursued, there were those in the Ministry of Education who expected the higher school to maintain sufficiently high standards in the seven areas to allow graduates not wishing to proceed to the university the opportunity to become middle-level engineers or medical practitioners. But the vision of the higher school performing the dual function of university preparation for some students and vocational training for others proved unworkable. Terminal courses in agriculture, commerce, engineering, and law were short-lived or never established.[14] The only "technical course" (senmon gakka) that attained a strong foothold in the higher school curriculum was a program for paramedics. Yet even this had limited impact on higher school life, since the medical departments were isolated from the main campuses, and all were eventually transformed into independent institutions.[15]

Although the vast majority of matriculants were bound for the university, the higher schools did not, initially, accept new students on an equal footing. Because of widespread scholastic inadequacies in the middle schools, many students, who performed marginally on the entrance examination, were accepted on condition that they take special remedial courses before entering the two-year "main course" (honka). By 1894 the general quality of matriculating students had risen markedly, and the remedial courses were quickly abandoned.[16] Thereafter, all uni-

14. Terminal degrees in agriculture and commerce were never awarded by the higher schools, and the number of students in law and engineering never exceeded a combined total of 250 for all the higher schools. Except for a small engineering program at the Fifth Higher School that lasted until 1908, the technical courses were phased out of the higher schools by 1900. An unsuccessful attempt by the Ministry of Education in 1894 to strengthen the "technical course" is discussed in the following chapter. See also Nakajima Tarō, "Kyūsei kōtō gakkō seido no hensen," I, in Tōhoku Daigaku Kyōikugaku-bu kenkyū nenpō, no. 11 (1963), pp. 13–14.

15. In three cases the medical departments were located in separate towns. See Nakajima Tarō, "Kyūsei kōtō gakkō seido no seiritsu," in Tōhoku Daigaku Kyōikugakubu kenkyū nenpō, no. 5 (1957), pp. 17–18. The dissolution of the higher school medical departments is also discussed in the following chapter.

16. Nakajima, "Kyūsei kōtō gakkō seido no seiritsu," pp. 15–17. While in effect, the remedial courses, depending on the individual, lasted from one to three years. In other words, they assumed the burden of the third, fourth, and fifth years in the middle schools.

versity-bound students were grouped together in a single, three-year "preparatory course" (*yoka*). Ministry of Education regulations did allow students a choice of three academic programs that fed into advanced university studies in literature, science, and medicine. Variations between programs should not be exaggerated, however, since every student, whether he planned to pursue German philosophy or chemical engineering at the university, received a liberal arts education, with the bulk of class hours devoted to Japanese and Chinese literature, pure (as opposed to applied) science, and most important, literary English and German. (See Appendix III, Table I.) Although the humanities-centered curriculum drew heated criticism throughout the prewar period, higher school regulations steadfastly upheld linguistic facility and literary taste (*bungakujō no shumi*) as special privileges of the university-bound elite.[17]

Concerned more with training gentlemen than with imparting knowledge, the early higher school faculty posed as men of impeccable moral standard and character. Apart from a handful of specialists in the department of medicine, the faculty was dominated by two interdependent groups. First, there were the much-venerated "old bushi types" (*kobushi no tenkei*), as the students called them, the ascetic pedagogues of Far Eastern philosophy and literature.[18] Draped in black kimonos, sporting long white beards, and alluding cryptically to the *Analects*, these living relics from the old domain academies reminded the students of their place in history. Balancing the museum-like image of the "old *bushi* types" was the much younger, though equally traditionalistic, group of headmasters and teachers of Western languages, who were more intimately involved in the upbringing of the students. In an effort to reduce the gap between teacher and pupil, some, like Kanō Jigorō, exchanged blows with their students in the kendo shed, while others, like Orita Hikoichi, bathed in the dormitory tub.[19] Physical proximity notwithstanding, the headmasters still maintained an air of aloofness, which kept them apart from their pupils even when they were soaking in the same water. The headmaster was an object of respect and occasionally of fear, but rarely of love.

17. Ishida Katsuo, "Kyūsei kōtō gakkō gakka katei no hensen," *Kokuritsu kyōiku kenkyūjo kiyō*, no. 95 (March 1978), esp. pp. 137–139.

18. *Kōryōshi*, p. 369; *Gokō gojūnenshi*, pp. 170–172; Ōura Hachirō, ed., *Sankō hachijūnen kaikō* (Tokyo, 1950), pp. 147–149.

19. *Shūgakuryōshi*, p. 361; Ōura, p. 59.

The Establishment of the First Higher School

On April 29, 1886, just two weeks after the issuance of the Middle School Ordinance, the Tokyo University Preparatory School was renamed and reorganized as the First Higher School (referred to more simply in Japanese as Ichikō).[20] Not only was Ichikō the first higher school to be founded, it was also earmarked by the Ministry of Education as the model institution whose policies would be emulated by the other academies.[21] The exemplary role of the school extended to the setting up of curriculum, drafting of student regulations, and building of a "fixed school spirit" (*ittei no kōfū*) around the metaphors of devotion to the nation and family unity. The one exceptional feature of Ichikō was its physical location in the heart of the capital city. Although the campus was moved in 1890 to a more secluded setting, Ichikō students never had easy access to the mountain streams and valleys of their brethren in the provincial higher schools.

Initially, both the Ichikō administration and the Ministry of Education were concerned that the image of the new school might be tarnished by the legacy of the old preparatory college, which, in the eyes of many educators, symbolized the selfishness and decadence of contemporary students.[22] To counter such suspicions, the Ichikō administration took swift and decisive measures to stiffen the regulations affecting all aspects of student life, from matriculation to graduation.

Of immediate significance was the intrusion of certain ascriptive barriers into the admissions procedures. Along with performing admirably on the entrance examination, the prospective Ichikō student was expected to be seventeen years old and blessed with "acceptable manners, health, and demeanor," as defined by the administration. Any impediment of speech, deformity of body, or idiosyncrasy of behavior constituted grounds for denying admission to even the brightest candidate. The prospective student was also required to pay a one-yen fee to take the entrance examination and a yearly tuition of twenty yen. Especially when compared with the private colleges, these rates were not extraordinary even though they represented a considerable hike over the thirty-sen examination fee and two-

20. *Rokujūnenshi*, p. 111.
21. Ibid., p. 119.
22. As described in Mori Ōgai, *Vita Sexualis*, pp. 61–102.

yen tuition in the former preparatory school.[23] At the same
time that they raised tuition and fees, the Ichikō administration
terminated the preparatory school program of granting scholar-
ships to needy students. As justification, the administration
noted that low fees and tuition "cannot improve the dignity and
grace of the applicants."[24] Nakagawa Gen, special assistant to
the Minister of Education during the 1880s and headmaster at
three successive higher schools between 1891 and 1911, added:
"Those of meager means will receive a lower education, those
of moderate means will receive a middle-level education, and
those of considerable means will receive an advanced education."[25]

There is little question that the fees and tuition at Ichikō,
which applied to all the higher schools, functioned as safeguards against uncontrolled social mobility. In the opinion of
educators like Nakagawa, the ambitious, though hopelessly
uncultured or impoverished, student was not meant for the
higher schools, and was better advised to enter a normal school
where the government paid all expenses so that lower-class
achievers might become reliable martinets in the primary school
classroom.[26] This does not mean that objective standards for
achievement at Ichikō were suddenly discarded for old class di-
visions. Competition for distinction on the entrance examinations increased steadily throughout the Meiji period, enabling
the higher schools to draw from a wider spectrum of the rural
and urban middle classes than was presumably the case in elite
boarding schools in the West.[27] Yet the new admissions requirements put the higher schools beyond the reach of the
working-class family and signaled an end to the early Meiji
practice of rushing fourteen- and fifteen-year-olds through the
gates of Tokyo University. As the institutions of state took firm
root at the end of the century, the urgency to produce a skilled
governing elite had slackened; consequently, the new higher
school administrations had ample time to choose their candi-
dates carefully and to remold their character after matriculation.

In pursuit of the latter goal, the Ichikō administration issued
a directive in October 1886, announcing its intention to guide all

23. *Rokujūnenshi*, pp. 45 and 159.
24. Toita, p. 141.
25. Kuda Katsuo, "Mori Arinori no kyōiku zaisei seisaku, *Kyōikushi kenkyū* 1 (Oct. 1955):28.
26. Ivan Hall, p. 419.
27. Kimijima Ichirō, *Daryō ichibanshitsu* (Tokyo, 1967), pp. 136–137.

students along "the important path outside the curriculum" (*gakkagai no yōdō*).[28] Against a background of faculty leniency and disinterest, the memorandum notified students that the school would assume responsibility for their deportment in loco parentis. During the succeeding two years, as the faculty drew up specific regulations backed up by "punishments" for those students who "rendered harm to the learning atmosphere,"[29] it became clear that Ichikō needed a creative and articulate spokesman who could do more than issue threatening memoranda. Precisely because he had this wider vision of the role of the higher school in the nation's future, Kinoshita Hiroji, a close associate of Mori Arinori, was appointed assistant headmaster of the school in 1888 and headmaster the following year. During his five-year tenure, Kinoshita left a permanent mark on the course of preparatory education in prewar Japan.

Kinoshita Hiroji and the Pedagogy of Seclusion

Kinoshita Hiroji was only thirty-seven when he arrived at First Higher, but he had already compiled a remarkably diverse and impressive vita. Born in central Kyūshū, the son of a Confucian scholar, Kinoshita was schooled in a small, family-run academy before enrolling in the famous domain school near his home, the Jishūkan. The early training in Confucian ethics and political ideals had an enduring effect on his distinguished career. In 1870, Kinoshita received a government scholarship to study at Tokyo University (then called Daigaku Nankō), where he pursued a law degree. Five years later, after graduating from the university, he was awarded a scholarship to continue law at the University of Paris. Upon returning to Japan in 1879, Kinoshita was appointed to a number of government commissions and taught for a while at Tokyo University before coming to Ichikō in the summer of 1888.[30]

Despite his training as a legal scholar and a foremost authority of French political thought, Kinoshita maintained an active interest throughout his life in educational policy, specifically in the tasks of higher school and university adminis-

28. *Rokujūnenshi*, p. 130.
29. Ibid., pp. 175–176.
30. Kinoshita stayed at Ichikō until 1893, when he returned to the Ministry of Education briefly before becoming the first president of Kyoto University in 1897, a position he occupied until 1908. He died in August 1910 at the age of sixty. Karasawa Tomitarō, *Kōshinsei*, pp. 237–240.

1. Kinoshita Hiroji (ca. 1890). Courtesy of Kōdansha

tration. Rather than converting him into a political or legal the-
orist, the experience at the University of Paris seemed to make
Kinoshita all the more wary of abstract speculation about human rights and natural law, which might justify the pretensions
of political radicals but contributed little to the stability of administration. In Kinoshita's opinion, France suffered from an
overdevelopment of theory and an underdevelopment of institutions.[31] By contrast, he was favorably impressed by the
gradual evolution of constitutional government in England
along with its supporting educational institutions: the public
schools and universities, which assured an orderly flow of cultivated gentlemen into parliament and the civil service. The incident that most deeply impressed Kinoshita during his four
years in Europe was a boat race between Oxford and Cambridge. The gentlemanly decorum and spirit of "fair play" per-
vading the event reminded Kinoshita of the "spirit of *bushidō*"
and brought him to the apparent recognition that the success of
liberal institutions in England rested on an underlying moral
edifice.[32]

To return to Japan in 1879, to the clamor for "people's rights"
and to the exhibitionism of student dandies was troubling.

31. Kinoshita Masao and Kinoshita Michio, "Ko Kinoshita Hiroji no omoide," in
Ichikō Dōsōkai kaihō 30 (Feb. 23, 1936):23–25.
32. Yamamoto Jūrō, ed., *Higo bunkyō to sono jōfu no kyōiku* (Kumamoto, 1956),
pp. 278–279.

Serving as adviser to the Ministry of Education and lecturer in legal studies at Tokyo University, Kinoshita observed the changing mores of student life. He was undoubtedly dismayed by the growing popularity of ballroom dancing among a group of students from Tokyo University and a nearby women's school who tried to imitate the "high collar" social gatherings at the Rokumeikan.[33] Kinoshita also witnessed a surge of campus political activity, notably in October 1883, when nearly two hundred students from both the university and the preparatory school boycotted graduation ceremonies. The immediate issue was the university's decision to enclose the entire campus within a high wooden fence, but there were broader implications, since the angry students also joined in a protest demonstration in Ueno Park in defiance of the government's new Law on Public Meetings.[34] Even if the "political youth" (*seiji seinen*) of the day had no intention of causing serious disruption, Kinoshita believed they were not fulfilling the duties of studenthood. Thus, he joined Mori Arinori and other leading educators who voiced concern over the lack of moral direction in higher education. In this spirit, he gladly relinquished his chair in law to become Ichikō's assistant headmaster.

Within weeks of his arrival at First Higher, Kinoshita delivered an important address to a student-faculty assembly which capsulized the emerging philosophy of preparatory education. Kinoshita opened his remarks by reiterating the ideal of the higher school "gentleman" (*kunshi*): "You students of First Higher will someday stand in the upper crust of society (*shakai no jōryū ni tachi*). Whether in politics, the arts, or scholarly affairs," the young assistant headmaster proclaimed, "you are the future leaders of Japan. Therefore, it is natural that your personal manners be impeccable and your aspirations noble so that you set a standard for other youth."[35] The system of higher education in Japan, Kinoshita continued, was founded on the belief that those students headed for the university possess "self-respect" (*jikei*), "decorum" (*reisetsu*), and "morals" (*shūshin*). Only when endowed with these qualities could a student become a "great man" (*taijin*) capable of fulfilling responsible duties in the wider arena of public life. The vocabulary and

33. Ōmuro Teiichirō, *Daigaku oyobi daigakusei*, pp. 38–39.
34. Terasaki Masao, "Jichiryōseido seiritsu shiron," in *KKGK*, no. 15 (January 1978), pp. 24–25.
35. *Rokujūnenshi*, p. 103.

content of these statements were reminiscent of classical Confucian formulations on the inseparable relationship between the cultivation of personal character and the execution of public duties.

Unfortunately, according to Kinoshita, there were disturbingly few well-mannered or high-spirited gentlemen among the ranks of Meiji students. "When I observe your everyday behavior," he told his slightly humbled audience, "I am appalled by the way you enter the classroom with your hats on, ignore proper etiquette towards passers-by on the street, and sing loudly wherever you go." More objectionable was the extravagant "student fashion" (*shoseifū*) that beguiled young men of their money, masculinity, and sense of public duty. The university and preparatory school students depicted in the popular fiction of Shōyō were stumbling, indecisive braggarts, whose total lack of energy ranked them with the most unseemly elements of the vulgar society. There was every indication, Kinoshita continued, that unless measures were taken to shield students from a world of extravagance and private indulgence, they might never succeed in "gaining the respect of society."[36] Having consulted with Mori Arinori, who was also "deeply concerned" about the "lack of trustworthiness" among students, Kinoshita made the following declaration:

> [F]or you students to lead a moral life by cultivating your spirit correctly, while living in a society that reeks with bad manners and obscenity, is a formidable task. I understand your distressing situation, but I believe it essential that you be resolute. In particular, I hope you will realize that when you take just one step off the campus, everyone is an enemy—that the higher school is, in effect, a castle under seige.[37]

The alarmist reference to a "castle under seige" (*rōjō*), which Kinoshita repeated on several occasions and to other higher school students around the country,[38] has the distinctly traditional connotations of the "closed-society" (*tojita shakai*) view of the world that has, for many Japanese historians, become a metaphor for Tokugawa feudalism.[39] It seems to hearken as

36. Ibid., p. 103.
37. Ibid., p. 104.
38. For example, just one month after his speech at Ichikō, Kinoshita issued a similar warning to the students of Fifth Higher. *Gokō gojūnenshi*, pp. 93–94.
39. Matsumoto Sannosuke, *Kindai Nihon no chiteki jōkyō* (Tokyo, 1974), p. 134; Kamishima Jirō believes that Kinoshita's policy of seclusionism was indeed rooted in the closed-world view of the Tokugawa domain or feudal village. Kamishima Jirō, *Kindai Nihon no seishin kōzō* (Tokyo, 1970), pp. 28–31.

well to a Confucian principle that human perfectability requires nurture in a carefully prescribed setting. Yet Kinoshita's theory of seclusion (*rōjōshugi*) or monasticism revealed not only his affection for the past but also his distress over social and political conditions in the late 1880s. While accepting the imperative that Japan should industrialize quickly as a condition for national strength, he believed that social and political changes should proceed at a much slower pace. Elites must maintain their self-respect and manliness before popular pressures and amusements. Hence, Kinoshita's design for turning the higher school into a castle, sheltered from the vulgarities of "ordinary, run-of-the-mill students" (*jinjō bon'yō no shosei*), echoes the sentiment of a galaxy of conservative critics (from Tocqueville to Karl Mannheim) who have lamented the diminishing insulation of cultural elites from the masses.[40] "To counteract rather than copy the defects of the day," said A. Lawrence Lowell, "is the greatest goal for higher education."[41] With this defensive conception of the school, Kinoshita was in full accord.

In achieving the essentially negative goal of transforming the campus into a *univers clos,* Kinoshita was greatly assisted in 1890 by the government's decision to move the entire campus from a congested quarter of Kanda to a far quieter, secluded setting atop Mukōga Hill in Hongō, where once stood the alternate residence of one of the Tokugawa retainers.[42] A giant wrought-iron gate and a high picket fence severed the school physically and psychologically from the city, with the effect of reifying Kinoshita's metaphor of a "castle under seige."

There was, however, a positive dimension to the plea for seclusion. The formulation that "one step off the campus everyone is an enemy" (*kōgai ippo mina teki*) was balanced by the comforting possibility that everyone inside the school was your brother or father. Once liberated from all social and cultural disorders, students and faculty could make of their cloistered community a surrogate family guided by the virtues of intimacy, propriety, and loyalty—virtues that were infelicitously absent from the developing urban society. Kinoshita bemoaned the primordial family, which in the post-Restoration era no longer

40. Harold L. Wilensky, "Mass Society and Mass Culture: Interdependence or Independence?" *American Sociological Review* 29, no. 2 (April 1964): 174.

41. Quoted in Henry Farnham May, *The End of American Innocence: A Study of the First Years of Our Times, 1912–1917* (New York, 1959), p. 57.

42. Nishizawa Kichi et al., eds., *Aa gyokuhai ni hana ukete: Dai Ichi Kōtō Gakkō hachijūnenshi* (Tokyo, 1972), p. 236.

provided children with proper social breeding (*shitsuke*). There-fore, the school had to assume the burden of "family educa-tion" (*katei kyōiku*). "We educators are acting in place of your parents," Kinoshita pronounced, and in return he asked stu-dents to treat their teachers as concerned fathers and their classmates as brothers.[43] Emerging as a utopian family of men, the school community would supersede the weakening nuclear unit as a source of student pride and identity.

Mindful that even a pseudo-family needed tight internal or-ganization, Kinoshita proposed, first, that all students attend a weekly lecture in ethics, and second, that as many students as possible live in residence halls on the campus. The new course would not only expound the Confucian virtues of "deportment, conduct, and decorum" (*zasa-shintai-reisetsu*) but also present correct classroom behavior and student-teacher interchange. Kinoshita hoped that the "ill-mannered and undisciplined ways" of earlier students would disappear as Ichikō pupils learned to take off their caps when entering the Ethics Lecture Hall and to bow politely to their teacher. To ensure that eti-quette was followed outside of class, he urged that students and faculty supervisors live together in a restructured dormi-tory. "The dormitory will allow us teachers a chance to become closer to you," he reassured his listeners, "and to help you with your homework. If the teachers live on campus, they can be with you day and night, and you can ask them questions about anything that may be on your mind."[44] Warm and soothing language notwithstanding, Kinoshita was undoubtedly at-tempting to gain authority over students who had lived in scat-tered rooming houses that were "dissolute beyond words."[45]

The immediate response to Kinoshita's address was less than enthusiastic. To be sure, a few students welcomed the idea of a family school cut off from society's perturbations; and among these was Natsume Sōseki, an upperclassman at the time of the inaugural address. "When attending the higher middle school," Sōseki wrote in a postgraduation essay, "my class-room became a home and my classmates became members of a family."[46] He added that the personalization of faculty-student relations should become a model for all secondary schools. Yet

43. *Rokujūnenshi,* p. 104.
44. Ibid., p. 106.
45. *Kōryōshi,* p. 1.
46. Natsume Sōseki, "Chūgakkō kairyōsaku," *Sōseki zenshū* 22 (Tokyo, 1957):117.

Sōseki spent little time in the dormitory, where Kinoshita divided residents into a hierarchy of paramilitary units under the supervision of dormitory inspectors (*shakan*) chosen from the faculty. One of the first issues of the monthly student publication, the *Society of Friends Magazine*, described life under faculty surveillance before the move to Hongō:

> The faculty inspectors, especially those from nonacademic departments, treated the students as if they were slaves. . . . To cite one example: at that time the inspector was always sticking his nose into the rooms and complaining about little infractions of the rules. One day, he stormed in without even saying hello. Seeing a stray piece of paper on one of the desks, he exploded: "Why do you leave your desk so messy? Clean it up immediately!" You can see from this incident how much the inspector interfered in every detail of our lives.[47]

The reliance on dormitory inspectors and a "deportment point system" (*gyōjōten seido*), whereby a student was given a certain total of points from which deductions were made for each breach of good manners, made Kinoshita appear to his earliest students as "an extreme legalist" (*kyokutan na kiritsuteki no hito*) who "despised laxity" and advocated "discipline from beginning to end."[48] This impression was reinforced by his encouragement of a physical-fitness program that consisted of "military exercises" (*heishiki taisō*) and infantry-style maneuvers (*kōgun*), held periodically in the countryside outside Tokyo. He even endorsed a proposal by one of his colleagues that all students begin the day with a cold bath.[49]

While these measures tended to restrict student behavior and to reduce greatly their freedom of access to the polymorphic world of politics and popular fashions, the students made little protest. After the first few months, they apparently concluded that their headmaster, though rigid, was sincere and that his proposals were ultimately in their interests as chosen young men destined, in Kinoshita's words, "to stand in the upper crust of society." One student, Noda Heijirō, explained in an early essay on "The Logic of the School Spirit": "Our First Higher School must produce geniuses (*saijin*) who can drive

47. Akanuma Kinzaburō, "Masa ni dai ni no jichisei kishukuryō o min to suru ni tsukite shokai o nobu," part III, *DIKGKZ*, no. 9 (Sept. 28, 1891), p. 11.

48. Minamigumo Shōnosuke, "Hitotsubashi jidai no kaiko," in *Ichikō Dōsōkai kaihō*, no. 24 (Jan. 25, 1934), p. 66.

49. Natsume Sōseki, "Chūgakkō kairyōsaku," pp. 113–114.

away society's sordid customs. There is no reason for our school to rear vulgar persons (*zokubutsu*) who merely glide with the breezes of the times." In Noda's view the headmaster's appeal for students to arm themselves as "warriors" in combat against society's vulgar currents (*zokuryū*) was well founded. Before assuming high office, students needed to strengthen their willpower. Self-discipline was a matter of public responsibility.[50] Noda Heijirō's remarks are one of the first intimations of an ideological bond between the students and their teachers which runs through much of higher school literature.

Nationalism and the Ichikō Spirit

Kinoshita Hiroji's fervent wish for Ichikō was the sealing of a spiritual covenant between school and nation that would shape the thinking of his students. The unity of school and nation required some pontificating by the headmaster on the virtues of the Imperial House and Japan's cultural tradition; but Kinoshita devoted most of his energies to the nurture of patriotism through a structure of nonverbal symbols that obviated the insipid maxims of a primary-school reader. Ichikō's "school spirit" (*kōfū*) was not a formula for recitation; it was a cultural ideology made up of an entire panorama of objects, events, and mannerisms to foster a desired mood or sentiment.[51]

The ubiquitous school symbol was the student uniform: a black Nehru jacket with brass buttons, matching cap, and white gaiters (for ceremonies only). Kinoshita insisted the students wear the uniform at all times, especially when venturing outside the campus. Of particular significance was the brass badge fastened to the front of the cap above the visor. In his ethics lectures, Kinoshita often referred to this badge, which bore imprints of an oak and an olive leaf, as representing "the spirit of Japan": the oak leaf signifying warrior prowess (*bu*) and the olive leaf symbolizing literary studies (*bun*); in a congruent interpretation the oak leaf symbolized Mars, and the olive, Minerva.[52] Together with the badge, Kinoshita requested that students have two white bands attached to their caps, sym-

50. Noda Heijirō, "Kōfūron," *DIKGKZ*, no. 3 (Jan. 27, 1891), p. 27.

51. In writing this paragraph I have been influenced by Clifford Geertz, "Ideology as a Cultural System," in David E. Apter, ed., *Ideology and Discontent* (Glencoe, Ill., 1964), p. 62.

52. *Rokujūnenshi*, p. 111.

bolizing honesty and purity.[53] The formal uniform was thus completed, save for that distinctive symbol of higher-school status acquired after the Russo-Japanese War: the long black cape.

Beyond his elaboration of the uniform, Kinoshita bolstered the symbolic world of the school with art. Combining financial help from the Ministry of Education with artistic advice from Okakura Tenshin, he commissioned ten pictures. Each portrayed a historical personality or event especially chosen by the headmaster to symbolize the great virtues and moments in Japan's quasi-mythological past. The most famous were portraits of Sugawara Michizane and Sakanoue no Tamuramaro, both of which hung in the Ethics Lecture Room. Sugawara Michizane (845–903), scholar and politician, served as a special councillor to the Heian Emperor Uda, while Sakanoue no Tamuramaro (758–811), a military hero, spearheaded a campaign against the Ainu in northern Honshū. Centuries after their deaths, the two men were mythologized as demigods representing scholarship (Sugawara) and warrior prowess (Sakanoue). For the students of Ichikō, these giant portraits were a powerful reinforcement for the Minerva and Mars symbols on the school badge. The other eight pictures commissioned by Kinoshita also dramatized the unity of the "way of letters" and the "way of the warrior," with some portraying scholar priests in quiet reflection, and others famous battles, like the ill-fated Mongol invasion.[54]

Among Kinoshita's symbolic creations, the school flag assumed special importance. To the students of Ichikō, the whole concept of a school flag was baffling, since spiritual allegiance to the former preparatory college had been virtually nonexistent. They were especially amazed when their headmaster, acting on the suggestion of Mori Arinori, laid out the design for a school flag which featured the character for country (*kuni*), embroidered in gold and framed by the olive and oak leaves. Heralded as "the flag which protects the country" (*gokokuki*), its symbolic import was described in an emotional speech by Kinoshita's colleague and successor, Kuhara Kyūgen:

> Our school must never be satisfied with the mere pursuit of higher learning; we must always recognize our responsibility to cultivate

53. According to Minamigumo, p. 66.
54. Nishizawa, pp. 6–8.

2. Assembling for the march to the Imperial Palace (1889). Courtesy of Kōdansha

national spirit through moral training. Because "the flag which protects the country" is created with this noble purpose in mind, it represents both the defense of the nation and the honor of the school (*kokka no hogo to gakkō no meiyo*). . . . Our flag inspires us to expose our bodies, if necessary, to cannon smoke and a rain of bullets. . . . It is, therefore, no different from a military flag.[55]

The official unveiling of the school flag took place on February 11, 1889, six days after the announcement of its design, in order to coincide with the date for the issuance of the new Imperial Constitution by the Meiji Emperor.[56] But Kinoshita planned for more than raising the flag on Constitution Day. During the week before the celebration, he suspended classes in preparation for the event. On one day, he gathered the entire student body on the athletic field where, standing on a classroom desk, he personally directed a succession of banzai cheers for the Emperor, which, according to Ichikō sources, he invented.[57]

On the morning of February 11, the students woke up early, put on their uniforms, and assembled at the front gate of the school for the two-mile march to the Imperial Palace. At the

55. *Rokujūnenshi*, p. 194.
56. Unless otherwise stated, the following details are from Minamigumo, pp. 68–74.
57. Minamigumo, p. 70; Nishizawa, p. 29.

head of the parade was the standard-bearer, elected by the students to carry the new flag for this august occasion. (The standard-bearer was Wakatsuki Reijirō, a future prime minister, who in later life looked back on this day as one of the most moving experiences in his life.)[58] The students carried a huge, heart-shaped placard inscribed with the English slogan "Our true heart." The early departure ensured that they would reach their destination before the expected throng of citizens who would watch the departure of the Imperial Entourage for Aoyama Field. When the gates to the Imperial Palace opened, a contingent of guards on horseback clomped across the bridge over the moat. Immediately, the Ichikō students began their prerehearsed cheers and waved their flag, while the carriages with important ministers and members of the Imperial household followed in succession. But as the Emperor's carriage passed over the bridge, the students stopped their staccato chants and bowed their heads in total silence. From inside his carriage, the Meiji Emperor reportedly nodded his head respectfully toward "the flag which protects the country" as he passed by the solemn assembly of Ichikō students. His motion of deference to their school flag on this day of national celebration would be permanently recorded in the annals of First Higher.

The unveiling of the school flag was the most dramatic event in a stream of patriotic celebrations. Every national holiday saw students marching around the school grounds or holding dinner assemblies in honor of the Imperial family. To label the early Ichikō students nationalists adds little to our understanding, since questions of national strength and security permeated the climate of opinion in the late nineteenth century. More noteworthy was the students' emerging self-conception as chosen guardians of the country in accordance with the symbolism of the school flag. The literal bent of this disposition was manifested in the utter seriousness with which students participated in civic rituals and also in their intolerance of any departures from ceremonial etiquette. The latter was dramatically illustrated when Ichikō's famous Christian professor of philosophy, Uchimura Kanzō, decided, for religious reasons, not to bow before the Imperial Rescript on Education at a school assembly in 1891. The attending students were first shocked, then

58. Amako Tomaru, *Heimin saishō Wakatsuki Reijirō* (Tokyo, 1926), pp. 174–175.

outraged. One student writer reported the incident in the school magazine: "Who among the Japanese people is unable to be moved to tears by this sacred ceremony? By refusing to bow, Uchimura Kanzō of this school has soiled the holiness of our ceremonial hall."[59] For several days after the incident, Uchimura was harassed mercilessly by his students, who even hurled rocks at his house while calling upon him to renounce his act of sacrilege.[60] Alarmed by the possible threat to Uchimura's well-being, Kinoshita asked his colleague to issue a statement to defuse the student anger. Uchimura obliged: ". . . for the sake of the school, the principal, and my students, I consented to bow."[61] Tempers immediately cooled, and things returned to normal at Ichikō. But no one would soon forget the gravity with which the students undertook their role as defenders of the Imperial regalia.

The Founding of the Provincial Higher Schools

Although this study focuses mainly on Ichikō, the four other original higher schools—Second, Third, Fourth, and Fifth Higher—did make important contributions to the cultivation of Japan's prewar and postwar elite.[62] Whereas Ichikō was always considered "the model throughout the country" (zenkoku no mohan),[63] its brother schools more closely exemplified the philosophy of preparatory education in one important respect: they were situated in quieter provincial settings, noted for natural beauty and historical reputation as centers of traditional learning and culture. As a consequence, the policy of seclusion in the provincial higher schools depended much less on artificial walls or "castle" metaphors and more on the natural barriers afforded by mountains, fields, and streams.

59. "Chokugo haitaishiki," DIKGKZ, no. 3 (Jan. 27, 1891), p. 42.

60. Kōryōshi, p. 1200.

61. Ryusaku Tsunoda, Wm. Theodore de Bary, and Donald Keene, eds., Sources of Japanese Tradition, vol. 2 (New York, 1967), p. 347; Uchimura Kanzō, Uchimura Kanzō chosakushū, vol. 18 (Tokyo, 1954), pp. 257–268.

62. In addition to the five originally authorized institutions, the government, in 1887, granted higher school status to distinguished middle schools in Yamaguchi and Kagoshima. Both schools were historically linked to former domain academies— Meirinkan in Chōshū and Zōshikan in Satsuma—which may have prompted the government to raise their status. However, the Yamaguchi Higher School was converted into a technical school in 1905 (before regaining higher school status in 1919), while the Kagoshima Higher School remained on the periphery of the elite track until it was renamed the Seventh Higher School in 1901. For more on this, see Nakajima, "Kyūsei kōtō gakkō seido no seiritsu," pp. 14–15; Toita, pp. 9–10.

63. Rokujūnenshi, p. 119.

The provincial higher schools were situated in four distinct regions of the country. Representing the Kansai region of central Japan was Third Higher (Sankō), founded two weeks after Ichikō on the grounds of the Osaka Middle School. Orita Hikoichi, who had pioneered in reforming preparatory education, was asked to continue as headmaster of the new higher school. Although he accepted the offer, Orita voiced immediate displeasure with the school's location: "Osaka may be a good place for transacting business," he quipped, "but it is hardly suitable for inspiring brilliance." [64] As long as Third Higher remained in a bustling entrepôt, the students would be "mesmerized by gaudy devices, frivolous games, and slick words." He thought a far better site was Kyoto, where "mountains, clear-running streams, and traditions of cultural refinement" constituted an "ideal setting for the proper cultivation of the students." [65] Mori Arinori concurred. Thus, with the help of local donations (and assurances from city officials that no brothels would ever be built in the vicinity of the campus), [66] Sankō was moved in 1889 to an idyllic site at the foot of Yoshida Hill on what was then the northern fringe of Kyoto.

The factors of environment, historical tradition, and local enthusiasm, which had been critical in determining the ultimate location of Sankō, were equally decisive in the foundation of Second, Fourth, and Fifth Higher. In choosing suitable locations, the Ministry of Education took its time, sponsoring numerous expeditions to the hinterland for nearly a year after the founding of Ichikō and Sankō. The towns winning government recognition were Sendai for Second Higher, Kanazawa for Fourth Higher, and Kumamoto for Fifth Higher. It is no exaggeration to say that these three towns had to win recognition by the government. The regional competition was fierce, with municipalities waging full-scale "invitation movements" (*yūchi undō*) [67] and public funding campaigns to elicit a favorable response from government officials. Thus, two months before the final decision on the site for Second Higher, civic leaders in Sendai appealed to local citizens to join a movement "to increase our prosperity and raise our level of culture." [68] Such en-

64. Sakakura, p. 106.
65. Ibid., p. 106.
66. Professor Kume Tadayuki, personal interview at Kyoto University on November 3, 1971.
67. Tomatsu Nobuyasu, *Shikō hachijūnen* (Kanazawa, 1967), p. 42.
68. Atoda Reizō, *Nikō o kataru* (Sendai, 1937), pp. 2–3.

thusiasm was appreciated by the government, since the success of the higher school as a character-building institution would depend in part on its charismatic hold on the local populace.

Tradition and natural beauty also weighed heavily in the choice of these three towns. Indicative of the cultural nationalism of the 1880s and in marked contrast to the commercial and diplomatic factors guiding the selection of the government foreign language schools a decade earlier, the Ministry of Education sought as locations for the higher schools towns that had been centers of scholarship in the Tokugawa period. Sendai, Kanazawa, and Kumamoto were all former castle towns with distinguished domain schools: the Gakuyōkendō, the Meirindō, and the Jishūkan. They also provided picturesque grounds for the schools. The extent to which the government was impressed by hills and streams was evident in Mori Arinori's special trip to Sendai, where he personally surveyed the prospective school-grounds, pointing out the location of specific buildings and even pacing off the ideal distance between the proposed front gate and the main hall.[69] For a man with such prodigious responsibilities to be tramping through fields and fording streams in an effort to plot the grounds for individual higher schools may seem extraordinary; but Mori Arinori believed that no effort should be spared in arranging the environment for the cultivation of future leaders.

The ambience of the provincial higher schools was a source of great pride for faculty and students. Believing that the character-building goals of preparatory education were more easily realized in the rustic atmosphere of Kumamoto or Sendai, administrators continually reminded students of their good fortune to live apart from the capital: "The Kyūshū district in which this school stands," noted Fifth Higher's headmaster in 1890, "has long nurtured the virtues of fortitude (gōki) and simplicity (junboku). . . . Kumamoto is as far removed from the gaiety and frivolity of the city as heaven from earth. This should be an ideal place, therefore, for establishing a higher school which cultivates youth for the better."[70] An early headmaster of Second Higher was similarly delighted that his students resided near the rugged terrain of northeastern Japan, away from the distractions of the big city: "A frightening place that devours peo-

69. Ibid., p. 8; Takahashi Tomio, "Kawaguchi no shiori" (Sendai, 1961), pp. 9–10.
70. Gokō gojūnenshi, p. 129.

ple's children" (*hito no ko o kuikorosu osoroshii basho*).[71] Mirroring the enthusiasm of their headmasters, the provincial higher school students wrote glowingly of their pastoral settings. Whereas high-picket fences artificially severed Ichikō from a vile urban surrounding, Sankō students maintained that no barriers were needed between the campus and "the unlimited beauty and history" of Kyoto's northern reaches.[72] Likewise, Fifth Higher students paid frequent homage to the rivers and mountains of Kumamoto, proclaiming that they lived in "a fortress of ginko trees rustled by the breezes of simplicity."[73]

The joy with which faculty and students greeted their provincial surroundings was linked to their faith in the rustic warrior gentleman as the character model for all higher school students. The tragedy of the post-Restoration era, lamented one Second Higher student, was the dwindling commitment to the Spartan values of the countryside as students flocked to Tokyo: "Those idiotic city students whom we have all heard so much about: they look upon the school as if it were a commercial establishment, and their teachers as if they were salesmen, and their tuition as if it were a market price."[74] City youth were invariably depicted in provincial higher school magazines as extravagant, weak-willed, and disrespectful of tradition. In contrast, the stalwarts of Kanazawa, Sendai, and especially Kumamoto saw themselves as upholders of samurai ideals rooted to the very countryside surrounding their schools. "Our school has an unmistakable spirit of warrior heroism," pronounced Nakagawa Gen when he served as Fifth School's headmaster, "since the area around us was once the stamping grounds of great medieval heroes . . . who fought so valiantly for the Emperor."[75] So too, the students and faculty at Second Higher honored the virtues of greatness and manliness (*yūdai gōken*) that guided the former samurai of northeastern Japan.[76]

71. Ishisaka Kinnosuke, ed., *Meizenryō shōshi* (Sendai, 1942), p. 83.

72. Quoted from an early Sankō student poem entitled "Environment Controls Our Character," in Dai San Kōtō Gakkō Kishukusharyōshi Henshūbu, ed., "Jiyūryōshi," pp. 119–120.

73. Quoted from the Fifth Higher school anthem in Genkōsha, ed., *Ryōka wa ikiteiru* (Tokyo, 1963), p. 179.

74. Sone Toranosuke, "Kōfū shūyōsaku," *Shōshikai zasshi*, no. 8 (Dec. 25, 1894), pp. 9–10.

75. "Nyūgakushiki ni okeru Nakagawa Gakkōchō enzetsu taii hikki," *Ryūnankai zasshi* 3, no. 24 (Oct. 1, 1894): 3.

76. Atoda, *Nikō o kataru*, p. 143.

Apart from distinctive rural settings and historical traditions, the four regional higher schools followed First Higher in the formation of educational policy. As at Ichikō, courses in Western languages and literature dominated the curriculum; the family served as the model of social organization; collective symbols reinforced institutional loyalty; and the school spirit resonated the values of national service. Regional pride in the provincial schools never swelled to the point of distracting students from their transcending duty to the country. This is suggested, first, in the speeches of educators and visiting critics, like Tokutomi Sohō, who lectured students on the importance of character building for the future "pillars of the nation" (*kokka no chūseki*) and, second, in the early essays of student leaders.[77] Surely Second Higher's Yamazaki Nobuki, in an 1896 "Treatise on the Academic Spirit," made the case as strongly as any educator, when he assailed contemporary youth for forsaking the samurai discipline of the feudal age (*hōken jidai no shifū*). Yamazaki urged his fellow students to reinstate the principles of the Mito school, emulate the public spirit of Restoration *shishi*, and rally the nation to greater heights.[78]

Much about the early higher schools made them appear as a reification of the domain academies: the physical location of three of the schools, the division of the curriculum between *bun* and *bu*, the emphasis on etiquette and family structure, the "old *bushi*" paternalism of the faculty, the concept of the school as a "castle under seige," and, most important, the frequent invocation of the samurai spirit and Confucian gentlemanly ideal. Yet, for all of this, in two significant ways the higher schools seem, in Joseph Levenson's terms, more "traditionalistic" than "traditional." First, the restoration of the gentleman did not actually signal a return of the feudal aristocracy. Students with samurai backgrounds, who represented over half of higher school enrollments in the early 1890s, decreased gradually during late Meiji and Taishō.[79] They were replaced by upstanding, but de-

77. *Shūgakuryōshi*, pp. 94–95.
78. Yamazaki Nobuki, "Gakufūron," pp. 1–10.
79.   Class Background of Higher School Students (1890–1892)

	1890	*1891*	*1892*
Nobles (Kazoku)	7	5	8

cidedly bourgeois, sons of businessmen, government bureaucrats, and rural landlords.[80] Whatever remorse the architects of the higher schools may have had about the breakdown of the feudal social order, no one was prepared to reconstitute hereditary criteria for matriculation. Competitive entrance examinations would always be the primary—though by no means the only—standard of judgment in determining who would enter the higher educational track. The higher schools were thereby placed in the curious position of nurturing a group of petty-bourgeois achievers with the traditional values and ethos of a dying aristocracy. Their attendance at a higher school would combat a crisis of deracination in middle-class youth by giving them a sense of historical continuity with the samurai and the ascriptive affectations of language and demeanor commensurate with their newly achieved status.

Finally, the higher schools were distinct from the domain schools because they were national institutions committed to the education of a national elite for a legal-rational state. The social and political context for summoning Confucian norms of public service and loyalty was significantly different at Fifth Higher in 1890 than it had been at the Jishūkan forty years earlier. No matter how much an "old *bushi*" pedagogue like Akizuki In'ei, Fifth Higher's preeminent Confucian scholar, affected an air of rustic simplicity, railed against the conveniences of materialistic civilization, and revered the archaic customs of the Kyūshū countryside, he steadfastly regarded his school as a national beacon serving youth from every corner of the land. For this to be more than a pipedream, the higher school faculty

Samurai Descendants (Shizoku)	2,049	2,283	2,293
Commoners (Heimin)	1,926	2,154	2,142

Note: These were the only three years that the Ministry of Education conducted a survey of class backgrounds in the higher schools. Figures include students enrolled in both the university-preparatory and the terminal medical courses. Monbushō, ed., *Monbushō daijūhachi nenpō* (Tokyo, 1967), p. 51; *Monbushō daijūkyū nenpō*, p. 38; *Monbushō dainijū nenpō*, p. 37. By 1931, the percentage of students of samurai descent at First Higher had decreased to one out of four students. See Kokuritsu Kyōiku Kenkyūjo, ed., *Nihon kindai kyōiku hyakunenshi*, vol. 4 (Tokyo, 1974), p. 1273. The provincial higher schools had an even lower percentage of students with samurai backgrounds in the prewar period. See Takaishi Shigekatsu, "Kyōdō kumiai no hata no moto ni," *Ryūnankai zasshi*, no. 202 (July 1, 1927), pp. 78–96.

80. Kimijima, p. 140; Tokyo Shōka Daigaku, *Gakusei seikatsu chōsa hōkoku* (Tokyo, 1934), p. 9.

was beholden to the quintessential symbol of industrialization, the railways, which, fortuitously, spread across the country in the late 1880s and 1890s. Ironically, by the turn of the century, steam engines hauled city boys to provincial Kumamoto for gentlemanly cultivation.

CHAPTER THREE

Seclusion and Self-Government

This magnificent monastery, hidden behind hills and woods, has long been reserved for the exclusive use of the students . . . in order that their receptive young spirits will be surrounded by an atmosphere of beauty and peace. Simultaneously the young people are removed from the distracting influence of their towns and families and are preserved from the harmful sight of the active life. . . . In addition there is the important factor of boarding-school life, the imperative need for self-education, the feeling of belonging together.

HERMANN HESSE, *BENEATH THE WHEEL* (1906)

An enormous society of boys between the ages of eight and eighteen governed by an unwritten code of its own making, an almost free republic of 100, 200, or 500 members, a club where even before adolescence a boy was imbued with the spirit of an aristocratic nation: such was the English public school.

ELIE HALÉVY, *ENGLAND IN 1815* (1913)

The Gothic walls seemed to shut off our college competitions from the cruder world outside us and fostered the illusion of an American Utopia.

HENRY CANBY, *ALMA MATER* (1936)

In the 1890s, Ichikō, Eton, and St. Paul's were more striking in their similarities than in their differences. In each case the school resembled a cloister purposefully set apart from a society in transformation; a surrogate family where an all-male faculty assumed both paternal and maternal responsibility; a training-ground for future leaders to acquire the affectations of gentlemanly character; and a museum where antique bathtubs and portraits of medieval saints united the present with a distant and wondrous past. Japanese students were, on the average,

two or three years older than their Anglo-American counterparts; their admission to Ichikō required considerably more individual initiative than was probably the case among the boys
at Eton and St. Paul's; their curriculum was centered around literary English and German rather than Greek or Latin; and their
concept of "righteousness" was shaped by Confucian rather
than Christian dictums. Yet such distinctions dwindled in significance in light of the shared view of the boarding school as a
sanctuary in an age of bewildering, often frightening, technological change.

The insularity and traditionalism of the boarding school
posed the same dilemma for educators in Japan as for educators
in the West: notably, the academy was torn between the affirmative goal of instilling manliness, or making boys into gentlemen, and the negative goal of guarding against precocity
whether in the form of academic streamlining, heterosexual intimacy, or direct participation in political movements.[1] In at-
tempting to satisfy both goals, the faculty was placed in the
awkward position of treating their students as neither little
boys nor grown men but as youth passing through an interim
stage in the life cycle: adolescence. The conception of adolescence as an institutionalized moratorium between childhood
and adulthood was not consciously identified with the boarding school until the turn of the century. Like Thomas Arnold,
Kinoshita Hiroji rarely invoked the term adolescence (*seishun*),
even though in arguing for the sequestration of his students
both from their parents and from adult society he was converting the higher schools into more than another layer of education. Implicitly, Kinoshita equated the school, as a total experience for remolding character, with an epoch in his students'
lives. The introduction of an additional stage in the life cycle,
defined by cultural preference rather than by physiological necessity, underscored the cross-purposes of an institution that
cultivated manliness yet deferred the acquisition of manly
responsibilities. The question was unavoidable: Why isolate
young men who were destined for leadership positions from
the very society they would lead?

More than in England or the United States, where acknowledged superiority in technology and industry made the tempo-

---

1. For a discussion of the concept of precocity, see F. Musgrove, *Youth and the Social Order* (Bloomington, Ind., 1965), pp. 51–57.

rary internment of the young elite less risky, the paradox of the boarding school created tension and divergence of opinion among educators and government officials in Japan. Moreover, unlike the Anglo-American boarding schools, the higher schools were, as national preparatory academies, under the administrative arm of the Ministry of Education and thus potentially more vulnerable to government pressure. This was especially true during the 1890s and early 1900s when the lines between vocational and liberal education were still being debated and when Japan was just entering its initial phase of industrialization.

The controversy over the goals of preparatory education was inadvertently sparked by the assassination of Mori Arinori on February 11, 1889;[2] the event threw the Ministry of Education into immediate disorder and robbed the higher schools of their staunchest and most powerful government supporter. Within two years, members of the newly established Diet leveled strong complaints against the government's allocation to the higher schools of 400,000 yen, an amount that constituted nearly one-third of the entire budget for the Ministry of Education.[3] To members of the Liberal party, this was an exorbitant sum for five boarding schools with a combined enrollment of under 4,500 students and with a philosophy of gentlemanly cultivation that was of small benefit to the productive capacity of the nation. In response, the Ministry of Education, under the leadership of Inoue Kowashi between 1893 and 1894, launched a campaign to promote applied science and industrial arts. Although a former confidant of Mori Arinori and the primary drafter of the Imperial Rescript on Education, Inoue seriously doubted the value of predominantly moral education for students beyond the compulsory level. In an address delivered to the Diet in May 1894, he warned that the nation was locked in an "industrial and technological struggle" for world recognition and that this was not the time for educators to disparage vocational training, especially with the imminent threat of armed confrontation with China.[4] The combination of international tension, industrial demands, and political agitation convinced Inoue of the necessity to issue numerous directives on voca-

2. The assassination of Mori is discussed in Ivan P. Hall, pp. 3–6.
3. Kaigo Tokiomi, ed., *Inoue Kowashi no kyōiku seisaku* (Tokyo, 1969), pp. 406–407; Toita, p. 18.
4. Tamaki Hajime, pp. 73–74; Kaigo, *Inoue Kowashi no . . .* , pp. 671–672.

tional education, including one ordinance pertaining exclusively to the higher schools.

On paper, the Higher School Ordinance of 1894 had sweeping implications.[5] It called for the revitalization of the floundering "technical course" (*senmon gakka*), replacing the "university-preparatory course" (*daigaku yoka*) as the central core of the curriculum, and it anticipated the eventual transformation of the higher schools into local vocational colleges with terminal programs for students who could then enter society directly as middle-level engineers, legal consultants, or medical assistants. If carried out to the letter, the Ordinance would have put an early end to the higher school pedagogy of seclusion and cultivation by a drastic reduction in the distance between nonelite professions and the school. But the plan was barely launched before it was scuttled altogether. With the notable exception of Third Higher, where concerted government pressure led to an overhauling of academic priorities during a six-year period of confused and often acrimonious experimentation,[6] the higher schools continued to graduate mostly university-bound students with a liberal arts degree. Finally, in 1897, when it was clear that Inoue's Higher School Ordinance had lost credibility, the Ministry of Education began to liquidate technical courses in every school, including Third Higher. In 1901 the higher-school medical departments were transformed into independent schools, and two years later all remaining technical courses were reconstituted along a separate academic track for advanced technical schools or colleges (*kōtō senmon gakkō*). (See Appendix III, Table 2.)

The failure of the Higher School Ordinance of 1894 was partially a consequence of the Ministry of Education's own reluctance to urge implementation. Declining health forced Inoue Kowashi to resign just two months after issuing the Ordinance, creating another vacuum of leadership.[7] For the next five years the Ministry pondered over several widely varying proposals for the secondary sector, including one—modeled after an ear-

5. For a complete discussion of the Ordinance, see Kaigo, *Inoue Kowashi no . . .* , pp. 405–465.

6. Sakakura, pp. 140–144.

7. Even while he was still healthy, Inoue was too deferential toward higher school administrators to bring about radical changes in the curriculum. He was much more the "senior statesman" than "self-conscious intellectual reformer," as Byron Marshall argues in "The Tradition of Conflict in the Governance of Japan's Imperial Universities," *History of Education Quarterly* 17 (Winter 1977): 389–390.

lier recommendation by Tokyo University's renowned professor of pedagogy, Emil Hausknecht—that sought to retain the middle and higher school as a single, eight-year preparatory academy.[8] Meanwhile, the combined opposition of higher school headmasters and many university faculty further slowed the momentum to realize Inoue's plan. But the coup de grace may have been administered by the pupils themselves. Higher school students had little interest in becoming middle-level technicians or doctors, ridiculed contemporaries who did, and resented any effort by the government to manipulate the curriculum or to transfer technical-course students from one institution to another depending on fluctuating resources in the departments of engineering and medicine. The student aversion to vocational training was manifested by low enrollment in technical courses, and enabled headmasters to ignore government directives by keeping humanities at the heart of the curriculum.[9]

The Higher School Ordinance is a seductive landmark, which can lead the historian of institutions into a documental cul de sac. Despite an outpouring of official reports from the Ministry of Education in the early 1890s, the history of the higher schools was not made in Inoue Kowashi's office. On the contrary, the actions of headmasters and students reflected a growing independence of fin de siècle higher schools from Tokyo. Throttled by the formalities of character building during the foundation years, the students emerged in the 1890s as articulators of the "school spirit" and as defenders of their own aspirations. Symbolizing this assertiveness was the self-governing dormitory, an institution which was conceived in the headmaster's office at Ichikō yet which ultimately catalyzed student consciousness.

8. Emil Hausknecht drafted a proposal for the Ministry of Education immediately after visiting one of the provincial higher schools between 1888 and 1889. (No one knew the whereabouts of this proposal until it was accidentally discovered in the winter of 1979 in the National Diet Library.) The initial response to Hausknecht's report was apparently cool. At least Nishimura Shigeki scoffed at the idea of adopting the German secondary school model in toto. (See Kaigo, *Inoue Kowashi no* . . . , p. 258.) However, by the turn of the century several educators, notably Toyama Shōichi, advocated reforms that closely paralleled the German secondary school system. (See Uchida Takeshi, "Meiji kōki no gakusei kaikaku mondai to kōtō gakkō seidoron," *Kokuritsu Kyōiku Kenkyūjo kiyō*, no. 95 [March 1978], pp. 5–28.) Although the higher school resembled the upper-level Gymnasium in its preparatory orientation, it never became an exact replica. Whereas the Gymnasium was a nine-year institution for day students, the Japanese higher schools, with two later exceptions, retained their unique identity as three-year boarding schools that were structurally independent of the lower secondary sector.

9. Toita, pp. 132–134, 186.

3. The Ichikō clock tower. Courtesy of Kōdansha

The "Glorious Manifesto"

In the spring of 1889, First Higher was officially moved from its original site in Kanda to its permanent site on Mukoga Hill near Tokyo University.[10] For Kinoshita Hiroji, the new location,

10. Nishizawa, pp. 16 and 21. While there is a gentle slope descending from Hongō toward Ueno, Ichikō was not situated on a real hilltop. "Mukoga Hill" was more a figment of student imagination than an actual incline.

graced by tall pine and cedar, corresponded to his concept of character building. He was impressed with the great red-brick quadrangle on the new campus, with its clock tower rising majestically in front of the main gate. Like the gothic towers of Eton and Harrow, the monumental architecture of the higher school inspired awe in students and faculty alike, a constant reminder of their special place in the social order. Of particular interest to Kinoshita was the provision on the new campus for residence halls that would accommodate all students. With the anticipated opening of the residence halls in March 1890, Kinoshita's vision of a self-contained and isolated community of students was becoming a reality.

During the fall of 1889, Kinoshita issued a memorandum expressing his hope that students would move into the new dormitory in March. The announcement ignited the first visible sparks of dissatisfaction with the new headmaster's policies. Students who were living in private housing held a series of meetings in November and December to consider the administration's proposal. Such a move would infringe on the freedom they had traditionally enjoyed in rooming houses. It had never mattered, as one student explained, what time they got up or ate their meals in private rooming houses; but in a dormitory every minute of the day would be subject to strict faculty regulations, as had been the case in the dormitory on the old Kanda campus.[11]

Although some students voiced displeasure over the possibility of a mandatory residence system (*kaikishuku seido*) at Ichikō,[12] no further elaborations on the official view were released from the headmaster's office. Finally, on February 24, 1890, only one week before the opening of the new dormitory, Kinoshita Hiroji called for an all-student assembly to explain in detail his idea of boarding-school life at Ichikō. The speech, which students dubbed the "Glorious Manifesto,"[13] would have a lasting effect on higher school culture.

As in his inaugural address, Kinoshita articulated his idea within the context of a national social environment, which he characterized in the most negative terms: traditional customs were "eroding," and "etiquette" (*ringi*) was "crashing to the

11. Minamigumo, p. 91.
12. The term (mandatory residence system) was not officially used until the late 1890s, although this is obviously what Kinoshita had in mind.
13. Moiwa Toyohei, *Ichikō tamashii monogatari* (Tokyo, 1925), p. 99.

ground." The worst offenders in this "surging wave" of "immorality" were the irresponsible, unmannered, and dissolute urban students. He warned, "If you wish not to be soiled by their evil ways, if you wish to keep your distance from their customs, then you must terminate any association with these [vulgar] students."[14] The dormitory would help in meeting this challenge, for it was constructed not for "convenience" but as "an impregnable fortress" (kinjō teppeki) isolated from the chaos of the outside world. Thus the dormitory, even more than the trees and the high picket fence that surrounded it, was the reification of Kinoshita's metaphor of a "castle under siege."

In contrast to the "evil ways and sordid customs" (akufū ozoku) of the outside world, life in the new dormitory would be dedicated to cultivating "pure moral sense" (junsui naru tokugishin), the pursuit of which would be guided by "four tenets" (shi kōryō):

> Build self-respect, and cultivate honor.
> Arouse affection, and cultivate the public spirit.
> Develop humility, and cultivate tranquility.
> Pay attention to hygiene, and cultivate cleanliness.

Kinoshita's explanation of the "four tenets" was cryptic and tautological. "Honor" (renchi) and "self-respect" (jichō) distinguished cultivated men from "beasts" (kinjū); the "public spirit" (kōkyō no kokoro) was required for the protection of the country; "affection" (shin'ai), reflected in "the beautiful atmosphere of a close-knit organization," should be the instrument for understanding and developing "the public spirit"; "humility," "tranquility," and "cleanliness" were necessary attributes of any organization committed to the ideals of public fellowship and "the mutual polishing of personalities." He proclaimed: "We must build a close-knit group through cooperative efforts and a common spirit; we must develop our honor, cultivate the public spirit, and plan for the dawn of moral righteousness."[15]

Similar platitudes had been invoked before. However, earlier Kinoshita had emphasized the role of dormitory inspectors in overseeing the process of cultivation; on this occasion, he was leaning in a different direction, as was made clear near the end of the speech.

14. *Kōryōshi*, p. 2.
15. Ibid., pp. 2–3.

To accomplish the goal of our four tenets, we cannot depend on harsh rules or the strong arm of a supervisor. You students must acknowledge your status and responsibility (*chii to sekinin*) and arouse the spirit of self-government. This will depend upon the way you interact as friends striving to admonish each other and polish each other's character. . . . I have complete confidence in you; and if you agree to govern your own affairs . . . , I will never interfere without your permission.[16]

In justification, Kinoshita noted that Ichikō was "the leader among the nation's higher schools" and that "no other school had garnered as much respect within the society." He also recommended that the role of the previous dormitory inspectors be reduced so that "the complete responsibility for order within the dormitory" would be borne by the students; they would form assemblies and decide on a contract (*kiyaku*), a set of organization articles to be submitted to the headmaster's office for final approval. Kinoshita concluded his speech with this pledge:

I propose the abolition of the previous system of dormitory supervision. In its place, you are encouraged to govern yourselves. If you accept this responsibility . . . , I fully believe we can accomplish the objectives of this dormitory. Will you strive toward this end?[17]

Self-Government as Educational Policy

Although Kinoshita pledged to reduce the power of faculty inspectors, scholars of educational administration and history in Japan view the reform as nonlibertarian and pervaded with "a strong odor of *bushidō*," to borrow Miyasaka Tetsufumi's blunt phrase.[18] Kinoshita was no crusader for academic freedom; the Uchimura Kanzō incident attests to that. And his language was redolent with Confucian allusions, suggesting further that self-government was another mechanism for gentlemanly cultivation, rather than an inducement for individual expression. Kamishima Jirō and Terasaki Masao have speculated that Kinoshita's conception of self-government was a revival of the semi-autonomous student confraternity attached to the Zōshikan or other Tokugawa youth groups (*wakamono gumi*) which were—

16. Ibid., p. 4.
17. Ibid.
18. Miyasaka Tetsufumi, "Kagai kyōikushi," p. 198.

most unlike the higher schools—integrated with the economic and social life of the village.[19] Having received his formative education in Kyūshū before the Restoration, Kinoshita was familiar with these organizations.

However traditionalistic the proposal for self-government may appear to the historian today, it should not be forgotten that to many government officials the reform was viewed as revolutionary.[20] "Revolutionary" is hardly the adjective to describe Kinoshita Hiroji; but his proposal was unusual in the context of stricter authority in all levels of the school system, of government scholars preparing drafts of the Imperial Rescript on Education, and of the vivid memory of student depredation in the old Kaisei Gakkō and Tokyo University Preparatory School. It is not surprising that the Ministry of Education was caught off guard. After informing Enomoto Takeaki, Mori Arinori's successor, of his intention to grant self-governing privileges to his students, Kinoshita waited more than a year for a response. Finally, on May 27, 1891, he received a curt note stating that the matter was still under consideration.[21] By that time, self-government was already a reality at Ichikō and was beginning to spread to the provincial higher schools.

If government officials feared that self-government at First Higher was an affirmative response to the residual clamor for "people's rights" or a capitulation to a specific set of student demands, they were sorely mistaken. Kinoshita had no sympathy for the self-aggrandizing claims of "political youth," and he compared the emerging political parties to the squabbling factions who undermined the Ming Dynasty.[22] Self-government was a defensive strategy to reinforce "status and responsibility," which distinguished higher school students from "ordinary youth." It was inextricable from the policy of seclusion, but unlike the threatening tone of the latter, self-government was presented to students as a special privilege or an incentive for good behavior. "It was never my intention to treat you like a bunch of rickshaw runners or stablemen," he later explained.[23] Nor was it his intention to run the higher school like a military

---

19. Kamishima, *Kindai Nihon no seishin kōzō*, pp. 28–30; Terasaki, "Jichiryōseido seiritsu shiron," pp. 42–43.
20. *Kōryōshi*, p. 5.
21. *Rokujūnenshi*, pp. 199 and 207.
22. Yamamoto Jūrō, ed., *Higo bunkyō . . .* , p. 278.
23. Karasawa, *Kōshinsei*, p. 239.

academy.[24] For the students to act like gentlemen, for them to replace their channels to the "vulgar world" with strong institutional loyalties, they needed a clear role in maintaining order and discipline within the community. Thus, after relying for nearly two years on faculty coercion to forge a tightly knit and well-ordered dormitory, Kinoshita felt the time was ripe for students to assume that responsibility on their own. He apparently believed there was little danger of a return to the brutal domination of younger students by upperclassmen, as had earlier occurred at the Kaisei Gakkō, since student leaders would govern by written contract and would be accountable to the "four tenets."

Besides enhancing the values of loyalty and responsibility, Kinoshita's motivation for transforming the management of the residence hall from a "proctorial system" (*shakan seido*) to a "self-governing system" (*jichi seido*) remains obscure. A laconic educator who exemplified the old *bushidō* maxim of action before words (*fugen jikkō*), Kinoshita Hiroji resisted ponderous explanations of his policies and left no letters or diary at the time of his premature death in 1910 that might have illuminated his intentions. Given his frequent expressions of confidence that the Ichikō students were "men who [would] preside over the politics of Japan" (*Nihon no seiji o ryōshitaru mono*),[25] Kinoshita's colleagues and successors consecrated the dormitory as a training-ground for statecraft. As Taniyama Shohichirō, the dean of students from 1898 to 1925, stated: "Behind the construction of the residence hall and the gathering of classmates under one roof was the attempt to make students understand the way to rectify and govern other people by first learning to rectify and govern each other."[26] The timeless formulation of the Confucian public service ideal was given a firmer historical footing by Seto Toraki, Ichikō's headmaster between 1913 and 1919, who equated "the spirit of the 'four tenets'" with "the spirit of the Imperial Constitution" (*kenpō no seishin*).[27] For Seto, the timing of the "glorious manifesto"—one year after the promulgation of the Meiji Constitution, four months before the first general election, and eight months before the convening of the Diet—was more than historical coincidence. The institutions of

24. *Rokujūnenshi*, p. 106.
25. Ibid., p. 107.
26. *Kōryōshi*, introduction, p. 1.
27. Ibid., introduction, p. 8.

the self-governing dormitory were meant to develop in tandem with the institutions of the constitutional state, with the former providing the reservoir of trained leaders for the latter. Whether or not Kinoshita actually linked the self-governing dormitory to the Imperial Constitution and bureaucratic agencies of state, the fact that at least a few of his later colleagues did so is a telling indication of how seriously they regarded the "glorious manifesto" as a statement of educational policy.

The Initial Response

In the immediate aftermath of Kinoshita's speech, a whirlwind of excitement blew through the corridors of First Higher. One student exclaimed: "Previously in our old dormitory we were burdened by rules and surrounded by inspectors who treated us like children, . . . but now our headmaster . . . is allowing us to transform the former system into a new order of self-government."[28] Another enthused: "We are so happy, . . . to be designated as unique among the schools of this nation is an absolutely joyful event (*zetsudai no kaiji*)."[29]

Such was the excitement that gripped students who believed that Kinoshita's change of policy was "a great revolution" (*dai kakumei*). But Akanuma Kinzaburō, an upperclassman of foresight and moderation, cautioned that the rapture of the moment should be tempered with the realization that those who govern themselves must bear full responsibility for their actions. Now was the time not for celebration but for making "substantial decisions." Akanuma observed: "If we accept this challenge with a frivolous mind today, in the future, when self-government proves unworkable, we shall be forced to come back to our headmaster cowering on bended knee, begging him to make rules and appoint supervisors to control our lives again." Consequently: "What kind of honor can we preserve in this society?" If the First Higher students were perceived as "lethargic youth," incapable of managing their own affairs, they would never "fulfill the Imperial will (*seishi*) under the Constitution and extend the nation's power and glory." Better to live under faculty surveillance, Akanuma concluded, than to be "ridiculed by the public."[30]

28. Ibid., p. 4.
29. Ibid., p. 5.
30. Ibid.

Akanuma's speech engendered an air of sobriety among the jubilant students. Realizing that they were on a stage and that many skeptics, both in and outside of government, were watching, they began to make serious preparations for the transfer of power. In his speech Kinoshita had impressed upon the students the need for a written document that would define the structures of government in the new dormitory and establish rules to maintain the spirit of the "four tenets." Excited by the prospect of drafting their own constitution only one year after the promulgation of the National Constitution, a committee of peers, under the leadership of Akanuma, was selected to hammer out a carefully worded contract (*kiyaku*). The final document gave a legal-rational basis for decision making that continued, despite situational deviations, until the demise of the school during the Allied Occupation.

Since the contract was subject to administration approval, the drafters were compelled to chart a prudent course between fulfilling the "duties of studenthood" and securing the rights to manage the dormitory without faculty interference.[31] Accordingly, much of the contract reiterated earlier faculty regulations aimed at insulating the higher school from the capital city. For example, departures from the campus for even the smallest errand must be reported to the gatekeeper; the curfew on ordinary school days was eight o'clock in the evening; and spending a night outside Independence Hall (Jichiryō), as they called their new place of residence, required special permission from student authorities. The contract also contained rules prohibiting smoking, spitting, and the reading of "obscenely romantic fiction" (*waisetsu ni wataru haishi shōsetsu*). One article stipulated that students wear their uniforms, however dirty, "from washup time in the morning to bedtime at night."

The most innovative section of the contract dealt with the structure of student government and the delegation of authority. The document called for two governing bodies, a General Assembly (Sōdaikai) and an Executive Committee (Iinkai). The General Assembly would be made up of approximately a hundred students, representing each of the rooms in the dormitory. (Throughout most of Ichikō's history it was customary for ten students to share each of the rooms, and it was the responsibility of each group of ten roommates to elect one delegate to

31. The following information is taken from *Kōryōshi*, pp. 6–10.

4. Strolling toward Independence Hall (ca. 1915). The black cape was a unique symbol of higher school status. Courtesy of Kōdansha

serve in the General Assembly.) The General Assembly was expected to meet once a month to consider amendments to the dormitory contract or discuss problems pertinent to the operation of the dormitory. Balancing the legislative powers of the General Assembly was the much smaller Executive Committee, whose ten members were selected in all-campus elections. (First-semester freshmen were restricted, however, from voting for members of the Executive Committee, although they were granted the privilege of sending representatives to the General Assembly.) The responsibilities of the Executive Committee included the supervision of daily business within the dormitory. Each Executive Committeeman was assigned a special area of responsibility, such as supervising the cafeteria, inspecting rooms for pernicious insects or inflammable objects, or checking the supply of utilities and the general maintenance of the building. Most significantly, the members of the Executive Committee had the authority to discipline peers who did not conform to the rules.

In theory, the distribution of authority between the General Assembly and the Executive Committee was a remarkable stroke in political artistry. Neither body could make changes in the contract without the consent of the other. Furthermore, no one could serve on both bodies simultaneously or serve on one body for more than a semester, although the reelection of incumbent representatives was permitted. The fact that the members of the Executive Committee and the General Assembly were elected in different ways also appeared to ensure a broad mandate. The glaring omission in the student government was provision for a separate judicial body. The students believed, rather idealistically, that departures from the norm would be rare and were best handled by the Executive Committee.

Even without a clearly defined judicial branch, the self-governing institutions of the Ichikō dormitory operated remarkably well during the initial months. Just four days after moving into the new hall, orderly elections were held for representatives to both the General Assembly and the Executive Committee. Spokesmen were elected within each governing body to meet with the administration in order to ease the transition from faculty to student control. Remarkably, the General Assembly and the Executive Committee exercised their authority independently. On one occasion during November 1890, the two governmental bodies clashed over the quality of food served in the cafeteria. Several members of the General Assembly precipitated a minor showdown by circulating a petition demanding better food. The Executive Committee immediately opposed the move, stating that any organized protest would be premature and unwise. The General Assembly, on the other hand, gave its unqualified support to the petition, and in the struggle that ensued, the members of the Executive Committee were forced to resign until new elections were held at the end of the month. The power wielded by the General Assembly was consistent with the principle of a working democracy, since this was the body that most closely represented the will of the entire student body.[32] For the time being, the students at Ichikō had demonstrated that they could meet the challenge of home rule.

The establishment of the governing institutions for Independence Hall was paralleled by a growth of social consciousness, expressed in the writings of student leaders, that undoubtedly surpassed the expectations of the faculty. Particularly noteworthy was Akanuma Kinzaburō's extended article on the recent development of the self-governing dormitory, which appeared in the new student periodical, the *Society of Friends Magazine*, during 1891. The essay placed the rise of self-government at Ichikō within the broad historical context of "the great revolu-

32. *Kōryōshi*, p. 10.

tion in social education" precipitated by Rousseau's *Emile*. Before Rousseau, according to Akanuma, students were the victims of "old-fashioned educational methods" (*kodai no kyōiku hōhō*), or learning through "external force" (*gaibu no kyōsei*), and it was only with the publication of *Emile* that the door was finally opened to the new ideal of "negative education," permitting the young to learn in an unrestricted atmosphere. Since Rousseau's death, a number of philosophers of education had contributed to the spread of child-centered learning, including Pestalozzi, Froebel, Spencer, and, by implication, Kinoshita Hiroji.[33]

Were many members of the Ichikō faculty capable of expounding on the ideals of Rousseau with the sophistication reflected in Akanuma's essay? Probably not. Nevertheless, Akanuma's outrage over "repressive education," while most genuine, was not an expression of equalitarian sympathies. Applied to primary schools, normal schools, or military schools, the "old-fashioned methods" of education were unfortunate, in Akanuma's opinion, but perhaps necessary. Applied to higher school students, such methods were almost criminal: "Who among the noble (*dōdōtaru*) students of the higher schools should be warned not to smear the school gates, or told how to make his bed, clean his room, and measure closet space for his clothes? How can students live respectably when burdened with these picayune rules? Such an oppressive system may be suitable for teaching primary-school students or training soldiers; but what useful purpose is served by imposing such indignities upon the noble students of the higher school?"[34] "There is no way for great men," he added, "to rise from a condition of serfdom."[35]

As evidence that higher school students deserved special treatment, Akanuma pointed to the recent triumph of the Ichikō students:

> The self-governing system of our dormitory has achieved impressive results in rearing a noble and brave determination among the students. It has aroused a spirit of cooperation and nurtured . . . an attitude of self-respect within each person. . . . No matter how

33. Akanuma Kinzaburō, "Masa ni dai ni no jichisei kishukuryō o min to suru ni tsukite shokai o nobu," part II, *DIKGKZ*, no. 7 (May 25, 1891), p. 15.
34. Akanuma, "Masa ni dai ni . . . ," part III, *DIKGKZ*, no. 9 (Sept. 28, 1891), p. 14.
35. Akanuma, "Masa ni dai ni . . . ," part II, p. 15.

much some may try to slander us, the success of our dormitory is an unshakable fact that *cannot be blemished by one speck of criticism.*[36]

Akanuma's concluding words of self-congratulation marked the beginning of a tradition among First Higher students of idolizing their accomplishments and conveniently overlooking their shortcomings. Exactly one year after the opening of Independence Hall, on March 1, 1891, the entire student body gathered for an anniversary celebration, in which speakers expounded on the magnificence of the self-governing spirit. So ecstatic were the participants that it was decided to make the anniversary celebration (*kinensai*) a permanent event in the Ichikō calendar. For future observances, streamers and banners would fly from the windows of the dormitory and special "dormitory songs" (*ryōka*) would be composed to highlight festivities. A sampling of lines from songs written during the 1890s and early 1900s conveys a sense of the exuberance and reverence with which the first generation of students viewed their place of residence: "Hurrah! Hurrah for Independence Hall! Our spirit is forever lodged in our commitment to self-respect and self-government!" "The union that is guided by the self-governing mind has the power of a rock that can break mountainous waves." "Our Independence Hall stands high above the world, overshadowing the colleges of Eton and Yale." "The root of the self-governing spirit grips like quack grass, and while days may pass and winds may blow, the flow of independence can never be curbed."[37]

The Demand for Self-Government and the Higher School Uprisings

For all their effusive self-praise, the Ichikō students never considered self-government the exclusive privilege of the residents of Independence Hall. Akanuma Kinzaburō conveyed the prevailing sentiment when, in the spring of 1890, he observed: "We must strive for good results because the provincial higher schools will be imitating us as they build their own self-governing systems."[38] With the emergence of school magazines in the

36. Akanuma, "Masa ni dai ni . . . ," part III, pp. 14–15. (Italics added.)
37. "Kishukuryō dai gokai kinensai kiji," *DIKGKZ*, no. 45 (March 2, 1895), p. 5; Genkōsha, ed., *Ryōka wa ikiteiru* (Tokyo, 1963), p. 49; Terasaki Masao, "Kyūsei kōkō ni okeru ningen keisei," Master's thesis, Tokyo University, 1959, footnotes, p. 49.
38. *Kōryōshi*, p. 4.

early 1890s, which greatly facilitated communication among students from different higher schools, it was reasonable for Ichikō leaders to assume that their model would be emulated in the provincial academies. Except for Third Higher, however, where Orita Hikoichi's conception of student responsibility and privilege mirrored the view of Kinoshita Hiroji, the path to self-government in the provincial higher schools was not smooth. Moreover, at no institution—including Ichikō—did the decade of the 1890s elapse without at least one serious confrontation between students and headmaster over the limits of self-governing authority.

The most interesting variant of the Ichikō model is evidenced at Fifth Higher (Gokō), where the idea of student autonomy originated in the commons and then spread to the dormitory.[39] So unpalatable was the food in the early Gokō dining hall that students, who were unaccustomed to institutional cuisine, staged sporadic cafeteria riots (*makanai seibatsu*) in which bowls of rice were hurled across the hall and kitchen staff sent scurrying out the windows. The ungentlemanly outbursts manifestly concerned the administration, which looked to Ichikō for ideas on how to rectify the situation without necessarily improving the menu. Intrigued by the experiment in Independence Hall, but in no mood to adopt self-government in its entirety, the Fifth Higher faculty opted to give students complete authority in the kitchen, to plan and prepare meals, while maintaining a rigid hold on the dormitory. Introduced in the winter of 1891, the "cook-for-ourselves system" (*jisui seido*) sparked considerable glee among students, who celebrated the following anniversary day with the clang of pots and pans. The novelty of governing the kitchen, however, was soon replaced by the drudgery of chopping vegetables; and an examination of essays in the school magazine between 1893 and 1897 reveals a growing discontent with faculty policy. Whereas in January of 1893, the "cook-for-ourselves system" was hailed as "a giant step toward the full realization of self-government and disciplinary authority," by the fall of 1897 students were complaining about serving as "prostitutes" to the stove.[40] Meanwhile, the administration tightened regulations in the residence hall; and when the dean of students delivered an especially stern speech in Oc-

39. *Shūgakuryōshi*, pp. 28–31.
40. "Suiji iin," *Ryūnankai zasshi*, no. 13 (January 1893), p. 43; "Jisuiseido to Shūgakuryōseido no kaikaku," *Ryūnankai zasshi*, no. 60 (Nov. 5, 1897), p. 56.

tober of 1897, describing youth as "a period for absolute sub-mission" (*zettai fukujū jidai*), angry students drew up demands for an extension of self-government from the kitchen to the dor-mitory.[41] Realizing they could no longer deny a privilege that was already being enjoyed by students at First and Third Higher, the faculty consented to begin the transformation from a proctorial to a self-governing system.

In the same year that Gokō students petitioned for an exten-sion of self-government, two major "uprisings" (*sōdō*), which shed light on developing student conceptions of honor and privilege, erupted on the campuses of the First and Second Higher schools. At Second Higher (Nikō), the turmoil centered around the policies of the headmaster, Yoshimura Toratarō, an important advocate of the higher school philosophy of gen-tlemanly cultivation, but an educator who was slow to appreci-ate self-government. By 1894, Nikō students were voicing dis-satisfaction with Yoshimura for maintaining a "rigid academic environment," which, they claimed, compared dismally with Ichikō.[42] They were also annoyed at their headmaster for com-plying with a government directive, linked to the Higher School Ordinance, that called for the transfer of medical stu-dents (seeking terminal higher school degrees as hospital assis-tants) from Third to Second Higher. Denied self-government by a headmaster who lectured on gentility but did nothing to oppose the "invasion" of his school by "crass technicians," the university-bound students vented their smoldering anger by picking fights with the unwelcome outsiders from Kyoto. In this inflamed atmosphere, Yoshimura made a serious error. On March 7, 1897, he announced the expulsion of two liberal arts students whose names were recorded on the registry of a local brothel. Upon discovering that the names were falsely signed by a pair of medical students, the majority of stalwarts, seeth-ing in "righteous indignation," organized a boycott of classes and demanded the resignation of their headmaster. When he refused, a special delegation of students, bearing a small sword, asked him to commit *harakiri* in their presence. When Yoshimura rejected this suggestion as well, the students threat-ened to withdraw from school and emigrate to Hawaii. Finally, the Ministry of Education dispatched an emergency team, led

41. *Shūgakuryōshi*, p. 81.
42. The details of the incident are taken from Ishisaka Kinnosuke, ed., *Meizenryō shōshi* (Sendai, 1942), pp. 10–24; Atoda, *Nikō o kataru*, pp. 110–116.

by Kinoshita Hiroji, which recommended that Yoshimura be quietly transferred to another school. The strike quickly ended and within months of the arrival of a new headmaster, self-government was institutionalized at Second Higher.

Just three months after the disturbance in Sendai, First Higher—idealized by Nikō and Gokō students as the progenitor of self-government—had an uprising of its own over a request by the Ministry of Education to open one of the wings of Independence Hall for occupancy by students from a neighboring normal school.[43] When the new headmaster, Kuhara Kyūgen, made a tentative agreement during the summer vacation in 1897, a band of outraged stalwarts returned from their homes around the country and staged a "live-in" demonstration to protest the "dismemberment" of Independence Hall. They vowed never to leave the premises until the administration rescinded its agreement. Struck by the utter seriousness of the protesters and their argument that sharing Independence Hall with prospective primary-school teachers would lead to "the downfall of the academic spirit" (*gakufū no metsubō*), Headmaster Kuhara backed down from his earlier decision and convinced the government to find other accommodations for the normal-school students.

There were perhaps a dozen such uprisings among higher school students in late Meiji involving alleged administration insensitivity to self-government, brawls between liberal arts and technical students, or government-directed transfers.[44] That the uproar was disturbing to some educators is evidenced in Takayama Chogyū's article, "The Logic of School Uprisings," published during the summer of 1898.[45] Takayama had taught English at Second Higher until he tendered his resignation, along with seven other faculty members, on learning of the decision to transfer Yoshimura Toratarō. His outrage over the government's action stemmed from a conviction that Second Higher students had broken the law and deserved to be punished. "Constitutionalism" (*hōchishugi*), Takayama submitted, could not survive if the government showed "favoritism" (*jōjitsushugi*) toward irresponsible youth. Heeding Takayama's alarmist warnings, two scholars have argued recently that the higher school protests, combined with the nearly two hundred

43. *Kōryōshi*, pp. 13–17.
44. See, for example, *Shūgakuryōshi*, pp. 71–72.
45. Takayama Rintarō (Chogyū), "Gakkō sōdōron," *Taiyō* 4, no. 14 (July 5, 1898): 30–36.

incidents in the normal and middle schools, contained "dangerous seeds for the social system" and should be examined within the broader context of late Meiji social movements.[46]

The epidemic of uprisings at the turn of the century does beg the scrutiny of social historians; but care must be taken not to lump, automatically, the disturbances on the higher school campuses with the more extensive and somewhat later turmoil that swirled through the normal and middle schools. Higher school students who rebelled against their administrations in the 1890s certainly had no intention of participating in a wave of student protest. The issue in the Second Higher strike was *accountability* to what the students perceived to be the philosophy of preparatory education. In their eyes, Yoshimura Toratarō (by denying self-government, admitting vocational students to the school, and falsely accusing two campus stalwarts of wrongdoing) was not abiding by the standard of a higher school administrator and should be removed from office. At Ichikō the students were similarly protesting the decisions that threatened the already established principle of higher school autonomy and seclusion. The protesting students would have shuddered at the suggestion that their actions might someday be grouped with the disturbances of normal or middle school students. As one of the leaders explained in an article written three years after the incident: "We had heard about the school disturbances that erupted across the country at that time. And we were adamant in our contempt for those bad practices (*heifū*), fully realizing that it was our obligation as residents of Independence Hall to transcend such immorality."[47] The demonstration against the partitioning of the dormitory was remarkable, the writer continued, because no student conducted himself in a way that reflected unfavorably on his duties (*honbun*) as a higher school student. Agreeing wholeheartedly with this assessment, an editor of the school magazine chimed in that the students had strained the outer limits of "responsibility" (*sekinin*) by allowing their headmaster time to avoid "losing face" vis-à-vis the government.[48] Indeed, Ichikō students laid ultimate blame for the incident squarely on the Ministry of Education. As one Shioya

46. Terasaki Masao, "Meiji gakkōshi no ichi danmen," *Nihon no kyōiku shigaku*, no. 14 (Oct. 5, 1971), p. 35; Tamaki Motoi makes a similar argument in *Nihon gakuseishi*, pp. 68–74.

47. Yoshida Kumaji, "Jichiryō ni taisuru yo ga kenkai no kako oyobi genzai," *DIKGKZ*, no. 95 (March 25, 1900), p. 3.

48. "Nanbokuryō jiken," *DIKGKZ*, no. 69 (October 15, 1897), p. 9.

Yutaka commented in 1899, the Higher School Ordinance, along with proposals to streamline the curriculum and open higher school facilities to students on other academic tracks, undermined the "school spirit" and delicate web of human relationships within the dormitory.[49]

Unlike Takayama Chogyū, a number of influential educators were apparently satisfied that the uprisings by their students were not inconsistent with the privileges and responsibilities of status. In mediating the dispute at Second Higher, Kinoshita Hiroji believed that the extension of student authority would instill a greater appreciation for law and constitutional procedures; that, in the words of one of Yoshimura's successors at Nikō, self-government was the best mechanism for "teaching students the great duty of preserving public order."[50] Likewise, Kuhara Kyūgen confided that unhappy students at Ichikō "did not exceed [their] status" (*gakusei no bun'iki o koezu*), their actions reflecting merely "a love for sincerity and self-government."[51] Along with their endorsement of self-government, sympathetic administrators seemed impressed by student demands to be treated differently from peers enrolled in the normal school, middle school, and technical course of the higher school. That Inoue Kowashi's plan to strengthen technical studies had the unintended effect of crystallizing the separate identity of university-bound students was ironically gratifying, especially to those headmasters who opposed the Higher School Ordinance of 1894. Although the uprisings disturbed many faculty, the liberal arts students—by refusing to share quarters with contemporaries they deemed undesirable—had at least taken the initiative in defining who they were and why they alone deserved the privilege of self-government.

By the turn of the century, a self-governing dormitory modeled after Independence Hall was flourishing in each of the higher schools. And whether the idea came from above, as at Ichikō and Sankō, or from below, as at Nikō and Gokō, the consequence was much the same: a magnification of institutional pride and an efflorescence of self-consciousness. The drafting of contracts, the establishment of miniature assemblies, the organization of school magazines, the staging of anniversary fes-

49. Shioya Yutaka, "Kōfū no suitai o ronjite sono shinkōsaku ni oyobu," *DIKGKZ*, no. 88 (June 15, 1899), pp. 12–13.
50. "Seinoryō kairyō shiki," *Shōshikai zasshi*, no. 41 (Oct. 15, 1900), p. 73.
51. *Kōryōshi*, p. 16.

tivals, and the composition of "dormitory songs" are emblematic of the beginnings of a distinct student subculture that is analytically separable from the faculty models for character building. Henceforth, the ordeal of becoming a gentleman would be balanced by the privilege of indulging in a self-regulating adolescent community that was institutionally contained.

Self-Government in Perspective

No other aspect of the higher school experience has elicited more satisfaction and pride among alumni than the traditions of the self-governing dormitory. Repeating a familiar refrain, the editors of a recent compendium of recollections put it this way: "The distinguishing trait of the old higher schools is the dormitory. Separated from their homes, the young stalwarts . . . lived together in the paradise of perfect self-government (*kanzen na jichi no tengoku*)."[52] Not every alumnus is so euphoric about the higher school dormitory, although enthusiasm usually exceeds that of the technical- or normal-school graduate, for whom the experience of living on campus was unlikely to be a "perfect paradise."[53] To be sure, the principle of self-government was also invoked in prewar normal and technical schools; but this was usually a guise for mutual spying among students and an incentive for "squealing" to school authorities, something which higher school headmasters actively discouraged as inimical to the ethic of manliness. The higher school dormitory may have been unique, therefore, as the fountainhead of the school spirit, the object of countless songs of praise, and the subject of elaborate "dormitory histories" (*ryōshi*), happily compiled by student annalists with each passing month.

Glowing recollections of life in the higher school dormitory are often combined with rather controversial assertions that self-government imbued students with an early respect for the legal-constitutional framework; that it nurtured debating skills; that it taught the importance of self-restraint, esprit de corps, and compromise in the smooth operation of the general assemblies and the "mock parliaments" (*gikokkai*) so popular after the

52. Yamamoto Kazuya, ed., *Waga seishun: kyūsei kōkō* (Tokyo, 1968), p. 36.
53. For descriptions of normal-school life, see Karasawa, *Kyōshi no rekishi*, pp. 44–66; Ivan Hall, pp. 424–437.

turn of the century.[54] In supporting the view that the dormitory was, in effect, a workshop for parliamentary democracy, alumni enthusiasts often recite the impressive list of legal theoreticians and liberal politicians who graduated from the higher schools.[55] While intriguing, such contentions suffer from *post hoc, ergo propter hoc* logic and fail to account for the higher school graduates who took little interest in defending constitutional liberalism either before or after World War II.

Self-government in the higher schools was neither the "charade" that Joseph Kett describes in American secondary schools between 1900 and 1920, nor the primitive organization of praepostors in the British public schools (where there were few, if any, written safeguards against a tyranny of age and muscles).[56] Still, the executive committees and general assemblies, despite their impressive structure and glowing assessments by alumni, were unable to overcome the fundamental paradox of preparatory education. Self-government may have served as a testing ground for rulers-in-training, but it also prolonged the period of incubation from the real tests of adult political and social life. The students knew this; they knew they were living in a state of abeyance and yet appeared in no mood to accelerate their entry into the world. "Our dormitory is a utopia (*senkyō*)," an Ichikō stalwart wrote in 1892, "where our days are beautiful, our spirit light."[57] In speeches and songs, parades and anniversaries, the early higher school students paid lavish tribute to self-government, less because it afforded practical training in the techniques of administration, and more because it gave them greater independence from the faculty, greater dependence on the peer group, and a new self-image of privileged youth standing at the top of the social order.

54. In an interview on May 3, 1976, Maruyama Masao stressed the seriousness of self-government at Ichikō in the 1930s; Maruyama's assessment was shared by most alumni interviewed for this project.

55. Lawyers and legal theoreticians who graduated from Ichikō include Okamatsu Santarō (1891), Minobe Tatsukichi (1894), Itokawa Masatetsu (1897), Suehiro Izutarō (1908), and Tanaka Kotarō (1911). For lists of legal authorities among Ichikō alumni, see Sakamoto Yasuyuki, ed., *Aa gyokuhai: Kyūsei kōtō gakkō monogatari* 1 (Tokyo, 1967): 27–28, 50, 57–59, and 89–91.

56. Joseph F. Kett, *Rites of Passage* (New York, 1977), p. 187.

57. Tachibana Nansei, "Kan o shirusu," *DIKGKZ*, no. 15 (March 27, 1892), p. 20.

CHAPTER FOUR

The Culture of Ceremony

The learning to be responsible, and independent, to bear pain, to play
games, to drop rank, and wealth, and home luxury, is a priceless boon. I
think myself that it is this which has made the English such an adven-
turous race; and that with all their faults . . . public schools are the cause
of this manliness.

EDWARD THRING, LETTER TO G. R. PARKIN (CA. 1875)

Adolescence is notoriously the time when the temptations of the flesh
multiply and when many youths, oppressed by their "animal impulses,"
seek to escape from the burden of guilt by adopting ceremonial patterns.

HAROLD LASSWELL,
PSYCHOPATHOLOGY AND POLITICS (1930)

By the turn of the century, the separation of the outer world of
Imperial Japan and the inner world of the higher schools was
quite striking, nowhere more so than in Tokyo, the ambivalent
home for the First Higher School. Although hardly a match for
Osaka as an industrial center, early twentieth-century Tokyo already had its share of factories whose belching chimneys were
beginning to "stain the crystalline purity of the atmosphere that
had enfolded Yedo of pre-Meiji times."[1] The sludge-filled ca-
nals, the flying cinders, the grind of machinery, the streets congested with carts of all kinds drawn by man and animal, the
notices pasted on telephone poles, calling for women to work in
suburban textile mills, were all impinging on a former way
of life that now lingered precariously in the back streets. The
worst offender to the memory of a quieter day was the electric
trolley with its zigzagging overhead wires casting sparks across

1. Robert P. Porter, *The Full Recognition of Japan* (London, 1911), p. 401.

the streets. One hundred miles of track were laid across the city between 1903 and 1905,[2] including one line that clanged and rattled by the main gate of Ichikō. About the new addition to the urban landscape, Nagai Kafū lamented, "The confusion at transfer points is remarkable, telling of a city that is splitting at the seams and has no tailor."[3]

The city was also growing by leaps and bounds. The population, under 700,000 at the time of the Restoration, soared to 2 million by 1900, then doubled over the next two decades. (The nation's population grew over the same intervals from approximately 35 to 45 to 55 million.) The exploding population was as much a function of internal migration as of increasing birthrates; and of those who flocked to the capital from the countryside, some were rural poor seeking employment in metropolitan factories, but many, and perhaps most, according to James White,[4] were ambitious youth, often the younger sons of landlords, who came to Tokyo with a middle or vocational school diploma, hoping either to extend their education or to work as salaried employees in the spreading maze of commercial and government offices. Late Meiji Tokyo was the fountainhead for Japan's "new middle class"—a heterogeneous mass of salaried bureaucrats, technicians, clerks, teachers, salespeople, plant foremen, and engineers—whose combined numbers approached 220,000 in 1910, a figure almost commensurate with the ranks of "old-middle-class" shopkeepers and businessmen.[5] The demographic transformation within the capital's middle stratum was an important index of Japan's burgeoning industrial-capitalist economy.

Instrumental to the rise of the new middle class was the expansion of secondary education and a popular reformulation of the ethic of self-improvement. Total attendance in the public and private middle schools swelled from approximately 10,000

2. Henry D. Smith, "Tokyo as an Idea," p. 57.

3. Edward Seidensticker, *Kafū the Scribbler* (Stanford, Calif., 1968), p. 33.

4. James W. White, "Internal Migration in Prewar Japan," *Journal of Japanese Studies* 4 (Winter 1978):81–119.

5. These figures, which come from Porter, p. 402, are presumably based on the Tokyo Municipal Census of 1908. In any case, precise occupational statistics for the late-Meiji period are impossible to ascertain. Estimates vary, but economists seem to agree that the proportion of white-collar workers in the labor force had risen to at least 18 percent by 1920. This growth paralleled the expansion of the middle and technical schools. See Robert Cole and Ken'ichi Tominaga, "Japan's Changing Occupational Structure and Its Significance," in Hugh Patrick, ed., *Japanese Industrialization and its Social Consequences* (Berkeley, Calif., 1976), pp. 66–67 and William W. Lockwood, *The Economic Development of Japan* (Princeton, 1968), pp. 129–131.

in 1890 to nearly 100,000 in 1905, while students attending the newly organized vocational schools at the secondary level approached 30,000.[6] In contrast, the enrollment in the higher schools and universities increased very little. Even with the establishment of two new academies at the turn of the century, Sixth Higher in Okayama and Seventh Higher in Kagoshima, there were still only 5,300 students, a figure corresponding to the available openings in Tokyo and Kyoto universities. The resulting numerical discrepancies between the universal primary school (with its 5.3 million students) and the middle school, and the middle school and the higher school, created competition of unprecedented ruthlessness.[7] Despite continuing government efforts to attenuate the drive for achievement by emphasizing the duties of mass citizenship in the primary schools and by channeling students into the less prestigious normal and vocational tracks, the struggle for survival on the main academic track was brutal. Proclaimed Inoue Tetsujirō in 1902, "Today, competition is the keynote of the field of learning, a place where examinations sort out the superior from the inferior. . . . The inferior are pushed to the rear and only the victorious advance from victory to victory."[8]

The application of the Social Darwinist ethic to the matriculation requirements for the advanced public schools placed an inordinate burden on the student with university aspirations, a burden made heavier by family and, in some cases, village expectations. Middle-class families were quick to identify the son who had the best chance of reaching the pinnacle of the school system; and from the moment he entered primary school, the "educational mamas" of late Meiji relentlessly lectured their chosen offspring on the social and economic benefits of a secondary and a higher education.[9] As social pressures mounted and academic competition intensified, middle school youth sought comfort outside the home and local school in a genre of popular literature which, by featuring biographic sketches of

6. Figures are taken from vols. 4 and 5 of Kyōikushi Hensankai, ed., *Meiji ikō kyōiku seido hattatsushi.* See also Appendix II for enrollments throughout the public school system in 1908.

7. This crush of competition is best illustrated in a comparison of entering enrollments at each ascending level of the main academic track. See Appendix III, Table 3.

8. R. P. Dore, ed., *Aspects of Social Change in Modern Japan* (Princeton, N.J., 1967), p. 136.

9. Nishizawa Kichi et al., eds., *Aa gyokuhai ni hana ukete* (Tokyo, 1972), p. 41. For a general discussion of this question, see George A. De Vos, *Socialization for Achievement* (Berkeley, 1973), esp. chap. 1.

"successful people" and pointers on how to prepare for entrance examinations, catered to the psychological needs of the "struggling student." [10] The bustling market for such dubious publications as *Who's Who in the Higher Schools* (*Kōtō gakkō hyōbanki*) and *Secrets for Taking the Higher School Examinations* (*Kōtō gakkō juken hiketsu*) indicates that the situation was becoming quite desperate by the end of the Meiji period. Moreover, with the scarcity of openings in the best schools, youths were inevitably forced to lower academic sights and turn attention to manuals offering advice on how to make the best out of less than superlative credentials within the sprawling reaches of the salaried bureaucracy. [11] If the early Meiji ethic of "rise up in the world" (*risshin shusse*) had a heroic, ennobling ring, the late Meiji ethic of "success" (*seikō*) connoted a far cruder enterprise of learning the techniques for academic survival and for ingratiating oneself with prospective employers.

Like the other higher schools, Ichikō stood in a most ironic position amidst the din of electric trolleys and the clutter of how-to-succeed manuals. As the cherished gateway to Tokyo University and the best government jobs, Ichikō was the supreme object of middle-class ambition and the raison d'être for literature pandering to parvenu youth. Many, if not most, students who entered Ichikō after 1900 had been avid readers of the popular tracts on success during their own middle school years. Nevertheless, once settled in Independence Hall, their attitudes appeared to undergo a complete metamorphosis as they quickly affected an image openly antagonistic to the former world of individualistic competition, possessive dreams, and nagging mothers. Renouncing the ethos of the petty-bourgeois achiever, the students sought a new identity in the fraternal and ascriptive bonds of the peer group: In order to seal those bonds and prevent a recurrence of the atomizing drive to get ahead, they perfected an elaborate array of primitive rituals.

The phenomenon known to prewar students and educators as "higher school barbarism" (*kōtō gakkō bābarizumu*) defies chronological brackets. Fraternal rowdiness and rites of passage

10. Dore, *Aspects of Social Change*, pp. 133–138; H. D. Harootunian, "Introduction: A Sense of an Ending and the Problem of Taishō," in Bernard S. Silberman and H. D. Harootunian, eds., *Japan in Crisis* (Princeton, N.J., 1974), pp. 18–20; the question is given its fullest discussion in E. H. Kinmonth, "The Self-made Man in Meiji Japanese Thought."

11. An example would be the guidebook for achieving success in Tokyo published in 1909 and discussed by Henry Smith, "Tokyo as an Idea," p. 59.

were part of the subterranean customs of samurai youth in late Tokugawa; in the post-Restoration era this behavior was translated into the roughneck style of provincial students at the Kaisei Gakkō and the preparatory schools. Even during the foundation years of the higher schools, when headmasters attempted to engineer the physical and social ambience for the prospective gentleman, higher school students joined in sporadic outbursts of uncontrolled roughhousing and camaraderie. Underlying such inchoate displays of energy were, first, a refusal by students to abide by the norms of conventional etiquette and, second, the apparent emotional need for physical solidarity among youth occupying the same social and historical setting.

After 1895 primitivism surfaced in the higher schools, not as a deviant tradition, but as an accepted way of life that flourished and perished with the institution. To an extent, the reliance on physical sacrifice and rites of initiation was an unexpected consequence of the pedagogy of seclusion and the rise of self-government, which legitimized antagonism between youth and conventional social norms and allowed freedom from adult supervision. The headmasters also gave indirect encouragement for primitive fraternization in their campaigns for "manliness" (*gōken*), "fortitude" (*gōki*), and pseudo-kinship ties within the school, all of which assumed greater importance than scholastic performance. Grades had little if any meaning throughout the history of the higher schools, expulsion for academic reasons was virtually an impossibility, and passage to the university was assured. (See Appendix III, Table 4.) Hence, students, who had withstood considerable academic pressure during later primary and middle school, might well respond to the scholastically carefree atmosphere of the higher schools in outlandish group behavior. The patterns of fraternal bondage, however, entailed much more than a release of pent-up frustrations. Indeed, student customs and rituals evolved over the years into a symbolic language that superseded the speeches and maxims of the faculty as the ideological bulwark of higher school consciousness.

The Rites of Masculinity

The initial response to self-government in the higher schools was marked by the drafting of carefully deliberated constitutions, the success thereof depending on the students' willingness to abide scrupulously by both the letter and the spirit of the bylaws. It is not surprising that strict adherence to legal precedent proved too boring and tedious for the majority of students, who preferred to throw a baseball or bellow out a "dormitory song" than to ponder the constitutionality of an action taken by a member of the Executive Committee. Given the difficulties in maintaining the integrity of formal political bodies, the students relied increasingly on unwritten custom and ritual to bring order to their lives. As ceremonial patterns evolved, events on the student calendar acquired a transhistorical (*chōjidaiteki*) quality, in one dean's words, or they were conventionalized to the extent of appearing impervious to social change.[12] For over a half-century, Japan was jolted by the crises of industrialization and the ravages of war, but the ceremonial side of higher school life changed very little, with initiation rites at the beginning of the school year, commemorative observances at the end, and athletic contests in between.

Student customs in the higher schools can be divided into two categories: rites of initiation and rites of intensification. The first includes those ceremonies for inducting freshmen into the community, while the latter comprises formal observances and day-to-day conventions, which strengthened group solidarity and esprit de corps. Actually, the line of distinction between the two is sometimes blurred, since every ritual involved the testing of willpower and inner strength. In this sense, they were all rites of masculinity, satisfying the need for self-validation and communal bondage within an isolated group of young men.

At Ichikō, the initiation ceremonies for incoming freshmen took place during the first weeks of each school year. At this time the new arrivals were subjected to a series of ritual ordeals designed to purge their middle school dispositions (*chūgakusei konjō*) of childlike dependence on the home and to prepare them for their new lives in the total institution of the higher school. After several months of initiation, recalled Watsuji Tetsurō, first-year students were so familiar with the "manly" rituals and customs of the school that no one could mistake them for the middle school "boys" who had recently left their homes in the countryside.[13] There had been little choice in the matter; either one switched loyalties and feelings of dependence from

12. Ōmuro Teiichirō, *Kōkō seikatsuron* (Tokyo, 1948), p. 3.
13. Watsuji Tetsurō, *Watsuji Tetsurō zenshū*, vol. 18 (Tokyo, 1963), p. 415.

family to the school, or one risked being ostracized by the peer group, something which few students could tolerate for very long.

The initiation of incoming freshmen was predicated on their physical separation both from their former way of life and, for a time at least, from the upperclassmen. The first of these conditions was automatically satisfied by the policy of seclusion, which practically eliminated casual social intercourse between those attending the school and the outside world. Separation of initiates from the rest of the student body was accomplished by herding all first-year students together in odd-numbered rooms within the dormitory, the even-numbered rooms being reserved for the seniors (*senpai*).[14] So segregated, it was impossible for freshmen to forget their common subordinate status as juniors (*kōhai*) within the student hierarchy of age and experience.

The first step in the actual induction of newcomers was the formal matriculation ceremony (*nyūgakushiki*) held at the beginning of the school year in each of the higher schools.[15] At Ichikō, the big day began at 8:30 in the morning with students lining up on the athletic field in full uniform. For the freshmen, this was the first opportunity to don the clothes symbolizing their new status. From the athletic field, the one thousand students filed into the Ethics Lecture Hall, the upperclassmen taking seats to the left of center aisle, the freshmen sitting on the right. Seated in a row of chairs on the stage were the members of the faculty, all draped in long black gowns for the occasion. Hanging majestically above the podium were the portraits of Sakanoue no Tamuramaro and Sugawara no Michizane, symbolizing the unity of warrior vigor and classical scholarship at First Higher. When students and faculty had taken their seats, a moment of dead silence was broken by the sound of unsteady footsteps creaking down center aisle. Grasping the heavy golden staff bearing the school flag, the senior member of the faculty, Imamura Yūrin, made his way slowly to the front podium. For the incoming freshmen, the sight of this aging vestige from the Meiji Restoration struggling over "the flag which protects the country" elicited astonishment and occasional tears.

The matriculation ceremony was strictly a faculty affair, usually highlighted by an address from the headmaster calling on

14. Ibid., p. 407.
15. Details are based on Kyūchiku Zenshi, *Jichiryō seikatsu* (Tokyo, 1907), pp. 16–17.

5. An executive committeeman addresses the Ichikō freshmen (1930). Courtesy of Kōdansha

the freshmen to be "respectful toward [their] seniors and diligent in learning about the school spirit." [16] With the conclusion of the headmaster's address, the faculty and upperclassmen (excepting the Executive Committee) withdrew from the assembly hall, allowing student leaders an opportunity to complete the first stage of the formal initiation. What transpired next was variously described as "the swearing-in ceremony" (*senseishiki*) or "dormitory entrance ceremony" (*nyūryōshiki*); [17] it was, in fact, an oratorical marathon in which members of the Executive Committee expounded for three to six hours on the virtues of Independence Hall. For the freshmen, who had already sat through the faculty speeches, the "dormitory entrance speeches" (*nyūryō enzetsu*) could be an excruciating rite of endurance, as they were forced to sit quietly, fully concentrating on the words shouted at them and resisting nature's urges.

Precedent and convention guided the content of the "dormitory entrance speeches." Addresses in the 1930s were almost exact replicas of those given forty years earlier. Invariably, they

16. "Shin kōyū shōkai," *DIKGKZ*, no. 29 (Sep. 27, 1891), p. 107.
17. At Ichikō students usually referred to this occasion as a "dormitory entrance ceremony." See Nishizawa, p. 128.

began with a recitation from the text of Kinoshita's "glorious manifesto." Committeemen then commented at considerable length on the "four tenets" of the dormitory, the policy of seclusion, and the responsibilities of self-government. Time was always allotted for a recounting of the great deeds of former upperclassmen, who endured untold hardship during the "dismemberment incident" of 1897 so that the young men of Ichikō might always enjoy the privilege of self-government.[18] The delivery of the speeches was as important as their content. A bland induction address was unheard-of at Ichikō or at any other higher school; every senior leader was expected to shout, whisper, gesticulate madly, and jump off the stage (if necessary) in an effort to convey the significance of institutional lore. He also glowered at the audience and challenged their masculinity. "You should beg me to call you boys (shōnen)," one speaker taunted the incoming freshmen in 1898. "If you want the upperclassmen to treat you as men (sōnen), how do you intend to prove yourselves? Never stoop to acting like girls. Be like Alexander the Great! Demonstrate your manliness (danshi no honshoku o hakki seyo)!"[19] Throughout this verbal barrage, the first-year students remained frozen in their seats, unable to move until the ritual bow before the school flag at the end of the ceremony.[20]

If the freshmen were fatigued by their day-long ordeal of listening to speeches, they still had to brace themselves for more challenges. Upperclassmen customarily intimidated the newcomers during their first days on campus, surprising them with blunt questions at any time or place (lavatory included). "Who are you? What's your name? Where do you come from? What are you doing here?" The questions would be rattled off in quick succession. In responding, the freshman was obliged to show due respect to his interrogator by answering obediently, with a minimum of carefully selected words. Any sign of an-

18. Kyūchiku Zenshi, p. 22.
19. "Shin nyūryōsei ni kigosu," DIKGKZ, no. 79 (Sep. 30, 1898), p. 75; another typical example can be found in "Nyūryōshiki," DIKGKZ, no. 149 (Oct. 3, 1905), p. 50. The same preoccupation with testing the manliness of incoming students is seen in the provincial schools. For example, at Second Higher the upperclassmen would challenge their peers to try to project their "bushi-like and manly features." "Kairyōshiki," Shōshikai zasshi, no. 44 (May 10, 1901), p. 94.
20. Both written and oral oaths of allegiance were required of freshmen in several of the provincial higher schools. See, for example, Dai Roku Kōtō Gakkō Seitoryō, ed., Rokuryō ryōshi (Okayama, 1925), p. 119; Yamamoto Kazuya, ed., Waga seishun kyūsei kōkō, p. 38; also Nishida Kitarō refers to a "swearing-in ceremony" (senseishiki). Nishida Kitarō zenshū, vol. 12 (Tokyo, 1966), p. 92.

6. An arm-wrestling tournament in Independence Hall (ca. 1915). Courtesy of Kōdansha

noyance could lead to more severe forms of harassment. "The incoming freshmen," wrote one sympathetic upperclassman at the turn of the century, "are petrified that the uttering of one unsolicited word will bring a blow to the head. . . . Therefore they listen attentively to their seniors, whether they are ridiculous or reasonable, and give the appearance of being obedient followers."[21]

As one might imagine, the catalog of ritual ordeals for incoming freshmen varied from school to school. In at least one of the provincial higher schools, there were, as Kurt Singer has described them, "excursions to graveyards and other haunted places" where freshmen were terrified by "mock apparitions."[22] Far less involved, yet more prevalent, were the little

21. Yoshogakujin, "Sōdaikai o ronzu," *DIKGKZ*, no. 76 (May 5, 1898), p. 91. For more examples of the intimidation of incoming students, see Fukita Junsuke, "Sono zengo," in *Ichikō Dōsōkai kaihō* (Oct., 1936), pp. 30–31; Kyūchiku Zenshi, pp. 59–60; Kusajima Shigure, *Ichikō jidai* (Tokyo, 1931), pp. 43–57. The "speak only when spoken to" custom that was imposed on incoming freshmen could become especially irksome in the cafeteria, where upperclassmen delighted in shouting at the cooks for second helpings while freshmen sat quietly before empty plates. For more on this, see *Watsuji Tetsurō zenshū*, vol. 18, p. 414; Ishikawa Sei's reminiscence in *Kōryō Komaba* 4, no. 2: 45; and Kusajima, pp. 57–77; Kyūchiku Zenshi, pp. 36–40; Abe Jirō's comments on the "storm" as a ritual of intimidation in *Abe Jirō zenshū*, vol. 13 (Tokyo, 1962), pp. 296–299.

22. Kurt Singer, *Mirror, Sword and Jewel*, p. 83.

7. Toughening the Ichikō freshmen (ca. 1915). Courtesy of Kōdansha

tournaments arranged by groups of upperclassmen, who challenged their underlings to spur-of-the-moment arm-wrestling or candle-blowing contests. (The latter were notorious for mustering wind from elsewhere than the lungs.)[23] But of all the ritual ordeals that awaited the newly arrived freshmen, none could rival the "welcome storm" (*kangei sutōmu*) in striking fear in the hearts of the uninitiated. Every incoming higher school freshman knew that sometime during his first weeks on campus he and his roommates would be attacked in their sleep by a roving band of upperclassmen. So wild were the tales of the midnight "storms" that many first-year students suffered through a few sleepless nights waiting for the inevitable ordeal. When the "storm" finally struck, it usually lived up to its reputation as an unforgettable rite of passage.

A typical "welcome storm" at any of the higher schools occurred between one and three in the morning, long after the lights in the dormitory had been turned off. The first warning signal was a sudden outburst of shouting voices, stamping *geta*, and washpans being banged in the downstairs hall. The freshmen, who realized their time had come, immediately sought

23. Ōura Hachirō, ed., *Sankō hachijūnen kaiko* (Tokyo, 1950), p. 91; "Kakuryō sawakai," *DIKGKZ*, no. 80 (Oct. 31, 1898), pp. 83–84.

8. A gathering "storm" at Hirosaki Higher. As explained in Chapter 7, Hirosaki Higher was founded during the post-World War I expansion. Courtesy of Yamauchi Naosuke

refuge under their bedding, pulling blankets and comforters over their heads. There they quivered in huddled masses while the crescendo of stamping feet and shouting voices made its way up the stairs. As the noise intensified, the wood-constructed dormitory trembled, as if struck by an earthquake. On reaching the top of the stairs, the attackers—clad only in loincloths (*fundoshi*) and headbands (*hachimaki*) and armed with kendo sticks, brooms, or buckets of cold water—burst into the rooms occupied by the freshmen. For the next few minutes the "stormers" kicked, beat, or jumped on top of the covered mounds lying helpless before them. They also hurled buckets of water into the room, often shattering a window or two in the process. When satisfied with their conquest, the attackers turned to their next prey, leaving behind a room full of battered and bruised underclassmen.[24] A Fifth Higher freshman describes the frightful condition of his room after the "storm":

24. Every higher school "dormitory history" has vivid descriptions of the "storms." Typical accounts of this rite of passage at Ichikō can be found in *Kōryōshi*, p. 1459; *Kyūchiku Zenshi*, p. 33; Deguchi Kyō, *Zenkoku kōtō gakkō hyōbanki* (Tokyo, 1902), pp. 22–23.

What a terrible sight it was after the storm! The broken glass was scattered everywhere in the corridor. In our room the broken pieces were strewn about over the *tatami*, on the bedding, and even in our pillows. But the water that had been splashed so liberally into our room had done even greater damage than the glass. My bedding was soaking wet, and certainly I could not sleep in it that night. My potted plant had been pulled up by the roots, and my friend had had his stomach trodden upon.[25]

The "storm" probably originated at First Higher around 1895 and spread quickly thereafter to each of the provincial schools.[26] It was never a monolithic ritual; attackers at one school might imitate the howling and barking of a dog pack, whereas at another they would set up rope traps in the hall to catch any underclassman in flight.[27] Moreover, by 1910, students had perfected a more convivial version of the ritual in order to celebrate a variety of occasions; there was a storm for anniversary day, a storm for graduation, a storm for victory on the athletic field, a storm for the completion of military exercises, and a storm for any night when students were overcome by the need to lose all inhibition in a wild frenzy of jumping, bellowing, shoving, and clinging. Still, the original purpose, which assumed overriding importance throughout the prewar period, was to test the manliness of the newly arrived freshman, rid him of his middle school dependence on the family, diminish his independent urge toward self-achievement, and enlarge his psychological need for incorporation within the community. The reasoning may seem contradictory, for contrived rituals of intimidation are not conducive to making someone want to belong to a group, and there were some students who were so terrified by the tales of midnight assaults that they simply fled home. But for the vast majority of newcomers, the mental strain of anticipation and the physical pain, which might linger for days after the attack, had the long-term effect of sealing allegiance to the institution. The injuries of the moment could be tolerated, even "welcomed," because the victim knew that he had proven his determination to stand on his own as a higher school man, that he had sustained the symbolic wounds necessary to validate his membership in the closed society of late adolescent males.

25. Graham Martyr, ed., *Ryūnan monogatari* (Kumamoto, 1930), pp. 143–144.
26. Deguchi, p. 93; "storms" are not recorded in *Kōryōshi* until 1898.
27. "Jiyūryōshi," p. 40; *Shūgakuryōshi*, p. 561.

9. Prelude to a Fifth Higher "storm" (1934). Courtesy of Ishida Ryōkichi

Having withstood the ordeal of the "welcome storm," the first-year student could look forward to happier times. As a full-fledged junior member of the student community, he now joined his seniors in an extensive array of collective rituals that promoted group solidarity and school spirit. Since these rituals of intensification included both periodic observances and day-to-day customs, they consumed much of the extracurricular time and energy of the students.

The periodic observance is the most easily identified form of

10. "Storming" down the corridor. Hirosaki Higher, courtesy of Yamauchi Naosuke

ceremonial behavior in the higher school dormitories. Included under this heading are the formalized gatherings that enlivened the schoolboy experience: "anniversary celebrations" (*kinensai*), "dinner assemblies" (*bansankai*), "farewell parties" (*sōbetsukai*), and "tea assemblies" (*sawakai*). All of these observances were scheduled for specific times and places, and all adhered to a conventionalized format for celebration, involving the sharing of food and drink, the singing of "dormitory songs," the recitation of school oaths, the performance of skits and sword dances, and the display of institutional totems. Although they allowed little room for experimentation or creativity, the periodic observances imbued the student with a sense of belonging to a long and venerable tradition.

The ceremonial format for a late-Meiji "tea assembly" conveys a sense of the mystery and excitement attending periodic observances. Beginning just after supper and continuing until the early hours of the morning, the "tea assembly" was generally divided into three parts, the first of which was set aside for lengthy speeches extolling the school spirit. When the voices of student and alumni orators finally ran dry (usually after three or four hours), the assembly happily turned its attention to the presentation of short skits and sword dances (*enbu*). Like the "costume parades" (*kasō-gyōretsu*) that highlighted anniversary-day festivities, the skits revealed a student fondness for caricature. The impersonations of an assortment of social groups, from simple fishermen on Awaji Island to smooth-operating businessmen in Tokyo, sparked uproarious laughter while implicitly fortifying the lofty self-image of the audience. The sword dances, in contrast, were both performed and viewed with an air of solemnity. Usually the lights were turned off in the assembly hall and candles lit in front of the stage before the lone dancer began his slow but powerful movements. As he danced, a narrator recited verses from the tales of legendary, medieval heroes, and the students surrendered completely to the phantasms of their mind.[28] In the words of one upperclassman describing a climactic performance at a "tea assembly" in 1896: "The swirling flashes of the sword conjured images of a swallow flying gracefully under a willow tree at night, and the deliberate style of the dancer reminded us of a hawk soaring by itself high in the sky."[29] With the completion of this staged fantasy, tea and crackers were served as a common substance or communion for a spiritually aroused assembly. The victuals also refueled the energies of the stalwarts in time for a joyous round of "dormitory songs." Finally, when the full repertoire had been faithfully sung, the "tea assembly" concluded with a singing of the national anthem and a rousing banzai for self-government and chastity.[30]

The rituals of collective affirmation extended far beyond the formalized observance of a "tea assembly" or an anniversary celebration. A day rarely passed without groups of students seeking to strengthen the social bond in some kind of informal ritual activity. For example, the room parties, or *konpa* (from the English company), were organized spontaneously by small groups of students at any time and in any room in the dormitory. They usually consisted of twenty or thirty students sitting around a table, nibbling on crackers, singing "dormitory songs," and listening to upperclassmen recite school folktales. It was not uncommon either for *konpa* merrymakers to cap off the evening with a round dance, or "fire storm." Unlike the "welcome storm," the "fire storm" was a spur-of-the-moment rite of exaltation. After igniting a small bonfire in the athletic

28. Ōmachi Yoshie, "Kenbu o ronzu," *DIKGKZ*, no. 3 (Jan. 27, 1891), p. 10.
29. "Kishukuryō sawakai," *DIKGKZ*, no. 58 (June 20, 1896), p. 72.
30. Ibid. For this discussion I have also relied on the detailed description in "Kishukuryō dai go kai kinensai kiji," *Dai Ichi Kōtō Gakkō Kōyūkai zasshi furoku*, no. 45 (March 2, 1895), pp. 5–10.

field and stripping down to their waists (or underwear), participants danced arm in arm around the soaring flames in a state of "fraternalizing ecstasy."[31]

Less dramatic were the little rituals governing everyday behavior that blended the individual student unwittingly into the rhythms of the community. Custom dictated the way a student must talk (in a manly, forceful tone), the way he dressed (in a worn-out, slightly tattered school uniform), the way he slept (in a mildewy bedroll that never saw the light of day), the way he studied after midnight (only by candlelight), the way he walked down the street (with a pronounced swagger), even the way he relieved himself in his bedroom without traipsing down to the appropriate ground-floor facilities (by simply opening the window). This last custom, called "dormitory rain" (*ryōu*), was one of a number of rituals that regulated the vital functions of higher school students.[32]

Looking over this list of customs, one is struck by the apparent urge among the students to seek conformity and companionship by maintaining what Watsuji Tetsurō has called an uncivilized (*hibunmeiteki*) level of existence.[33] In part, the uncivilized lifestyle was a consequence of living in a dormitory that offered its residents few amenities: the ramshackle wooden structures were cold and dreary in the winter, hot and infested with insects in the late spring and summer. At the same time, the students actively contributed to the contamination of the dormitory by rejoicing in their own filth. The longer a stalwart wore his uniform without washing it or the longer he left his bedroll on the floor without airing it, the more likely he was to win the respect of his peers. Like their contemporaries in the Victorian public schools, the late Meiji higher school students championed their artificial state of "relative deprivation"[34] as a test of manly determination to live unselfishly in fraternal har-

31. Singer, p. 32; descriptions of the "konpa" can be found in *Kōryōshi*, pp. 1461–1462.

32. The ritual of "dormitory rain" probably first appeared at Ichikō in 1895 or 1896, according to "Jiyūryōshi," p. 29. And by the time of the publication of Deguchi's *Zenkoku kōtō gakkō hyōbanki* in 1902, the ritual had already gained considerable notoriety. (See especially pp. 24–25.) The student fascination for elimination is suggested in a number of other rituals and superstitions about ghosts inhabiting certain toilets on campus. See, for example, Kondō Kōichirō, *Kōfū manga* (Tokyo, 1917), pp. 3–4; Deguchi, pp. 237–238; Ōura, p. 91; *Shichikō omoideshū kōhen*, p. 439.

33. *Watsuji Tetsurō zenshū*, vol. 18, p. 407; Tsuji Jirō, "Kōryō no omoide," *Ichikō Dōsōkai kaihō*, no. 36 (Jan. 27, 1938), p. 45.

34. The term is used in John Wakeford, *The Cloistered Elite: A Sociological Analysis of the English Public Boarding School* (New York, 1969).

11. Firelight celebrations at Hirosaki Higher (left) and Ichikō (right). Courtesy of Yamauchi Naosuke and Kōdansha.

mony. Nothing was more effective in enhancing the sense of belonging to the community than the awareness among students that they must join together in withstanding the adversities of uncivilized life. This explains why the rite of "dormitory rain," the ultimate expression of higher school primitivism, was commonly viewed as the most satisfying ritual of intensification.[35] For what could be more deeply affecting than to stand shoulder to shoulder, seniors with juniors, answering nature's call in the light of the moon while singing a favorite "dormitory song":

> When my friends are sad
> I will cry.
> When I am happy
> My friends will dance.
> Behold, the flaming red of our school flag.
> It is dyed o'er the fumes
> Of our seething blood
> As we are moved
> By the spirit of life.[36]

---

35. Miyagi Otogorō, "Ichikō jidai mukashi gatari," *Ichikō Dōsōkai kaihō*, no. 35 (Nov. 15, 1939), p. 15.
36. Genkōsha, ed., *Ryōka wa ikiteiru* (Tokyo, 1963), p. 56.

The Exercise of Asceticism

Even without witnessing the nocturnal rituals of "dormitory life" (ryō-seikatsu), visitors to the Ichikō campus at the turn of the century were amazed at the strenuous level of activity among students.[37] Whether they were strutting back and forth between classes, slamming their rice bowls on the cafeteria counter for refills, or scribbling Chinese couplets on the ceiling of Independence Hall, the students were conspicuous in their exertions. Idleness was tantamount to sin in the 1890s and early 1900s, when an outbreak of influenza or, in 1904, of typhoid fever could not keep some stalwarts from "storming" through the dormitory regardless of faculty expostulations. Epitomizing the students' attitude of unrestrained exertion (tetteishugi) was their devotion to athletics. From sunup to sundown—before, between, or after classes—the crack of bamboo swords and baseball bats filled the air on Mukōga Hill. Sport dominated the extracurriculum of the early higher schools, and the rituals of "club life" (bu-seikatsu) complemented the rituals of "dormitory life" in forging the collective solidarity of the student community.

Before the foundation of the higher schools, students and ed-

37. Ishii Mitsuru, *Nitobe Inazō den* (Tokyo, 1935), pp. 275–280.

ucators viewed sport as "only a game." The handful of student athletic clubs in existence prior to 1886 consisted of poorly organized baseball teams and crews, which were called "off-campus recreational clubs" (*kōgai yūgibu*),[38] an appellation that underscored both their independence from the institution and their lack of serious purpose. This carefree attitude toward strenuous outdoor activity was overhauled by the architects of the higher schools, who, in accordance with the *bun-bu* formula, stressed the importance of physical training as part of the formal curriculum. Initially, the early administrators were reluctant to permit students to organize their own extracurricular sports clubs, fearing a return of the undisciplined precedent of the off-campus "athletic meetings." But as the higher school developed into a self-contained institution, and with the extension of self-governing privileges to the students, the idea of developing an athletic program attracted attention. By the early 1890s, most higher school administrators had come to agree with the opinion expressed in Shōyō's novel that sport could serve as a safe outlet (*morasu michi*) for adolescent energies, provided all activities were sponsored directly by the school and made use of school facilities.[39] In this way, higher school athletics were clearly distinguished from the "off-campus recreational clubs" of previous years.

Without faculty encouragement, the athletic program in the higher schools might never have been implemented, but their success was ultimately assured by the enthusiasm of the students. Not only did the students take the initiative in organizing the clubs, they also pushed for the creation of an extracurricular confederation to provide a common source of funds for all activities. The idea originated at Ichikō in October of 1890, when students obtained consent from the faculty to organize the Society of Friends (*Kōyūkai*), a body which served, thereafter, as the cover organization for all institutionally sanctioned clubs. Similar bodies were formed in each of the provincial schools over the next five years.[40]

At the founding of the extracurricular confederations, faculty and students invariably spoke of the need for a balanced program of cultural and athletic activities.[41] A survey of the list of

38. Takahashi Samon, "Kyūsei kōtō gakkō ni . . . , (II)," p. 32.
39. Tsubouchi Shōyō, p. 125.
40. *Kōryōshi*, p. 240; Miyasaka, pp. 195–197.
41. Sakakura, pp. 128–129; *Gokō gojūnenshi*, p. 425; *Kōryōshi*, p. 240; Toita, p. 85.

clubs within each of the original confederations reveals, however, an overwhelming preference for athletics. The Society of Friends at Ichikō originally sponsored nine clubs, seven of which were sports clubs (baseball, crew, judo, kendo, archery, tennis, track) while only one was intellectual, the Literary Club, which was responsible for the school magazine. A ninth club was organized to plan school excursions. In a similar vein, athletic clubs dominated the extracurriculum in the provincial higher schools, including Sankō, considered by many to have set the highest standard of culture for its students, where five of the original seven clubs were devoted to sports.[42]

At first glance, the popularity of sports in the early higher schools might be ascribed to the apparent anti-intellectualism of the students. At Ichikō, for example, students often spoke of the need for an "athletic school spirit" (*undō kōfū*) that was consonant with their ideal of manliness.[43] When a small group of students proposed the addition of a debate club to the Society of Friends in the early 1890s, they were greeted by outright hostility from many of their peers. "The vast majority in the Society of Friends," wrote Yanaihara Tadao, "were not pleased by the idea of debate. They considered the essence of the school spirit to lie in sport, while regarding debate as entertainment for frivolous dandies (*keihakushi*) and dangerous to the collective ethos."[44] Only after the Ichikō debaters went to ridiculous lengths to accommodate the "athletic school spirit" (by agreeing, for example, to debate the rise of the Oxford crew) did forensics gain a foothold in the Society of Friends in 1899.[45] Attempts to organize music and poetry clubs fared even worse and achieved no respectability on campus until after the Russo-Japanese War. Such examples suggest that the 1890s was an inhospitable decade for student intellectuals; that indeed, if a stu-

---

42. Sakakura, p. 129.

43. Two representative essays on the "athletic school spirit" at Ichikō during the mid-1890s are Nakauma Kō, "Kōfū to undōka to no kankei o ronjite Kyōto ensei ni oyobu," *DIKGKZ*, no. 34 (Feb. 27, 1894); and Jikokyoan Shami (an obvious pen name), "Wagashuguan shujin ni ataete undō no en o toku," *DIKGKZ*, no. 43 (Jan. 8, 1895). The authors of both articles talk about the righteousness of action and sacrifice over idle contemplation. As Jikokyoan puts it: "Abandon what you call knowledge and cultivate instead the essence of accomplishment and greatness through your devotion to sports" (see p. 89). Similar articles can be found in provincial higher school magazines; for example, at Second Higher, "Izukuka rōshitsu ni . . . ," *Shōshikai zasshi*, no. 31 (Oct. 31, 1898), pp. 40–42.

44. *Kōryōshi*, p. 297.

45. Matsubara Kazuo, "Kōronkai no ryūsei o nozomite mankō no shishi ni tsugu," *DIKGKZ*, no. 63 (Jan. 30, 1897), p. 13; Yanaihara Tadao, "Benron bushi," in *Kōryōshi*, p. 301.

dent could neither swing a bat nor thrust a bamboo sword, he was hard pressed to cheer those who could or suffer the indignities of a pariah.

However, the anti-intellectualism of the early higher school students should not be exaggerated. The students were undeniably a most literate group, whose verbal skills were perfected in classroom studies of literature and foreign language. Even the articles in the *Society of Friends Magazine* which praise the athlete and attack the idle intellectual are written with considerable grace and precision.[46] To say, therefore, that the students were a hopeless band of Philistines stretches the point. Furthermore, the most illustrious men of letters on the higher school faculties during the 1890s were just as enthusiastic about sport as their students. Takayama Chogyū, for example, spearheaded the drive to organize a baseball team at Second Higher in 1896, and Natsume Sōseki is often cited as one of Ichikō's most ardent sports fans.[47]

The popularity of sport was undoubtedly rooted in the faith that physical training perfected human character. With rare exception, student leaders praised the athletic club for replacing the fragmented image of the pale, bookish, self-serving, and occasionally debauched student with a robust and determined prototype—the higher school man. Like the young roughnecks of early Meiji, the higher school stalwarts believed that an internal battle was raging for control of their spirit, a battle between the manly values of the school (vigor, willpower, self-restraint) and the effeminate values of the outside society (enervation, weakness, self-indulgence). More than other campus rituals, sport was the embodiment of the former and the prophylactic against the latter. The founding members of the Ichikō Kendo Club explained: "Ichikō's school spirit honors diligence, thrift, and the martial ethos (*kinken shōbu*); our club, with its mottoes of righteousness (*seigi*), embodies the essence of this spirit. . . . By cultivating simplicity and manliness (*gōken*), we can oppose the frivolity of the vulgar world and lead the nation's youth."[48] The thrust of the kendo sword was a thrust at the seductive world that surrounded and threatened Ichikō's bastion of masculinity.

46. For example, the articles by Nakauma Kō and Jikokyoan cited above.
47. Takase Naotomo, ed., *Shōshikai zenshi* (Sendai, 1937), pp. 350–361. In Nippon Taiiku Kyōkai, ed., *Supōtsu hachijūnenshi* (Tokyo, 1958), there is a special section on "Sōseki and sports," unpaged.
48. *Kōryōshi*, p. 369.

In the battle for control of the senses, sport was a test of endurance similar in function to the dormitory rites of passage. Inevitably, the higher school athlete was expected to follow a Spartan routine of early morning alarms, cold baths, marginal nutrition, and hours upon hours of uninterrupted practice. Ōtsuyama Kinnosuke recalls the "fierce practice sessions" for the Sankō Kendo Club in which each participant received his share of elbow welts, ear-deafening blows to the head, and occasional jabs to the midsection that made one "jump with pain."[49] The privations of an ordinary day's practice were compounded at specially designated periods for intensive training. New recruits for the Ichikō crew, according to Takami Jun, were sometimes required to practice for seven straight days and nights with hardly any sleep or food.[50] Worse yet were the celebrated "winter exercises" (kangeiko)—a two- or three-week period in the middle of winter earmarked for a grueling succession of predawn practice sessions. Judo and kendo athletes in particular were renowned for maintaining a stiff upper lip as they jogged in their bare feet over a frost-covered turf at four or five in the morning.[51]

Besides appealing to Spartan needs, sport was a powerful vehicle for "uniting the public heart" (shūshin o hitotsu ni su), as one student wrote in 1895.[52] In every respect, club life maximized the individual's feelings of dependence, on first the team, then the school, and ultimately, the nation. Any athletic activity in the higher school was considered a collective endeavor, even when the actual competition involved matches between individuals, as in kendo and judo. To underscore this point, sports clubs adopted mottoes that called upon the members to dedicate themselves to the ideals of "self-renunciation" (botsuga) and "total sacrifice" (tettō tetsubi gisei).[53] Further enhancing internal solidarity was the custom of having senior club members share the same suite of rooms in the dormitory and of

49. Ōura, Sankō hachijūnen kaiko, p. 107.

50. Takami Jun, "Kaiketsu Teroren no shi," Hashimoto Otsuji, ed., Kishi Michizō tsuitōroku (Tokyo, 1963), p. 347.

51. Kōryōshi, pp. 371–372; "Kangeiko," DIKGKZ, no. 32 (Jan. 8, 1895), p. 94. An excellent description of the rigors of athletic life at Ichikō can be found in Tsurumi Yūsuke's "Ichikō jidai no omoide," Kōryō Komaba 1, no. 1 (Oct. 27, 1959):26; also Sakakura, p. 171.

52. Nakamura Kōhei, "Kōfūron zoku," DIKGKZ, no. 46 (April 22, 1895), p. 6.

53. Dai Yon Kōtō Gakkō Jishūryō Ryōshi Hensan Iinkai, ed., Dai Yon Kōtō Gakkō Jishūryōshi, p. 51; Dai Roku Kōtō Gakkō Seitoryō, ed., Rokuryō ryōshi, p. 180; Kōryōshi, p. 379.

12. Celebrating an athletic victory on the steets of Hirosaki. Courtesy of Yamauchi Naosuke

holding periodic "training camps" (*gasshuku*) during vacation, when teammates lived in virtual isolation on campus for two or three weeks of solid practice. So intense was the esprit de corps resulting from such traditions that the club took on the appearance of a small community within the larger community of the school.

Still, the club never existed apart from the school. Much of the incentive for intensifying the social bond among teammates came from preparing the club for battle against their counterparts from a rival institution. By the turn of the century, athletic rivalries among higher schools were blossoming, and as competition intensified, the pressure on the athletes to uphold the honor of the institution became enormous. On the eve of important contests, the entire school community gathered for special "tea assemblies" or send-off ceremonies, where fiery speakers attempted to rouse the players to victory. If the team emerged triumphant, athletes and rooters joined in a frenzied celebration highlighted by a "victory storm." But if the team were defeated, a pall of gloom swept over the campus, and despondent athletes huddled together and sulked for days on end, sometimes even shaving their heads out of humiliation.[54]

If defeat brought the athlete to the brink of despair, the promise of victory inspired him to supererogatory feats of courage. Like the Tom Browns of Rugby and the Dink Stovers of Yale, the mark of a higher school hero was his prowess on the playing field combined with an indomitable loyalty to the alma mater. Every school had its pantheon of heroes whose noble deeds were permanently inscribed in the folklore of the institution. At Ichikō, the most revered upperclassman was Moriyama Tsunetarō, an outstanding pitcher on the baseball team who pitched a shutout against a team of visiting Americans in 1903. In preparing for this game Moriyama—known to the early Ichikō stalwarts as the "ball god" (*kyūshin*)—relentlessly heaved his fast ball against the brick wall of the clubhouse. Under the pressure of his mighty arm, the wall, after several days, began to give way, and one or two bricks actually caved in, leaving a gaping hole for later generations to view with amazement. Next to the hole in the wall, an inscription called attention to "the traces of Moriyama's fierce training."[55]

There are numerous other stories of athletic prowess at Ichikō, which were passed along by word of mouth from upperclassmen to lowerclassmen and were eventually collected in a fascinating volume, published in 1925, entitled *The Tales of the Ichikō Soul* (*Ichikō tamashii monogatari*). Among those immortalized are two gallant members of the crew who swam the icy water of the Sumida River on a midwinter's night in 1899 in order to report precisely on the tricky currents to their fellow crew members. Inspired by their valiance, the Ichikō crew went on to defeat the Tokyo School of Commerce in their annual boat race. Another favorite tale describes the heroism of a judo athlete, who refused to let knowledge of his father's imminent death deter him from scoring an impressive victory in a crucial meeting—further evidence that the "family school" was overshadowing the primordial family. And then there is the story of Ichikō's most dedicated cheerleader, who, despite being bedridden with a terminal case of tuberculosis, devoted his last gasping energies to queries about how the baseball club was faring in its crucial confrontation with Sankō. After receiving

54. Yamamoto Kazuya, p. 59; Terasaki, "Kyūsei kōkō ni okeru ningen keisei," footnotes, pp. 56–57.
55. Nishizawa, p. 37; Professor Maruyama Masao also retold this story during an interview in Princeton on May 3, 1976.

word that Ichikō had won, he quietly passed away, singing praises to the alma mater. The story is appropriately rendered in English as "Victory or Death." [56]

"To abandon himself body and soul to the game," in Huizinga's phrase, was the mark of a higher school hero. [57] However, in its extreme form heroism became indistinguishable from martyrdom. Higher school lore is replete with tales of the judo-club enthusiast who suffered a shoulder separation rather than give up on the mat, or of the fever-stricken baseball player who refused to skip a day's practice. More disturbing are instances of over-exhaustion and sheer recklessness. Members of the Second Higher crew, for example, repeatedly took risks on the unpredictable coastal waters off Sendai. In March 1903 two crew members drowned when their boat capsized in treacherous waters; two years later a third student drowned during a furious practice session. [58] By far the worst incident took place during winter practice on December 28, 1934, when a launch capsized far from shore, drowning all ten crew members. As in the other incidents, the victims became instant heroes; classmates and teachers talked about the "inspiration" (kangeki) of ten athletes dying together while struggling to keep their boat afloat. Even the headmaster, who might be expected to interject a cautionary note on the value of winter exercises, opened his eulogy to the fallen crew members in almost glowing terms: "The true way of boating is exemplified in the harmony of the manly spirit when the individual oarsman merges indistinguishably into the crew of one boat. We can see in this tragic incident the supreme devotion and martyrdom to this principle by ten members of the Second Higher crew." [59]

Although never quite dropping to the nadir of American college sports (in 1905 alone eighteen American students lost their lives on the football field), [60] athletic competition and training in the higher schools were obviously more than a game. As a test of manliness, as a mechanism for intensifying school loyalty, and as a stage for making heroes, sport assumed vital importance in the ceremonial culture of the student community. At the same time, the sports club played a key role in "dormitory politics" (ryō no seiji), functioning as a primary organ of recruit-

56. Moiwa, Ichikō tamashii monogatari, pp. 1–29 and 327–344.
57. Johan Huizinga, Homo Ludens (Boston, 1955), p. 21.
58. Takase Naotomo, ed., Shōshikai zenshi (Sendai, 1937), pp. 473–475.
59. Atoda, p. 157.
60. Frederick Rudolph, The American College and University, p. 375.

13. Manly determination: the victorious Archery Club. Hirosaki Higher, courtesy of Yamauchi Naosuke

ment into the student government.[61] From the encomiums he received for his exploits on the playing field, and from the experience he acquired as a member of a club managed completely by participating students (except for the martial arts, there were

61. Tezuka Tomio, *Ichi seinen no shisō no ayumi* (Tokyo, 1966), pp. 54–59.

14. Cheering the Ichikō baseball team at the height of the prewar rivalry with Sankō. Courtesy of Kōdansha

no faculty coaches), the higher school athlete was a natural candidate for office in the general assembly or executive committee.

National Prestige and Sport at Ichikō

Along with its influence on the internal structure and values of the student community organized athletics served as a conduit between school and society. The celebrated rivalries between the First and Third Higher baseball teams and between the Third and Fourth Higher judo clubs captured wide public interest and were covered extensively in regional newspapers. In addition, the big athletic event was the one occasion when ordinary citizens were allowed into the academic cloister as rooters for the local higher school. Thus more than other campus rituals, sport communicated to the outside world and thereby shaped popular images of the higher school students as a strong-willed, self-abnegating, and honorable elite. The laudatory perception derived in part from the wonder of sport itself in late Meiji Japan. Participation in outdoor games was a unique status privilege in the 1890s, when working-class youth could not dream of spending five or six hours a day playing baseball or wrestling in the judo hall. Whereas military calisthenics was routinized throughout the compulsory and normal-school sectors, sport in Meiji Japan was the exclusive preserve of the higher school, the private college, and the university. Fully aware of this distinction, students were quick to seize upon the sporting event as an opportunity to display honor and good form in full public view.

Sport at Ichikō developed faster than in any of the brother schools; and until the early 1900s, when most of the "inter-high" rivalries originated, Ichikō teams played many of their games with neighboring technical schools or private colleges. The students attending these rival institutions, although hardly lower class, were singled out for lack of gentlemanly attribute in Kinoshita Hiroji's addresses; hence, the athletic confrontations with Ichikō often revealed certain underlying social tensions. The heated competition between Ichikō and the Tokyo School of Commerce (later called Hitotsubashi) illustrates this point. Beginning in 1889, the two schools competed in a series of highly publicized boat races that were romanticized by the Ichikō students as a reenactment of the Punic Wars, with the Tokyo School of Commerce symbolizing the Carthaginian lust for business and material extravagance and with Ichikō standing for the manly virtues of Rome.[62] The faculty at First Higher seemed intent on making the most of the social cleavage between the schools by rewarding their victorious crew in the spring of 1889 with copies of *Hamlet* and Matthew Arnold's *Literature and Dogma*.[63] Presumably, the award lay well beyond the intellectual grasp of the crass vocationalists at the commercial school, although it is problematic whether the Ichikō crew members were prepared for such a heavy dosage of *Kultur*.

If the "Punic Wars" were fought to preserve social rank within the society, then the baseball games between Ichikō and resident American teams in the treaty port of Yokohama had even broader sociopolitical implications, which buttressed the notion among First Higher students that "the athlete [is to the school] what the warrior is to the country (*undōka wa kore o kuni ni hisureba gunjin nari*)."[64] Baseball was the fastest growing college sport in the 1890s, and the strongest team was fielded by First

62. Moiwa, p. 331.
63. From "Sōseki to supōtsu," in Nippon Taiiku Kyōkai, ed., *Supōtsu hachijūnenshi.*
64. Nakauma, "Kōfū to undōka . . . ," p. 13.

Higher.[65] Once the Ichikō players either had defeated or were convinced of their superiority over such rival private colleges as Meiji Gakuin, Keiō, and Waseda, they began, as early as October 1891, to issue challenges to the American team representing the exclusive Athletic Club in Yokohama's foreign settlement. For five years the Ichikō students attempted to arrange an international match; yet the Americans always sent back a negative response, softened only by manifestly lame excuses about baseball being "our national game" and about the physical hazards of undersized Japanese schoolboys confronting a group of hearty Yankees.[66] To the Ichikō students the condescending refusals to play were shocking evidence that Americans in Yokohama were not viewing the Japanese as their equals and were, in effect, reaffirming the illegal and patently discriminatory privileges of the unequal treaties. Thus, a simple game of baseball assumed the dimensions of a struggle for national dignity.

Finally, after five years of fruitless inquiries, the perseverance of the Ichikō players was rewarded. With the help of an intermediary, the first official baseball game between an American and a Japanese team was arranged for May 23, 1896, to be held on a playing field in Yokohama which had, heretofore, been strictly off limits to everyone outside the Western community.[67] Considering the unprecedented nature of the game and the residual cultural biases of many in the settlement, it is not surprising that when the Ichikō players entered the park to begin their pregame warm-ups, they were greeted by jeers and catcalls from the foreign spectators. Undaunted by their uncivil welcome, the First Higher team went on to wallop the Yokohama Athletic Club by a score of 29 to 4; when the latter pleaded for an immediate rematch two weeks later, the students delivered their opponents an equally decisive defeat, 32 to 9. And so the series continued, with eleven more games spaced over a period of eight years. Of these Ichikō emerged victorious in nine games, while losing only two "squeakers" by one- and two-run margins. The total tally over the entire series of 230 runs for

65. Baseball was first introduced to Japan in 1873 when two American teachers organized a team at the Kaisei Gakkō. Over the next two decades, the sport spread quickly among students in the private colleges and foreign language schools, including the Tokyo Preparatory School. For more details on the early history of Japanese baseball, see Hirose Kenzō, *Nihon no yakyūshi* (Tokyo, 1964), pp. 1–8; Kimijima Ichirō, *Nihon yakyū sōseiki* (Tokyo, 1972), chaps. 1–3; Kubota Takayuki, "Gakusei yakyū oyobi shōnen yakyū," Ōbunsha, ed., *Yakyū taikan* (Tokyo, 1949), pp. 49–51.

66. *Kōryōshi*, pp. 649–651.

67. Hirose, p. 8; Kimijima, *Nihon yakyū sōseiki*, pp. 13 and 85.

First Higher and a paltry 64 for the Americans gave pause as to whose "national game" baseball really was.[68]

The poor showing by the Americans was utterly humiliating, especially since the Yokohama Athletic club recruited additional players from the crews of several United States battleships (including the *Detroit*, the *Kentucky*, and the *Yorktown*) that were periodically moored in the settlement harbor. In contrast, the triumphant showing of a succession of First Higher teams aroused the public spirit. The games, according to one account, were "sensational news," and in the wake of each lopsided win, the Ichikō players were mobbed by grateful citizens, who viewed the contests as a symbol of Japan's liberation from the unequal treaties.[69] For their part, the Ichikō athletes delighted in recognizing their achievement as "victories for the Japanese people" (*hōjin no kachi*) and boasted freely of the will to play each game as if "the name of the country" (*kokumei*) was at stake.[70] Just as the Battle of Waterloo was won on the playing fields of Eton, the First Higher students believed that their triumphs in baseball accelerated Japan's rise as a military power in the Pacific. Yet, in accepting newspaper praise for their "great victories" (*taishō*) and unselfish devotion to the nation, the students also enhanced their own social standing. The fine line of distinction between service to the country and self-interest is exemplified in the lyrics of Ichikō's famous "Baseball Club Rouser" (*Yakyūbuka*),[71] written in 1905 in commemoration of the Yokohama Series.

I

Among literary and martial arts pursued
In the righteous air of the First Higher School,
Baseball stands especially high
With its spirit of honor that refuses to die.

---

68. Figures are compiled from the individual accounts of each game in *Kōryōshi*, pp. 651–679. The score for one game, between Ichikō and the battleship *Yorktown* on June 8, 1897, was not given in the above source and was found instead in "Waga gun daini beigun to tatakau," *Undōkai* 1, no. 2 (July 1897), p. 5.

69. The term "sensational" is used to describe the reaction of Second Higher students to the games in Nakayama Yoshio and Etō Takehito, *Ten wa Tōhoku yama takaku* (Tokyo, 1966), p. 239; the second game received front-page headlines in *Asahi Shinbun*, June 7, 1896; the gratitude of Japanese citizens is described in "Itsuwa," *Dai Ichi Kōtō Gakkō Kōyūkai zasshi furoku*, no. 58 (June 20, 1896), pp. 17–18.

70. "Yokohama ensei kiji," *Dai Ichi Kōtō Gakkō Kōyūkai zasshi furoku*, no. 58 (June 20, 1896), p. 4.

71. Genkōsha, *Ryōka wa ikiteiru*, p. 76.

II

The crack of the bat echoes to the sky
On cold March mornings when we chase balls on the ice.
Year in and year out, through wind and rain,
Enduring all hardship, we practice our game.

III

While the years have seen many a foe
Come to our school yard where strong winds blow,
Upon touching the sleeves of our armored knights
We turn them away, speechless with fright.

IV

The valorous sailors from the *Detroit, Kentucky,* and *Yorktown*
Whose furious batting can intimidate a cyclone
Threw off their helmets, their energies depleted.
Behold how pathetically they run away defeated.

V

Courageously, we marched twenty miles south
To fight the Americans in Yokohama.
Though they boast of the game as their national sport,
Behold the games they have left with no score.

VI

Ah, for the glory of our Baseball Club!
Ah, for the glitter it has cast!
Pray that our martial valor never turns submissive
And that our honor will always shine far across the Pacific.

The Significance of School Rituals

As in the West, the history of education in Japan has been dominated by institutional studies and biographies of educators,
while the configurations of student culture have received far
less attention. In commenting on the broader significance of
higher school rituals and athletics, we must first consider why
the subject has largely escaped serious investigation. Two
points come to mind. First, there is a strong feeling, even
among alumni loyalists, that the ritual life of the higher schools
was too primitive, too bizarre, or even too inscrutably Japanese
to warrant scholarly attention.[72] That students relieved them-

72. Karasawa Tomitarō speaks of the uniqueness of the Ichikō ethos in terms of "a
Far Eastern heroic air" (*tōyōteki gōketsufū*). See Karasawa, *Gakusei no rekishi*, pp. 83 and
89.

selves out the second-story window, ran barefoot in the snow for "winter exercises," or, as occurred at early Fifth Higher, slaughtered stray dogs for a sacrificial stew,[73] is all interesting material for popular memoirs but hardly suitable for more refined academic tastes. Congruently, scholars are reluctant to delve into student customs, which they regard as exhibitions of youthful nonsense and of little consequence to either the historian concerned with Japan's early industrialization or the sociologist interested in the career development of the prewar elite. Sober-minded bureaucrats, the argument insists, had long since abandoned their juvenile inclinations to dance and sing and heave baseballs against brick walls. So why examine school rituals which, at best, are irrelevant and, at worst, embarrassing?

The assumption that higher school primitivism was uniquely Japanese can be refuted from a cross-cultural perspective. Contemporary accounts of the Victorian public schools and New England colleges reveal distinct similarities with the student lifestyle in Japan. The intimidation of underclassmen, the worship of manliness and self-sacrifice, the adherence to a plethora of unwritten customs—"notions" as the Wykehamists called them—these were undoubtedly on Joshua Fitch's mind when he criticized the British public schools in 1897 for their "low standard of civilization," their "deep-seated indifference to learning for its own sake," and their production of "healthy animals."[74] Similarly, G. Stanley Hall, in his essay "Student Customs" published in 1902, described the American college as a "polymorphic human seminarium" of "overflowing animal spirits," which he variously categorized as "savagery," "infantilism," and "downright babyism." Like Fitch, Hall found intriguing and unsettling the fact that initiation rites, secret totems, athletics, and other forms of "sub-civilized life" should surface in the great seats of higher learning.[75] In their own inexorable urge for primitive communion on an elemental level of sacrifice, elimination, and physical exercise, the higher school stalwarts were no more peculiar or eccentric than their Ameri-

73. Miyajima Shin'ichi, ed., *Ryūnan monogatari* (Kumamoto, 1962), p. 102. This anecdote was also repeated in an interview with Professor Oda Ryūta of Saga University, who attended Fifth Higher between 1903 and 1906. The interview was conducted at Saga University on April 13, 1971.

74. Joshua Fitch, *Thomas and Matthew Arnold* (New York, 1897), p. 106.

75. Stanley Hall, "Student Customs," in *Proceedings of the American Antiquarian Society*, vol. 14 (1902), pp. 83–95.

can and British peers. Indeed, while it was common in the higher schools to identify rituals with the uncouth mannerisms of the masterless samurai, there were students and educators who firmly believed that the "storm," for example, was an imitation of hazing practices in Western fraternities and residence halls.[76]

Granting that the customs of the higher schools, even if not directly inspired by Western models, were not peculiarly Japanese, one wonders why students in the industrializing countries made life so difficult for themselves. Why resort to primitive injunctions when one might easily sit back and enjoy the conveniences of modernity and the privileges of social status? With sporadic exception, the higher school students of Imperial Japan preferred walking to riding the electric trolley, dirty uniforms to freshly laundered ones, risking bodily injury in a "storm" or judo match to languishing in a neighborhood cafe. Since few students came from impoverished homes, the argument that economic factors determined such habits is not convincing. Nor can we substantially attribute the ritual life of the community to the dictates of the headmasters. Throughout the history of the higher schools, most headmasters viewed the "storm" and the rite of "dormitory rain" with some uneasiness and occasionally outright disapproval.[77] Admitting that it was better for boys to dance around bonfires than to patronize brothels (at least the dormitory and athletic rites prolonged dependence on the institution and postponed heterosexual intimacy), few headmasters were ever able to reconcile the pedagogical view of the gentleman with the phenomenon of students jumping up and down in their underwear.

Whether or not all the rituals won the hearts of the faculty, they were significant to the students in giving meaningful shape to conceptions of identity and status. Ceremonial culture in the higher school strengthened the collective solidarity of the student community while increasing its spatial and social separation from the surrounding society. The banalities of a college subculture may well derive from student efforts to adopt, as Robert Sheldon noted at the turn of the century, "some mode of

76. *Shūgakuryōshi,* p. 146; Takahashi Samon, *Kyūsei kōtō gakkō kenkyū* (Tokyo, 1978), pp. 374–375; Yanaihara Tadao has compared the higher school "storm" with the "tossings" in the British public school, although the latter could be far more violent. See Yanaihara Tadao, *Yanaihara Tadao zenshū,* vol. 24 (Tokyo, 1965), p. 662.
77. Aoe Shunjirō, *Kanō Kōkichi no shōgai* (Tokyo, 1974), pp. 165–167. The attitude of Nitobe Inazō will be discussed in chapter 7.

life which is different from that of the family and average citizen."[78] Seen in this light, the totemic observances, the animal sounds, the secret handshakes, and other cap-and-gown eccentricities are really inchoate expressions of class privilege. Ironically, in this instance, privilege was conferred in an ambience of Spartan denial. The worst fear of higher school students at the turn of the century was to relax, let down their defenses, and bend under the influences of sensual temptation and "materialistic civilization" (busshitsuteki bunmei). "The value of a man," said one of Ichikō's most illustrious student leaders in 1905, "is first recognized after he has dealt with adversity" (jinbutsu no shinka wa bankon-sakusetsu ni ōte nochi hajimete shirubeshi).[79] And striking a harmonious note, a Fifth Higher stalwart called upon his peers to struggle with meager provisions like "old warriors" in order to preserve "the dignity of students" from a society in turmoil.[80] Realizing that physical comfort and convenience could destroy their spiritual claims to status, students expended prodigious energy in erecting and overcoming artificial barriers—winter exercises, candlelight study, cold baths—to counteract the sloth that comes with progress.

The primitive and physically taxing nature of higher school rituals gave the students a set of unequivocal guideposts in demarcating status, but it also permitted them to inspire the "vulgar society" at a distance. If the old bushidō metaphors appeared out of step with history, they were in fact no more so than the "muscular Christianity" that permeated the Victorian public schools. In his appeals to the "fighting life" (sentōteki seikatsu) and warnings against the softening effects of urban, middle-class civilization, the athletic hero at Ichikō was, like his counterpart at Rugby or Yale, the ideal spokesman for an age when the application of Darwinian analysis to human affairs allowed little tolerance for the weak, the effeminate, the hedonistic, and even the scholarly.[81] "People who devote their lives to scholarship," according to a Gokō athlete in 1895, "are inanimate objects. We must be adventurers, never succumbing to the life of scholarly lassitude."[82] As sportsmen fighting to the bitter end, the students were able, rather ingeniously, to create

78. Henry D. Sheldon, Student Life and Customs (New York, 1969, reprint), p. viii.
79. "Dai ichi gakki zenryō sawakai kiji," DIKGKZ, no. 151 (Nov. 25, 1905), p. 95.
80. Shūgakuryōshi, p. 77.
81. Rudolph, pp. 380–381.
82. Shūgakuryōshi, p. 364.

the illusion of adventure for a populace that desperately wanted to believe in the manliness of its future leaders. The huffing and puffing on the athletic field was extremely important, for the students were, in reality, most unadventurously interned in an academic cloister and contributing very little to the society. They were absolved of most responsibilities to serve in the military, to participate in community assistance programs, or to add anything to the productive capacity of the economy.[83] Without sport, there was little they could do to call attention to themselves as a hard-working, self-abnegating, and, as demonstrated in the Ichikō-Yokohama Series, public-spirited elite who could lead Japan at a time of intense international rivalries.

The rituals of the dormitory and the athletic field also had implications for the personal growth of the students. Asceticism was a way of life in the higher schools. In the spirit of the early Meiji roughnecks, the higher school heroes were inevitably ascetic heroes, like Ichikō's ace pitcher, Moriyama Tsunetarō, or Natsume Sōseki's literary protagonist from Fifth Higher, Sanshirō, who, when forced by circumstances to share the same hotel sleeping quarters with a female stranger, built a partition of twisted sheets between himself and his unwanted bedmate under the pretext of repelling fleas.[84] Such behavior is not unusual among middle-class youth, especially in a society where adolescence is institutionally contained and protracted. And while Spartan norms are potentially repressive and the basis for the most prejudicial attitudes toward the opposite sex, there are psychologists, including Peter Blos and Anna Freud, who view asceticism among male and female youth as the first, and hence the most primitive, ego support in the emergence of an integrated personality.[85] Ascetic norms can pave the way for more complex syntheses of identity by moving youth beyond their infantile dependence on the family and by preserving the internal solidarity of the age-group in a transitory state between childhood and adulthood.[86] When students were initiated into a higher school community, they were acutely aware not only

83. The annual or biannual military maneuvers (kōgun) were never viewed as a serious public duty. Nishizawa, pp. 136–137.

84. Natsume Sōseki, Sanshirō, trans. Jay Rubin (Seattle, 1977), pp. 7–9. Sanshirō is actually a Fifth Higher graduate who is entering Tokyo University.

85. Anna Freud, The Ego and the Mechanism of Defense (New York, 1962); Peter Blos, On Adolescence: A Psychoanalytic Interpretation (New York, 1962), p. 183.

86. Kenneth Keniston, "Psychological Development and Historical Change," in Theodore K. Rabb and Robert I. Rotberg, eds., The Family in History (New York, 1973), p. 147.

of advancing their academic careers but, more important, of entering an immediately painful yet ultimately gratifying stage in their lives. As one senior at Fifth Higher remembered, his first days on campus were "dark" and gloomy, for he had been wrenched from his "kind parents' home" and placed in an "unkind world" of tight-lipped upperclassmen. In hindsight, however, he realized that "Fifth Higher is not such a childish place as my mother middle school. We higher school boys must be independent. We must no longer depend on another man's assistance."[87]

While students gained independence of their own past, they remained very dependent on each other and the institution they inhabited. Through the choreography of collective rituals, the breakdown of family allegiance was balanced by an intensification of allegiance to the school, thus forestalling any inclination toward a jaggedly independent concept of self. Indeed, one can argue that something of a regression was taking place; that students who were reared to achieve on their own, in the spirit of the late Meiji literature on personal success, suddenly, on entering the higher schools, reverted back to ascriptive norms which contradicted the rational demands for specialization and performance in an industrializing society. Be this as it may, Japan was entering a new stage of industrial development in the early 1900s, a stage which made the archaic brotherhood mentality of the early higher schools less anomalous. After the turn of the century, industry and bureaucracy expanded at such an accelerated rate that the need for individual achievers was diminished by the need for good company men, people who took themselves more seriously as "functions of institutions" than as headstrong "go-getters."[88] As a "reservoir of solidarity" that could be reactivated at a later time, the higher school was ideally suited to meet the personnel demands of a maturing industrial state.[89] For in many ways, the prewar and postwar civil service was an extension of the athletic club, requiring team players willing to struggle for long hours in uncomfortable settings while heeding the principles of seniority, fair play, honor, and unswerving loyalty. Even the "storm," the ritual that appears so absurdly out of keeping with career devel-

87. Martyr, pp. 37–38.
88. The problem of youths behaving as "functions of institutions" is discussed in Stephen Spender's "The English Adolescent," *Harvard Educational Review* 18 (1948): 229–239.

opment, was once singled out by Hatta Yoshiake, Vice-President of the South Manchurian Railway in the 1930s, as his most significant experience in preparing for the rigors of foreign service.[90] The eagerness to make personal sacrifices in carrying out public duties, to remain loyal at all times to one's peers, and to blend into the habitual rhythms of collective life was as critical to the smooth operations of a government ministry as it was to a higher school dormitory.

Observing the ceremonial activities of his students at Fifth Higher for more than a decade, Graham Martyr concluded in 1930 that life in the higher schools was indeed a "good training" for future careers. "If one may make comparisons," Martyr pointed out, "I should be inclined to say that Fifth Higher is the Winchester of Japan as far as psychology is concerned."[91] No one was better qualified to make this comparison, since Martyr was himself a Winchester graduate. Yet the question here is not limited to the resemblance of the students of one higher school to those in one public school. Rather, one is impressed by the way in which ceremonial culture in the higher schools, like the house rituals in the British public schools or the archaic drinking and dueling customs in German fraternities, provided students with a "social education," as Weber has called it, for bureaucratic service.[92] This was not an education measured empirically by academic achievement, but one that had a considerable influence, nevertheless, on the development of personality within a newly risen elite. However outlandish they were in external appearance, the higher school rituals had undeniable functional value in featuring a set of ascriptive behavioral norms that strengthened collective identity and common purpose long before students entered public service.

89. S. N. Eisenstadt, *From Generation to Generation* (New York, 1964), p. 239.
90. Sakamoto Yasuyuki, p. 35.
91. Martyr, pp. 77–78.
92. Weber, *From Max Weber*, p. 387.

CHAPTER FIVE

Public Tyranny

We looked upon every trumpery little custom and habit which had obtained in the School as though it had been a law of the Medes and Persians, and regarded the infringement or variation of it as a sort of sacrilege.

THOMAS HUGHES, *TOM BROWN'S
SCHOOLDAYS* (1857)

English public schools . . . have largely sterilized intelligence by making it cringe before the herd. This is what is called making a boy manly.

BERTRAND RUSSELL, *EDUCATION AND
THE SOCIAL ORDER* (1932)

In late June of 1900, an illuminating meeting took place in the headmaster's office at Ichikō between Kanō Kōkichi, then in his second year as the school's chief administrator, and Hatoyama Haruko, the well-bred mother of a newly matriculated seventeen-year-old named Ichirō.[1] Accounts show the laconic headmaster sitting stiffly at his desk while Mrs. Hatoyama launched into an impassioned description of her involvement in Ichirō's education: how she had aroused him every morning before dawn to get an early start on his studies; how she had coached him before the entrance examinations for middle and higher school; how she had been filled with pride when Ichirō earned a place in the freshman class at First Higher. The excitement over her son's carefully nurtured achievement was tempered, however, by the sudden realization that he must now leave home. Mrs. Hatoyama had heard frightening stories about un-

---

1. Details of this incident are taken from Hatoyama Ichirō, *Hatoyama Ichirō kaikoroku* (Tokyo, 1957), pp. 66–70; Naruse Mukyoku, "Dai Ichi Kōtō Gakkō hihan," *Shinchō* (June 1950), p. 55; Aoe, pp. 189–190; Nishizawa, p. 41.

sanitary conditions in the dormitory, unsupervised rituals of initiation, and "clenched-fist punishments" for students who were not accepted by their peers; and she was worried for her son's health and happiness. Since the family, which lived in Tokyo, had provided an excellent environment for study, she wondered if Ichirō could be granted a dispensation to live at home. To this request, Headmaster Kanō had a curt and unambiguous reply: "If you do not want your son living in the dormitory, then please find another school for him."[2] One month later Ichirō was among the three hundred freshmen initiated into Independence Hall. And despite his mother's fears, he apparently survived the boarding-school experience in good shape to embark on a career that led to Tokyo University, the House of Representatives, the Cabinet, and in 1954, the office of Prime Minister.

The meeting between the bachelor headmaster and the proud yet worried mother hints at the potential for misunderstanding between the higher school and the family. Like so many parents who cheered their sons as they struggled up the academic "ladder of success," to use Herbert Passin's phrase, Hatoyama Haruko could not, apparently, reconcile the Meiji ideology of self-improvement with communal life in the higher schools. What distinguished an advanced student from a student in the primary grades, she thought, was the freedom to exploit learning for its practical value. She assumed that the contribution of the higher school to her son's education was limited to the classroom, that extracurricular activities among peers were at best idle amusement and at worst injurious to the fragile health of a boy who had never ventured from his mother's side. In contrast, Kanō Kōkichi believed that the "social education" in the dormitory was of greater significance than the academic education in the classroom precisely because it obliterated the private bonds between mother and child and thus cleared the way for the rise of a civic-minded and group-oriented gentleman. As a scholar-educator for whom celibacy was a measure of public commitment, Kanō was unmoved by the entreaties of a woman who was, in his opinion, a captive of private sentiment, crudely opportunistic, and insensible to the higher school code of manhood. If mothers were repelled by the filth and primitivism of Independence Hall, they were perfectly free to enroll

2. Nishizawa, p. 41.

their sons in the preparatory track for a private college, like Keiō or Meiji Gakuin, where lavatories were sanitary, students reasonably well-dressed and groomed, and the curriculum tailored to professional goals. The rude lifestyle at Ichikō was the price one had to pay for social status. In the end, the ideological factors obviously outweighed Mrs. Hatoyama's fears.

Seen in its most favorable light, the "social education" in the higher schools was an important ingredient in the formation and replenishment of a discrete status group, which served as a dependable source of national leadership for over five decades. Considering the vicissitudes of Japan's international position and domestic economy, there is little question that the presence of a small, self-conscious elite, forged from the common stock of higher school rituals, lent an air of stability to the most uncertain times. Whatever the crisis, either at home or abroad, one could rest assured that the future leaders of the land were cultivating a firm sense of honor, of noblesse oblige, and of communal identity in the corridors of Independence Hall and the playing fields of Mukōga Hill. And yet, as Hatoyama Haruko seemed to sense, the sudden isolation of students from their families, plus the explosive chemistry of fraternal camaraderie, could lead, under certain conditions, to the destruction as well as the building of character.

Whether in the form of insurrections against the faculty, town-and-gown strife, or campus-centered political movements, research on the student in history has tended in recent years to concentrate on patterns of rebellion.[3] Given the conventionalized nature of college subcultures, the scholarly trend is wholly understandable. "Student life doesn't alter much over the generations," Tokutomi Roka observed in 1900. "Days and months slip by, so long in prospect, so short in recall; you flip over the leaves of your calendar, day by day, week by week, and with the speed of a dream the year's end confronts you."[4] Academic calendars, periodic observances, recurring athletic rivalries, all give the campus subculture its "transhistorical" atmosphere and make the historian especially eager to discover rebel groups whose struggles against established formats pro-

3. Among recent books that take this approach are Alexander DeConde, ed., *Student Activism* (New York, 1971); Seymour M. Lipset and Philip G. Altbach, eds., *Students in Revolt* (Boston, 1969); Lewis S. Feuer, *The Conflict of Generations* (New York, 1969); Steven J. Novak, *The Rights of Youth* (Cambridge, Mass., 1977); Seymour M. Lipset, *Rebellion in the University* (London, 1972).

4. Tokutomi Kenjirō, p. 184.

vide insight into the effect of broader social changes on student life. The succeeding chapter in this study was written with such thoughts in mind. But in the search for disruption and agitation, one must not overlook the possibility that energy released on campus under the banner of rebellion, and often in full public view, may be insignificant in comparison with coercive pressure, or outright force, that is uneventfully absorbed by the student community. Youth groups, including those independent of adult authority, can revert to a fiercely conformist social order in which members are held strictly accountable to collective norms and mores. More often than not, the "fraternity man," as Weber called him, is imprisoned by "the rigid and compelling conventions" of his own making.[5]

The problem of youth and internal repression may be most acute within communities of schoolboy elites, where the cultivation of status honor is often indistinguishable from a narcissistic urge for self-idolization. Removing its social identity from the masses through elaborate rites and ceremonies, the college fraternal organization can entertain visions of rising above the everyday world to a rank of collective sacred. Once this occurs, the attention of the group will turn to the defense of sacred totems associated with the organization, which will lead to an inevitable surrender of personal autonomy. To venture on one's own in this situation is a matter no longer of personal choice but of defying religious sanctions. Such was the dilemma that confronted the higher school dormitory in the early 1900s.

Defense of the Sacred

With self-government a fait accompli, higher school students in late Meiji perfected a world view based on categorical distinctions between the realm they inhabited and the realm that lay endlessly beyond the school gates. The sword dances, the costume parades, the sacrificial communions, the games, and the "storms" had a spellbinding effect on the participants, suffusing the mind with dualistic visions of purity within the community and profane sensuality outside. The theme was repeated with liturgical consistency by orators at "tea assemblies": "Cut off from the vulgar world (*sezoku*) and based on sa-

5. Max Weber, *From Max Weber*, p. 390.

cred grounds (*seichi*), we steadfastly resist the frivolity and effeminacy of the surrounding society. . . . Who dares to deny that the shining history of Independence Hall is sacred (*shinsei*)?"[6] And if the message could not be conveyed by ritual or spoken word, the students sought reaffirmation in "dormitory songs" like Ichikō's famous *Aa gyokuhai*:[7]

> From our vantage atop Mukōga Hill
> We the stalwarts of the five dormitories,
> Our ambitions soaring to the sky,
> Gaze down upon a vulgar world
> Which revels over moonlight reflections
> Of cherry blossoms in its sake cups
> And which is addicted to the dreams of ordinary life.

Enthralled by the metaphorical possibilities for expressing their world view, students conjured an elaborate mythology. At Ichikō, they compared the institution to Monte Cristo or the temple of Mars; at Fourth Higher, students imagined that a "fiery chariot," presumably drawn by a team of white stallions, soared through the skies above the school's "sacred precincts," announcing the "coming" of Transcendental Dormitory; at Fifth Higher, students fantasized that their school slogan, "rugged simplicity" (*gōki bokutotsu*), was a "holy oracle" invoked originally by "the god of Tatsuta Mountain"; and students in virtually every school worshipped the lush vegetation on their campuses, which thrived on earth sanctified by generous deposits of "dormitory rain."[8]

Through song, dance, myth, and rites of elimination, the students had, by the turn of the century, transformed the higher school into a sacred cosmos. And once the idea of inner purity was firmly imbedded in the collective consciousness, concern shifted to devising mechanisms that would preserve the imaginary edifice. The formal rules and regulations found in the dormitory contracts were considered inadequate for this task. The "sacred school spirit" (*shinsei naru kōfū*) required the protection of negative injunctions that formed an "unwritten constitution" (*fubun no kenpō*).[9] Although discordant with the legal-rational

---

6. Ichiryōsei, "Funpunroku," *DIKGKZ*, no. 140 (Oct. 25, 1904), p. 61.

7. Genkōsha, *Ryōka wa ikiteiru*, p. 52.

8. Dai Yon Kōtō . . . , ed., *Dai Yon Kōtō Gakkō Jishūryōshi*, p. 23; Shūgakuryōshi, p. 143.

9. Tsurumi Yūsuke, *Ko* (Tokyo, 1970), p. 17; Oguri Fuyō, *Seishun*, in *Nihon Gendai Bungaku zenshū*, vol. 11 (Tokyo, 1968), p. 280; *Shūgakuryōshi*, p. 126; students also used the expression "unwritten laws" (fubunritsu) to convey this idea. Tezuka, p. 52.

structure of the dormitory, the taboo emerged in late Meiji as the primary weapon for defending school from society, manliness from effeminacy, sacred from profane. How the students relied on negative injunctions in preventing, first, outsiders from defiling sacred objects within the school and, second, insiders from adopting vulgar manners and affectations deserves our consideration.

The defense of the higher school cosmos against external threats is clearly documented. We have already discussed the "uprisings" in the 1890s, which reflect on the extreme sensitivity of students to any outside interference. In this case, the violators of the "sacred" were officials of the Ministry of Education or school administrators who dared to impinge on the extraterritorial authority (*chigai-hōken*) of the self-governing dormitory. Beyond the uprisings, the history of the higher schools is filled with "incidents" (*jiken*) sparked by intrusion from outside.

The first and perhaps most famous of these was the Imbrie Incident, which took place at Ichikō during a baseball game with Meiji Gakuin in April 1890. As was customary for all athletic events, a band of rooters from Meiji Gakuin was given permission to enter the campus just before the start of the game. The invitation did not extend, however, to a late-arriving American professor of English from the rival school who, upon finding the main gate to the campus closed, decided to scale the fence in order to catch the last innings. Moments after surmounting the barrier that separated the inner sanctum of Ichikō from the capital city, Imbrie was apprehended by an enraged delegation of judo club members, one of whom tossed a small stone or piece of tile, which struck the unwitting professor in the face.[10] Exaggerated reports of how Professor Imbrie was severely beaten and even "stabbed" by the attacking students sent shock waves through the Western community, which immediately condemned First Higher as an "uncivilized" bastion of antiforeignism and samurai-style "barbarism."[11] In their own defense, the Ichikō students argued that the fence surrounding the school was "sacred" and that any outsider, be he foreigner or Japanese, must pay the consequences for violating

10. Moiwa, *Ichikō tamashii monogatari*, pp. 104–106; *Kōryōshi*, p. 642; Nagasawa Denroku, "Inburi jiken no omoide," *Ichikō Dōsōkai kaihō*, no. 38 (Nov. 30, 1938), pp. 24–26.
11. For the reaction of the foreign community, see *Japan Weekly Mail*, May 24, 1890, pp. 524–525, 527–528; Clarence Brownell, *Tales from Tokio* (New York, 1899), pp. 73–76. (The latter mistakenly refers to William Imbrie as Charles Eby.)

a taboo. While distraught by the violence that had taken place, Kinoshita Hiroji, as the architect of Ichikō's policy of seclusion, supported the students, and in the end no disciplinary actions were taken against the judo club vigilantes.[12]

More worrisome than blatant trespass was the surreptitious entry of the school grounds by curious members of the opposite sex. The contempt for women and the values they were perceived to represent (softness, weakness, deception) was, as we have seen, at the heart of the higher school ethos. Safely ensconced in their oasis of manliness, the early contributors to the *Society of Friends Magazine* were proud that the school walls could, as one writer put it, "withstand forever the arrows of Apollo."[13] Whether or not the arrows of love ever penetrated the Ichikō fortress, intrepid young women did steal onto the campus on rare occasions, creating an enormous furor. The first of the "female incidents" (*onna jiken*) took place at Ichikō in the spring of 1891, when a woman was discovered in attendance at a special assembly for sword dances. The infuriated stalwarts immediately halted the dances, closed down the main lecture hall, and poured several bags of salt over the seats in a rite of "repurification."[14] Suspicion that the woman in attendance was secretly invited by a campus "softy" prompted this remark from the student essayist Noda Heijirō: "I wonder if the one who informed this woman of the sword dance is man enough to stand on his own with clenched fists prepared to challenge the campus ruffians." Predictably, no one stepped forward.[15]

Other "female incidents" that rocked First Higher included the unwelcome appearance of the famous actress Mori Ritsuko at the anniversary celebrations on March 1, 1916. While the gates of the school were customarily opened to the public for a few hours on Anniversary Day, the sight of a "vulgar actress" on sacred turf was simply too much for the stalwarts to bear. In the weeks that followed, Mori's brother, an Ichikō freshman, was hounded (and probably beaten) by his classmates. Overcome by shame, he committed suicide on May 3 of the same year.[16]

12. Nagasawa, pp. 25–26.
13. Yamauchi Fuyuhiko, "Rōjōshugi o ronzu," *DIKGKZ*, no. 119 (Sep. 25, 1902), p. 1.
14. Hoshina Kōichi, "Kōryō jidai no omoide," *Ichikō Dōsōkai kaihō*, (June 15, 1927), pp. 16–17.
15. Noda Heijirō, p. 24.
16. Shimamoto Hisae, *Meiji no joseitachi* (Tokyo, 1966), pp. 210–211; Toita Yasuji, "Monogatari kindai Nihon joyūshi," in *Fujin Kōron* (June 1978), p. 268.

The fortress mentality of the students and their extreme defensiveness toward the opposite sex was exacerbated by rumor in the popular press. As a group, journalists were not always friendly toward higher school students, perhaps because many were graduates of private universities and had some reason to be annoyed by the social pretensions of the Imperial University elite. Curious to know what was happening in the "castle schools," yet forbidden from doing any investigative reporting, a few journalists jumped at the opportunity to print hearsay about the amorous affairs of campus stalwarts. In one incident, occurring in the fall of 1902, the *Yomiuri* press latched onto a story that several students at a Tokyo women's secondary school received love letters from Ichikō stalwarts. The insinuation produced a vitriolic disclaimer (allegedly written by Abe Jirō): "The thousand stalwarts, who resist the turbidity of this world (*yo no kondaku*), will never cease being angry and upset over this [false accusation]." [17] Several years later at Fourth Higher, students were similarly aroused over the depiction of a Shikō student as the romantic protagonist in a serialized popular novel written for the *Osaka Mainichi*. As at Ichikō, the students vehemently denounced the newspaper story as misrepresenting the higher-school principles of asceticism and warrior valor, and eventually forced the publisher to terminate the series. [18]

If students were touchy about their public reputation, they were even more so about dishonorable conduct within their own ranks. In fact, so shocking was this possibility that the earliest residents of Independence Hall, despite Kinoshita's warning to be on guard against violations of the "four tenets," refused to address the question of disciplinary procedures. Although the authority to punish was clearly in their hands, the mere thought of a student court somehow tainted the image of a school where the spirit of "public opinion" (*yoron*) should arbitrate any dispute. "There is no need for us to have closely defined laws to punish the bad and praise the good," proclaimed a student leader at a "tea assembly" in 1891. "It is only through the spirit of public opinion that we can do this. Therefore," he

17. "Kokuhaku," *DIKGKZ*, no. 122 (Dec. 20, 1902), p. 65; according to Abe Yoshishige, this disclaimer was written by Abe Jirō. Abe Yoshishige, *Iwanami Shigeo den* (Tokyo, 1970), p. 57.

18. Tomatsu, *Shikō hachijūnen*, pp. 43–44, 59, and 68; Dai Yon Kōtō . . . , ed., *Dai Yon Kōtō Gakkō Jishūryōshi*, pp. 40–45.

continued, "our laws exist outside the law; and in the absence of written law our higher laws are executed. We practice the law which comes from heaven" (*tenju no hōritsu*).[19]

Leaving disciplinary problems to the vagaries of "public opinion" or the "four tenets" would seem to set a foreboding precedent even though a remarkable uniformity of purpose marked the first few years of the self-governing experiment. Nonetheless, by the turn of the century, there were signs of strain within the student community, the obvious one being an increase in the number and the level of destruction of the "storms." Originally a ritual of initiation or victory celebration, the "storm" had degenerated by the early 1900s into a nightly ordeal of violence and sometimes homosexual predation.[20] A handful of courageous writers, at First and Second Higher in particular, decried the "storm" as anathema to the high ideals of the self-governing dormitory;[21] yet such protests were to little avail, since the ritual was part of the sacred culture of the dormitory and many of its greatest practitioners were revered athletes or even members of the executive committees. Despite formal prohibitions in later years, the higher school students were never able to control the nocturnal urge for rampage.[22]

The majority of students at the turn of the century were less concerned, anyway, by the "storm" than by two forms of privatization creeping into the community. First, there were student intellectuals who favored reading and contemplation over boisterous public rituals. (The crisis they precipitated is discussed in the next chapter.) More upsetting was the spreading "virus of selfishness," reflected in a weakness for finer pleasures. "When we compare the conditions in our school today with those of a few years ago," wrote an irate stalwart at Second Higher in 1898, "we now have one small group of students who are prone to extravagance."[23] The discovery of a "small group" in their midst who secretly courted pleasure offended the Spartan sensibilities of higher school roughnecks and called forth a battle

19. *Kōryōshi*, p. 11.

20. Hakugansei, "Undō kōfū to tekken seisai no kachi to o ronjite Kyōfūkai o nanzu," *Shōshikai zasshi*, no. 49 (May 6, 1902), pp. 22–42.

21. For example, Wagashuguan, "Kōyūkai zasshi dai sanjūkyūgō o yomu," *DIKGKZ*, no. 40 (Oct. 28, 1894), pp. 67–80; Dōkasen, "Fūu no koe," *DIKGKZ*, no. 82 (Feb. 18, 1898), pp. 92–101. (This latter article was partly censored.)

22. See, for example, the dispute precipitated by a violent "storm" at Ichikō in 1924: *Kōryōshi*, p. 129.

23. Atoda, p. 51.

cry, like the Second Higher declaration of 1898, for "gentlemen of integrity and simplicity (*gōchoku shitsuboku no shi*) . . . to resist impure habits and rid the school of all luxury."[24]

In higher schools across the country, student leaders launched similar campaigns to stamp out self-indulgence and rekindle the school spirit. Specific remedies included a toughening of the dormitory rites of passage—known as the "suppress the freshman policy" (*shinnyū assei seisaku*) at Ichikō; a series of temperance drives; and a few halfhearted efforts to discourage homosexuality in the dormitories, something which was publicly frowned upon though privately tolerated. An article appearing in the *Society of Friends Magazine* in the fall of 1900 gently remonstrated the overzealous stalwarts who "entice our most beautiful boys with sweet words and then lead them into that mysterious world."[25]

The prominent manifestation of student concern for defending the dormitory against the seeds of internal decay was the creation of special watchdog committees. At Second Higher in 1898, for example, groups of concerned students met in "sacred places" on campus to talk about ways "to revitalize the school spirit while opposing the luxury of the day."[26] When friendly persuasion proved inadequate in discouraging wayward lads from submitting to their baser instincts, students formed, in 1902, the Society for Moral Reform (Kyōfūkai), a constabulary dedicated to upholding the principles of "manliness" (*gōken*), "fraternity" (*yūai*), and "nobility" (*kōketsu*).[27] In the campaign "to rectify student degeneracy," the charter members made clear their intention not only to offer "advice" but also "to mete out punishments."[28] Delighted by the idea of students punishing each other, the faculty left to the discretion of the Society for Moral Reform all questions of corrective action.

At the same time that the Society for Moral Reform (later called the Righteousness Society) was formed at Nikō, similar organizations cropped up at Fourth, Fifth, and most important, First Higher. Because of its urban location, the need for watchdog committees at Ichikō was especially pronounced. As early as 1895, a Society for Moral Restoration (Kōfūkai) was orga-

24. Ibid., p. 54.
25. Keifūshi, "Keifūroku," *DIKGKZ*, no. 100 (Nov. 5, 1900), p. 69.
26. Atoda, p. 71.
27. Ibid., p. 82.
28. Ibid.

nized to safeguard against any future slackening of resolve. However, the Society, functioning as a glorified pep club, never dealt effectively with specific disciplinary problems. When two students showed disrespect toward the school flag in 1895, the Society responded by reporting the incident to Kinoshita Hiroji.[29] To many Ichikō stalwarts, this willingness to run to the headmaster at the first sign of trouble was unmanly and totally out of keeping with the spirit of self-government. As a result, a second watchdog committee, the Mainstream Society (Chūkenkai), was organized in the spring of 1898. Like the Society for Moral Restoration, the Mainstream Society existed independently of the formal ruling bodies in the dormitory. Its members were selected from the ranks of second-year students and had the responsibility of preventing "the slightest hint of dandyism" from infecting life on Mukōga Hill. In pursuit of this goal, the "Mainstreamers" favored the use of force when necessary: "The Mainstream Society has no personal sentiment; what has to be done is done blindly!"[30] With this ominous declaration, the Society set itself the task of maintaining public order.

Just at the time of the founding of the Mainstream Society, Kanō Kōkichi was appointed Ichikō's headmaster. As a scholar of Far Eastern philosophy and a practicing ascetic, Kanō embodied the saintly ideal of the higher school teacher.[31] His philosophy of higher education was capsulized in a literate discourse, "On Moral Education" (Tokuiku ni tsuite), written during his first months at Ichikō and published in two installments in the Society of Friends Magazine. Essentially, Kanō subscribed to the traditionalist view that learning, especially for a young elite, must be removed from the worldly values of pragmatism (kōrishugi) or competitive achievement (kyōsōshugi). Like Kinoshita Hiroji, Kanō was a staunch advocate of higher school monasticism, and yet he surpassed Kinoshita by grounding this principle in a theory of the convergence of "actuality" (jissai) and "logic" (ronri). "Actuality" for Kanō was not everyday life but a realm of true experience, attainable in a school dedicated to "moral enrichment." The convergence of "actuality" and "log-

---

29. Kōryōshi, p. 1166.
30. Ibid., p. 1162.
31. For a detailed biography of Kanō Kōkichi, see Aoe, Kanō Kōkichi no shogai. A description of Kanō's "other worldly" renunciation of sensual pleasures can be found in Abe Yoshishige, ed., Kanō Kōkichi ibunshū (Tokyo, 1958), p. 21.

15. Kano Kōkichi (ca. 1900). Courtesy of Kōdansha

ic," in other words, was dependent upon the spatial separation of school from society.[32]

Kanō's philosophic ramblings delighted campus intellectuals who were already looking for a more erudite justification of seclusion than could be extracted from Kinoshita's metaphor of "a castle under siege."[33] He began to worry the stalwart majority, however, when his air of saintly detachment seemed to conflict with the authority of the Mainstream Society. Specifically, as a devotee of the classical ideals of asceticism and contemplation, Kanō was not amused by the rowdiness of a "storm" or a "cafeteria uprising," and when it came time for the students to consider amending the contract in 1900, he publicly speculated on the wisdom of giving the administration responsibility for punishing disrupters of the peace. Although a few student intellectuals, feeling that their position in the community might be more secure under faculty supervision than when it was left to the mercies of their athletic peers, welcomed Kanō's suggestion, the majority feared that their headmaster was bent on destroying Independence Hall. "The authority to punish," one observed, "must of necessity accompany self-government like a shadow."[34]

32. Kanō Kōkichi, "Tokuiku ni tsukite (II)," *DIKGKZ*, no. 89 (September 30, 1899), pp. 1–4.

33. "Hihyō," *DIKGKZ*, no. 90 (Oct. 30, 1899), pp. 46–47.

34. Ōshima Masanori, "Shinkei no ben," *DIKGKZ*, no. 99 (November 1, 1900), p. 6.

A standoffish, quiet man, Kanō Kōkichi was certainly in no mood for a confrontation with his students. Nor had he meant his remarks to be more than a suggestion for restoring the school spirit. Ideally, he explained in a later "tea assembly" address, students should live together as a perfect family, each member sharing of the "same mind" (dōshin). To act morally was to act in the collective interest of the fellowship; excessive privatization should be avoided. Kanō put the matter starkly at the end of his address:

> It is difficult for an organization to survive when its members hold secrets (himitsu). If a member of this community has a secret, and if that secret is harmful [to the public fellowship], then punishments must be imposed to wash those secrets away.[35]

The leaders of the Mainstream Society could not have expressed it better. The issue then was not over who should be punished but who should do the punishing. After initial hesitation, Kanō accepted the precedent of student jurisdiction. The revised dormitory contract of 1900, to which he lent his full support, reaffirmed the "right" of students to punish each other.[36] Kanō further strengthened the hand of student leaders by declaring that residence in the dormitory was mandatory. What had previously been custom at Ichikō was now official policy. And, as was revealed in the case of Hatoyama Ichirō, even the parents of Japan's most prominent families could not dissuade the Ichikō administration from herding their sons into Independence Hall.

While Kanō reinforced the powers of student disciplinarians, supporters of the Mainstream Society contributed long, theoretical articles to the Society of Friends Magazine on the problem of punishment. In general, the dominant view was to continue the tradition of judging an individual's culpability on the basis of public feelings rather than legal procedures. There was a great difference, wrote Saitō Yoshie, the most articulate spokesman for the Mainstream Society, between "criminal sanctions" (keihōjō seisai) and the "discipline of friends" (kōyūkan seisai). The former applied to the masses, whose behavior was neces-

---

For further discussions of the negative student reaction to Kanō's tentative proposal for restoring faculty supervision, see Kiyama Kumajirō, "Gisatsu no Jichiryō," DIKGKZ, no. 103 (January 25, 1901), pp. 1–18, and Kōryōshi, pp. 18–19.

35. "Dai jūikkai kishukuryō kinensai," DIKGKZ, no. 105 (March 25, 1901), p. 107.
36. Kōryōshi, pp. 19–24.

sarily regulated by "formal law."[37] However, if such laws were applied on Mukōga Hill, another member argued, they would "destroy the righteousness of self-government."[38] Authority in the dormitory emanated from the spirit of the "four tenets" and "the intimate feelings of love" within the community. Whereas "criminal sanctions" were directed against "a false, superficial, and vulgar social mind," the "discipline of friends" was rooted in the sanctity of fellowship.[39] Despite the platitudes, Ichikō's legal theoreticians did not rule out the use of physical force, even for the discipline of friends.

Since students revered public sentiment over law, all punishable "crimes" in the dormitory were against Ichikō's unwritten constitution. To draw up a list of specific offenses in any higher school dormitory is to impose order on a murky realm of ritual interdiction. It is almost impossible to define the precise deed which at any time might incur the wrath of the "public." We do know that an individual acting independently of the community and against the grain of "manliness" or "family harmony" was apt to be punished. Flaunting one's individuality, for example, by indulging in fancy clothes and toiletries or by speaking out in the name of Nietzsche against the political hierarchy of the dormitory was always risky business in the early higher schools. Eating or drinking or "storming" by oneself was also universally scorned; and any stalwart receiving a box full of goodies from his family was obliged to share them with his roommates.[40] In a similar vein, it was customary for students to share each other's belongings. Clogs, towels, handkerchiefs, books, and pens continually circulated in the dormitory. And individuals who were overly sensitive about their personal possessions could be punished for defying the order of "house communism," to borrow Nitobe Inazō's phrase.[41] But the most severe strictures applied to courtship: To send or receive a love letter in the dormitory was strictly taboo; to visit a girl friend or a brothel was even more taboo; to attempt to conceal one's liaison by sneaking out of the dormitory in the middle of the night and scaling the "sacred fence" was probably the worst offense of all.

37. Saitō Yoshie, "Seisai shikō no dōki," *DIKGKZ*, no. 111 (November 30, 1901), pp. 2–3.
38. Ōshima Masanori, "Shinkei no ben," p. 4.
39. Saitō Yoshie, "Seisai shikō no dōki," pp. 2–3.
40. A vivid example of this behavior is found in Tsurumi Yūsuke's schoolboy novel *Ko*, p. 17.
41. Nitobe Inazō, *The Japanese Nation*, p. 194.

While affecting a wide range of behavior, one single thread runs through these interdictions: the disdain for privatization. Consequently, public safety committees like the Mainstream Society, acting in defense of the unwritten constitution, had complete authority to invade the privacy of any resident in the dormitory. They intercepted and opened letters, searched rooms, read diaries, and appointed special inspectors (*ten-ken'in*) to keep a ready eye on the activities of any suspicious individual. In addition, the inspectors conducted nightly roll calls to see that each student was in his properly assigned bedroll.[42]

Regrettably, the operations of the Mainstream Society did not stop with surveillance. An identified offender was summarily punished. If the "sentiment" of the committee members was inclined toward a light punishment, the offender might simply receive a tongue-lashing. If, on the other hand, the wayward student was considered guilty of sacrilege against the school spirit, the Mainstream Society had the solemn responsibility to recommend the "clenched-fist punishment" (*tekken seisai*)—the higher school version of a public lynching.

The Myth of Innocence

First Higher's most awesome rite of sacrifice and intensification took place on the athletic field after the sun had set.[43] With the sounding of a bell, the students of Independence Hall would file onto the athletic field, where they formed a giant circle around an inner circle of Mainstream and Executive Committee members along with assorted captains from the athletic clubs. In the center, silhouetted against the flicker of a paper lantern, stood a lone, often trembling figure. All eyes would bear down upon the accused as the chairman of the Executive Committee announced the verdict of the Mainstream Society. Mr. X had violated the school's code of honor by entering into an illicit af-

---

42. Izumiyama Sanroku, *Tora daijin ni naru made* (Tokyo, 1953), p. 38; Kume Masao, *Gakusei jidai* (Tokyo, 1971), pp. 121–140; Moiwa, *Ichikō tamashii monogatari*, pp. 29–47; Nihon Keizai Shinbunsha, ed., *Watakushi no rirekisho*, vol. 7 (Tokyo, 1970), see sections by Tazaki Yūzō, pp. 41–92.

43. Since the "clenched-fist punishment" was never spelled out in any of the "contracts" for the self-governing dormitories, we must depend on literature and memoirs for detailed descriptions. The details in this account are taken from Kume Masao, *Gakusei jidai*, pp. 121–140; Moiwa, pp. 29–47; Izumiyama, pp. 38–39; Ishikawa Sei, "Kōryō kaisō (3)," *Kōryō Komaba* 5, no. 1 (January 1963):61–62; Oguri Fuyō, *Seishun*, pp. 287–288.

fair with a neighborhood prostitute, or Mr. X had slandered the school song in a "tea assembly." If there was tangible evidence, a confiscated picture or letter, it would be held up for all to gasp at. Finally, the chairman would expound on the virtues of Ichikō's tradition; how the upperclassmen had sacrificed private pleasures for the public good; how, with tears in their eyes, the stalwarts must now apply the sacred "clenched-fist punishment."

Completing his statement, the chairman would step aside, making way for the head of the Mainstream Society, who usually had the honor of delivering the first punch. Standing directly in front of the culprit, he might ask for a confession, which, if given, could lessen the severity of the blows. Then, announcing his name and position in the dormitory, the chairman of the Mainstream Society would strike the offender three times. Thud, thud, thud—the sounds could be heard in succession. His job completed, the chairman would step aside for each fellow member to declare name and rank and add three blows. And when they were finished, two or three representatives from the Executive Committee would be given their turn. And when they were finished, the ritual was turned over to the captains of the athletic clubs, whose blows were the most feared of all. Thud, thud, thud—the offender might topple over and could therefore be kicked.

Throughout this ordeal, the public stood frozen as if in a trance. It was all so captivating: the darkness, the flickering lantern, the wind, the moon, the tears, the blood. They were not beating an enemy; they were beating a friend whom they loved. They were beating the evil that had crept into his heart. They were beating the evil that could creep into their own hearts. That is why the school leaders were shedding tears with each strike at their classmate. Everybody was sincere. It was awful, but it was beautiful.

The "clenched-fist punishment" had occurred among students at the Kaisei Gakkō in what Inoue Tetsujirō described as an overflow of "samurai spirit."[44] Yet it was the higher school students who institutionalized the punishment and wove it into the ceremonial fabric of the subculture. Although the social context and extent of violence are not comparable, the for-

44. Inoue Tetsujirō, "Meiji shōnen . . . ," pp. 61–62.

malized school-yard beatings of late Meiji bear certain similarities, as suggested by Naruse Mukyaku, with lynchings in the Old South.[45] Notably, the scheduling, the use of the audience, the glorification of the past, and the reinforcement of public ties against a common victim are attributes that underlie both forms of ritual "justice."

That the school-yard beatings were never intended as spontaneous outbreaks of collective violence is underscored by lengthy exegeses in the *Society of Friends Magazine*, explaining how to and how not to participate in one of these sordid affairs. In his article entitled "The Theory of Punishment," Saitō Yoshie specified that those who administered the "clenched fist" should be firmly resolved and intensely sincere. The test of sincerity, he explained, was whether the properly authorized committee members could "apply violence with tears" (*naite bōryoku o kuwae*). The "beauty" of physical punishment, according to Saitō, was in the mixture of the blood of the accused with the tears of the accuser; if the accuser did not cry, he was not displaying sincerity and should therefore be barred from further participation.[46] Oddly enough, Ichikō annalists, who scoured the library for evidence to support their vision of justice, singled out George Washington as the ideal disciplinarian. Washington, they claimed, on the basis of legendary accounts, was moved to tears by the execution of John André—Benedict Arnold's ill-fated yet ever gallant accomplice—whose death warrant he had signed. Similarly Ichikō stalwarts, according to the anonymous author of "Weeping, They Hung John André," were to emulate Washington's combination of firmness and deep sensibility.[47]

Beyond the tales of compassionate execution, the fist law was justified as being in the interest of both the victim and the community. The selfish student who went on a drinking binge or met illicitly with a prostitute defamed his social status. He needed punishment to cleanse his heart, regain his honor, and reassimilate into his "mother school." The fist law also contained "the multiplier effect," whereby one student's misdeed spread like a contagious disease. Anyone was vulnerable to the temptations of the flesh, so when a culprit was caught in the

45. Naruse Mukyoku, p. 56.
46. Saitō Yoshie, "Seisairon," *DIKGKZ*, no. 98 (June 15, 1900), pp. 6–7; Saitō Yoshie, "Seisai shikō no dōki," pp. 3–4.
47. "Naite Jon Andā o kiru," *DIKGKZ*, no. 82 (Feb. 18, 1898), pp. 102–103.

act, his retribution became a kind of "sacrifice" to purge the community soul.

Our concentration on Ichikō does not mean that students in other higher schools acted more kindly toward individualists. The Society for Moral Reform at Second Higher also resorted to fist laws. Indeed, not only could an offender be beaten and expelled from the dormitory at Second Higher, but, on occasion, his desk and chair, along with other belongings, were thrown out the window into the courtyard below.[48] Similar incidents of public outrage have been recorded at Fifth Higher, where those who soiled the school's reputation faced the "clenched-fist punishment" or "bedroll crunch" (futongan).[49] While precise information as to exact time, place, and participants in these chastisements is difficult to obtain, it would appear that their frequency was increasing at the turn of the century as the strains within the student community mounted.

The destructiveness of the "storm," the campaigns against "individualism," the rise of public safety committees, the reliance on brute force to protect the name of the school: these startling realities do cast doubt on the utopian view of the Meiji higher schools as the best of all possible worlds. Indeed, when focusing on this darker side of the higher school experience, one is tempted to conclude that by 1900 the self-governing dormitory, despite its libertarian charter, operated as a miniature autocracy. This was the view held by the most illustrious foreigner to teach in the Meiji higher schools, Lafcadio Hearn. Writing in 1904, Hearn looked back at his teaching experience at Fifth Higher with considerable dismay: "In this quietly and coldly ordered world there is little place for the joy of youth. . . . Everybody watches everybody: eccentricities or singularities are quickly marked and quietly suppressed." Hearn was at a loss to explain "all this repression" in the "higher official schools," except as a continuation of "the training at samurai schools."[50]

Without denying Hearn's suggestion of historical continuity between the domain academies and the higher schools, there would seem to be more compelling reasons for the tyrannical

48. Takahashi Samon, "Kyūsei kōtō gakkō ni okeru kōfū no seiritsu to hatten III," KKGK, no. 8 (April 1975), p. 26.

49. Shūgakuryōshi, p. 24.

50. Lafcadio Hearn, Japan: An Attempt at an Interpretation (Boston, 1923), pp. 464–465.

inclinations of late Meiji higher school students, which can be placed in a broader historical context. Certainly one contributing factor was the posture of the faculty. Portraying himself as a disciple of Thomas Arnold and Noah Porter, Kanō Kōkichi praised the "communal life" (*kyōdō seikatsu*) in the dormitory at Ichikō as the best place for privileged young men who were "relatively pure human beings" (*hikakuteki junketsu na ningen*). Admitting the possibility for depredation in a community run entirely by adolescents, Kanō remained confident: "Since the students are always watching each other, they cannot let a person get away with anything that is too bad."[51] Besides, Kanō believed that "communal life" had the built-in potential for self-correction, that any disturbance in the dormitory would resolve itself over time. He, like many of his colleagues, could therefore justify a timely retreat to the study whenever a "storm" or "clenched-fist punishment" was brewing.[52]

Along with their faith in self-criticism and self-rectification, higher school administrators tended to view the rowdiness of a "storm" or even the violence of a "clenched-fist punishment" as less damaging to the gentlemanly ideal than dandyism or flaunting individualism.[53] Better that the boys be guilty of "a little manly roughness" (*otokorashiki tashō no sobō*), as Kinoshita Hiroji put it, than to fall back into their mother's laps or to seek out maternal substitutes on city streets. The values of honor and self-respect, according to Miyoshi Aikichi at Second Higher, required students to live as "brothers" locked into the indestructible social unit of the dormitory.[54] When selfishness, lust, or excessive attachment to primordial kin threatened this unity, then the most drastic measures could be sanctioned to remedy the situation.

This much having been said, we cannot conclude that the patterns of tyranny in the higher school were choreographed by the headmasters. There were chief administrators, including Orita Hikoichi at Third Higher and later Nitobe Inazō at First

51. Aoe, p. 209.
52. Ibid., pp. 166–167; this standoffish attitude is also apparent among other higher school administrators and faculty at the time, who believed it would be more in keeping with the manly ethic of the dormitory to let the students punish each other with a minimum of adult intervention. See especially Ishisaka, p. 89; also "Ichikō Bungeibu no kaiko," *Kōryō Komaba* 16, no. 2 (October 1974), on the attitude of Professor Taniyama at Ichikō, pp. 261–262.
53. Nitobe Inazō, who succeeded Kanō as headmaster, put it this way: "To be a student is to be plain in habit and taste. . . . Dandyism is a heinous offense in the society of learning." Nitobe Inazō, *Japanese Nation*, pp. 192–193.
54. Ishisaka, ed., *Meizenryō shōshi*, p. 88.

Higher, who were clearly repulsed by the "clenched-fist punishment" and discouraged students from resorting to violence. Even Kinoshita Hiroji, in one of his last speeches at Ichikō, delivered on March 1, 1893, called upon campus stalwarts to balance firmness with compassion and to be ever cognizant of "the fate of Jean Valjean" in Hugo's *Les Miserables*.[55] Although the faculty bears some responsibility, the students ultimately made the decisions to organize public safety committees and to inflict corporal punishment on their peers.

Why was a schoolboy elite, with all the sobering advantages of knowledge and culture, so vulnerable to tyranny and repression? The argument of cultural relativists like Inoue Tetsujirō that the higher school students merely perpetuated the aggressive traditions of pre-Restoration samurai is unconvincing.[56] Predatory behavior and violent mastery among students (and the studious disregard thereof by faculty) are certainly not unique to late Meiji Japan. The violence of the "clenched-fist punishment" or "bedroll crunch" are equaled, if not exceeded, in the "tossings," "floggings," "paddlings," and "brandings" that have won dubious notoriety in the annals of British and American student life. Even the ritualized circumstances in which these ordeals took place bear remarkable similarities.

A more compelling explanation for the drift among higher school students toward public tyranny lies in the ceremonial milieu of the dormitory and the predilection for absolute distinctions. The polarization of sexual characteristics was especially perilous, for it catered to the worst insecurities of young men who had just come of age. Students continuously admonished each other on the importance of maintaining an aggressive and unkempt appearance so as not to entice the opposite sex. According to one Ichikō student in 1900, young men who attracted young women by washing their faces and cutting their hair were, in a spiritual sense, "too dirty to write about."[57] This denial of heterosexual inclinations resulted in further prohibitions against any activity that smacked of effeminacy, whether it was speaking softly, dressing meticulously, composing po-

55. "Kishukuryō kinenbi," *DIKGKZ*, no. 25 (March 27, 1893), p. 74.

56. Inoue Tetsujirō, pp. 61–64. Equally unconvincing is the relativist argument of Francis Hsu that an "English public school culture" with its patterns of "male bonding" cannot be found in the Japanese (or Chinese) experience. Francis L. K. Hsu, "Prejudice and Its Intellectual Effect in American Anthropology: An Ethnological Report" in *American Anthropologist* 75 (1973):14–15.

57. "Henpen," *DIKGKZ*, no. 100 (November 5, 1900), p. 68.

etry, or dreaming of knights and fair maidens. So calcified were the distinctions between manly and unmanly behavior that the individual was left no mode for dissent, no right of appeal before an executive committee, no way to transcend the peer group and petition the administration directly.

Beyond the reification of collective ideals, the higher school students may have fallen victim to what Erikson calls the "inborn proclivity" of youth for totalistic solutions to the quest for self. From this perspective, the cruelty which late adolescents perpetrate upon nonconformists can be explained as a "necessary defense against a sense of identity loss." [58] In an academic community, which is explicitly dedicated to the cultivation of ideal men rather than engineers or plumbers, the question of "identity loss" takes on the added meaning of a collapse of status and honor. Given the convergence of high social and psychological stakes, it is not surprising that gentlemen-in-training should stoop to very ungentlemanly means in maintaining conformity to ascriptive norms of behavior and social rank. To do otherwise would be tantamount to an admission that the gentleman has the same prosaic urges to buy comic books, spend a night at a brothel, or bask in the warmth of maternal kindness as any ordinary young man. "Tossings," "brandings," and "clenched-fist punishments" are reminders that this is not the case.

Talk of dark "inborn proclivities" as evoked in Golding's *Lord of the Flies* should not lead us to the conclusion that the totalistic inclinations of students in the Meiji higher schools were irreversible. Primitivism, harsh asceticism, and cruelty are not the only "necessary defenses" open to the adolescent in the quest for identity. There are nonaggressive defense mechanisms that make use of the mind rather than the body, but they thrive in adolescent communities where the right to intellectualize goes hand in hand with the right to swing a baseball bat. Fortunately, the early 1900s saw the rise of a group of student intellectuals who were eager to enlarge the sphere of private behavior in the higher schools and, in a few cases, to speak out as rebels against the tyranny of the peer group.

58. Erik H. Erikson, *Identity, Youth and Crisis* (New York, 1968), pp. 87–88, 132, 191, and 210.

CHAPTER SIX

The Higher School Catharsis

"Now put it to me straight," said Stover, looking past La Baron
straight into Reynold's eyes. An instinctive antagonism was in him, the
revolt of the man of action, the leader in athletics, at being criticized by
the man of the pen.

OWEN JOHNSON, *STOVER AT YALE* (1912)

But now Törless became stubborn. He himself felt that he had not put
his case well, but both the antagonism and the misguided approval he had
met with gave him a sense of haughty superiority over these older men
who seemed to know so little about the inner life of a human being.

ROBERT MUSIL, *YOUNG TÖRLESS* (1906)

Whatever the cause—the cross-cultural influence of Social Darwinism, the closed boarding-school environment, or the adolescent need for physical activity—one finds a resemblance
among the popular schoolboy types in the late Victorian public
schools in England, liberal arts colleges in America, and higher
schools in Japan. In all three countries, the college or the boarding school was an athletic haven where healthy boys flexed
their muscles, rarely stopping for self-reflection. The heroes of
Tom Brown's Schooldays, Stover at Yale, and *Tales of the Ichikō Soul*
share a common identity as crusaders for the public good who
put the welfare of the house or the school above their selfish
personal interest. As young men of action driven by the urge to
test and retest their manliness, they embody the ideals of an aggressive nationalism that sanctioned the control of the weak by
the mighty and, indirectly at least, fueled imperialist ambition.

The domineering presence of the public-spirited athlete in an
age of Social Darwinism raises worrisome questions about the
quality of school life for those whose strength dwelled in the

mind rather than the body. What was the fate of slender youths of poetic sensibility in a community that worshipped the likes of Dink Stover, Stalky, and Moriyama Tsunetarō? The response on the Anglo-American side to this question appears quite bleak. At least one book and numerous memoirs document the misery of young writers in the British public schools who spent their waking hours seeking refuge from taunting, teasing, and bullying classmates.[1] While Jonathan Gathorne-Hardy argues that British intellectuals may have needed the adolescent experience of confronting oppression in order to stand on their own in later life, the writers themselves (including Forster, Orwell, Meredith, and Connolly) displayed little affection for their alma maters, even in retrospect.[2] American authors have undoubtedly been more charitable about the colleges they attended, although Sinclair Lewis fled the "crushing mold" and "dread mysteries" of Yale in 1903 for the more congenial atmosphere of Upton Sinclair's literary commune.[3] And F. Scott Fitzgerald, after making a futile attempt at football (all 138 pounds of him), came to the distressing realization in 1917 that "Princeton is stupid!"[4]

The response of Japanese writers to the higher schools varies according to date of enrollment. Those who graduated before the Russo-Japanese War (1904–1905) were often quite unhappy. The curriculum gave little attention to new developments in modern literature, and out-of-class activities were dominated, as we have seen, by campus sportsmen. The discomfort of young writers was conveyed in letters and short critiques, usually published anonymously or under pseudonyms, in the school magazines. At Ichikō, for example, the first stirrings of protest were revealed in the critiques of a mysterious "Wagashuguan" who, in October of 1894, appealed to his classmates to stop ridiculing the "nonathlete" (hiundōka) and to read more books, instead of aimlessly "wasting energy" on the athletic field.[5] Those apprentice writers who attended the higher schools after the Russo-Japanese War, on the other hand, had a far more sanguine view of their schooldays. Many, in fact, surpassed their athletic peers in showering praise on the alma

1. John R. Reed, *Old School Ties: The Public Schools in British Literature* (Syracuse, N.Y., 1964).

2. Jonathan Gathorne-Hardy, *The Old School Tie* (New York, 1977), p. 209.

3. Mark Schorer, *Sinclair Lewis* (New York, 1961), pp. 106–107, and 127.

4. Robert Sklar, *F. Scott Fitzgerald* (New York, 1967), p. 16.

5. Wagashuguan, "Hihyō," *DIKGKZ*, no. 40 (Oct. 28, 1894), p. 77.

mater. The disparity between the response of a Wagashuguan in the 1890s and the ever more positive assessments of Abe Jirō and Abe Yoshishige in the early 1900s and Kawai Eijirō and Yanaihara Tadao a decade later suggests that the higher schools were undergoing a transformation from within. The dimensions of social change in late Meiji and the suffering it entailed for some students is the subject of this chapter.

Japan's victory in the Russo-Japanese War is often heralded by historians as marking the fulfillment of the long-standing dream for national security and equal standing with the Western powers. On the battlefield of Mukden and in the Straits of Tsushima, the nation demonstrated once and for all the capability of "playing our game," as Theodore Roosevelt put it.[6] The "game" included more, of course, than military victory. By 1905 Japan was the first non-Western nation to enter as an equal into a bilateral security pact with a Western power, the first non-Western nation to establish modern colonial regimes, the first non-Western nation where the combined gross national income from industry and commerce surpassed agriculture.[7] Yet these accomplishments, though remarkable, were undertaken at enormous cost in human life and spirit. There was no rejoicing in the streets of Tokyo when the Treaty of Portsmouth was announced, only rioting by an angry mob that believed the nation's sacrifice was not sufficiently compensated in territorial acquisitions.

Symptomatic of the mal du siècle gripping the country in the wake of the Russo-Japanese War was the behavior of youth. With international recognition of Japan as a "first-class country" (ittōkoku), the collectivist ideology of state rang hollow to the ears of ambitious youth who believed the days of self-sacrifice were over.[8] Now more than ever the measure of human worth was in terms of material riches as young people in hamlets and small towns across the land intoned the slogan of the postwar era: "success" (seikō).[9] But the maturing industrial-capitalist state placed institutional limits, as we have seen, on the extent to which the multitudes of "success youth" (seikō seinen)

6. Elting E. Morison, ed., *The Letters of Theodore Roosevelt*, IV (Cambridge, Mass., 1951), p. 724.

7. Takahashi Kamekichi, *The Rise and Development of Japan's Modern Economy*, trans. John Lynch (Tokyo, 1969), p. 324.

8. Harootunian, "The Problem of Taishō," pp. 14–21; Oka Yoshitake, "Nichiro sensōgo ni okeru atarashii sedai no seichō (jō)," *Shisō*, no. 512 (1967), p. 141.

9. Sumiya Mikio, "Kokuminteki buijon no tōgō to bunkai," in *Kindai Nihon shisōshi kōza*, vol. 5 (Tokyo, 1972), pp. 19–20.

could advance within the social order. The framework for competition was "stunted," to use Kamishima's term, and the possibilities for youth of modest background to enter the normal schools, let alone the middle or higher schools, were sufficiently remote to reduce the credibility of the revitalized postwar success ethic.[10] Thus, while a majority of youth struggled on without getting very far, a distinct minority dropped out of the race altogether in utter despair. These were the "anguished youth" (hanmon seinen) who individualized their failure to achieve in conspicuous displays of inactivity and melancholia. In the eyes of alarmed government officials and social critics, both the "success youth" and their "anguished" counterparts were suffering from "civilization sickness" (bunmeibyō), a malady of prosperity which struck young people in advanced industrialized nations.[11]

Higher school students, as they denounced the materialism of "success youth," were among the first to exhibit these symptoms of "anguish" at the turn of the century. Unlike many of their cohorts, however, the spiritual turmoil of the young elite did not stem from immediate academic pressures or even from premonitions of career failure. Rather, it was generated by an evolving realization that both the "athletic school spirit" and the family state offered the sensitive youth very little in his psychological and philosophic struggle for meaning in life. Like the adolescent heroes in the neo-romantic literature of Hermann Hesse, Thomas Mann, and Robert Musil, the anguished students of the late Meiji higher school posed as misunderstood geniuses in search of subjective authenticity against the combined obstacles of a domineering peer group and a meaningless ideology of state. We begin our examination of the ensuing tensions between intellectual and athlete by surveying the changing temper of the higher schools reflected in the role of student writers and the influence of a new pedagogical style.

From Customs to Consciousness

The higher schools were conceived of as a time for building character, an academic hiatus free of the heavy course requirement of either the middle schools or the Imperial universities.

10. Kamishima Jirō, "Meiji no shūen," in Hashikawa Bunzō and Matsumoto Sannosuke, eds., Kindai Nihon seiji shisōshi, vol. 1 (Tokyo, 1971), p. 389.

11. Kenneth B. Pyle, "The Technology of Japanese Nationalism: The Local Improvement Movement, 1900–1918," Journal of Asian Studies 33 (November 1973): 62.

We have seen that this ideal in practice created a playground for Philistines, a regression to a lifestyle of primitivism. In the later Meiji period, ironically, several of the conditions that allowed this regression also afforded an opportunity for expansion of intellectual horizons. Consider the principle of seclusion. To the extent that the identity of an artist or a philosopher requires distance from workaday tribulations, the isolation of the higher school could just as well stimulate the imagination as the urge to fraternize. Also, the antimaterialism of the students and their effusive sensibilities to natural beauty were hidden conduits for aesthetic expression. Starting with the composition of "dormitory songs" and verses describing their pastoral settings, the students were but a small step away from writing odes to pine trees and cherry blossoms. Certainly, they had the vocabulary and writing skills to make that transition. For despite their allegiance to such slogans as "action before words," the early stalwarts waxed eloquent on "simplicity" and "warrior valor." [12]

Indeed, a few could do more than that. The student community of each higher school had, from the beginning, a small body of gifted writers, usually members of the literary club that edited the school magazines, who discharged their public duties by articulating the orthodox view of the "school spirit." At Ichikō this group of resident intellectuals included Akanuma Kinzaburō, Noda Heijirō, Nakamura Kōhei, Kitazawa Teikichi, and Tsukuda Toyōo, all of whom contributed articles, justifying the physical exertions of their peers, to the *Society of Friends Magazine* in the 1890s. Besides praising the flag, the Mars-and-Minerva badge, and other institutional totems, the philosophic pillars of the "school spirit" went to great exegetical length to demonstrate how the "four tenets" were part of a noble historical legacy;[13] how collective life in the dormitory combatted the fallacy of seeking success (*risshin shusse no meisō*);[14] how sport ennobled the human spirit;[15] how the voice of justice (*seigi no koe*) was hidden beneath the ruckus of the "storm" and the pounding of a "clenched-fist punishment."[16] The disquisitions

12. For example, "Kangeiko," *DIKGKZ*, no. 43 (Jan. 8, 1895), pp. 94–95; Yuasa Shōnosuke, "Jūdō," *Shōshikai zasshi*, no. 3 (Dec. 22, 1893), pp. 31–37.

13. Takeda Tarōji, "Kyōka oyobi gakufū," *DIKGKZ*, no. 35 (March 22, 1894), p. 28; Kitazawa Teikichi, "Kishuku kyōikuron," *DIKGKZ*, no. 83 (Jan. 31, 1899), pp. 16–21.

14. Kitazawa, p. 17; Bungeibu iin, "Jichiryō no sei," *DIKGKZ*, no. 39 (Oct. 7, 1894), p. 27.

15. Nakauma Kō, "Kōfū to undōka . . . ," pp. 11–16.

16. Kakureishi, "Tenrai," *DIKGKZ*, no. 106 (April 30, 1901), pp. 19–36; Tsukuda Toyōo, "Aete kōyū shoshi ni uttau," *DIKGKZ*, no. 81 (November 1898), pp. 10–12.

on athletics and character building suggest that although Japanese students in the 1890s were just as energetic as their American peers, they were not, as Henry Seidel Canby described his generation at Yale, "strenuous without thought to ask the reason why."[17]

Along with defending the old certitudes of sport, school, and nation, the early student ideologues insisted that their teachers remain faithful to the humanistic ideals of moral education, and they protested vigorously any signal from the administration that the academic focus might shift toward vocational training or that stiffer grading standards might be instituted. In 1894 and again in 1898, the editors of the *Society of Friends Magazine* spoke out strongly on the dangers of "utilitarianism" (*jitsurishugi*) and careerism creeping into the classroom at First Higher. Nothing would render greater injury to the righteousness of status (*taigi meibun*) than for Ichikō students to use their education as a tool for attaining petty ambitions. The middle school practice of "cramming all night" for examinations had no place at First Higher, according to the editors, where students had the cherished right to benefit from "true cultivation" (*shin-shūyō*). Hence the editors demanded that the faculty consider ways to ensure that "examination study" would never intrude on higher school life.[18]

The unceasing attacks on utilitarian knowledge and the materialist ethic of self-improvement[19] were implicitly self-serving, coming as they did from students who had already achieved so much and whose distaste for competitive examinations rarely, if ever, elicited proposals to change the rules for academic achievement in the primary and middle schools. In light of the Higher School Ordinance of 1894, however, the fear of losing the integrity of the curriculum was still genuine, and to make matters worse, students were worried about the strength and will of an aging faculty to hold the line against external assaults. By the turn of the century, the "old *bushi* types" were performing a largely ceremonial role in the higher schools, reading the Imperial Rescript on Education and holding the school flag at special assemblies. Their classes in Chinese literature and philosophy were, apparently, less than inspiring as were the courses taught by middle-aged foreign language teachers, who

17. Joseph Kett, *Rites of Passage*, p. 175.
18. Bungeibu iin, "Kakumon," *DIKGKZ*, no. 79 (Sept. 30, 1898), p. 4; Bungeibu iin, "Jichiryō no sei"; Tsukuda, p. 8.

confined their lessons to linguistic analysis of literary classics. Criticism in school magazines of mechanical teaching methods, arid classroom discussions, and an absence of "love" between pupils and their older teachers leaves the impression that some students were yearning for a new approach to learning that was guided neither by vocational training nor by rigid character-building models.

It was precisely their ability to enliven the classroom by challenging the students to think for themselves that accounts for the popularity of a new breed of higher school teachers in the late 1890s and early 1900s. As a group the new teachers were distinguished from the "old *bushi* types" by their younger age, their post-Restoration education (many in fact were among the earliest graduates of the higher schools), their remarkable erudition and intellectual creativity. When one thinks of the intellectual as a higher school teacher, the names of such luminaries as Uchimura Kanzō, Doi Bansui, Takayama Chogyū, Natsume Sōseki, Nishida Kitarō, Kuriyagawa Hakuson, and Kuwaki Genyoku first come to mind. All taught courses in philosophy, German, or English, and all, with the exception of Uchimura, found the relaxed higher school ambience ideal for launching illustrious academic or literary careers. More important, when these young teachers came to the higher schools, they did so as intellectual missionaries of a new wave of thought, inspired by the early romantic literature of Kitamura Tōkoku and Shimazaki Tōson, the pioneering theological tracts on Christianity, and the magnetic presence of Professor Raphael Koeber, the great attraction in the Philosophy Department at Tokyo University between 1893 and 1914. Koeber proselytized on behalf of German philosophy among a surprising number of gifted late Meiji and Taishō writers (including Nishida, Takayama, and Kuwaki); and the charge that he thundered forth in the classroom undoubtedly made a lasting impression on those who introduced Kant and Schopenhauer to the higher schools: "My students are all philosophers, and as philosophers they are soldiers fighting with spiritual arms for the expansion of the *Zeitgeist*." [20]

The missionary zeal of the young philosophers and writers who joined higher school faculties in late Meiji is apparent in their out-of-class endeavors to organize study groups. The pi-

19. One of the strongest attacks on the success ethic is found in Kitazawa, "Kishuku kyōikuron," esp. pp. 16–19.
20. Kubo Masaru, ed., *Kēberu hakushi zuihitsushū* (Tokyo, 1970), p. 179.

oneer in this effort was probably Uchimura Kanzō, who in 1888 helped to organize the Ichikō Christian Youth Society, a fifteen-member group that held weekly discussions of the nature of religious experience. Although ridiculed by their athletic peers as "a society for weaklings" (*yowakimono no kai*), the young Christians continued to meet after their mentor's precipitous departure in 1891.[21] More successful projects were undertaken by Takayama Chogyū at Second Higher and by Nishida Kitarō at Fourth Higher. When Nikō's Literary Club was on the brink of dissolution in 1896, Takayama rallied students to the club's defense and even donated some of his own money to help sustain its operations. He also presented a series of extracurricular lectures on the history of philosophy, which fired the imagination of attending students, who thanked him profusely for uncovering "the mysteries of the cosmos" and "the secrets of the inner life."[22] Similarly, Nishida Kitarō, during his eight years at Fourth Higher, organized a number of small reading groups, including the Dante Society, the Goethe Society, and the Sartor Resartus Society.[23]

For all the efforts of the late-Meiji philosophers and writers in organizing study groups and propagating their own world view, one must be careful not to overestimate their influence on the higher school students. After all, Uchimura Kanzō was literally driven out of Ichikō; Takayama Chogyū abruptly resigned from Second Higher in a huff over the student strike; Natsume Sōseki was rather standoffish while teaching at First and Fifth Higher; and even Nishida Kitarō was anxious to find a university job after eight years in Kanazawa. The galaxy of writers who either taught or gave lectures to higher school students is remarkable indeed; yet they were not as important to the students as a group of less renowned disciples of Raphael Koeber. I speak of the "teachers of life" (*jinsei no kyōshi*), to borrow Asukai Masamichi's sobriquet,[24] those students of philosophy who joined the higher school faculties at the turn of the century and who retained their positions, in some cases, until death, three to four decades later. They were the quintessential "*sen-*

21. *Kōryōshi*, pp. 1199–1201.
22. "Dai san gakki shigyōshiki," *Shōshikai zasshi*, no. 25 (May 18, 1897), p. 46; "Takayama hakushi iku," *Shōshikai zasshi*, no. 53 (March 8, 1903), p. 52.
23. Tomatsu, *Shikō hachijūnen*, p. 70; Lothar Knauth, "Life is Tragic," *Monumenta Nipponica* 20:346.
24. Asukai Masamichi, "Kokuminteki bunka no keisei (I)," in *Iwanami kōza Nihon rekishi*, vol. 18, (Tokyo, 1963), p. 302.

sei"—men like Ichikō's Iwamoto Tei and Suge Torao, Nikō's Awano Kenjirō, and Gokō's Yamagata Motoharu—powerful symbols of continuity in the 1920s and 1930s but catalysts for change three decades earlier.

In certain respects, the "teachers of life" bore a closer resemblance to the "old *bushi* types" on the faculty than did the scholar-artists who passed through the higher schools on their way to national fame. For one thing, many were bachelors who lived in a detached personal world completely out of touch with middle-class conventions. Awano Kenjirō is reputed to have worn the same coat and necktie for most of his forty years at Second Higher, and Iwamoto Tei feasted on the same concoction of meat and vegetables every time he sat down for dinner. (Students were welcome to share his habitual repast so long as the menu was not altered.) Although immersed in the written works of every culture and prone to read philosophic tracts while walking to school, the "teachers of life" were not publishing scholars. Students called Awano "the Sōseki who doesn't write," and when pressed to explain his epistolary reticence, Awano would say, "To bequeath a book is to bequeath shame to posterity."[25] And so they refused to write, leaving it to novelists like Sōseki (whose portrayal of Hirota Sensei in *Sanshirō* was reputedly inspired by the "philosophical smoke" of Iwamoto's unceasing cigarettes)[26] to document all the idiosyncrasies of personality and world view. Still, the "teachers of life" left an indelible impression on their students, which, as Mitani Takanobu explains, was largely "intangible."[27] Like the older faculty, they were genuinely concerned about the spiritual presence of their students, but rather than summoning Confucian models of the gentleman, they stressed the importance of cultivation from within, of self-examination, and of seeking new meaning in life in a realm of philosophy and art. Whereas Kinoshita Hiroji and Nakagawa Gen concentrated on character building (*shūyō*), the "teachers of life" encouraged students to discover for themselves the existence of an inner soul in a program of self-cultivation or cultural enrichment (*kyōyō*).

In their formal capacity as classroom instructors, the "teach-

25. Nakayama Yoshio and Etō Takehito, *Ten wa Tōhoku . . .* , pp. 72–73.

26. Mitani Takanobu, "Iwamoto Tei sensei no omoide," *Kōryō Komaba* 12, no. 2 (April 1970):27.

27. Ibid., p. 28.

ers of life" defied every rule of academic protocol. They were known to commence German classes by launching a discussion of Aeschylus; to write complex mathematical problems on the board for which they had no solution; to begin class when it should normally end; to lose grade books; to refuse questions; to refuse answers; to fail an entire class year after year.[28] Iwamoto Tei was especially notorious for this last peccadillo, which irritated the anonymous and ever humorless officialdom in the Ministry of Education.[29] Yet, warnings from above did not prevent Iwamoto from continuing to apply his inscrutable grading standards on Ichikō students, who delighted in being his victims. What better way to parody the middle-class standards of success than to fail, gloriously, in Iwamoto's philosophy and German courses? At the same time, by underlining the absurdity of learning by standardized format, Iwamoto and company steered the students toward a new intellectual horizon where achievement was measured not in a grade but in the pursuit of a higher level of consciousness. They tried, in effect, to jolt the conventional mental habits of a middle-class mind, though they offered no easy formulas for the attainment of philosophic insights to replace old ways of thinking. The students must read the great philosophers; they must think and struggle on their own to grasp the elusive truth, which, as Iwamoto put it, was like a "moon shadow" (*tsukikage*) dancing across an open lake.[30]

Between 1898 and 1905, students in all seven national higher schools were affected in some way by the challenge of self-discovery and the philosophic insights of the "new thought wave" (*shinshichō*): an amorphous mixture of Christianity, historical idealism, and German neoromanticism. Across the country, student intellectuals heralded a "new age," often striking a chiliastic theme. "We are riding a new wave of hope," proclaimed an Ichikō student in a spirited piece on "Greeting the Twentieth Century" (*Dai nijusseiki o mukau*), "we are shaken by the great ocean of truth (*shinri no taikai*) that is borne by the coming century. . . . So let us cultivate the true self (*shinga*) in perfect harmony and with healthy expectation as we awaken

28. Nakano Yoshio, "Kyūsei kōkōteki naru mono," *Tenbō* 72 (December 1964), pp. 110–117; Tezuka Tomio, pp. 52–54.
29. Sakamoto Yasuyuki, pp. 22–23; Nishizawa, p. 258.
30. Hasegawa Saiji, "Iwamoto Tei sensei goroku," *Kōryō* 16, no. 2 (October 1974): 184.

to the new age."[31] Were the newly awakened student writers, who now declared themselves "Welt-Mann" or "Kultur-Mensch," merely parroting the ideas of established intellectuals or striking out on their own? Evidence from school magazines suggests that the latter comes closer to the truth. The earliest essays on individualism appeared in higher school magazines within three or four years of Kitamura Tōkoku's pioneering "Theory of the Inner Life" (1893) and well before Takayama Chogyū's discourse "On the Aesthetic Life" (1901). Nor can we give exclusive credit to the "teachers of life" for this intellectual and spiritual breakthrough. In systematically organizing their thoughts on Kant and the meaning of religious experience, the student writers and debaters accomplished something that men like Awano Kenjirō and Iwamoto Tei could never do. It was thus a combination of external stimulation and internal awakening, along with the obvious advantage of splendid library and publishing facilities, that made it possible for a Sankō junior named Tsukamoto Ryūgai to write his perceptive analysis "On Nation and Individual" in 1900, or for a Fifth Higher senior named Yoshida Osao to deliver a talk on "Personalistic Religion and Humanity" two years later, or for one Akase Yayoki of the same school to find enough material on philosophy and education in 1910 to write an "Intellectual History of Fifth Higher."[32]

At Ichikō the "new thought wave" first surfaced in a trickle of essays published in the *Society of Friends Magazine* between 1897 and 1900 under such titles as "The Theory of Inspiration" (*Kankaron*), "A Private View of Life" (*Jinsei shikan*), and "Students and Spiritual Training" (*Gakusei to seishin shūyō*). The essays were theoretical and burdened with hairsplitting distinctions between "the will of self-existence" (*jiko-sonzai no ishi*) and "the consciousness of self-existence" (*jiko-sonzai no jikaku*).[33] The pressing question, of course, was whether there could be a "self-existence" (conscious or willful) in a school where young men grunted on the athletic field and "stormed" in the dormitory. Early Ichikō intellectuals were understandably cautious about disclosing any "contradiction" between their own private life as writers and the public rituals of the community, prefer-

---

31. "Dai nijusseiki o mukau," *DIKGKZ*, no. 103 (Jan. 25, 1901), p. 89.

32. Akase Yayoki, "Ryūnan shisōshi," *Ryūnankai zasshi*, no. 137 (Dec. 20, 1910), pp. 26–46.

33. Uzawa Fusa'aki, "Gakusei to seishin shūyō," *DIKGKZ*, no. 83 (Jan. 31, 1899), pp. 1–5.

ring instead to call attention to the universality of student aspirations to rise above "material wants" and "vulgar people."[34] Accordingly, drawing upon Uzawa Fusa'aki's essay of 1899, the exploration of Kant and Hegel was simply "another method of spiritual training," which could coexist with judo, baseball, and "tea assemblies."[35] This accommodating view was shared by a group of moderate innovators who conscientiously attempted to elevate the campus subculture beyond what Wada Ichirō called "l'état de barbarie."[36] The time had come, another wrote in 1900, to break free from complete subservience to "custom" (*shūkan*) and to recognize that the "sacred aspects" (*shinsei naru tokoro*) of the school were of the mind as well as of the body.[37]

However, not all students were able to expatiate on the inner self in one breath and march off to a campus pep rally in the next. For the most sensitive or "anguished youth," innovation only intensified the strain of reconciling private claims with the public demands of the dormitory. Their alternatives were either to withdraw quietly from participation in group activity or to declare themselves rebels. Most chose the former course and in sufficient enough numbers by 1900 that alarmed stalwarts condemned the "retreatism" (*taihoshugi*) and "pessimism" of their bookish peers. Writing in 1901, one student leader warned that Ichikō was being overrun by agonizing dilettantes who followed in the footsteps of the Seven Sages of the Bamboo Grove.[38] As the phenomenon of personal anguish and withdrawal spread among higher school students, Ichikō was rocked by a sensational incident that left a permanent mark on the attitudes of the young elite.

The Suicide of Fujimura Misao

The week of May 10, 1903, was perhaps the most extraordinary in Ichikō's sixty-year history. It began with the Baseball Club registering a 26 to 0 romp over a team of American sailors from the battleship *Kentucky*, the flagship of the U.S. Pacific Fleet, and ended with the discovery that a sixteen-year-old freshman

34. Iwasaki Kun, "Nihon gendai gakusei no shichō," *DIKGKZ*, no. 86 (May 5, 1899), p. 32.
35. Uzawa, p. 15.
36. Wada Ichirō, "Shisōkai no funkyū to gojin no taido," *DIKGKZ*, no. 116 (April 25, 1902), p. 3.
37. Ichiryōsei, "Funpunroku," *DIKGKZ*, no. 140 (Oct. 25, 1904), p. 61.
38. Kakureishi, "Tenrai," *DIKGKZ*, no. 106 (April 30, 1901), p. 21.

named Fujimura Misao had committed suicide by jumping from a three-hundred-foot precipice into the churning basin of Kegon Waterfall. A thorough search of the scene revealed that, before taking his spectacular leap to self-destruction, Fujimura had peeled off a section of bark on the trunk of an oak tree that stood near the edge of the cliff, and on the smooth surface underneath, he had written his own epitaph with the title "Feelings at the Precipice" (*Gantō no kan*):

> Ensconced in the vastness of space and time,
> I, with my meager body, have tried to fathom the enormity of this universe.
> But what authority can be attributed to Horatio's philosophy?
> There is, after all, only one word for truth: "incomprehensible."
> My agony over this question has brought me, at last, to a decision to die,
> And yet now, standing at the precipice,
> There is no anxiety in my heart.
> For the first time, I realize that great sorrow is at one with great happiness.[39]

News of Fujimura's suicide and the metaphysical epitaph he left behind became a national sensation almost overnight. Newspapers across the country carried the story; and pictures of the delicate-featured sixteen-year-old probably became as familiar to the man on the street as those of an Ōkuma Shigenobu or an Itō Hirobumi. In part, the popular interest was spurred by the image of someone jumping into the raging torrents of the nation's most spectacular waterfall. Even more intriguing, though, was the specter of an elite student from Japan's premier character-building institution forsaking family, school, and country to resolve his own personal struggle with the riddles of existence. Fujimura's suicide appeared to be purely "egocentric," reflecting a total inability to find meaning beyond his inner turmoil. For a citizenry that was bracing for a second major war in less than ten years, that had been reared to accept "altruistic" suicide as the honorable course for self-destruction, and that was accustomed to looking at First Higher as the fountainhead of national "vigor," the news of Fujimura's suicide was bound to generate excitement.

39. Fujiwara Tadashi, "Aa bōyū Fujimura Misao kun," *DIKGKZ*, no. 128 (June 15, 1902), pp. 76–77. The details leading up to the suicide are discussed in this article (pp. 74–77) and in Azuma Suehiko, "Fujimura Misao no omoide," *Kōryō Komaba* 10, no. 4 (October 1968): 13–14.

16. Fujimura Misao (ca. 1902). Courtesy of Kōdansha

The incident is especially noteworthy for its impact on a large segment of youth—including middle-school, normal-school, and perhaps some working-class youth—who were, apparently, the principal consumers of the postcards, picturebooks, and other marketable souvenirs that were spawned by the suicide, and who, in a few instances, even succeeded in duplicating Fujimura's act.[40] Putting the event in its broadest context, Nakano Yoshio argues that a rising suicide rate among youth at this time is symptomatic of the "first industrial revolution" and the establishment of a "capitalist system" that failed to satisfy the "spiritual demands of youth."[41] Earl Kinmonth has pushed the discussion beyond such sweeping generalities by noting that it was not only the "spiritual demands of youth" that had to be satisfied, but also the more prosaic need for a job, or at least a respectable job.[42] Even among university graduates, the prospects for self-fulfillment in one's occupation were dimming, and the road ahead must have looked even bleaker to those with a normal-school or middle-school degree, who

40. Katō Hidetoshi suggests there were as many as 200 suicidal leaps into Kegon Waterfall during the eight years following Fujimura's death. Katō also discusses the "sensationalism" surrounding the event in "Jisatsu sutairu no hensen," Ōhara Kenshiro, ed., *Jisatsu* (Gendai no esupuri) (Tokyo, 1966), pp. 227–228.
41. Nakano Yoshio, *Roka Tokutomi Kenjirō dai ni bu* (Tokyo, 1972), p. 290.

knew they could never become more than petty functionaries. Fujimura's suicide could thus be seen by middle-class young people, who were already showing signs of disenchantment with the Meiji dream of personal success, as emblematic of their own doubts about the future.

The immediate reaction among higher school students, however, revealed a desire to remain aloof from the popular clamor over the incident. At Ichikō, where the suicide had its most direct impact, many stalwarts were aghast at all the publicity, which they felt communicated a false impression of a school that had just regained its international standing on the baseball field. As reproduced in newspapers and popular literature, Fujimura's story seemed to make a mockery out of the traditional image of Ichikō as a stamping ground for "great gentlemen" (*taijin kunshi*) eager to sacrifice for the country. More disturbing to campus stalwarts was the possibility of further repercussions within the student community, where the suicide might inspire student intellectuals to amplify their private claims and strengthen their resolve to withdraw from public rituals. The concern of "dormitory politicians" was especially apparent during the initiation rites in the fall of 1903, when Ichikō's greatest orator and guardian of tradition, Aoki Tokuzō, repeatedly urged the incoming freshmen to view Independence Hall as a "single family" (*ikko no kazoku*) and the most beautiful thing under heaven (*tenka no zetsubi*). No mention was made of Fujimura, who was obviously regarded as an undesirable role model for the newcomers. The speech was published in the fall issue of the *Society of Friends Magazine* along with a vitriolic attack on "yellow peril" propaganda in the West and a patriotic call to arms by one Suita Junsuke in an essay on "War" (*Sensō*). Voicing what was probably the majority view at Ichikō, Suita struck out at those who harbored doubts about the national mission, proclaiming: "We are men who worship war and cheer imperialism!" (*gojin wa teikokushugi o shōwashi, sensō o ōka suru mono nari*).[43]

The traditionalist charges to sacrifice self for school and coun-

42. Earl H. Kinmonth, "The Quest for Success and the Discovery of Self in Late Meiji Japan," paper presented at the Association of Asian Studies annual meeting in March 1977, pp. 13–14.

43. Aoki Tokuzō, "Shinrai no tomo ni yosu," *DIKGKZ*, no. 129 (Oct. 2, 1903), pp. 8–14; Suita Junsuke, "Sensō," ibid., p. 3; for other militaristic articles or poems, see issues no. 135 and no. 138 during the following year.

try were balanced by equally impassioned defenses of the inner life. Sympathetic to his existential struggles and disposed to occasional spells of *Weltschmerz* of their own, the friends of Fujimura Misao contributed a series of powerful eulogies to the *Society of Friends Magazine*. Determined to rescue the suicide from the sensationalistic grasp of the popular press, the eulogists justified the act in language that only a well-educated person could appreciate. Reacting to an article in the *Yomiuri Newspaper* insinuating that the suicide was occasioned by a failure in love (*shitsuren*), one sympathizer issued a furious sally against those who would stoop to describing Fujimura in "base and vulgar prose" (*rōretsu naru gebun*) or pander to the "curiosity of society" (*seken no kōki*).[44] How could a young man who "searched for the secret of life" and "embarked on a voyage known only to God" be bothered by a girl friend?[45] The desire for love, money, or fame played no role in a suicide that, as Fujimura's best friend pointed out, was pure and "sincere" and beyond the limited imagination of the uncultured populace (*zokuryū*).[46]

To bolster their case for a philosophic suicide, the eulogists commended Fujimura's understanding of art and literature. They spoke of his affection for Yokoyama Taikan's portrait of Ch'ü Yüan, the ancient Chinese poet whose melancholia led to a suicidal drowning;[47] they pointed out his fondness for Wordsworth's dictum that "Nature never betrays those who love her";[48] and finally, they noted with pride that Fujimura's reference in his epitaph to "Horatio's philosophy" was based on a deep insight into the relationship between Hamlet and his best friend in Shakespeare's tragedy. Whereas Horatio functioned easily in the arena of everyday life, never stopping to question "the pipe for fortune's finger," Hamlet sought meaning in an extra-worldly universe of unanswered questions and non sequiturs. When Fujimura stated the rhetorical question "What authority can be attributed to Horatio's philosophy?" he was empathizing with Hamlet's own reaction to his friend's self-assuredness: "There are more things in heaven and earth, Hora-

44. Meikotsu, "Funpunroku II," *DIKGKZ*, no. 129 (Oct. 2, 1903), p. 78.

45. Arai Tsuneo, "Fujimura Misao kun o tomurau no uta jusshu," *DIKGKZ*, no. 128 (June 15, 1903), pp. 59–60.

46. Fujiwara, "Aa bōyū . . . ," p. 78.

47. Misada Jirō, "Fujimura Misao kun o chōsu," *DIKGKZ*, no. 128 (June 15, 1903), pp. 67–68.

48. Fujiwara, "Aa bōyū . . . ," p. 79.

tio, than are dreamt of in your philosophy."[49] Thus Fujimura, like Hamlet, was posing existential questions for which Horatio's down-to-earth philosophy had no answers.

To his friends and admirers, not only at Ichikō but at the other higher schools as well, Fujimura was Hamlet tormenting himself over "to be or not to be"; he was Ch'ü Yüan renouncing the world of corruption and extravagance; he was Faust standing above the steaming caverns, imperturbable in the face of death; he was the Nietzschean prototype of the creative artist whom Chogyū had lionized in his theory of the aesthetic life. Fujimura Misao was an uncommon man, a misunderstood genius, an aesthetic hero whose ruminations were light-years beyond the mental capacities of the masses. He was a very special person, who communicated with equally special people. His act was a fulfillment of Chogyū's charge to "transcend the present age" (*gendai o chōetsu*), and it was an utter travesty to think that commonplace youth should have the effrontery to try to venture on his extraordinary path.[50]

In fact, so profound was the spirit that moved Fujimura to suicide that even his closest friends believed themselves unworthy of following in his footsteps. Lamented Abe Yoshishige: "O Fujimura, spare us your laughter while you soar through heavenly clouds, for our legs are still bound to this earth."[51] For Abe and other young intellectuals, this was a heart-wrenching admission, which drove them into lonely nooks in the library for hours upon hours of brooding over the works of Chogyū, Goethe, and Nietzsche. A few, like Hayashi Hisao and Iwanami Shigeo, withdrew from the campus altogether to deserted huts in the mountains. For forty days, Iwanami suffered alone in his island retreat on Lake Nojiri, nourishing his soul on questions of life and death. Finally, after a visit from his mother, he gave up his hermitage, announcing that he was not yet prepared to follow Fujimura. (Nor would he ever be, for Iwanami went on to become a leading publisher.)[52]

49. Ibid., p. 80. The ability of Fujimura's friends to back up the reference to Horatio's philosophy was aimed at countering the skepticism of men like Inoue Tetsujirō who had publicly scoffed at the epitaph as intellectual nonsense. Abe Yoshishige, *Waga oitachi-jijoden* (Tokyo, 1970), p. 342; Itō Sei, *Nihon bundanshi*, vol. 7 (Tokyo, 1966), pp. 143–144; Watsuji Tetsurō, *Zenshū*, vol. 18 (Tokyo, 1963), pp. 298–299.

50. Moiwa, pp. 149–150.

51. Abe Yoshishige, "Fujimura Misao kun o omou," *DIKGKZ*, no. 128 (June 15, 1903), p. 73.

52. For an excellent biography of Iwanami, see Abe Yoshishige, *Iwanami Shigeo den* (Tokyo, 1970). Iwanami's philosophic retreat is discussed in Ibid., pp. 65–79.

By emphasizing the exceptional nature of the suicide, and its misapprehension by society, the friends of Fujimura Misao were giving the event a certain dignity that even campus stalwarts would find difficult to impugn. There was never a hint in any of the dedications that the incident signaled a disaffection toward the school spirit. Quite the contrary, certain aspects of the suicide seemed very consistent with the Ichikō style. Fujimura, for example, was said to have tied a bandana from head to chin in order to secure his school cap, suggesting that the eagerness to leave the "vulgar world" was coupled with a reluctance to sever his higher school identity.[53] More interesting was the curious affinity between Fujimura's "to be or not to be" ruminations and the "no condition" (*nō kondishon*) attitude of the higher school athletes. Both were living at the brink of death in their pursuit of absolute purity. Finally, however one viewed the suicide, it was difficult not to be impressed by the fervent outpouring of emotion from Fujimura's friends. Loyalty to a friend was a treasured virtue in the higher schools, and never had it been expressed so eloquently as in the wake of the great suicide. "Ah, Misao, my dear friend Misao," wrote Abe Yoshishige of the youth he knew and loved so well, on the first anniversary of the suicide:

> It's been one year since I lost you; yet never a day passes when I am not thinking of you. When I am close to nature, I think of you; when I am with people, I think of you; when I am alone, I think of you. Your voice should not be heard by anyone, yet my ears often hear you. Your face should never be seen again, yet I see your image everywhere. . . . Oh, why do I long for you so?[54]

The phrasing was more explicit than many stalwarts were accustomed to, but in the monastic setting of Ichikō, where unisexual friendships intensified over time, such sentiments might elicit considerable sympathy. The comrade-in-arms mentality of the sportsman and Abe's vision of romantic friendship were not that far apart. Taken together, therefore, the talk of death, metaphysics, and romantic friendship had a broad and irresistible appeal among higher school students. While many felt threatened, Naruse Mukyoku was undoubtedly correct when he observed: "Even within the athletic clubs, which cham-

53. Azuma, "Fujiwara Misao no omoide," p. 14.
54. Abe Yoshishige, "Waga tomo o omou," *DIKGKZ*, no. 137 (May 28, 1904), p. 36.

pioned heroism and the ethic of *bushidō*, there were concealed Hamlets."[55]

We shall probably never know the exact philosophic or personal reasons that prompted Fujimura Misao to take his life. What seems clear is that his close friends and sympathizers were anxious to transform a spectacular, national event into what Ōmuro Teiichirō has called a unique "higher school phenomenon."[56] Their perception of the suicide as a philosophic epiphany, guided by a "sacred will" and known only to themselves, extended social distance and reinforced institutional charisma.[57]

The reaction to the suicide also pointed to an expanded vision of adolescence as something more than a period of physical vigor when uncontrollable physical urges called for harsh ascetic training. In the early 1900s, the term "adolescence" (*seishun*) first appeared in the pages of higher school magazines, defined by self-conscious students as an "opportune period" for educated youth to wrestle with speculative issues and to establish "pure" (unisexual) friendships.[58] No one suggested that the outburst of anguish and philosophic analysis was a psychological defense of youthful innocence. But students and teachers alike began to perceive Takayama Chogyū's dictum to "transcend the present age" as having implications for educated youth that went beyond matters purely intellectual or artistic. In overcoming the physical world around him, the student also affirmed his right to pose ultimate questions and to create an imaginary universe that was important to his quest for a meaningful identity.

Moreover, the discovery of adolescence as an intellectual as well as a physical phenomenon enlarged private claims within the school. By pleading their affliction with the "anguish disease," student intellectuals were at last able to grasp an alternate mode of adaptation to life in a total institution: withdrawal. While the staunchest defenders of public unity in the school initially bemoaned the sight of fellow students hibernating in the library, the stalwarts soon learned that Ichikō, or any other higher school, could survive an epidemic of *Weltschmerz* and maybe, in the end, be all the better for it.

55. Naruse, "Dai Ichi Kōtō Gakkō hihan," p. 57.
56. Ōmuro Teiichirō, *Seishun no shiseki* (Tokyo, 1955), p. 55.
57. Fujiwara, p. 78; Moiwa, pp. 149–150.
58. Tago Kazutami, "Fujimurasei no jisatsu o ronzu," *Shōshikai zasshi*, no. 57 (Nov. 18, 1903), especially p. 9.

Yet, learning to accept the migration of students to the inner depths of the soul was one thing; countenancing "extreme individualists" who used the opportunity for withdrawal as a launching-pad for outright rebellion was quite another. Even in the wake of Fujimura Misao's suicide, one can discern no softening of public hostility in the higher school dormitories toward anyone disposed to assault the sacred traditions of the institution. The story of Uozumi Kageo, the most notorious of higher school rebels, underscores the distinction between withdrawal into the self and active assertion of the self against the public rituals of the dormitory.

Attack on the Sacred:
Uozumi Kageo at Ichikō

The true rebel, wrote Albert Camus in his seminal essay on the subject, is driven by a "revulsion at the infringement of his rights and a complete and spontaneous loyalty to certain aspects of himself."[59] He is, by this definition, a solitary figure, who marches to his own drum, heeding the authority of an unyielding inner conscience. The rebel is not a visionary romantic who waves banners up and down the street proclaiming an end to tyranny and oppression. His eyes are fastened, rather, on "the most concrete realities" of immediate and pressing concern in everyday life. Thus the rebel launches his protest against those tissues of authority "where the living heart of things and of man are found": home, village, school, or job.

Despite persisting myths about rebellious youth, few adolescents emerge as true rebels within their own subcultures. As a mode of adaptation among youth, rebellion presents an especially difficult course of action, for it requires a firm stand against the peer group at an age when the need to belong to a gang, a fraternity, or a team is often overwhelming. In Independence Hall, as in other higher school dormitories at the turn of the century, a growing minority evidenced dissatisfaction with the traditional rituals of the campus. Some, like the friends of Fujimura Misao, expressed discontent by temporarily withdrawing into their own philosophic cocoons. Other, more outspoken critics submitted essays to the school magazine which attacked the "athletic school spirit" for its celebration of physi-

---

59. Albert Camus, *The Rebel* (New York, 1951), pp. 14–15 and p. 298.

cal prowess. Yet, even this latter group included few individuals who could be classified as rebels.[60] Most used pen names for their articles, and all relied on a turbid writing style that blunted the cutting edge of their attack. This was not the case with Uozumi Kageo.

When Uozumi Kageo arrived at Ichikō in the fall of 1903, he found the school in its most unsettled state since the foundation. Memories of Fujimura Misao were still vivid; the baseball team had lost several of its stars through graduation, sparking dire predictions for a sudden downfall;[61] recent epidemics of typhoid fever had taken the lives of five students, including a former chairman of the Executive Committee; and the intellectual climate in the school was fractured by a vibrant debate over the proper balance between private claims and public demands. Typical of the philosophic ferment among student intellectuals was Abe Jirō's "Attitude toward Contemplation and Ideals,"[62] an abstrusely theoretical essay in defense of the inner self against the authority of history, society, and church. Though eloquently written, the essay made no mention of Independence Hall.

Contributing to the agitated atmosphere at Ichikō during Uozumi's freshman year was the outbreak of hostilities with Russia. Reminiscent of their response to the Sino-Japanese War, the Ichikō stalwarts projected a strong patriotic front in hopes of inspiring plebeian soldiers on the battlefield. On February 8, 1904, four days after the government declared war, the Executive Committee decided to forgo decorations for the coming anniversary celebration so that extracurricular fees could be donated to the army. Students were also asked to contribute ten sen a month as an ongoing contribution to the war effort. Both proposals won hearty approval in the General Assembly.[63] Three days later the entire student body gathered for a winter "tea assembly" devoted to patriotic speeches by faculty and students. While the "teachers of life" remained silent, "old

60. Representative of the first stirrings of protest are Wagashuguan, "Kōyūkai zasshi dai sanjūkyūgō o yomu," *DIKGKZ*, no. 40 (Oct. 28, 1894), pp. 64–80; Dōkasen, "Fūu no koe," *DIKGKZ*, no. 82 (Feb. 18, 1898), pp. 92–101. The latter describes the "storm" as "the attacks of a pride of lions on a flock of quivering sheep" (p. 93).
61. The predictions were well founded, as Ichikō lost to Waseda and Keiō in the spring of 1904 and again in the fall of 1906. *Kōryōshi*, pp. 168–170.
62. Abe Jirō, "Risō meisō no taido," *DIKGKZ*, no. 138 (June 28, 1904), pp. 1–10. There were also signs of a backlash, and by the fall of 1904 there were even speeches in the "tea assemblies" to ban individualism. See *Kōryōshi*, pp. 24 and 33.
63. *Kōryōshi*, p. 29.

bushi types," like Imamura Yūrin and Aoyama Shioya, issued blistering attacks on the Russians and called upon the students to rally behind the men in action. Of the six student speakers, only one, Arai Tsuneo, interjected a cautionary note about "war fever." The assembly was climaxed with the singing of a chauvinistic number, specially written for the occasion by Aoki Tokuzō, entitled "The Attack Russia Song" (*Seiro no uta*).[64]

Uozumi Kageo was quite dismayed by the patriotic clamor of his classmates and took the occasion of the first anniversary of Fujimura Misao's suicide to express his strong feelings about war and individual rights in his "Theory of Suicide" (*Jisatsuron*) written for the *Society of Friends Magazine*. Although he had been a close friend of Fujimura's, the essay was not a panegyric but an impassioned defense of the right of any person to decide for himself the ultimate philosophic question: whether to live or whether to die. For the man tormented by life's unanswered riddles, the decision to commit suicide was a supreme act of sincerity. Uozumi's sympathy for self-immolation did not extend, however, to the battlefield. To expose oneself to a "rain of bullets" was an act of "cowardice," since the victim surrendered to a cause that had no meaning for the inner self. "Indebtedness to the fatherland" (*kunkoku no on*), he argued, "is a superstition (*meishin*), which is engraved upon the hearts of innocent children by their primary school teachers."[65]

In respecting the sincerity of the philosophic suicide over the gross inanity of sacrifice on the battlefield, Uozumi did not suggest that all men of good will must follow in the footsteps of Fujimura Misao. Adumbrating a proposition that would appear in Sōseki's late novels,[66] Uozumi concluded his essay by citing three alternatives for overcoming the existential predicament facing modern man: (1) philosophic suicide, (2) madness, (3) religious faith. For Uozumi, both lunacy and suicide were out of the question. He had his own religious faith, a personal vision of Christianity, which compelled him to struggle through life, knowing, like Sisyphus, that he might never climb the moun-

64. "Sawakai kiji," *DIKGKZ*, no. 134 (Feb. 25, 1904), pp. 70–74. Another indication of the patriotism of the students is seen in the victory celebration on campus at the end of the war. See "Dai san gakki zenryō sawakai," *DIKGKZ*, no. 168 (June 20, 1905), pp. 137–145. For patriotic atmosphere at Sankō where the students went on strike against a German professor who slighted the Japanese war effort, see Ōura, pp. 78–79.

65. Abe Yoshishige, ed., *Setsuro ikō* (Tokyo, 1974), p. 57. All of Uozumi's writings are included in this book.

66. As interpreted by Edwin McClellan, "An Introduction to Soseki," *Harvard Journal of Asiatic Studies* 22 (1959), esp. p. 200.

17. Uozumi Kageo (ca. 1905). Courtesy of Kōdansha

tain of eternal truth.[67] Predictably, there was a small eruption over Uozumi's article when it was submitted for publication. Statements equating "indebtedness to the fatherland" with "superstition" were especially offensive to Headmaster Kanō, and attempts were made to censure such inflammatory language.[68] That the piece ended up being published in almost its entirety, at a time when the nation was at war, is remarkable, although Uozumi was ostracized thereafter by many of his peers.

A full exposition of Uozumi's philosophy appeared the following fall in an essay "On Individualism" that was as impressive for the way it was written as for the ideas it contained. The essays for the *Society of Friends Magazine*, like those for other higher school publications, were written in an ornate and often recondite style that permeated everything from accounts of baseball games to the first tentative probes into epistemology. Whatever the subject, the fondness for quotations in foreign languages, puns, and literary allusions made much of student writing, and perhaps intentionally so, unreadable to all but the learned. While Uozumi was hardly disposed to the vernacular,

67. Abe Yoshishige, ed., *Setsuro ikō*, p. 63.
68. When Uozumi got wind of these efforts to censor his article, he abruptly quit his position as one of the editors for the school magazine. Abe Yoshishige, *Waga oitachi*, p. 358.

his essay on individualism presented a series of incisive statements that were free of the esoteric witticisms and long-winded digressions of his fellow student writers.

The theme of "On Individualism" is reminiscent of Thoreau's dictum that "a corporation has no conscience," for Uozumi, like Thoreau, was concerned about the kinds of compromises individuals must make in their eagerness to belong to organizations. Whether a business, a club, or a school, the unit inevitably adopted its "organizational will" (*dantaiteki ishi*) that encroached on the member's autonomy. For the individual crushed by the "rotting creeds and ceremonial parchments" of the organization, the sole recourse, according to Uozumi, was to speak out for the sanctity of the inner self. Every man had the right, indeed the obligation, to attack the institutional authority that threatened his autonomy. The "spirit of resistance" (*hankotsu no seishin*) was, for Uozumi, the essence of individualism and the force behind the historical dialectic. "Constructionism" (*kensetsushugi*) remained a frivolous dream without "destructionism" (*hakaishugi*).[69] In this latter view, Uozumi appeared to affirm quite consciously, the Nietzschean concept of "eternal recurrence" that casts the historical creator in the role of the destroyer of existing values.

Uozumi's theory of iconoclastic individualism was especially noteworthy because it affected both the way he wrote and, more important, the way he behaved with his peers. From the moment he entered Independence Hall, Uozumi was repulsed by the "primitive" (*genshiteki*) lifestyle of the residents. Recalling the agony of his freshman year, he complained that life in the dormitory was "neither communal living nor a society built upon individual rights, but simply a case of living together in a flock" (*gunkyo*). The unending tumult of "storms" and raucous singing made it impossible for Uozumi to sleep, or even think, except on those rare occasions when everyone on his floor was off to class or engaged in some extracurricular activity. At such times, he would retreat to his room, sit down on his bedroll, and contemplate for as long as he was left alone.[70]

To his seven roommates, Uozumi was a complete oddball. His ghostly pallor and delicate features made him curiously effeminate in a world that had traditionally worshipped manliness. While his roommates upheld the Ichikō standards of mes-

69. Abe Yoshishige, ed., *Setsuro ikō*, pp. 83–92.
70. Ibid., p. 316.

siness and filth, Uozumi bathed regularly and tried to keep house in his corner of the room, arranging his books neatly and even airing his mattress. On one occasion he horrified those around him by tidying up one of the public lavatories, something which apparently had never been attempted before. But Uozumi was unperturbed by the hostility he engendered among some of his classmates, particularly among his roommates, whom he disliked intensely.[71]

In the Literary Club there were some who admired the sincerity of his convictions, but Uozumi had very few close friends at Ichikō. He was not interested in ingratiating himself with a wide circle of acquaintances, choosing instead to single out one individual with whom he could share his inner secrets and feelings. While attending middle school, Uozumi considered Fujimura Misao his confidant; after Fujimura's death, Uozumi's attention turned to Egi Sadao, a classmate at Ichikō who was two years his junior. Egi was one of the new breed of philosophically inclined athletes. During the afternoons he was known to all as a tireless stalwart on the school's judo squad. But if he was a sportsman by day, Egi was a poet by night and susceptible to the long brooding spells that afflicted other "anguished youth" on campus. For his part, Uozumi was fascinated by the "internal war" raging in Egi's soul as he swung between athletics and poetry in his quest for truth and sincerity. By the same token, Egi was equally impressed by Uozumi as a brilliant visionary. Presumably, the two youths spent many hours strolling about the campus and discussing the problems that were tormenting each other's mind. Moved by these private conversations, Uozumi decided to publish two letters to Egi in February and June of 1904.[72]

Romantic letters to imaginary or deceased friends (as we saw in Abe Yoshishige's tribute to Fujimura Misao) were considered perfectly acceptable contributions to the school magazine. What distinguished Uozumi's "Letters to a Friend" was that almost everyone in the dormitory knew that the "friend" in question was Egi Sadao. Furthermore, the letters were very personal, revealing secrets which apparently embarrassed some of the readers. For example, Uozumi began his February letter with the following question: "Why is it that when my heart thinks of

71. Ibid.; Abe Yoshishige, *Waga oitachi*, p. 370; Miyamoto Kazukichi, "Bōyū Uozumi Kageo kun," *DIKGKZ*, no. 202 (Feb. 11, 1911), p. 9.
72. Abe Yoshishige, *Waga oitachi*, p. 369.

you, it begins to throb feverishly? At times I meet you face to face; at times I see you in my dreams. Will my soul ever stop convulsing over you?" The passage continued with more explicit language: "Is love something which is confined only to persons of different gender (*ai wa isei no aida nomi ka*)? If this be so, then we are embarked on a love which many might deny." Uozumi went on to describe some recent experiences: "I will never forget the evening of January 28 when I took your hand and you kneeled down in front of me with tears falling to the ground. Oh, your words at that time were sincere and the preciousness of that moment will never leave my mind. You are lachrymose; the turbulent blood of adolescence (*seishun no chi*) rages within you. But does not the consciousness of the meeting between our two souls bring transcendental melodies to your ear?" [73] And on another occasion: "Do you remember that night I embraced you? God to whom I prayed then is your Father too. You cried then over my expressions of sincerity. Can you believe too that my love flows from God?" [74]

Uozumi's overblown romanticism was a foreshadowing of the kind of literary expression that would be so popular among higher school students in the Taishō period. Unfortunately, in writing such an explicit confession, he was a little ahead of his time. Although distorted forms of sexual inversion were known to occur within the ritualized context of the "storm," students at Ichikō were upset over reading about an ongoing private relationship that touched on inclinations that had always been concealed behind a cloak of rationalization. No stalwart wanted to be made conscious of the possibility that the fun he was having wrestling with his roommates might be driven by some unconscious emotion. The joy of Mukōga Hill was that it was pre-Freudian. As two of his closest friends later commented, Uozumi had the irritating trait of exposing aspects of school life that had always been glossed over as "innocent" or playful. [75]

While Uozumi's flamboyant personality and outspoken declarations produced many enemies during his Ichikō days, the animosity did not burst into an outright counterattack until he wrote his most controversial essay in October 1905: "An Interpretation of the Problem of the School Spirit Based on the Principle of Individualism and a Proposal for the Liquidation of the

73. Abe Yoshishige, ed., *Setsuro ikō*, p. 202.
74. Ibid., p. 204.
75. Abe Yoshishige, *Waga oitachi*, pp. 369 and 383; Miyamoto Kazukichi, p. 8.

Mandatory Residence System." As the author explained in his introduction, the essay was meant as a contribution to the emerging debate over the relevance of the "almighty school spirit" (*bannō kōfū*) to the private claims of philosophic youth. Specifically, Uozumi centered his discussion around an attack on three of Ichikō's cherished traditions—monasticism, sport, and mandatory residence—with the hope of separating "myth" (*meishin*) from reality, "fallacy" (*gobyū*) from truth, and "contradiction" (*mujun*) from logic. By romanticizing and idealizing school activities, students at Ichikō had, in Uozumi's opinion, distorted reality far beyond the limits of empirical observation and were, in effect, denying "the principle of the dialectical change of ideas in history."[76] They had surrendered their freedom as individuals to a symbolic system whose only claim to authority was the sacred veil that covered it. To Uozumi the time had come to unmask the customs of the past, to strip them of their extra-worldly claims and lay them bare for scrutiny in the open air of reason and rationality.

The first principle to come under Uozumi's fire was monasticism (*rōjōshugi*). Springing from the "fallacy" that "the standards of today are lodged in the past,"[77] "monasticism," according to Uozumi, was rooted in an "old *bushidō* ethic," which should have perished with the Meiji Restoration. The cloistered world of Independence Hall reminded him of those diehard defenders of the Bakufu who barricaded themselves in Kan'eiji Temple when the Imperial armies took over Edo. By upholding this feudal mentality of the Shōgitai, the Ichikō students had erected a spiritual wall between themselves and the world outside, rendering the school inaccessible to the winds of intellectual change. Thus denuded of historical relevance, monasticism had endured on Mukōga Hill as a hollow ritual or illiterate article of faith (*fubun no shinjō*), pleasing to those surviving reactionaries from Japan's antiforeign past. Summoning the iconoclastic spirit of John Huss, Uozumi called for the repudiation of monasticism as an ideology that had long outworn its historical welcome.[78]

Along with monasticism, Uozumi denounced the primitive youth (*yaseiji*) who ran the school.[79] Lacking culture and taste,

76. Abe Yoshishige, ed., *Setsuro ikō*, pp. 114–115.
77. Ibid., p. 116.
78. Ibid., p. 117 and 119.
79. Ibid., p. 121.

these ruffians ordered their lives around a set of mindless rituals. They intoned the "four tenets" and sang "dormitory songs" in the style of "high priests chanting hymns of praise." Worst of all, they inflated the importance of sport. "There is no connection between a declining school spirit and the sagging fortunes of an athletic team," Uozumi asserted, in an obvious criticism of those who saw sport as the institution's major attraction. Quite the contrary, he argued, the recent defeats suffered on the athletic field and paralleled by the inner-worldly battles of "anguished youth" were encouraging signs that Ichikō was at last breaking out of the shackles of the past. Sport was just a hobby (*shumi*) chosen out of "personal preference" and insignificant to questions of human worth.[80]

Unlike earlier critics, Uozumi did not let his criticisms dangle in the thin air of righteous indignation. He realized that the authority of doctrines rested on the power of institutions and that criticisms of sport, monasticism, or primitivism would simply fall on deaf ears if allowed to stand by themselves. Any attack on higher school tradition had to be leveled ultimately at the overriding authority of the dormitory. Accordingly, Uozumi turned his attention in the concluding pages of his essay to exposing "the myth of the sacred theory of the mandatory residence system" (*kaikishuku seido shinseisetsu no meishin*).

Proponents of mandatory residence at Ichikō believed that the experience of living in the dormitory afforded students valuable opportunities for "communality" (*kyōdōtai*) and "self-government" (*jichi*). Uozumi rejected these as myths, arguing that the "fair name of community" (*kyōdō no bimei*) was a euphemism for "condemning the individual" and "destroying the personal self (*jinkaku*)"; that "self-government," rather than expanding personal freedom, was a disguise for the "iron chains" of a "penitentiary" (*kangoku*).[81] By heaping respect on such vacuous slogans as "communality" and "self-government," the students had fallen victim to a tyranny of their own making. Pronouncing the rules of the dormitory "dogmatic scripts" and accusing those defenders of tradition of being out of touch with the times and basically "sick," Uozumi concluded with this proposal: "Showing our respect for the freedom of the individual and the integrity of the inner conscience, I hereby submit that

80. Ibid., pp. 119, 123, 124, 126, and 316.
81. Ibid., p. 128.

we take immediate steps to abolish the mandatory residence system in our dormitory."[82]

Toward a New Synthesis of the School Spirit

By dissecting the school spirit with the cool precision of a scientist, carefully separating fact from myth, Uozumi Kageo touched a raw nerve within the collective consciousness of the student body. Moreover, since he refused to soften his words with flowery metaphor or esoteric quotations, no one expected that campus diehards would cushion their language in response. And indeed they did not. During the weeks following publication of his proposal, Uozumi was accused of being a lunatic, a crybaby, a dandy, and a traitor. His enemies were obviously waiting to jump on him in light of his previous articles and notorious behavior around campus; and this essay was the last straw.

Primarily, the diehards attacked Uozumi for institutional slander. He betrayed the legacy of former upperclassmen, disregarded the sanctity of the "four tenets," demeaned athletics. The students also held Uozumi liable for subverting what Aoki Tokuzō called "the mission of the Yamato people" (*Yamato minzoku no shimei*).[83] Fukui Rikichirō, a future chairman of the Executive Committee, elaborated: "When you criticize the values of monasticism, diligence, martial valor, community, and self-government, you are not simply criticizing school spirit. Do you not realize, Uozumi, that our school flag is the quintessence of loyalty and patriotism (*chūkun aikoku*)?"[84] Other traditionalists hammered away at the same themes: that Independence Hall was the "noble embodiment of family and nation"; that the spirit of Ichikō insured "the preservation of national genius"; that "the conquest of the entire world was the mission of the Ichikō stalwarts"; and that anyone who so contemptuously slighted the organizational ethos of the school was, in effect, denigrating the "national polity."[85] Even Uozumi's specific proposal to abolish mandatory residence was construed by his critics as an insult to the "national society." To live outside

82. Ibid., p. 129.
83. "Dai ichi gakki zenryō sawakai kiji," *DIKGKZ*, no. 151 (Nov. 15, 1905), p. 95.
84. Fukui Rikichirō, "Iwayuru kojinshugi no kenchi ni tachitaru kōfūkan o hyōsu," *DIKGKZ*, no. 151 (Nov. 25, 1905), p. 21.
85. "Kōfū mondai enzetsukai," *DIKGKZ*, no. 152 (Dec. 15, 1905), pp. 60, 78, 80, and 81.

the dormitory, Fukui explained, was like living in a foreign country.[86] It was not simply a question, then, of Uozumi's disliking the "storm" or asking to be left alone to sulk over the problems of human existence. The heresies he voiced were perceived by the stalwarts as devastating in their implication, posing a serious threat to the entire communal, "family-school" ideal that had guided students for nearly two decades. Instinctively, they rallied around the ultimate sanction for institutional tradition: the inseparability of the "school spirit" and the "spirit of national devotion."

The extent of hostility against Uozumi was apparent in a "tea assembly" held shortly after the publication of his controversial article, where even the moderate, philosophically inclined chairman of the Executive Committee, Tsurumi Yūsuke, admonished the young rebel for his inciteful language and brazen disregard for the conservative sensibilities of his fellow students.[87] Uozumi sat through the entire assembly, listening to one after another of his critics, hoping perhaps that someone might rise in his defense. But no one did. Finally, he gained permission from the chair to speak in his own behalf. The palpable sincerity with which he poured forth his views, rapping his boney knuckles on the podium for emphasis, moved the reporter for the *Society of Friends Magazine* to compare him to "young Luther"; "You, Uozumi, with your frail constitution and hoarse voice, have fought fearlessly for your private beliefs before a hostile audience; such a display of courage arouses some respect, even among those of us who strongly oppose your ideas."[88]

But Uozumi's self-defense, no matter how sincerely it was delivered, intensified the hostility against him. A chorus of voices, coming mostly from the athletic clubs, were now calling for the "clenched-fist punishment"; and their demand was seriously considered by political authorities in the dormitory.[89] The beating, fortunately, never took place. For one thing, some of the leading diehards believed the fist law an inappropriate response to a transgression akin to treason. The school-yard beating was intended, after all, as a ritual of reassimilation; and campus stalwarts had no desire to bring Uozumi back into the

86. Fukui, p. 28.
87. "Dai ichi gakki zenryō sawakai kiji," pp. 93–94.
88. Ibid., pp. 97–98.
89. Uozumi says this in his own diary. Abe Yoshishige, ed., *Setsuro ikō*, p. 120.

"family," even after a public thrashing. Better to send him to a hospital for "extended treatment," to paraphrase one rough- neck, than to waste effort over a "clenched-fist punishment."[90] At the same time, the young intellectuals in the dormitory, while disagreeing with Uozumi's brand of "extreme individual- ism" (kyokutan na kojinshugi), were not pleased by the prospect of seeing a fellow writer kicked and beaten on the athletic field. Some, including Abe Yoshishige, even wondered if the sickly rebel could survive such an assault.[91] Acting to prevent the un- thinkable, a delegation of moderates organized a special "lec- ture meeting on the problem of the school spirit" in order to give vent to the fulminating reaction against Uozumi. The organizers hoped that a public debate might establish new com- mon ground between philosophic moderates and athletic die- hards and thus pave the way for a reunification of the campus community around an expanded vision of the school spirit.

The special forum was unprecedented in Ichikō's history. Never before had an individual student sparked so much con- troversy to warrant such an assembly; and never before had "the logic of the sacred school spirit" (kōfū shinseiron) come un- der intense public scrutiny. (Also adding to the noteworthiness of the occasion was the roll call of bright young men who were to become cultural and political leaders in their later years.) The speakers represented the full spectrum of opinion in the contro- versy, ranging from a dozen unrelenting spokesmen for the maintenance of tradition to Uozumi and his one unqualified supporter, Egi Sadao. In between the extremes was a group of moderates, represented by Abe Jirō (who attended as a visiting Tokyo University student), Abe Yoshishige, Tsurumi Yūsuke, and Maeda Tamon, all of whom were sympathetic to philo- sophic idealism but remained safely theoretical in most of their remarks.

As one might expect, the traditionalists focused on Uozumi as an individual whose "dangerous ideas" and "destructive be- liefs" threatened the interrelated pieties of family, state, and school. Uozumi, in turn, struck back with the same unremitting determination. At one point during the debate, he enjoined his listeners to stop the "sophistry" and "return to the inner self" (jiko shinrei ni kaere).[92] Exemplifying the ethic of ultimate ends,

90. "Kōfū mondai enzetsukai," p. 81.
91. Abe Yoshishige, Waga oitachi, p. 386.
92. "Kōfū mondai enzetsukai," p. 83.

Uozumi Kageo could make no compromise with campus stalwarts; nor could he substantially strengthen his base of support among those who shared some of his views. As he admitted in his diary, he was too much of an individualist to suit even his closest friends.[93]

By all accounts, the moderates carried the debate and won the audience. Avoiding any mention of Uozumi by name and steering clear of the highly inflammable issue of patriotism, the moderates focused their remarks on the possibilities for harmony and spiritual renewal. Abe Jirō spoke of the need for an "idealistic school spirit" (*risōteki kōfū*), which would "spring naturally" from the hearts of all the students; Abe Yoshishige graciously complimented the athletes for their "sincerity," observing that "sportsmen too must stand for spiritualism"; and Maeda Tamon, referring to himself as a "harmonizer" (*chōwasha*), confided that he could see the day when philosophers and athletes, individualists and traditionalists, would "join hands for the sake of the school spirit." Not everything the moderates said was pleasing to the diehards: Abe Jirō expressed his distaste for the "storm"; and Abe Yoshishige came out flatly against the "clenched-fist punishment" as an insult to the higher school ethos.[94] But even in criticizing the tradition, the moderates employed a soft, conciliatory language, revealing an earnest desire to reach the most obstinate roughnecks.

Despite their criticisms, the moderates accepted the self-governing dormitory and the collective, political framework for organizing student life at Ichikō. Though reluctant to join in the sacralizing of that framework or to identify it as the building-block of the "family state," the philosophic youth were certainly willing to live within it. As Maeda explained: "The mandatory residence system is a fact. We must of course attempt to make as good use of this system as is possible; but I am not going to complain about a system that already exists."[95] Maeda's remarks suggest a futile resignation on the part of student intellectuals; but this negative attitude was countered by a positive belief that the dormitory, while far from perfect, did allow for individual expression, which would be lost once students dispersed into the surrounding society. Abe Yoshishige expressed his "great approval" of Ichikō's monastic tradition, pre-

93. Abe Yoshishige, ed., *Setsuro ikō*, pp. 320–322; Abe Yoshishige, *Waga oitachi*, p. 369.
94. "Kōfū mondai enzetsukai," pp. 78–84.
95. Ibid., p. 83.

sumably because it insulated sensitive students from mind-numbing, popular banalities.[96] Other commentators hinted that without the framework of self-government and monasticism in the higher schools, there would never have been a discovery of the inner self.

The moderate position received further elaboration in extended articles by Abe Yoshishige ("My View of the School Spirit") and Tsurumi Yūsuke ("My Theory of the School Spirit") which appeared in the *Society of Friends Magazine* at the end of the year.[97] Both writers were primarily concerned with accommodating the new spirit of individualism within the traditional framework of the dormitory. Implicitly, they accepted Maeda Tamon's formula that the school spirit represented a cohesive amalgamation of the philosophic insights of all students while remaining distinguishable from and superior to the feelings of any single individual.[98] Conflict within the dormitory could be reduced, Tsurumi and Abe pointed out, if individualists and traditionalists looked beyond their surface differences to a transcending perception of the "personal self" (*jinkaku*). Unlike the anarchic self-assertion of a rebel or the flaunting extravagance of a dandy, the cultivation of the "personal self" required stamina, "sincerity," and dedication to the improvement of human relations. As the antithesis of egoism, the "personal self" was an ideal that should inspire athlete and philosopher alike and point the way toward a "new school spirit."

The events that rocked Independence Hall in the fall of 1905 have been hailed by school annalists as a watershed in the history of First Higher, "a giant step forward in the development of the school spirit" from a stage of rustic primitivism to a sophisticated metaphysical norm.[99] Some have even suggested that Ichikō experienced both a political and a spiritual "reformation" during the early 1900s,[100] an assertion that would be more convincing if Uozumi had emerged victorious in his assault on "barbarism" and "monasticism." Yet one cannot slight the genuine feelings of many sensitive Ichikō students in the fall of 1905 who were convinced that their world was changing for the better; that, specifically, the legitimacy of self-discovery *within*

96. Ibid., p. 82.
97. Abe Yoshishige, "Waga kōfūkan," *DIKGKZ*, no. 152 (Dec. 15, 1905), pp. 8–23; Tsurumi Yūsuke, "Yo no kōfūron," *DIKGKZ*, no. 151 (Nov. 15, 1905), pp. 1–20.
98. "Kōfū mondai enzetsukai," pp. 83–84.
99. Ibid., p. 85.
100. *Kōryōshi*, p. 249.

the organizational framework of the dormitory had been affirmed for posterity. As evidence for their optimism, they looked with justifiable pride on the school debates. Instead of allowing a group of roughnecks to silence Uozumi on the athletic field, the young stalwarts of Mukōga Hill were learning the virtue, as one writer put it, of "quietly exchanging manly opinions."[101] The view was best summed up by one of the editors of the school magazine: "By debating in the style of great gentlemen (*taijin kunshi*) striving to solve a mutual problem, we have witnessed the true sincerity of the Ichikō stalwarts. We will record this event in our school's history and glory in it for years to come."[102]

The Higher School Crisis in Perspective

Ichikō students were not alone in their painful reexamination of institutional traditions after the turn of the century. Similar debates over the philosophic claims of individuals versus the public demands of the dormitory fellowship erupted in each of the provincial schools. At Third Higher, "the problem of the school spirit" centered in the debate club, where campus intellectuals criticized athletes for their self-confinement and lack of culture.[103] In Fifth Higher, campus intellectuals, many of whom had come to Kumamoto from cities outside Kyūshū, organized a "cultural movement" in the immediate wake of Fujimura's suicide. Their philosophic zeal stirred fear in the hearts of some Kyūshū stalwarts, who, under the leadership of Ōkawa Shūmei, campaigned against the admission of "dandies" to Gokō.[104] At Fourth and the recently opened Sixth Higher, the confrontation between philosophers and Philistines occurred somewhat later, though with no less intensity.[105]

In none of the above confrontations did the crisis focus upon a revolutionary individual as it did in Ichikō. To find a parallel situation, one must turn to Second Higher, where in May 1902

101. "Kōfū mondai enzetsukai," p. 84.

102. *Kōryōshi*, p. 317.

103. Andō Katsuichirō, ed., *Dai San Kōtō Gakkō Benronbu bushi* (Kyoto, 1935), pp. 38–41, 53–58. A more serious confrontation between athletes and intellectuals is reported as occurring in 1907, p. 95 of above.

104. *Shūgakuryōshi*, p. 373; Akase Yayoki, "Ryūnan shisōshi," pp. 44–45.

105. Dai Yon Kōtō Gakkō Jishūryō Ryōshi Hensan Iinkai, *Dai Yon Kōtō Gakkō Jishūryōshi*, pp. 46–47; Ide Takashi, *Tetsugaku seinen no shuki*, Ide Takashi chosakushū, vol. 6 (Tokyo, 1969), p. 160; Kobayashi Hiroyuki, *Rokkō monogatari* (Okayama, 1969), pp. 184–189.

a scathing attack on the "athletic school spirit" appeared in the school magazine. Like Uozumi, the author condemned the traditional school spirit as a lifeless vestige of a "feudal age," which must be destroyed in the name of individual rights. In addition, the author charged campus roughnecks with using the "storm" as a masquerade for their own "improper sexual activities," under the unspoken assumption that "homosexuality arouses vigor" (*dōsei no ai wa genki o kobushi*).[106] Worse yet, fist laws imposed by the public safety committee prohibited "the natural interchange between persons of the opposite sex."[107] "Since residing in this dormitory," the writer complained, "a number of my fellow students have been punished for displaying an interest in women. But I have not heard of any punishment for those who engage in violent homosexual assaults (*dōsei jūkō*)."[108] While the critic was no advocate of heterosexual indulgence, he denounced the hypocrisy of stalwarts who cruelly branded the romantic dreams of philosophic youth as "selfish," yet took undue advantage of young and defenseless freshmen in the chaos of the "storm." Since he used a pen name, the identity of the Second Higher rebel remains obscure.

Attacking the Philistine traditions of college subcultures has always been a favorite pastime of writers and artists, that is, once they have safely graduated from the school that was persecuting them. What has been called the "tradition of criticism" associated with both the British public school and the German Gymnasium is not a record of students protesting against their headmasters, but one of well-known authors bitterly recalling their own schooldays, when they were tyrannized by their peers.[109] This is not the same thing as students speaking out as students in a critical reassessment of their subculture. One wonders if the turn-of-the-century students at Eton or Andover (or at Oxford or Yale, for that matter) ever confronted the issue of individualism versus "house rituals" with either the fervor or the consciousness that informed so many of the "debates on the school spirit" in the Meiji higher schools. The surge of essays on self-discovery and the "new school spirit" that filled the

106. Hakugansei, "Undō kōfū to tekken seisai no kachi to o ronjite Kyōfūkai o nanzu," *Shōshikai zasshi*, no. 49 (May 6, 1902), p. 34.
107. Ibid., p. 33.
108. Ibid., p. 34.
109. As extensively discussed in Reed, *Old School Ties*, and W. R. Hicks, *The School in English and German Fiction* (London, 1933).

pages of every higher school magazine was more than a frivolous outpouring of adolescent intellectualization. Students were reading and thinking and critically analyzing the culture they had inherited, within the broadest philosophic context. And this in itself may be unique in the annals of student history.

There were also concrete benefits to accrue from the debates. The reliance on fist laws and other violent means to resolve dissension within the student community began to disappear during late Meiji. Thereafter physical punishment was reserved for the most flagrant disrupters whose private behavior was a source of universal discord.[110] At the same time, the expression of personal opinion on most issues, especially theoretical issues, became a matter of course among higher school students; and debate, which was formerly prohibited at Ichikō, gained a new respectability as the noblest of extracurricular activities. During the Taishō period, no student writer or speaker could expect to have his say without eliciting a countervailing argument from at least one critic.

For student intellectuals, therefore, the higher school crisis was an enlightening experience, bringing a gush of fresh air into an institutional setting that had begun to rigidify from within. Yet, in opening the doors of their dormitories to philosophy and the arts, the campus intellectuals were also imposing limits on their self-expression. If there was one clear message from the late Meiji debates, it was that anarchic individualism, as proselytized by Uozumi Kageo, could not be tolerated in the community of students. Torn between the ethic of ultimate ends and the ethic of responsibility, the moderates accepted the structure of the dormitory while sidestepping the traditionalist notion that this organizational framework was a microcosm of the family state. To the moderates a confrontation between the private authority of the writer and the public authority of the Executive Committee was unnecessary. The self-awakening of the apprentice writer, they believed, added strength to the school spirit and to the claim that Ichikō students stood above the throng of middle-class youth whose "small ambitions" (*shōnaru hōfu*) catered to a vulgar quest for success.[111] Whether an athlete or a writer, the Ichikō student,

110. The "clenched-fist punishment" was formally abolished at Ichikō after a great dispute during the fall of 1922. See *Kōryōshi*, pp. 99–103.
111. Tsukuda Toyoo, "Aete kōyū shoshi ni uttau," *DIKGKZ*, no. 81 (1898), p. 8; Kitazawa Teikichi, "Kishuku kyōikuron," p. 17.

as Tsurumi Yūsuke explained, belonged to a separate "class" (*kaikyū*) defined by broad philosophic horizons that extended beyond family and society to the "universe" (*uchū tenchi*).[112] In Tsutsumi Biro's words: "The task for the great man (*daijōfu*) is to investigate the original meaning of life (*jinsei no daiichigi*) while avoiding small and beguiling things. He must enlarge his aspiration and deepen his erudition."[113] Yet, as they redefined higher school greatness in philosophic terms, the moderate intellectuals felt beholden to campus athletes and political leaders who safeguarded the borders between school and society, allowing Mukōga Hill to become a sanctuary for creative genius.

The involved deliberations of the moderate innovators are especially interesting in light of a comparable dilemma, albeit on a much larger scale, involving the tacit accommodation between the late Meiji intellectual and the imperial-bureaucratic state. Whereas an earlier generation of intellectuals, represented by the Meiji Six Society, had served as celebrated spokesmen or advisors for an emerging state, the generation of Tōkoku, Tōson, and Chogyū stood before a government whose legal and bureaucratic institutions were hardening and whose ideology of the "family state" threatened to nationalize social and intellectual life. Given the awesome powers of the state in all public matters and the ever-contracting sphere of individual action, the late Meiji writers were faced with the hard choice, as H. D. Harootunian has observed, of refusing "to act politically" as "the precondition to freedom, individualism, art, and culture."[114] Only by disassociating thought from politics were writers assured of maintaining a separation of, and avoiding a confrontation between, their private claims and the public demands of the Meiji state. Thus, they attempted to construct a safe framework which would guarantee complete freedom in all nonpolitical matters affecting art and philosophy while allegiance to the state, if not actively pronounced, was nonetheless assumed.

Similarly, the philosophically and artistically inclined students in the late Meiji and Taishō higher schools soon learned that to be a writer and a resident of the dormitory required a tacit understanding with student authorities. To repeat the caveat of the Ichikō Christian Youth Society, writers must not

112. Tsurumi Yūsuke, "Yo no kōfūron," p. 8.
113. Tsutsumi Biro, "Jikaku," *DIKGKZ*, no. 105 (June, 1901), p. 45.
114. H. D. Harootunian, "Between Politics and Culture," in Bernard S. Silberman and H. D. Harootunian, eds., *Japan in Crisis*, pp. 114–115.

meddle in "dormitory politics" (*ryō no seiji*),[115] which had no aesthetic or religious value and were better left in the hands of campus strong men. In this way, the higher school subculture may have contributed to the socialization of prewar intellectuals to the role of nonpolitical writers or scholars. The valuable experience gained as an accommodating intellectual in the boarding school could be put to good use in later life, when one had to face again the problem of balancing private claims with public demands—except that in this latter instance the demands emanated from the state rather than the school.

115. *Kōryōshi*, p. 1201.

CHAPTER SEVEN

From Meiji to Taishō:
Broadening Perspectives and
Enduring Traditions

The great men of culture are those who have had a passion for diffus-
ing . . . the best knowledge, the best ideas of their time; who have labored
to divest knowledge of all that was harsh, uncouth, . . . exclusive; to
humanise it, to make it efficient outside the clique of the cultivated and
learned, yet still remaining the best knowledge and thought of the time,
and a true source, thereof, of sweetness and light.

MATTHEW ARNOLD, *CULTURE AND ANARCHY* (1869)

A man was intended by nature to marry at eighteen. The average vil-
lager, clerk, pit-boy, work-boy begins "walking out" with a girl at the age
of fifteen or sixteen; the public school boy has no such opportunities of
courtship. Three hundred boys are spending three-quarters of their lives
in a monastic world. . . . They have never any chances of seeing girls of
their own class and of their own age. At a particularly susceptible period,
therefore, they have no natural objects for their affections.

ALEC WAUGH, *PUBLIC SCHOOL LIFE* (1922)

The late Meiji "debates on the school spirit" (*kōfū ronsō*) never
came to a decisive conclusion. Questions about the lines of de-
marcation between the private and public spheres sporadically
agitated the student community through World War II. Rarely a
year went by when the athletic stalwarts and the literary students in some higher school were not accusing each other of
failing to meet their respective obligations. Disputes would
often erupt over the cornering of extracurricular funds by the
sports clubs or the saturation of the school magazine with phi-

losophy, short stories, and poetry by literary students. At times the debate could become vituperative (as in the aftermath of a particularly destructive "storm" in June 1924, which did greater injury to the inhabitants of Independence Hall than the great earthquake one year earlier).[1] But the occasional tensions between athlete and writer were, in perspective, one of the higher school's greatest sources of strength and vitality. Vigorous argument sublimated the pugilistic tendencies of campus strong men, gave all students a safe avenue for dissent, and put an end to the compulsive conformity of an earlier age. Since the creative quest for identity cannot take place in a bland, unchallenging environment, the rise of debate among late-Meiji higher school students is an important indication that personality grew with the institution.

However, the growth of the student was not paralleled by notable advancements in the disposition of many government officials and social critics toward youth in industrial society. Railing against the inadequacies of the nation's young was a popular pastime of certain critics, as we have seen, well before the turn of the century. But in the wake of Fujimura's suicide, the trickle of criticism turned into a torrent. Conservatives, including Ōtsuka Motoe and Miyake Setsurei, denounced youthful "anguish" as a threat to the state;[2] progressives, including Taoka Reiun and Tokutomi Roka, worried that the combination of spiritual despair and excessive affection for wealth among the young might vitiate drives for social reform.[3] Critics of every political temper seemed in agreement with Sawayanagi Masatarō's assessment in 1905 that Japanese students had lost their "vitality."[4] The youth of Taishō Japan, as Tokutomi Sohō lamented eleven years later, lacked a galvanizing principle around which to rally their energies. Consequently, they were hopelessly divided among disparate shades of materialistic, anguished, debauched, nonchalant, and exemplary types.[5]

1. Miraculously, none of the students living in Independence Hall were injured during the earthquake; and the dormitory never caught fire. See *Kōryōshi*, pp. 114–115; the 1924 debate on the "storm" is recorded in ibid., pp. 128–129.

2. Ōtsuka Motoe, "Jisatsu to seinen," *Taiyō* 6, no. 2 (July 1, 1903):207–213; Oka Yoshitake, "Nichiro sensōgo . . . ," p. 139.

3. Harootunian, "The Problem of Taishō . . . ," pp. 20–21; Marius Jansen, "Changing Japanese Attitudes Toward Modernization," in Marius Jansen, ed., *Changing Japanese Attitudes Toward Modernization* (Princeton, 1965), p. 80.

4. Oka Yoshitake, "Nichiro sensōgo . . . ," p. 140.

5. Harootunian, "The Problem of Taishō . . . ," p. 10; Henry Smith, *Japan's First Student Radicals*, p. xi.

Ironically, the diversification of youth culture that Tokutomi found so upsetting in 1916 was one product of the capitalist-industrial state he longed for three decades earlier. Between 1914 and 1919 the gross national product expanded by more than a third, the extraordinary growth attributable in large part to foreign trade and the accumulation of an export balance of nearly 1.2 billion yen.[6] The rise in gross national product was paralleled by an enormous increase in factory laborers, who numbered nearly 1.7 million by the end of World War I (with young women still constituting the bulk of the working force in the key textile industry). Since profits reaped by urban industrialists had little impact on village life in Aomori, the prosperity of early Taishō was to a considerable extent illusionary. Still, with nearly 40 percent of the population living in small towns and cities by 1925, and with the continuing explosion of the new middle class (which, depending on who is included, constituted between 15 and 20 percent of the entire work force at the end of World War I),[7] Japan entered a new age in the 1920s, when an ethic of production was beginning to give way to an ethic of consumption. For the new middle class, at least, the traditional virtues of saving and self-denial that had propelled the nation into the industrial revolution in early Meiji yielded after World War I to the raspy voices of the Victrola and the gentle buzz of electric fans.

Taishō culture was a complex superstructure of political parties, mass communication, consumer marketing, and special-interest groups. Labor unions rallied beneath towering billboards plastered with advertisements for Lion Toothpaste and Kirin Beer; Model T Fords shared city streets with honey-wagons; suffragettes campaigned in kimono. The variegated culture offered the sons and daughters of the wealthy (and moderately wealthy) an unprecedented range of choices. There were movie theaters, cafes, dance halls for the Charleston, miniature golf courses, beauty parlors, department stores, and much more to suit the fleeting tastes and fancies of the "modern girls" (*moga*) and "modern boys" (*mobo*) of Taishō Japan. And there were bookstores stocked with a baffling array of "pure literature" (*junbungaku*), proletarian literature, comic books, sports magazines, and popular weeklies. The difficulty in arriving at deci-

6. William Lockwood, *The Economic Development of Japan*, p. 39.
7. Lockwood, p. 130.

sions on what to read and how much to spend for a V-neck sweater added to the uncertainty of growing up in urban Japan.

Beginning with the discovery in the late-Meiji press of the "problematic characteristics" of coming of age (depression, hedonism, volatility, self-immolation), the government took an alarmist position vis à vis the nation's young. Rather than accepting the stress and strain of youthfulness as a natural outgrowth of the complex society they had created, government leaders pounced upon the uncertainties of the young as symptomatic of private indulgence, decadence, and even political subversion. In the strident admonition to students in 1906, which guided official policy through World War II, the Minister of Education declared: "Today's students are satisfied with small successes, lured by luxuries, and anguished by idle dreams, neglecting completely their duty to society." Worse yet: "Dangerous thoughts (*kiken shisō*) are infiltrating the world of education, threatening to shake the very foundation of our school system. . . . Those entrusted with the responsibility to educate must pay careful heed to stamping out extremist biases and damming the flow of social poison."[8] The strong words were backed up initially by "preventive action," as Kenneth Pyle puts it, to make sure that "civilization sickness" did not spread beyond the new middle class to the rural and urban working force.[9] The prophylactic measures undertaken between 1907 and 1910 included the extension of compulsory primary education from four to six years; the redrafting of ethics textbooks to give greater emphasis to the ideology of the "family state"; the nationalization of rural "youth groups" (*seinendan*) that had evolved within the traditional village; and the establishment of a vast rural and urban network of local reservist associations for the army.[10] Taken together, these measures made certain that the great masses of young people, from ages six to thirty-six, would tread a straight and narrow path as they came of age in Taishō Japan.

But where are the higher schools on this diversified land-

---

8. Terasaki Masao and Satō Hideo, "Keizai no hatten to kyōiku no seibi," in *Kyōiku-gaku zenshū* 3 (Tokyo, 1970):107–108.

9. Kenneth Pyle, "The Technology of Japanese Nationalism," p. 53.

10. Ibid., pp. 62–63; Wilbur M. Fridell, "Government Ethics Textbooks in Late Meiji Japan," *Journal of Asian Studies* 24, no. 4 (August 1970):825–826; Richard J. Smethhurst, *A Social Basis for Prewar Japanese Militarism* (Berkeley, 1974), pp. 22–37.

scape of rural youth mobilizing for patriotic service, of "modern boys" lining up for the latest Harold Lloyd or Gloria Swanson feature, of socialist parties drifting to the left, of government expanding the electorate on one side and tightening police controls on the other? In the following discussions, we shall examine how the institution survived another reform movement after the Russo-Japanese War and how the students responded to the breezes of Taishō culturalism (*kyōyōshugi*) and Marxism in ways that strengthened their hold on social status.

The Higher Schools Reexamined and Reaffirmed

The government's policy of liquidating the uncertainties of growing up by placing rural and small-town youth under the wing of adult-sponsored organizations had a familiar ring, for the higher schools were also conceived as custodial institutions to defend against the "fashions of the world." The suicide of Fujimura Misao and the heated debates over the ideas of young rebels raised questions, however, in the Ministry of Education and the Diet about their effectiveness in fulfilling this original purpose. Four months after Fujimura's suicide, Kikuchi Dairoku (a former Minister of Education) warned an assembly at Sixth Higher that students and teachers had better get back to the business of learning foreign languages without fretting over abstract philosophic problems.[11]

For nearly fifteen years following Kikuchi's address, a slew of government conferences and committees proposed specific recommendations for reforming higher education. Repeatedly in the debates that ensued, members of the Diet and distinguished educators resurrected versions of Inoue Kowashi's scheme for a streamlined higher school curriculum tailored to vocational needs.[12] Why should the preparatory academies and universities detain young men of promise into their middle and even late twenties, overeducating them and leaving them ripe for psychological anguish or political radicalism? A streamlined curriculum, many thought, would push the student elite into

11. Dai Roku Kōtō Gakkō Seitoryō, ed., *Rokuryō ryōshi*, p. 89.
12. One of the most heatedly debated proposals was Minister of Education Komatsubara Eitarō's plan for collapsing the middle and higher schools into a single, seven-year institution that provided vocational training and university preparation. Komatsubara's plan, originally submitted in 1910, is reprinted in Kyōiku Hensankai, ed., *Meiji ikō seido hattatsushi*, vol. 5, pp. 1166–1168. For a full discussion of related proposals, see pp. 1139–1204.

productive work by the age of twenty or twenty-one. Toward this end, and perhaps influenced by Charles W. Eliot's lectures in Japan during the fall of 1912, several leading educators recommended sweeping reforms based on the reputedly more efficient, unilinear model for advanced technical and liberal arts education in the United States.[13] However, high government officials, especially in the House of Peers and the Privy Council, seemed more alarmed by such utilitarian proposals that would dissolve the higher schools into expanded "vocational colleges" than they were by the "youth problem" that sparked the debate in the first place.[14] Moreover, influential spokesmen in Tokyo University and the upper-level bureaucracy opposed any substantial changes in the structure of the higher schools. In this group were such renowned pillars of conservatism as Inoue Tetsujirō, Hozumi Yatsuka, Yamakawa Kenjirō, and Matsuzaki Kuranosuke, who apparently had confidence that the higher school community, despite the dallying of a few with "dangerous thoughts," was basically sound and should be left alone.[15]

The question of higher school reform was finally resolved with the formation in 1917 of the Special Council on Education, whose reports became the basis for comprehensive ordinances on higher education issued the following year. On the matter of preparatory education, the Council submitted statements, in January and May 1918, which reaffirmed the importance of "general education" (*futsū kyōiku*) in the higher schools and called for a simplified division of majors between the arts (*bunka*) and the sciences (*rika*). In backing up its recommendation, the Council argued that "the refined and profound level of general education" in the higher schools was an ideal "foundation" for university studies; that the higher school performed a critical service by amassing the brightest students from diverse regions of the country "under a fixed school spirit" (*ittei no kōfū no moto ni*); that the cultivation of the "gentleman" (*shinshi*) or "man of valor and frugality" was the best safeguard against the spread of frivolity and dandyism (*fuka keichō*) among the young elite.[16] The Council recognized the higher schools as the func-

13. I refer especially to the proposals by Kikuchi Dairoku (July 1914) and Takeda Sanai (September 1915), which are reprinted in ibid., pp. 1186–1191.

14. Ibid., p. 1192.

15. Kokuritsu Kyōiku Kenkyūjo, ed., *Nihon kindai kyōiku hyakunenshi*, vol. 4, pp. 1210, 1248.

16. Kyōikushi Hensankai, *Meiji ikō kyōiku . . .* , vol. 5, pp. 224–230.

18. After a snowfall. Hirosaki Higher, courtesy of Yamauchi Naosuke

tional equivalent to the French lycée, the German Gymnasium, and the British public school: "An institution which provides the highest level of general education for young men and which is dedicated to the perfection of national morality." [17] "Even if there were no university," the Council submitted, "the higher school would retain its raison d'être." [18]

Although the report endorsed the basic philosophy of higher school education, it did contain proposals for two important modifications. [19] First, the Special Council recommended that new higher schools be established in coordination with the anticipated expansion of the Imperial universities. By 1918, there were eight higher schools, and over the next decade seventeen new national schools (along with four private and three municipal academies) were founded and named after the towns in which they were located. This tripling of the higher schools appeared to signal a move away from the narrow elitism of the Meiji period. Also, coming at a time when the demand for a highly educated stratum of civil servants was beginning to level

17. Ibid., p. 236.
18. Ibid., p. 237.
19. A third proposal for a seven-year curriculum that would encompass the middle school was never adopted in the national higher schools.

off, the expansion seemed out of line with the employment market.[20] The demoralizing effects of the newly opened higher schools should not be exaggerated, however. Considering a parallel growth in the general population, the enrollment in the national higher educational track during the 1920s was still a tiny fragment of the male population of comparable age.[21] While expansion did raise immediate questions about the availability of excellent jobs for the educated elite, the concern was far more pressing in the universities, where students stood at the threshold of adult careers. Removed by time and space from the worries of the world, Taishō higher schools continued to promote a carefree ambience.

Ironically, the insulating effect of the higher school experience was most pronounced in the new "name schools," many of which were founded in isolated provincial settings that surpassed the older "number schools" in natural beauty. New higher school towns like Saga, Matsumoto, Yamagata, Matsue, and Hirosaki were virtually untainted by the afflictions of industrialization; and the urban students who flocked to these provincial retreats developed the same appreciation for "culture" and the same fierce loyalties toward institution and peer group that typified the older "number schools." They also perpetuated, quite self-consciously, the distinct customs long associated with the older academies: the tattered uniforms; the philosophic magazines; the *konpa*; the self-governing dormitory which poured forth song and "rain."

A more significant and potentially threatening modification of higher school policy concerned the problem of "dangerous thoughts." Before the Russo-Japanese War, the Ministry of Education found little cause to censure student essays or speeches; but this attitude changed with the 1906 admonition on student thought. Since the Special Council on Education was committed to general education over technical studies in the higher schools, the possibility of undesirable philosophies seeping into the curriculum or extracurriculum was ever pres-

20. Smith discusses this problem in *Japan's First Student Radicals*, pp. 17–18.

21. The matriculation figures in Appendix III, Table 3, suggest that increasing primary school enrollments made the higher school expansion negligible. Moreover, the total number of students attending the higher schools actually decreased after the Ministry of Education ordered the reduction of enrollment in December 1931. (See Nishizawa, p. 278.) Thus, while 16,227 students attended national higher schools in 1929, 14,201 students were in attendance in 1934. (See Nakajima, "Kyūsei kōtō gakkō seido no hensen, part 2," appendix.)

ent. Limiting education to "refined and profound learning" required discrimination by teachers and students over what should be read and what should be left alone. To a large extent, this problem could be resolved, as the Council explained, by the hiring of "superior teachers" who were exemplars of cultural taste. Yet the Council also left the door open for more direct government intervention when it suggested "responsible officials should attempt, in an appropriate way, to provide healthy literature (*kenzen naru yomimono*) for the students."[22]

Exactly what might be "an appropriate way" to assure "healthy" reading habits was never spelled out; the Council was obviously in no mood for hard-nosed measures that impinged on student or faculty autonomy. Still, the statement was at least a veiled warning that the Ministry of Education would not stand idly by while student intellectuals flirted with ideological heresies.

The protracted debates in government circles before and during World War I were almost unnoticed by most students and faculty in the higher schools. Absorbed by the fantasies of poetry, friendship, and sport, students had little inclination to speculate on what was happening in the Ministry of Education. Equally oblivious of the reports and counter-reports were the "teachers of life," apparently deemed too absent-minded and eccentric to serve on government panels. The higher schools were not, however, without public spokesmen during the critical decade following the Russo-Japanese War. In the tradition of Kinoshita Hiroji and Nakagawa Gen, the headmasters continued to play their role in bridging the gap between school and government. The most commanding public figure of the period was the successor to Kanō Kōkichi at Ichikō: Nitobe Inazō. His seven years as headmaster restored the school's national prestige and gave a great boost to student moderates who were striving for a resynthesis of the school spirit.

Nitobe Inazō at Ichikō:
"Sociality" and the Well-rounded Gentleman

In background, experience, and demeanor, Nitobe Inazō was unlike any of his predecessors.[23] Whereas Kinoshita and Kanō

---

22. Kyōiku Hensankai, ed., *Meiji ikō kyōiku . . .* , vol. 5, p. 233.

23. Born in 1862, the third son of a high-ranking samurai, Nitobe grew up in the heat and enthusiasm of the Meiji Restoration. In 1875, he entered the Tokyo English

projected a traditionalist image, Nitobe stood out conspicuously as a cosmopolitan and renaissance gentleman. By the
time he arrived at Ichikō in 1906, Nitobe had already achieved
considerable renown as an international scholar with advanced
degrees from Johns Hopkins and Halle universities, an educator at Sapporo Agricultural College and Kyoto University, a
colonial administrator in Taiwan, and an author of several well-
known books. (The latter included two popular English volumes which were written expressly to introduce Japanese
character and traditions to a curious Western audience.) Although formally trained as a specialist in agricultural technology, Nitobe considered himself a man of the age, with expansive interests ranging from Christian theology to Japanese
bushidō to his self-appointed role as "a bridge across the Pacific." Most important, he was an impassioned advocate of the
humanistic standards of *Bildung* and *Kultur* as the measure of
greatness.

The contrast in personal style between Nitobe and Kanō was
especially striking. Kanō was the bachelor recluse known only
to a small circle of scholars and writers, while Nitobe had influential friends around the world, and was married to the daugh-
ter of a prominent Quaker family in Philadelphia. The two
headmasters also presented an entirely different appearance to
their students. Kanō was simple and frugal in his life, never car-
ing about clothes and instinctively uneasy before a camera.
Nitobe, on the other hand, affected an air of patrician elegance
as he strode to school with his hair immaculately groomed, or
as he sat at his desk leaning pensively against the right index
finger in a calculated pose for school portraits. The stiff-upper-
lip attitude of his predecessor was nowhere to be found in
Nitobe's genteel mannerisms, mellow voice, and punctilio.

For Nitobe, the first months at Ichikō were something of a
shock. Here on the campus of Japan's most prestigious university preparatory school was an isolated community of students,
immersed in a subculture that seemed totally immune to the

Academy and then attended Sapporo Agricultural College between 1877 and 1881,
when he became a Christian. After studying one year at Tokyo University, Nitobe embarked on a career as an international scholar, spending three years at Johns Hopkins
and then earning a doctorate in two years at Halle University. He served as a member
of the faculty at Sapporo College and as a government administrator in Taiwan before
his tenure at Ichikō from 1906 to 1913. In his later life Nitobe served with distinction in
various roles as Under-Secretary of the League of Nations, President of Tokyo Women's
College, and member of the House of Peers. He died while on tour in Canada on October 15, 1933. For more details, see Kitasawa Sukeo, *The Life of Dr. Nitobe* (Tokyo, 1953).

19. Nitobe Inazō in gentlemanly repose (ca. 1910). From Dai Ichi Kōtō Gakkō Kishukuryō, ed., Kōryōshi (Tokyo, 1925)

mores of civilized society. "Barbarism" or "animalistic vitality" (*dōbutsuteki genki*)[24] were the only words to describe the way students dressed in worn-out uniforms and battered geta, bellowed out "dormitory songs" while walking between classes, used a sleeve for a handkerchief, or stripped to their underwear for a "storm." As if such displays were not enough, Nitobe was also appalled by the brooding withdrawal of students into the truncated philosophies of German neoromantics. The combination of barbarism and philosophic pessimism strained the forbearance of the new headmaster. Future national leaders must adhere to certain codes of social acceptability and be broadminded in their attitude toward thought and culture. Acting on his own conceptions of how a higher school student should behave, Nitobe made a number of widely heralded suggestions intended to raise Ichikō to a "higher level of vitality," to transform a "barbaric" community into a "cultural association."[25]

Nitobe's proposals for civilizing First Higher fell under three headings: cleanliness and sanitation; student-teacher relations; social communication and noblesse oblige. The first entailed a futile campaign to clean up and beautify the campus. Believing

24. Yanaihara Tadao, ed., *Nitobe Hakushi bunshū* (Tokyo, 1936), pp. 311–316.
25. Ibid., pp. 315–316; *Yanaihara Tadao zenshū*, vol. 24 (Tokyo, 1965), pp. 662–666.

that the stalwarts had no justification for living in and exulting in their own filth, Nitobe appealed to the government to remodel Independence Hall and plant cherry trees along the walkways leading to the classroom buildings. Although he got the cherry trees, the proposal to renovate the dormitory was rejected for lack of funds, leaving Nitobe no alternative but to ask that students launch their own cleanup campaign to alleviate the indignities of roach-infested hallways, dust-covered windows, and fetid lavatories. The response to this charge was less than overwhelming. By this time primitivism was so much a part of the subcultural ethos of the dormitory as to make cosmetic appeals an exercise in futility. The run-down appearance of the dormitory and its inhabitants would always be embarrassing to Nitobe; and only after a reassuring visit from General Nogi Maresuke, who saw "vitality" and "masculinity" beneath the unkempt surface, was he willing to let the matter rest.[26]

While his "cleanliness edicts" (seiketsuhō) fell on deaf ears, Nitobe did succeed in breathing new life into the academic curriculum. Rather than playing the role of the traditionalist headmaster who remained aloof from his students, Nitobe sought to break down pedagogical barriers by personally offering the required ethics course for incoming freshmen. The course, which had previously been a forum for senior members of the faculty to preach on Confucian pieties, was transformed into a lively discussion of Western philosophers and history. Nitobe's teaching methods were superb, and soon students who had never displayed much intellectual curiosity were scrambling for front-row seats at the weekly lectures.[27] So enthusiastic was the response, in fact, that the new headmaster felt obliged to rent a special flat across the street from the school, where he could accommodate the demand for additional discussion of philosophic problems.

Despite his interest in Western philosophy, Nitobe was not a "teacher of life." Unlike Iwamoto Tei or Kuwaki Genyoku, whose proclivity for speaking in the most abstract and complex terms left the majority of students in a constant state of bewildered fascination, Nitobe tried to be concrete and direct in his delivery, never hesitating to spin off the simplest English

26. Ishii Mitsuru, Nitobe Inazō den, pp. 275–284.
27. Morito Tatsuo, "Kyōikusha to shite no Nitobe sensei," in Maeda Tamon and Takagi Yasaka, eds., Nitobe Hakushi tsuiokushū (Tokyo, 1936), pp. 324–325; Yanaihara Tadao zenshū, vol. 24, p. 670.

homilies to underscore his points. ("To thee all men be heroes, every woman pure, each place a temple" and "Life is too short to be little" were among his favorites.) The distinctly upbeat, though slightly insipid, tenor of his lectures was indicative of Nitobe's Victorian idealism and his belief that youth who were exposed to the most optimistic and forward-looking literature could be remolded into better human beings. Armed with Carlyle, Tennyson, Longfellow, or Goethe, they could control the "animalistic vitality" or "subconscious" spirit that was fomenting from within. "Even when sleeping," Nitobe told his students "to dream with a clear and pure heart" uninterrupted by "storms" or the brooding thoughts of neoromantic philosophy.[28] When caught in the throes of anguish over "a morsel of Schopenhauer or a thin slice of Nietzsche," the student should first take a cold bath and then launch into *Sartor Resartus*. "He [Carlyle] can best help you in making resolutions, in forming decisions of character at this great crisis of life [adolescence]. Read him! and whether you outgrow him or not, you will be forever thankful for a sober and not sombre, for a solemn and not a sullen, view of life, nature, and God."[29]

Nitobe's homespun philosophy elicited a few sneers from the faculty. After hearing the new headmaster's version of Teufelsdröckh's metaphysical journey, Iwamoto Tei commented: "What a clamor he makes over *Sartor Resartus*!"[30] Fortunately, Nitobe took himself more seriously as an educator than as a philosopher; and he defended his homiletic teaching style as the best means of communicating with a broad cross-section of students. In his opinion, the "teachers of life" and the "old *bushi* types" were too distant and inscrutable. Repeating a familiar higher school idea, but giving it a slightly different thrust, Nitobe declared to his students: "The school must be run like a family. I want you to be my children. I want to be friends with you. I want to increase the level of intimacy."[31] "Intimacy" (*shinmitsu*) and "friendship" (*yūjō*) were favorite expressions reflecting Nitobe's view that the influence of personality (*jinkaku no kunka*) was the primary medium for character development. Unless students felt free to visit his office or

28. Yanaihara, ed., *Nitobe Hakushi bunshū*, pp. 307–308.
29. Kimijima, p. 157; Yanaihara, ed., *Nitobe Hakushi bunshū*, p. 139 (English Section).
30. Hasegawa Saiji, "Iwamoto Tei sensei goroku," p. 185.
31. "Dai ichi gakki sawakai kiji," *DIKGKZ*, no. 172 (Dec. 20, 1907), p. 60.

home at any hour of the day, Nitobe believed he could not discharge his duties as headmaster.[32]

Nitobe's person-centered approach to teaching dovetailed with another of the headmaster's pedagogical ideals: the concept of "sociality" (soshiarichī). The term was introduced to the Ichikō students in an important address on "Monasticism and Sociality" in December 1906.[33] Embellishing his statements with English terminology from Giddings's *Principles of Sociology*, the headmaster argued that a moral education strikes a harmonious balance between the polarities of "restraint" and "culture," "self-suppression" and "self-development." The history of Ichikō revealed a one-sided emphasis on "restraint" or the theory of rejection (kotonakareshugi) epitomized in the castle-school metaphor or, as he called it, "monasticism." Agreeing with the psychological "efficacy" of sequestering students "at a time in their lives when it [monasticism] can best meet their individual spiritual and ethical needs," Nitobe wondered whether seclusion had been overemphasized; whether a "means" for satisfying spiritual ends had not become an end in itself. The students were overly "exclusive," worshipping the "law of continuity" as they "crowded" together in their dormitory. To encourage a synthesis of the "personal self," Nitobe believed that students must balance "monasticism" with the open-minded and positive attitude of "sociality."

When Nitobe Inazō spoke of "sociality," he was not distracted by visions of cocktail parties and poolside chats. He did believe in patrician manners and gentility, and to an extent, his exhortations that students "be sociable" and "cheerful" were aimed at freshening appearances and helping old ladies cross the streets; but there was more to the principle than good manners. "Sociality" was the capacity for "spiritual sympathy" which brings two human beings together as friends; it was the ability to communicate on an idealistic level of "pure" thought and emotion through letters and great books; it was the hallmark of the well-rounded gentleman who was "inclusive" in his attitude toward life.

Nitobe repeated his ideas about balancing "monasticism" ("the law of continuity") with "sociality" ("the law of diver-

32. Tokyo Joshi Daigaku Nitobe Inazō Kenkyūkai, *Nitobe Inazō kenkyū* (Tokyo, 1969), p. 455.
33. Nitobe Inazō, "Rōjōshugi to soshiarichī to ni tsuite," *DIKGKZ*, no. 163 (Jan. 30, 1907), pp. 13–16.

sity") to a student body that was initially split over whether to accept or reject the charge. Moderate intellectuals (led first by Tanaka Tōru, Watsuji Tetsurō, and Morito Tatsuo, and later by Kawai Eijirō and Yanaihara Tadao) welcomed the progressive views of their headmaster and believed that the presence of Nitobe Inazō at Ichikō added momentum to the drive for a comprehensive school spirit. Yanaihara observed: "Under Kinoshita we cultivated the fiery red spirit of the *bushi*; under Kanō Kōkichi a stoic atmosphere of serious study prevailed; and now under the leadership of Headmaster Nitobe, we students can, without inhibition, tend to the spiritual cultivation of our personalities."[34] In Tanaka Tōru's view, Nitobe was the first headmaster to make conscious distinctions between mechanistic cultivation and spiritual cultivation, between the physical restraints of seclusion and the "cultural restraints" imposed by great works of literature.[35] And Watsuji Tetsurō applauded Nitobe for putting an end to the "primitive era" (*genshi jidai*) of roughnecks "driven by homosexual desires" (*dōseiteki yokujō ni kararete*) and for opening the way to a new spiritual essence.[36]

The reaction against Nitobe came largely from athletic stalwarts, who feared that the ethic of "sociality" might be a disguised form of egalitarianism. It was not only the headmaster's call for open-mindedness toward people from different classes and nationalities that worried the stalwarts, but the way he conducted himself in public. In a manner that was thought unbecoming to a headmaster at Ichikō, Nitobe submitted numerous articles during his tenure to the popular, bimonthly magazine *Industrial Japan* and to several women's magazines. Whatever the audience, he appeared to invoke the same theme on the importance of character training and "sociality" for harmony and order. To their horror, some stalwarts were convinced that Nitobe made no distinction between the ideals of Ichikō and the instructional needs of the populace.

The resentment erupted suddenly in a "tea assembly" on March 1, 1909, when two students (Suehiro Izutarō and Ishimoto Eikichi) accused their headmaster of being "a man who tries to please everybody" (*happōbijin*). Exclaimed Suehiro to

34. *Kōryōshi*, p. 319.
35. Tanaka Tōru, "Shinrai shokun no shimei o ronjite tokkanshugi ni oyobu," *DIKGKZ*, no. 179 (Oct. 10, 1907), p. 3.
36. Watsuji Tetsurō, "Seishin o ushinaitaru kōfū," *DIKGKZ*, no. 174 (Feb. 29, 1908), pp. 13–23.

the assembly, which included Nitobe: "It is time to eliminate the confusion between sociality and flunkyism." The two critics also took the occasion to lambaste Nitobe for daring, in the name of "chivalry" and "sociality," to set up special grandstands on the athletic field for the comfort of ladies at the coming intramural games. "The Western custom of showing respect to women at the expense of masculinity will lead us down the path to degeneration," Suehiro fumed. And Ishimoto added a stern warning that the stalwarts would tear down any special seating arrangements before the games ever commenced.[37] Nitobe handled the attacks against him with consummate showmanship. Stepping up to the podium after Ishimoto and Suehiro had had their say, the headmaster pulled a crumpled sheet of paper from his pocket and read a prepared statement of resignation. He had written the statement after taking office, he explained, with the intention of submitting it at any time he believed his services were not appreciated. Amidst sniffles that could be heard across the assembly hall, Nitobe said his one departing wish was that in twenty or thirty years his students would remember him with the same affection that Tom Brown remembered Dr. Arnold.[38]

The rally of emotional support for Nitobe in the aftermath of his dramatic performance made it impossible for him to resign, if indeed that was ever his intention. Whatever the case, the accusation that he was a "populist" was far from the mark. In one of his widely read books, *A Guide to Life* (*Yowatari no michi*), published in 1912, Nitobe stated bluntly: "Society preserves order through the existence of classes. . . . If we esteem nothing but equality, forgetting the existence of class hierarchy, we can never preserve the order of society."[39] The concept of "sociality" was merely an extension of his view of status hierarchy, capsulized in a favorite dictum: "associate with superiors" (*chō-ja ni majiware*).[40] "Sociality" was meaningful only if one were socializing with the right people, that is, with persons who had already cultivated their inner selves. "Since you are students,"

---

37. "Dai jūkyūkai kishukuryō sōritsu kinensai kiji," *DIKGKZ*, no. 185 (March 31, 1909), pp. 91, 96.
38. Ibid., pp. 96–98; Sugimoto Ryō, "Watashi no sannen ni gakki," *Kōryō Komaba 9*, no. 3 (October 1967):14–18.
39. Miwa Kimitada, "Crossroads of Patriotism," Ph.D. dissertation, Princeton University, 1967, pp. 247–248; *Nitobe Inazō zenshū*, vol. 8 (Tokyo, 1970), p. 100.
40. Nitobe, "Rōjōshugi to . . . ," p. 16; Morito Tatsuo, "Kyōikusha to shite no . . . ," pp. 332–333; Miwa Kimitada, pp. 218–219.

he explained, "there is no need to associate directly with society, but you must try to make contact with superior persons, be they great teachers or upperclassmen."[41] In defending his own activities as a writer for popular magazines, Nitobe reminded his students that "sociality" was a two-way path.[42] It required inferiors to seek moral guidance from superiors, but it also required men of culture to make themselves available to a broad segment of the population. Like Matthew Arnold, Nitobe believed that cultivated elites had a solemn obligation to be purveyors of "sweetness and light" to the unenlightened masses. Out of a sense of noblesse oblige, he appealed directly to the people, and he hoped his own students, after perfecting their inner sensibilities, would follow the same path into the public realm.

After deftly turning the protest against him to good advantage, Nitobe Inazō basked in the affection of his students for his remaining years at Ichikō. In the eyes of his most fervent disciples, he was a spiritual prophet who guided educated youth out of the doldrums of a closed-minded and primitive nationalism to a loftier vision of the personal self: the hallmark of Taishō intellectual culture.[43] While such generalizations have validity (by 1910 student writers at distant Fifth Higher were singing Nitobe's praise),[44] two qualifications should be kept in mind. First, the conception of the personal self was already part of the intellectual heritage of the higher schools when Nitobe arrived at Ichikō. Putting the weight of the headmaster's office behind the resynthesis of the school spirit certainly hastened the higher school "reformation,"[45] but Nitobe was not the grand progenitor of social and intellectual change. Indeed, a few student intellectuals found Nitobe's pontifications quite uninspiring. In his short story "Handkerchief" (written in 1916, just three years after graduating from First Higher), Akutagawa Ryūnosuke depicts Ichikō's Christian cosmopolitan as a man obsessed by mannerisms, a man who read Strindberg and Wilde in order to keep up with his literary students.[46] (Along

41. Kōryōshi, p. 1177.
42. Ibid., p. 1177.
43. Kokuritsu Kyōiku Kenkyūjo, ed., Nihon kindai kyōiku hyakunenshi, vol. 5, pp. 1261–1262; Morito, "Kyōikusha to shite no . . . ," p. 318; Matsukuma Toshiko, Nitobe Inazō (Tokyo, 1969), pp. 208, 222.
44. Akase, "Ryūnan shisōshi," p. 27.
45. The students used the English term (Kōryōshi, p. 249).
46. For an English translation, see Kojima Takashi and John McVittie, Exotic Japanese Tales (New York, 1964).

with Akutagawa, the latter included Yamamoto Yūzō, Kikuchi Kan, Tsuneto Kiyoshi, Kume Masao, Matsuoka Yuzuru, and Kurata Hyakuzō.)

Second, personalism and nationalism were not mutually exclusive for Nitobe Inazō. The development of personality (*jinkaku*) was the sine qua non for the growth of "civic responsibility."[47] Nitobe never strayed from the ideal of the higher school as a training ground for national leadership. And though he took little pleasure in reading the Imperial Rescript on Education, leaving such sterile tasks to "old *bushi* types" like Taniyama Shohichirō, Nitobe could be quite explicit about the expected role for his cultured students in an expanding empire. One year before his resignation, he wrote an introduction for the first edition of the student history of Independence Hall, stating that "the people who govern others must first govern themselves (*ta o osamuru kokumin wa mazu onore o osamuru*). Today the Japanese colonial lands are expanding to the West and north, and in the future they will expand to the south. I believe it is crucially important that there be proper training in the governing of other peoples."[48] An ideal practice ground for this noble enterprise, he explained, was Independence Hall, where boys were learning the art of political leadership and acquiring a knowledge of foreign languages and international culture. For Nitobe, the concept of "sociality" and noblesse oblige extended beyond national boundaries. Just as men of culture could inspire the masses in Japan, so too could they bring their power of enlightenment to bear on the less fortunate peoples of the Korean peninsula and southeast Asia. In this sense, Nitobe was, as Komishima Jirō and Miwa Kimitada have argued, a "cultural Darwinist."[49]

Nitobe Inazō was a unique figure in the distinguished line of headmasters at Ichikō. During his seven-year tenure, he wrote for popular journals, served on government commissions, embarked on a lecture tour of six American universities, and published books in English, German, and Japanese. As an international celebrity with liaisons to the Ministry of Education, Nitobe was singularly qualified to be the public defender of the higher schools at a time when the demands of technology and

47. *Yanaihara Tadao zenshū*, vol. 24, pp. 154 and 157; vol. 27, pp. 266–270.
48. *Kōryōshi*, introduction, pp. 5–6.
49. Kamishima Jirō, *Kindai Nihon no seishin kōzō* (Tokyo, 1970), pp. 202, 241; Miwa, pp. 343–349.

the nationalization of youth groups were threatening the ideals of gentlemanly cultivation. With his knowledge of both the British public school and the German Gymnasium, he argued compellingly on Japan's need for government by men of culture (*bunkajin*). That the Special Council on Education ultimately defined the higher school as the functional equivalent of the humanities-centered boarding school in the West is at least partly due to Nitobe's proddings.[50] His speeches at Ichikō are best viewed, therefore, in light of the broader audience of government officials and educators who were critically reevaluating the purpose and goal of preparatory education. In calling for a redefinition of the gentleman as a well-rounded personality ("sociable," "inclusive," and capable of harmonizing human relations in an age of materialistic conflict), Nitobe was not reforming the higher schools as much as he was justifying their existence.

The Spirit of the Taishō Higher Schools: The Triumph of the Personal Self

During the debates of the early 1900s, the majority of students—athletes and intellectuals—agreed in the persisting notion of the higher school as a spiritual entity that conferred status on the chosen few. Controversy arose over the nature and manifestation of the "school spirit": the traditional stalwart believed in the nobility of a comrade-in-arms psychology nurtured on the athletic field, while moderate intellectuals argued that the spirit of the school was as strong as the culture and personality of the individual student. By 1910 the debates had subsided, and the importance of culture and the inner self to the uniqueness of the higher school was widely acknowledged. At a dinner assembly in honor of the Ichikō baseball team in May 1911, the transitional sentiments of the higher school stalwart were reflected in Executive Committeeman Nakajima Takanao's charge to embrace the antinomies of self-sacrifice (*gisei seishin*) and self-awakening (*jiko kakusei*), club loyalty and soul-to-soul friendship, physical training and culture. "In this world where human relationships are frozen by the progress of science,"

---

50. For example Nitobe was a member of the advisory panel that opposed Komatsubara Eitarō's proposal in 1910 for a streamlined and vocation-oriented higher school. See Kyōikushi Hensankai, ed., *Meiji ikō kyōiku* . . . , vol. 5, pp. 1172–1177.

Nakajima asserted, "the soul-to-soul friendship and spirit of sacrifice at Ichikō gives us a sense of everlasting life."[51]

The wholistic approach to self-cultivation drew a wide and enthusiastic following among Taishō higher school students, who refused to surrender to a machine civilization that viewed people as extensions of material objects. The Meiji Restoration, asserted one Second Higher student in 1916, had produced an "external, materialistic revolution," but the coming "Taishō Restoration" would eventuate in an "internal revolution of mind and spirit."[52] At Ichikō the vanguards of this spiritual revolution came from the Debate Club. Although the club had sponsored the forums during the Uozumi controversy, the members revealed their intention in 1909 to transcend the fruitless "battles between individualism and institutionalism" and concentrate instead on the exploration of the personal self: "Today the Debate Club is moving quickly in the direction of religious and spiritual matters. . . . Our attention to problems of the external world is diminishing, and there is a feeling that we should remove ourselves from direct involvement in dormitory politics."[53]

The new club orientation was exemplified in a talk given by its chairman, Morito Tatsuo, in 1909 on "The One-Day Flower" (*Ichinichi no hana*). Reflecting the false modesty that was so typical of student writing during the Taishō period, Morito made the following confession:

> Intelligent young people like yourselves may become people who will obtain high positions and status in government and go on to lead the society; but a humble person like me prefers to be like one small lily in the cavernous depth of the valley which blooms and withers without recognition by man. Although the lily blooms but one day, it does so with the splendor of a May garden.[54]

Morita was voicing an existential concern for "being" and self-fulfillment in a private life. He was also declaring an aspiration to cultivate the inner self as inconspicuously as possible, without the *Sturm und Drang* that had propelled an earlier generation of students.

51. "Dai san gakki zenryō sawakai kiji," *DIKGKZ*, no. 207 (June 15, 1911), pp. 101–102.

52. Kikegawa Hiroshi, "Shidō kaikyū taru no sekimu," *Shōshikai zasshi*, no. 106 (June 1916), p. 257.

53. *Kōryōshi*, pp. 316 and 323.

54. Ibid., p. 323.

20. Outside reading at Hirosaki Higher. Courtesy of Yamauchi Naosuke

The importance of "being" over "doing" had a special attraction for Taishō higher school students, who were less confident than their Meiji forebears about occupational prospects and were fascinated by the semimystical aura of self-exploration and personal enlightenment. Everyone had a self (*jiga*), but very few persons could cultivate the self or, as one Nikō student put it, "listen carefully to the words which are secretly spoken from the fountain of the *individuum*."[55] To be so sensitive to the voice from within, one had first to be liberated from all external distractions of the temporal world. The personal universe of the higher school student was an ideal realm, symbolized by Morito's white lily and unaffected by the laws of empiricism or technocracy.

The journey into the recesses of the inner self was put in archetypal form, as a guide to student readers, in seminal works by two Taishō writers, who were themselves deeply affected by the late-Meiji higher school experience. I refer to Abe Jirō's *Santarō's Diary* (*Santarō no nikki*) and Kurata Hyakuzō's *Setting out with Love and Understanding* (*Ai to ninshiki to no shuppatsu*), published respectively in 1914 and 1917. The two books, along with

55. Ishimoda Tadashi, "Nikōsei no shisō no kaibō," *Shōshikai zasshi*, no. 145 (May, 1930), p. 12.

Nishida Kitarō's *Study of Goodness* (*Zen no kenkyū*), were "higher school bibles," must reading for all students during the 1920s and 1930s and hence deserving of our attention.

Abe Jirō began writing the self-probing essays and vignettes which make up *Santarō's Diary* in 1908, one year after graduating from Tokyo University and three years after his speech at Ichikō during the Uozumi controversy. The fact that he wrote the first section as an apprentice writer in his late twenties gives the admittedly "immature" and "imperfect" ramblings a certain authenticity to young readers. The book is not a day-by-day diary but "an intimate record of my inner life," as expressed by his shadow self and narrator, Aota Santarō.[56] The kaleidoscopic collection of reminiscences, internal dialogues, portraits of imaginary friends, and philosophic discourses on "internal morality," "love," "death," and "dream houses" represent a spiritual testimony to the private and lonely struggle of one youth, who is "searching for the light" within his inner self.

In writing *Santarō's Diary*, Abe makes clear that he, unlike Uozumi Kageo, is not asserting "the authority of the self" (*jiko no ken'i*) but merely probing "the content of the self" (*jiko no naiyō*). The problem with young rebels is that they act without appreciating the depth of their inner spirit. "The power to lead the true country of the self," he explains, "is not the power of a man moving around in a bold manner; rather it is the power to push forward and sink into the inner self."[57] Accordingly, Santarō broods at his desk for hours while his "inner voice" berates him for worldly thoughts. However much time he allots for reading, contemplating, and occasionally chewing his fingernails, Santarō is proud to stand above the common "children of society" (*shakai no ko*) who accept the banalities of everyday life. At least he is a "truth seeker" (*gudōsha*) who will someday discover the inner light, entitling him to become a "missionary" (*dendōsha*) for spiritual enlightenment.[58] Although the detail in *Santarō's Diary* is not strictly autobiographical, the sequence of selections mirrors Abe's own rise from an unknown "truth seeker" to a grand "missionary" for Taishō youth.

Kurata Hyakuzō's *Setting out with Love and Understanding* is also a highly personal collection of short essays which disclose the internal struggles and changing philosophic perceptions of

56. Abe Jirō, *Gōhon Santarō no nikki* (Tokyo, 1962), introduction, p. 11.
57. Ibid., p. 104. See also pp. 140–142.
58. Ibid., pp. 285–289.

a youth on the road to self-discovery. Half of the book was written while Kurata was still a student at Ichikō between 1912 and
1915; and three essays were first published in the *Society of
Friends Magazine,* creating an immediate sensation among his
classmates.[59] Several of the themes in *Setting out with Love and
Understanding* dovetail with *Santarō's Diary*: the disdain for materialism, the spiritual quest for identity, the importance of a
private life and personal relationships. But Kurata is far more
direct and emotionally involved in his writing than Abe Jirō.
Calling himself a *Naturkind,* Kurata trumpets an ideal of "instinctive spiritualism" or "absolute purity" (*tettei tetsubi jun'itsu*)
that is not amenable to conventional social mores. Fearing that
the concept of "sociality" embraced an artificial code of morality, Kurata chides Nitobe Inazō and his followers for failing to
recognize that the inner self is lodged in Nishida Kitarō's unmitigated state of "pure experience" and "whole being."[60]

Kurata's excursus is primarily concerned with the intensity of
experience, specifically the experience of love as a vehicle for
self-discovery. In his approach to the problem of love, a pattern
of development emerges from the author's changing perceptions, which document the growth of a late adolescent. Published originally in the *Society of Friends Magazine* in 1912, the
book's first essay, "Longing," is a confession of the homophilic
love between the author and his best friend, Nakamura Sannosuke. Their Platonic "union of souls" is temporarily fractured
over philosophic definitions of "purity" and "pleasure" until it
is rehealed by a shared reading of Nishida's *Study of Goodness.*[61]
Then, overcome by heterosexual love in the fall of 1913, Kurata
intellectualizes his feelings in the essay "Struggling to Discover
Self within the Opposite Sex." Yet, just when he thinks he has
found the ideal woman, Kurata's *bella donna* closes the door on
her romantic suitor, triggering a torrential confession, "The
Path Walked by a Person Who Has Lost His Love." "How can I
rescue my inner self?" Kurata wonders in the introduction to
this climactic essay, which appeared in the *Society of Friends
Magazine* in the winter of 1914. The sole recourse is to admit that
"instinctive love flares up like the coals on a fire" but cannot
sustain a lasting personal relationship.[62] Recognizing the "fal-

59. *Kōryōshi,* pp. 268–269.
60. Kurata Hyakuzō, *Ai to ninshiki to no shuppatsu,* in *Sekai kyōyō zenshū,* vol. 3
(Tokyo, 1963), pp. 76, 83; for analysis of Nishida Kitarō's thought, see pp. 34–54.
61. Ibid., pp. 15–34.
62. Ibid., p. 90.

lacy" of uniting instinct with spirit, Kurata turns to an idealized conception of "Christian love" or "love of neighbor" (*rinjin no ai*), which exists outside the physical realm.[63] Like Abe, Kurata ultimately combines his vision of a private life and personal relationships with a transcending ideal of social harmony.

Taishō and early Shōwa higher school students never grew tired of reading Abe Jirō and Kurata Hyakuzō. Well-used copies of their books were so ubiquitous in the dormitories that they—along with the black cape of the uniform, the tall *geta*, and the school flag—became part of the symbolic structure of the subculture. Why were these books so popular? One reason is the authors' understanding of the psychological state of their anticipated audience. Kurata introduced his book as a "monument to my adolescence" (*jibun no seishun no kinenhi*) and a "present" for "those youth who will follow me and who will have the same sincerity, purity, and courage that I had."[64] Besides understanding the potential for philosophic questioning among adolescents, Abe and Kurata made social sense out of the spiritual tribulations of sensitive boarding-school students.[65] They generalized the personal voyage into the inner self and transformed it into a theoretical expression of the collective sentiment and ideals of the student elite. The more obscurantist or unintelligible were their writings, the more they flattered their readers. For to immerse oneself in the ruminations of Abe or Kurata was to enter into a spiritual covenant with the authors that placed the Taishō student on a pedestal above the "children of society," who "crawled" through life without discovering the inner self.[66] Thus the fulfillment of the adolescent need for a philosophy of life became a prerogative of status; and thus the quest for identity became inseparable from the quest for social ideology.

"The Ichikō student," Akutagawa Ryūnosuke is quoted as saying in the early 1920s, "is more philosophic than Kant."[67] Certainly, many students considered themselves amateur phi-

---

63. Ibid., pp. 95–103, 149–161.
64. Ibid., pp. 10–11.
65. My thinking on the issue of literature and consciousness is influenced by Lucien Goldmann, "The Moral Universe of the Playwright," in Elizabeth and Tom Burns, eds., *Sociology of Literature and Drama* (Harmondsworth, 1973), pp. 311–317; Diane Laurenson and Alan Swingewood, *The Sociology of Literature* (New York, 1972), esp. chap. 3.
66. Abe Jirō likens those who blend with society to snakes. *Santarō no nikki*, p. 23.
67. Sō Sakon, "Ai to ninshiki to no shuppatsu, Dai Ichi Kōtō Gakkō IV" (Seishun fudoki 80), *Shūkan Asahi* (Jan. 27, 1978), p. 103.

losophers as they bellowed forth the anthem that resounded through all the higher schools in late Meiji and Taishō: "Dekanshō (Descartes, Kant, and Schopenhauer)! Dekanshō! Half the year we live with them. The other half we sleep."[68] The appetite for philosophy was more than a matter of singing a song, however, or of reading epics like *Santarō's Diary* and *Setting out with Love and Understanding*. A sampling of the essays and short stories from any combination of school magazines in the 1920s reveals that student writers were earnestly attempting to duplicate the struggles of Aota Santarō in their own lives. For example, at about the same time that the school magazine at Fifth Higher featured "The Transition from an Unconscious to a Conscious Existence," "From a Diary," and "A Talk with a Friend," the readers of the newly established magazine at Yamagata Higher enjoyed "The Social Significance of Isolation in Nature" and "Spring Melancholia," while contributors to the Sixth Higher magazine wrote on "Environment and Real Existence," "The Consciousness of Objects," and "To a Departing Friend." Not to be outdone, one Suzuki Yasuzō of Second Higher moved his classmates with "Recollections of a Lonely Evening: Skepticism Over the World View of New Idealism."[69] Whether in poetry, romantic short stories, or neo-Hegelian excurses, the "favorite enterprise" of Taishō students, according to Ōmuro Teiichirō, was the analysis of personal feelings and "the investigation into the fundamental problems of thought and existence."[70]

As one might imagine, this ground swell of interest in art and philosophy necessitated an expansion and modification of the extracurriculum. The well-established literary clubs could no longer accommodate the burgeoning number of amateur writers. Nor could they guarantee space in the school magazines for every cultural group on campus to communicate its aesthetic or philosophic view. Thus, in accordance with Nitobe Inazō's

68. John K. Fairbank, et al., eds., *East Asia: The Modern Transformation* (Boston, 1965), p. 544.

69. Saeki Gendō, "Muishikiteki seikatsu yori ishikiteki seikatsu e no tenkō," *Ryūnankai zasshi*, no. 198 (July 1, 1926); Honji Tadao, "Nikki no naka yori," *Ryūnankai zasshi*, no. 202 (July 1, 1927); Saegusa Hirone, "Yūjin to no hanashi," *Ryūnankai zasshi*, no. 200 (Dec. 1, 1926); Tanaka Yukio, "Shinzen kakuri no shakai igi," and Sakamoto Etsuo, "Haru kanashiku," in *Yamagata Kōtō Gakkō Kōyūkai zasshi* no. 11 (1923); Sawada Saburō, "Genjitsu seikatsu to kankyō," *Dai Roku Kōtō Gakkō Kōyūkai zasshi*, no. 68 (July 7, 1924); Tamaki Takashi, "Taishō no ishiki ni tsuite," and Miwa Katsuo, "Sarinishi tomo e," in ibid., no. 70 (Feb. 28, 1925); Suzuki's article is discussed in Takase Naotomo, ed., *Shōshikai zenshi* (Sendai, 1937), p. 532.

70. Ōmuro Teiichirō, *Kōkō seikatsuron*, p. 66.

21. The English Literary Society at Hirosaki Higher. Courtesy of Yamauchi Naosuke

"principle of diversity," an array of small literary and philosophic circles sprouted on the campuses. Since each had its pamphlet or small magazine, the total annual output of printed essays, short stories, and poetry from the Taishō higher schools was prodigious. Along with the mushrooming of study groups was an expansion of clubs devoted to music, painting, history, drama, and nature viewing. The aggregation of these diverse activities under one roof brought the higher school dormitory close to Nitobe's ideal of a "cultural association."

Simultaneously, the traditional rituals of "dormitory life" were modified in response to the expanding cultural interests of the students. Now, the *konpa* was as likely to become a "bull session" on "pure experience" as a traditional accounting of institutional folklore. "The battlefields seemed limitless," recalled Akutagawa of his lengthy disputes with Ichikō classmates over everything from Whitman's poetry to the meaning of creative evolution.[71] It was not uncommon either in the 1920s for younger faculty to shed their black gowns and join their students for *konpa* charged with philosophic argument and overflowing cups of sake. Paralleling the changing format of *konpa*

71. Howard Hibbett, "Akutagawa Ryūnosuke and the Negative Ideal," in Albert M. Craig and Donald H. Shively, eds., *Personality in Japanese History* (Berkeley, 1970), p. 432.

22. Formal instruction. Hirosaki Higher, courtesy of Yamauchi Naosuke

was the rise of a new genre of "dormitory songs." With the organization of music clubs, the lyrics and melodies of student compositions softened noticeably after World War I. Exemplifying this trend toward lyricism was the famous "Circling Lake Biwa Song" of Sankō.[72] Composed in 1919, the song tells of a group of Sankō students "drifting at the mercy of the waves" and communing with "rippling waters and rising mist." The song contains no reference to school spirit or athletic prowess, and the undulating melody is better suited to the violin than to the beating rhythms of a drum.

Accompanying these innovations was the broadening perception of the school as an intimate network of friends, or what one Sixth Higher student in 1919 called "an ideal community of true persons."[73] Unlike their Meiji forebears, the Taishō higher school students attached great meaning to horizontal, "I-thou" relationships, which thrived in private without seriously undermining the public, vertical hierarchy of "juniors" and "seniors." In countless essays and vignettes, students explored one an-

72. Ishii Kahei and Morita Yoshiaki, *Kurenai moyuru* (Tokyo, 1965), p. 13.

73. Ugata Junzō, "Ryōseikatsu o tsuranuite," *Dai Roku Kōtō Gakkō Kōyūkai zasshi*, no. 53 (June 30, 1919), p. 25; also see Ichii Keikichi, "Jichiryō no mokuteki," *DIKGKZ*, no. 202 (Feb. 11, 1911), p. 8.

23. A young teacher joins a "Konpa." Hirosaki Higher, courtesy of Yamauchi Naosuke

other's innermost feelings, sorting out the complex bundle of emotions that drove a friend to sit alone under a tree one day and to laugh and sing the next. Given the ages of the students and their limited access to young women, the residence halls overflowed with sexual energy. Yet, in contrast to the Meiji period, when sensitive youths complained of "storms" turning into homosexual assaults, the Taishō students appear to have vented their love for each other in a torrent of words, with little spillover—aside from arms wrapping around shoulders—into more explicit physical acts.

The diversification of club life and increasing sensitivity to personal relationships did not spell an end to campus primitivism. Athletic rivalries between higher schools continued at a feverish pitch through the prewar period; and higher school students in the 1920s were still unable to resist the nocturnal urge to peel off their clothes for a "storm" or open the windows for a rite of "dormitory rain." Concurrently, intellectual youth in the Taishō higher schools conformed to traditional standards of dress and behavior. Their frequently shaggy hair and tattered uniforms suggested that they were no more willing than their athletic peers to abide by conventional middle-class etiquette.

24. Roommates relaxing on open bedrolls. Hirosaki Higher, courtesy of Yamauchi Naosuke

Moreover, they were equally ill at ease with their feminine cohorts. Even when writing of heterosexual love in school magazines, students were idealistic in the manner of Kawabata Yasunari's Ichikō protagonist, who can watch and ponder, but cannot touch the pretty dancer from Izu. There were a few "decadents" among student writers, notably at Sankō, who violated ascetic taboos. But most students interested in philosophy and art were "wild intellectuals" (*yaseiteki chishikijin*), to borrow another phrase from the prewar educator Ōmuro Teichirō, who, like Aota Santarō, pushed forward into a self-oriented world of thought, refusing to compromise on appearance or to ingratiate the opposite sex.[74]

In the "dormitory histories" and school magazines published between 1910 and 1930, the Taishō higher school students proclaimed themselves the beneficiaries of historical progress. Here they referred not to the breakthroughs in heavy industry, mass transportation, and consumer marketing, but to "the progress of spiritual civilization" (*seishinteki bunmei no shinpo*)[75]

74. Ōmuro Teiichirō, *Kōkō seikatsuron*, p. 45.
75. "Shunu gōgō," *Ryūnankai zasshi*, no. 125 (June 20, 1909), p. 111.

25. Freedom and long hair. Hirosaki Higher, courtesy of Yamauchi Naosuke

manifested in the growth of the school spirit from the rigid character-building models of the foundation period to the graduated stages of primitivism, athleticism, individualism, personalism, and self-cultivation. By the late 1920s "the life of the self" (*jiga no seikatsu*) was such an integral part of the higher school experience that few students, including the heartiest athletes, would admit ignorance of the categorical imperatives or the nature of "pure experience." And for good reason: the triumph of the personal self was the apotheosis of status. Anyone with money could join the "modern boys"; and anyone who read one of the popular storybooks on higher school life could imitate a "storm" (an object of fascination for thousands of middle school students).[76] But to duplicate the intricate cultural style of the higher school students, to expatiate upon the aesthetic values of love and beauty, to write in neo-Kantian idiom: these were tasks that lay well beyond the grasp of most Taishō youth.

Leftist Students and Higher School Tradition

We [at City College in the 1930s] experienced our radicalism as a privilege of rank, not as a burden imposed by a malignant fate. It would never

76. Akutagawa Ryūnosuke notes the fascination among middle-school students, in *Akutagawa Ryūnosuke zenshū*, vol. 7 (Tokyo, 1958), p. 20.

have occurred to us to denounce anyone or anything as "elitist." The
elite was us—the "happy few" who had been chosen by History to guide
our fellow creatures toward a secular redemption.

IRVING KRISTOL, "MEMOIRS OF A TROTSKYIST" (1977)

A discussion of student thought in the Taishō higher schools would be incomplete without some mention of the impact of critical social theory on the campus subculture. Since an excellent study of Japan's first generation of leftist students, with a focus on Tokyo University, has been written by Henry D. Smith,[77] there is no need to rehearse the sequence of events and characters that highlighted the "movement." Suffice it to say that student interest in social reform and Marxism was born at the end of World War I (in the immediate aftermath of the Rice Riots, the Bolshevik Revolution, and the beginning of Yoshino Sakuzō's campaign for "democracy") and continued into the early 1930s, when government suppression forced a dwindling band of activists to operate in secrecy. During this period, the center of organization was in the universities, notably Tokyo and Kyoto universities, yet even there the total number of students who actually joined leftist societies never exceeded 3 percent, and was usually considerably less.[78] With such small memberships, it is not surprising that the influence of the student left on the course of political events before World War II was, as Smith has argued, "negligible if any."[79] And perhaps one reason to account for this lack of political influence by students, who prided themselves on being part of a critical "intelligentsia," was that so many educated leftists began formulating their beliefs within the conservative, and most unrevolutionary, setting of the higher schools.

The budding interest in social theory among higher school students in late Meiji and Taishō was a natural outgrowth of the broadening cultural horizons of the campus community. Once students took the plunge into philosophy and theory, they considered it their obligation, as well-informed gentlemen and as exponents of Nitobe's "law of diversity," to become acquainted with the full sweep of intellectual history, including contemporary social thought. At Ichikō, interest in social theory was first evidenced in the winter of 1911, when the Debate Club invited

77. Henry Smith, *Japan's First Student Radicals* (Cambridge, Mass., 1972).
78. Ibid., p. 139.
79. Ibid., p. 266.

the Christian humanist and writer, Tokutomi Roka, to speak at a special student assembly. Although Tokutomi used the occasion to decry the government's handling of the Great Treason Trial and to implore his listeners to serve the Emperor outside the established political apparatus, the Debate Club members quickly reassured their headmaster and alarmed government officials that they were impressed only by Tokutomi's "sincerity" (seii) and his concluding charge to "cultivate the personal self."[80] During the year following the Tokutomi incident, a small group of Debate Club enthusiasts continued to be attracted to humanist critics, including Yoshino Sakuzō and Kawakami Hajime, who believed that the key to reforming society and mitigating the costs of industrialization lay in the moral regeneration of man.[81] The extent to which late Meiji and early Taishō student critics were genuinely concerned by the plight of society's underlings and the extent to which they were searching for a more encompassing vision of the personal self is difficult to distinguish.[82]

In the years immediately following World War I, there was a surge of popular ferment and a proliferation of reform organizations that, initially at least, shared a vague yearning for universal suffrage and a more parliamentary form of government. The Ichikō students were not so insulated in their "castle school" as to be unaware of the social and political upheavals outside. In the dormitory history, the entry for 1919–20 begins with the statement that the "signal fires of revolution" (kakumei no hōka), ignited in Russia and Germany, heralded "a turning point in world history." Like other world powers, Japan was entering a "new age" (shinjidai) of massive industrial output, burgeoning cities, and a "labor problem (rōdō mondai) heretofore unseen in our country."[83] While the school annalist later conceded that popular pressure for the extension of democratic freedom at this "stage" in history was "only natural," he ex-

80. Kōryōshi, p. 327; Kenneth Strong's introduction in Tokutomi Kenjiro, Footprints in the Snow, pp. 37–38; Nihon Keizai Shinbunsha, ed., Watakushi no rirekisho, vol. 13 (Tokyo, 1963), pp. 117–119.

81. Tetsuo Najita, "Some Reflections on Idealism in the Political Thought of Yoshino Sakuzō," in Bernard S. Silberman and H. D. Harootunian, eds., Japan in Crisis, pp. 29–66; Gail Lee Bernstein, Japanese Marxist: A Portrait of Kawakami Hajime, 1879–1946 (Cambridge, Mass., 1976).

82. Shinobu Seisaburō argues that students were striving to discover the personal self by resolving social and labor problems. See Shinobu Seisaburō, Taishō demokurashii shi (Tokyo, 1958), pp. 794–795.

83. Kōryōshi, p. 61.

pressed fear that men of responsibility might be captivated by the fashions of the day (*ryūkō ni toraware*) and thus lose sight of the "spirit of noble tradition" (*tōtoki dentō no seishin*). "When the world is in this state [of turbulence]," the writer continued, "it is our responsibility to let the public know about [Ichikō's] righteous history (*seigi no rekishī*), which is colored by the beauty of tradition."[84] It was in this spirit that Ichikō stalwarts celebrated the thirty-year anniversary of the opening of Independence Hall, on March 1, 1920. Capping the festivities was an "anniversary dinner assembly," which saw many old graduates come to the podium to pay homage to the "four tenets," the "flag which protects our country," and the indomitable "school spirit." Abe Jirō delivered the keynote address on the "significance of traditions from a philosophic perspective."[85]

In a school of nearly a thousand, there may have been a dozen students who participated actively in the "democracy movement" of 1919 by campaigning for suffrage among workers in Tokyo.[86] Years of singing "dormitory songs" about the "vulgar society," however, made the "to-the-people" campaign as unrealistic for the Ichikō stalwarts as it was for their older university peers. And like the latter, the higher school student activists soon abandoned their populist slogans and refocused attention on the "inner-campus movement" (*kōnai undō*) in order to raise the consciousness of the "intelligentsia" (*chishiki kaikyū*) before it ventured back to the factories. In reality, the "social studies research club" (*shakai shisō kenkyūkai*), which was the organizational unit for this internal movement, became one of the maze of philosophic and literary societies that flourished on higher school campuses.

The Ichikō Social Studies Research Club was founded in November 1919 with fourteen charter members.[87] The stated purpose of the group was "the study of social problems" through reading, discussion, and lectures by eminent professors. The latter would include a galaxy of Taishō liberals (Kawai Eijirō, Ōyama Ikuo, Yoshino Sakuzō, Abe Isoo, Nitobe

84. Ibid., p. 75.

85. Ibid., p. 74.

86. According to *Kōryōshi* (p. 1288) there were about fourteen political activists at Ichikō, but how many of these actually joined ranks with the Shinjinkai is unclear. The origins of the Shinjinkai at Tokyo University and their early "evangelistic impulse" to go directly to the people are discussed in Smith, chap. 3.

87. *Kōryōshi*, p. 1288. Unlike Ichikō, the debate club provided the structure for leftist activity, as seen in Nagamatsu Eiichi, ed., *Mizutani Chōzaburō den* (Tokyo, 1963), pp. 9–11; Kikukawa Tadao, *Gakusei shakai undōshi* (Tokyo, 1947), pp. 144–147, and 227–230.

Inazō), whose idealistic lectures on such topics as "The Conceptualization of Social Problems" or "Social Problems and Existence" could bring hundreds of students to club meetings. However, regular gatherings for the discussion of socialist writers were more sparsely attended, and this worried the active membership. Feeling pressed to allay the fears of skeptical peers, the Social Studies Research Club strained to demonstrate the respectability of its activities as a natural extension of the Ichikō tradition. "Monasticism" and "self-government," they reminded fellow students, should never become a barrier to the free exchange of ideas or an excuse for closed-mindedness. On the contrary, the self-governing dormitory was established to protect students from arbitrary government or faculty regulations that would truncate their philosophy of life. Accordingly, the founding members of the Social Science Research Club assured their classmates: "We bear a grave responsibility to follow a single path for defending the autonomy and intellectual freedom of Independence Hall!"[88] Although they introduced new theories and vocabulary for the analysis of history and philosophy, the Ichikō leftists were rarely iconoclastic on matters pertaining to the alma mater. Instead, they tempered any criticism of house rituals with glowing acknowledgments that "the three years of our life on this hill are truly utopian"; that it was the special mission of their club to preserve the privilege of self-government; that the members were "burning with the spirit of sacrifice for our Independence Hall."[89]

It is tempting to say that these lavish claims of allegiance were merely cover for underground plots and schemes, which was the initial view of the Ministry of Education. But the lifestyle of student leftists was actually in the best tradition of the higher school stalwart. Social studies research groups adhered to the same ceremonial format of other clubs and fraternal groups in the dormitory, staging periodic *konpa*, and occasionally setting aside a weekend for communal living (*gasshuku*) patterned after the athletic training camp. Moreover the Spartan standard of student leftists rivaled that of any athlete. "Idleness is a sin; pleasure is selfish; decadence is cowardly!" These were the proud mottoes of Ichikō activists in 1925 as they com-

88. *Kōryōshi*, p. 1287.
89. Ibid., pp. 1290 and 1292. Similar effusions of institutional loyalty were made by members of the Sankō Debate Club, who attempted to justify their sociological studies within the framework of the school motto: "freedom." ("Jiyūryōshi," p. 76; Ishii and Morita, pp. 453–454.)

mitted themselves to a "manly" life of "total research in social studies."[90] The asceticism and emphasis on group bondage among leftist students helps to explain why social studies research groups were able to attract so many athletes to their ranks. In a recent article in the Ichikō alumni bulletin on "Judo and the Communist Party," Suzuki Hajime argues that students in the martial arts were as likely to become socialists as right-wing defenders of the kokutai.[91] Moreover, according to Smith, the stoic traditions of "communal living" and the friendship networks that originated in the higher schools were continued by student leftists throughout their university years. Long after they had entered Tokyo University, members of the Shinjinkai were split into friendship factions based on associations in the Ichikō Judo Club, or the Sankō Debate Club, or the Urawa Higher Literary Club.[92]

Together with their commitment to the ascetic life and community of friends, the higher school leftists engaged in a variety of on-campus activities designed to improve their standing and self-image. Members of the study societies, for example, were at the forefront of mutual assistance organizations (kyōsaibu), which collected funds from students, faculty, and alumni for needy students whose families had been stricken by natural disaster or economic depression. "House communism," to use Nitobe's phrase again, was always characteristic of the higher school community, and the mutual assistance organizations seem to have been an extension of this ideal. Higher school leftists also participated in a national federation of student Marxists (Gakusei Rengōkai) founded on the Tokyo University Campus in late 1922. Through affiliation with the federation, isolated study groups of five or ten students were able to extend horizontal contacts with sympathetic peers across the country, although these links proved rather fragile in the face of the combined opposition of higher school and university administrators.[93]

More ambiguous was the role of campus leftists in the outbreak of uprisings that swept through the higher schools (and many other schools) between 1926 and 1932. In almost every in-

90. Kōryōshi, p. 1319; also see pp. 1292, 1297, and 1310.

91. Suzuki Hajime, "Jūdō to Kyōsantō," Kōryō Komaba 10, no. 3 (July 1968):54–55. The appeal to athletic values is also apparent at Seventh Higher. See Sakudō Yoshio and Etō Takehito, eds., Hokushin naname ni sasu tokoro (Tokyo, 1970), p. 153.

92. Smith, pp. 41, 171, 178–179, and 252.

93. Ibid., pp. 187–194.

stance, large numbers of discontented students called for campus "alliances" or "strikes" as if adhering to a radical strategy for mobilization. Yet, on closer examination, the uprisings in early Shōwa appear to have had little ideological basis, conforming instead to the "accountability pattern" discussed in chapter 3. While widespread economic dislocation and the prospects of future unemployment may have contributed to student uneasiness (especially in the universities and technical schools, where the step into the job market was imminent), the higher school uprisings usually centered around the personality and policies of the headmaster. At Matsuyama Higher in 1926, where the first in this new wave of uprisings took place, the students went on strike over the sudden and arbitrary ruling by the headmaster to fail anyone who did not attend classes for more than a month. (Being absent from class had always been viewed as a student privilege.) At Second Higher, one year later, students rose up in arms over Headmaster Okano Yoshisaburō's decision to assert greater control over the extracurricular confederation, thus, in the words of one protester, "destroying the history of Meizen Dormitory, trampling on the tenets, and denying us our freedom."[94] The ensuing strike forced the Ministry of Education to transfer Okano to Sixth Higher, where, two years later, students staged another strike over his hardline policies and defiance of tradition.[95] And so the pattern was repeated at a number of academies, where the headmaster was accused either of restricting student freedom (Sankō, 1927) or of being insensitive to an epidemic of dysentery in the dormitory (Yamagata, 1928) or of actually embezzling funds from the coffers of the extracurricular confederation (Hirosaki, 1929). Even in those instances when a strike was called in reaction to a stiffening administration posture toward leftists, as at Matsue Higher in 1929, the protesters might first announce, "We are entering into this strike with a pure and sincere heart, as Japanese and as students without any ideological motivation."[96]

Whatever the role of leftist strategy in these uprisings, it is clear that there could never have been all-campus strikes, often

94. Kikugawa, pp. 400–401, 405–406; Atoda Reizō, *Nikō o kataru*, p. 116.
95. Kobayashi Hiroyuki, p. 291.
96. Etō Takehito and Fujita Gōshi, *Suishō meguru-kyūsei kōtō gakkō monogatari Matsue Kōkō hen* (Tokyo, 1967), p. 40. For details on the strike at Sankō in 1927, see Kuwabara Takeo, *Kuwabara Takeo zenshū*, vol. 7 (Tokyo, 1969), pp. 36–37. For the strike at Yamagata, see Yamagata Kōtō Gakkō Gakuryōshi Hensan Iinkai, ed., *Gakuryōshi* (Yamagata, 1938), pp. 86–87; and for Hirosaki, see *Kokū ni habataki: Hirosaki Kōtō Gakkō gojūnenshi* (Tokyo, 1970), pp. 153–154.

backed by alumni and in some cases by faculty, without the help of a few bungling headmasters.[97] The failing of an administrator like Okano Yoshisaburō was that he, in the words of the Second Higher strikers, "ignored the personal self."[98] Even Takayama Shūgetsu, who served at the time as a student supervisor under the direction of the Ministry of Education, admitted that a primary cause for all the commotion in the higher schools was the shallow "political ethos" of several headmasters, who were mere administrators and lacked the stature of a Nitobe Inazō, a Orita Hikoichi, or a Kanō Kōkichi.[99]

The higher school uprisings, whether or not they were politically motivated, should not divert our attention, however, from the principal activity of student leftists: study. To be a member in good standing of a research group required an enormous allotment of time for reading from selected texts and for joining in marathon discussions that could last through the night. Coming to Marxism by way of Taishō humanism, as the students did, it is not surprising that the emphasis in the discussion groups was on "being" over "doing." Yet, unlike the idealists, who were accused of "peeling the self to nothingness," the journey into Marxist theory and literary criticism was directed toward the spiritual awakening of a "new self" suspended in the realm of proletarian consciousness. The leaders of the Ichikō Social Studies Research Club elaborated: "With the spirit of a group of religious truth seekers who recognize new social phenomena, we shall polish our personalities, criticize every value, and, thereby, gain release from our deadlocked selves. We shall move forward convinced that new beliefs, truths, morals, and literature will light our path."[100]

Disclaimers notwithstanding, one suspects that the "polishing" of a "new self" was not that far removed from Abe Jirō's "personal self," and it probably required even more rigorous gymnastic feats of the mind. With such topics as "Breaking out of Metaphysics and Entering into the Dialectic" or "Pure Consciousness and Illusion," candlelight discussions among student leftists extended the outer limits of abstraction. It was, as Smith has put it, "intellectualization" for entry into the Marxist

97. Kuwabara suggests that there was great faculty sympathy for striking students at Sankō in 1927; see Kuwabara, p. 37; likewise, Atoda Reizō seems somewhat sympathetic toward the student strike at Nikō in the same year; see *Nikō o kataru*, pp. 115ff.

98. Kikugawa, p. 405.

99. Takayama Shūgetsu, *Kōtō gakkō to sakei mondai* (Tokyo, 1932), pp. 127–129.

100. *Kōryōshi*, p. 1295; see also Ishimoda Tadashi, "Nikōsei no shisō no kaibō," p. 11; Karasawa, *Gakusei no rekishi*, p. 243.

academic establishment.[101] For numerous historians, literary critics, and novelists, the theoretical debates that enlivened the social studies research clubs constituted a philosophic baptism. Yet the abstract and often obscurantist tenor of the discussions—however meaningful they were to the intellectual growth of the individual—steered students away from the physical objects of their study: the working classes.

Thus intimations of belonging to an "intelligentsia" or vanguard of the revolution became the source of both philosophical complexity and political immobility. Though they were repressive and sometimes crude, the "thought guidance" officials in the Ministry of Education were by no means the sole cause for preventing student Marxists from "going to the people." The students also blocked their own way by succumbing to the web of higher school monasticism, elitism, intellectualism, and asceticism. They could condemn social inequities, but with a choice of words that reaffirmed their social distance. It is the ultimate irony, therefore, that the liberal academic ambience that gave students the freedom to call themselves Marxists probably served the same function as Kinoshita's "castle-school" metaphor in keeping them apart from the working classes. For in the end, the student leftists, like Nezhdanov in Turgenev's *Virgin Soil*, found it impossible to "simplify" themselves.

101. Smith, pp. 264–270; discussion topics taken from *Kōryōshi*, pp. 1295–1315. For more samples of the intellectual gymnastics of higher school Marxists, see Shiryō Shikō Gakusei Undōshi Kankōkai, ed., *Shiryō Dai Yon Kōtō Gakkō gakusei undōshi*, (Tokyo, 1976), esp. pp. 234–263.

CHAPTER EIGHT

The Higher Schools and Japanese Society

*What talk do we commonly hear about the contrast between college edu-
cation and the education which business or technical or professional
schools confer? . . . You are made into an efficient instrument for doing a
definite thing, you hear, at the schools; but apart from that, you may
remain a crude and smoky kind of petroleum, incapable of spreading light.
The universities and colleges, on the other hand, although they may
leave you less efficient for this or that practical task, suffuse your whole
mentality with something more important than skill. They redeem you,
make you well-bred; they make "good company" of you mentally.*

WILLIAM JAMES, "THE SOCIAL VALUE
OF THE COLLEGE-BRED" (1970)

*Were I to deduce any system from my feelings on leaving Eton, it might
be called* The Theory of Permanent Adolescence. *It is the theory that
the experiences undergone by boys at the great public schools . . . are so
intense as to dominate their lives and to arrest their development.*

CYRIL CONNOLLY, *ENEMIES OF PROMISE* (1938)

As a unique institution for university preparation and character
building, the higher schools continued to flourish through the
holocaust of World War II. They did not, however, survive the
Allied Occupation. In March 1946 the United States Education
Mission submitted its landmark Report to General Douglas
MacArthur's staff, recommending the expeditious adoption of a
single-track school system conforming to the American model.
The aim of the new guidelines was to develop "a system of education for life in a democracy" that would "rest upon the recognition of the dignity and worth of the individual," regardless of

sex.[1] In every instance, classroom learning would "encourage equality, the give-and-take of democratic government, [and] the ideal of good workmanship in daily life." In pursuit of this goal, the Mission believed it imperative that "higher education . . . become an opportunity for the many, not a privilege for the few." "In order to increase the opportunity for liberal education at higher levels," the Report continued, "it would be desirable to liberalize to a considerable extent the curriculum of the preparatory [higher] schools leading to the universities . . . so that a general college training would become more widely available."[2]

Reading between the lines, some Japanese observers believed that the higher schools were, in effect, singled out as irresponsible institutions and even seedbeds for ultranationalism.[3] Certainly members of MacArthur's staff, already uncomfortable with reports by former Ambassador Joseph C. Grew on the militaristic tendencies of Japanese students, were disturbed by the paradoxical combination of filth and gentlemanly pretense in the higher schools.[4] Worse yet, in their eyes, were the reported instances of local higher school students assuming the role of constables, admonishing and even getting into brawls with American servicemen.[5] Such haughtiness was deemed completely out of keeping with the expected attitude of a defeated nation and did little to endear the boarding schools to United States officials.

Yet the final decision to liquidate the higher schools came not from MacArthur's staff but from a group of forty Japanese educators on the special Educational Reform Council (Kyōiku Sasshin Iinkai), which was organized to establish concrete guide-

1. *Report of the United States Education Mission to Japan*, Department of State Publication 2579, Far Eastern Series 11: Washington, D.C., 1946, pp. 8–9, 24.

2. Ibid., pp. 58 and 61. Lulu H. Holmes, who was Advisor on Women's Higher Education, later put the case against the higher schools this way: "The only avenue to the university level . . . , these *kōtō gakkō* were highly selective in their admission practices, they were costly, and they admitted no women, so they constituted a real block to university education for most students." See Holmes's article "Changes in Higher Education for Women in Japan, 1946–48" in *Daigaku Fujin Kyōkai kaihō*, no. 68 (October 20, 1967), p. 2.

3. This view seems to underlie much of the ensuing debate over the fate of the higher schools. See, for example, Kaigo Tokiomi and Terasaki Masao, *Daigaku kyōiku, Sengo Nihon no kyōiku kaikaku*, vol. 9 (Tokyo, 1972), pp. 78–81.

4. Joseph C. Grew, *Report from Tokyo* (New York, 1942), pp. 50–51.

5. The refusal of higher school students to be intimidated by unmannered American servicemen was suggested in interviews with Takahashi Seigo (Tokyo: Feb. 9, 1971), Kamimura Yukinori (Kagoshima: April 8, 1971), Oda Ryūta (Saga: April 13, 1971); Sō Sakon, p. 100.

lines for the enactment of the Mission's recommendations. Realizing the impossibility of transforming a school for cultivation and personal refinement into an academic service station for "good workmanship in daily life," the Council majority concentrated immediately on the issue of abolition. They were opposed by a distinct minority, including Abe Yoshishige, Amano Teiyū, and Yamazaki Kyōsuke, who argued that the higher schools were not "guilty" of abetting militarism; that, indeed, their basic philosophy was pedagogically sound.[6] The "sacrifice of the higher schools," according to Amano, was too "painful" to endure; and speaking in a broader context, Abe saw no reason for experimenting with progressive ideals which had yet to be fully realized in the United States.[7] The majority of Council members, many of whom were affiliated with private and technical colleges, remained unimpressed by the last-ditch effort to save the higher schools. The final report noted only that the decision to abolish caused "some regret."[8]

In the spring of 1949, the higher schools were officially dissolved, and the facilities and staff were incorporated into a greatly expanded network of public universities. Today, with 40 percent of all Japanese youth between the ages of eighteen and twenty-two attending a university or a junior college, the goal of the Education Mission to increase the availability of higher education is being realized.[9] Still, bitterness lingers among many alumni who will never accept the abolition of the higher schools as a historical necessity. Rather, they speak out strongly on the logic of reviving the old higher schools (*kyūsei kōkō fukka-*

6. For the view of the conservative minority who wanted to preserve the higher schools, see Hidaka Daishirō, "Kyūsei kōtō gakkō haishi no keii," *KKGK*, no. 5 (August, 1975), pp. 56–60; Kaigo and Terasaki, *Daigaku kyōiku*, pp. 78–80; Amano Teiyū, *Kyōiku shiron* (Tokyo, 1949), p. 47; for more on Amano's attitude, see Amano Teiyū, "Ichikō no saiken," *Kōryō Komaba* 11, no. 2 (April 1969); Hidaka and Amano were interviewed on October 14 and 15, 1971.

7. Amano's remarks are quoted in Kaigo and Terasaki, *Daigaku kyōiku*, p. 80. Abe's more general reflections are found in his "Address to the U.S. Education Mission," *Society* 64, no. 1649 (August 3, 1946), p. 2.

8. The Japanese Educational Reform Council, *Education Reform in Japan* (Tokyo, 1950), p. 14. For discussions of the progressive influence on educational reformers during the Occupation, see Victor N. Kobayashi, *John Dewey in Japanese Educational Thought*, Comparative Education Dissertation Series, no. 2 (Ann Arbor, 1964), chap. 5; James Robinson, "Academic Freedom and the Occupation of Germany and Japan," *Bulletin of Concerned Asian Scholars* 6, no. 4 (Nov.–Dec. 1974), esp. pp. 51–52, and 58; Nagai Michio and Nishijima Takeo, "Postwar Japanese Education and the United States," in Akira Iriye, ed., *Mutual Images: Essays in American-Japanese Relations* (Cambridge, Mass., 1975), pp. 169–187.

9. In 1975 the percentage of youth in college was 38.4, according to *Japan Report* 23, no. 1 (Jan. 1, 1977):2–3.

tsuron) as Japan approaches the twenty-first century.[10] Their determination in this revival campaign is strengthened by two convictions: first, that the higher schools were a bastion of liberalism through World War II; and second, that the schools contributed more to national integration, strong political leadership, and high cultural standards than any other institution before or after the war. In short, many alumni believe that Japan's position in the world today is a tribute to the enduring higher school spirit; and they fear that graduates of the giant "multiversities" of contemporary Japan are incapable of replenishing the ranks of the old higher school guard.[11] Were the higher schools immune to totalitarian appeals? Should they be restored? After considering the philosophy of cultivation in the context of the 1930s, I shall address these questions.

Pure Learning in an Age of Disenchantment

The exigencies of industrialization had always played havoc with the character-building policies of the higher schools. During Japan's early phase of industrial development from the 1890s to World War I, the higher schools were continually scrutinized by government officials, who wondered if the institutions were in keeping with the pace of modernization and the demands of commerce and industry. After World War I the external pressure slackened, only to be reintensified during the

10. Typical of the bitterness over the liquidation of the higher schools is Nakagawa Zennosuke's statement in October 1968: "The most unsavory and injurious policy during the Occupation was the reform of the educational system. The dissolution of the old higher schools," Nakagawa continued, "was extremely unfortunate for Japan." (Yamamoto Kazuya, ed., *Waga seishun . . .* , p. 82) While some unhappy alumni would like to see the alma mater reconstituted exactly as it was, the most articulate spokesmen for revival acknowledge that the only realistic way to bring back the spirit of the old higher schools is to revamp the structure of the existing public universities. For a complete discussion of this issue see the two symposiums on "Kyūsei kōkō fukkatsuron," in *Nippon rettō* 2, no. 1 (January 1, 1970):43–67. In recent years, as the possibility for restoring the higher schools in toto becomes increasingly remote, alumni loyalists have begun to turn their attention to the preservation of higher school sources. See Kōzu Yasuo, "Kai daihyō aisatsu," *KKGK*, no. 1 (July 1974), pp. i–ii. Still, a poll of higher school alumni in the spring of 1977 revealed that only 1 percent of respondents believed that the postwar system of higher education was an improvement over the prewar system. For a discussion of the poll, see Takahashi Samon, "Kyūsei kōtō gakkō ni okeru kōfū," *Kokuritsu kyōiku kenkyūjo kiyō*, no. 95 (March 1978), pp. 159–60. Thus even today, many alumni would like to see a revival of at least the philosophy, if not the exact structure, of the old higher schools. This view is most recently expressed in Ōkuma Hideo, "Kyūsei kōkō haru ka naru seishun," *Bungei Shunjū* (April 1979), esp. p. 209.

11. Kōzu, pp. i–ii; Yamada Eisaku, "Nihon keizai to Kōryō seishin," *Kōryō Komaba* 6, no. 1 (November 1964):20.

1930s. When unemployment among liberal arts graduates of the universities climbed, briefly, to 50 percent during the Depression, criticism of the *Humanitäts* ideal reached a crescendo. "Under the current social and economic conditions," declared Professor Abe Shigetaka of Tokyo University, "I have grave doubts about the wisdom of allowing our present higher schools to retain their unique obligations." [12] The cultivation of gentlemen seemed a costly, anachronistic exercise to those who wanted quick remedies for the social and political crises of the decade. Thus, between 1928 and 1937, advisory councils to the Ministry of Education proposed, once again, the transformation of the higher schools into a streamlined and science-oriented preparatory school or a vocational institute for commerce, industry, and agriculture. [13]

The threat of "vocationalization" loomed ominously on the horizon as higher school faculty and their sympathizers in the universities gazed upon an unfriendly world in the 1930s. Never before had Kinoshita Hiroji's metaphor of a "castle under seige" taken on such a real and urgent meaning. Suddenly, the intricately crafted principles of character building and cultural enrichment were in danger of being completely overwhelmed by the uncontrollable forces of economic depression, militarization, mass mobilization, and outright interference in campus affairs by "thought police," dispatched by the government to investigate the operations of underground Marxist study groups. Threatened by the nationalization of social life, articulate spokesmen for the higher schools rose to the defense.

The rally to preserve the cultural integrity of the schools was launched through alumni magazines and academic symposiums. Supporters claimed that the academy offered a "complete education" (*kansei kyōiku*), as Yoshida Kumaji called it, that could be neither circumvented nor abbreviated in the name of efficiency. [14] The idea of diluting the curriculum with vocational studies was utter folly, for the higher schools were *not* "a place

12. Quoted in Nakajima Tarō, "Kyūsei kōtō gakkō . . . ," part II, p. 60; for a discussion of student unemployment in the 1930s, see Karasawa, *Gakusei no rekishi*, pp. 211–215, and Kokuritsu Kyōiku Kenkyūjo, *Nihon kindai kyōiku hyakunenshi*, vol. 5 (Tokyo, 1974), pp. 578–588.
13. The various proposals for either reforming or abolishing the higher schools are discussed in Nakajima Tarō, "Kyūsei kōtō gakkō . . . ," part II, pp. 41–50; Kokuritsu Kyōiku Kenkyūjo, *Nihon kindai kyōiku hyakunenshi*, vol. 5, p. 1239; Robert King Hall, *Education for a New Japan* (New Haven, 1949), pp. 228–230, 244–245.
14. Iwanami Shigeo, ed., *Iwanami kōza kyōiku kagaku*, vol. 17 (Tokyo, 1933), pp. 40–41.

for perfecting talent that can be used by others" (*tanin ni mochii-rareru yō na jinzai no yōseijo*) but "a place for producing great men who can use other people" (*hito o mochiiru yō na daijinbutsu no umareru tokoro*). There were no shortcuts or simplistic formulas for achieving this "noble educational goal." [15] Unlike the purely functional demands of the vocational school or the research-oriented university, character development in the higher schools required an ideal physical setting, excellent teachers, libraries filled with great books, and as Obara Kuniyoshi pointed out, an overall cultural ambience that was sensitive to the psychological needs of "the critical period" called "adolescence." [16] Professor Haruyama Sakuki of Tokyo University concurred:

> The three years of higher school life in our country are the freest and happiest time imaginable, allowing us to glory in the unrestricted sensations of adolescence (*seishun*). . . . To eliminate this higher school experience, or to curtail it in any way, will depress the spirit of university graduates and make their characters small. [17]

In making this argument, which was squarely in the tradition of Orita Hikoichi, Kinoshita Hiroji, and Mori Arinori, the defenders of the higher schools had latched onto a powerful new weapon. The leisurely ethic of self-cultivation and the protracted experience of adolescence were now a psychological imperative. Leadership at the national level required precisely those elements for developing personality that made the higher schools unique: time, space, and emphasis on cultivating moral self-reliance. National leadership depended on "complete human beings" (*zenningen*), whose sense of right and wrong was independent of mass ideology. The primary-school and youth-school morality of the "family state" was simply inadequate to the psychological tasks of "human development" (*ningen kei-sei*). Such were the views of the higher school headmasters who assembled for an emergency conference in October 1937. Fearing the imminent dissolution of their institutions and the end of pure learning, they drafted a strong petition to the government on the importance of liberal culture (*ippan kyōyō*) and personal cultivation (*jinkaku tōya*) for the university-bound elite. [18] Al-

15. Minamigumo, p. 68; Suzuki Noboru, "Kyūsei kōtō gakkō no dokuritsu to honshitsu," *KKGK*, no. 6 (August 1975), p. 48.

16. Iwanami Shigeo, ed., *Iwanami kōza kyōiku kagaku*, p. 20.

17. Haruyama Sakuki, *Gendai no shūyō to kyōiku* (Tokyo, 1934), p. 328.

18. Kokuritsu Kyōiku Kenkyū-jo, *Nihon kindai kyōiku hyakunenshi* vol. 5, pp. 1240–1241, and Takahashi Samon, "Kyūsei kōtō gakkō ni okeru kōfū," p. 156.

though besieged by proposals to reform or liquidate the higher schools, the Ministry of Education must have been swayed by the united opposition of the headmasters, for the higher schools were left virtually unscathed until the end of the war. As was the pattern since 1900, the government, when faced with a hard choice, ultimately accepted the existing structure and philosophy of higher education.

The successful defense of liberal education in the 1930s from outside intervention is also attributable to the rededication of faculty and students to the humanistic ideals of culture and self-cultivation. At the forefront of the new pedagogical offensive was the thirteen-volume "student series" (*gakusei sōsho*) edited by one of Tokyo University's most famous liberal scholars, Kawai Eijirō. Published between 1935 and 1941, the "series" included volumes on *Student Life, The Student and Self-Cultivation,* and *The Student and Philosophy,* with contributions from Abe Yoshishige, Kurata Hyakuzō, Abe Jirō, Tsurumi Yūsuke, Kuwaki Genyoku, and other members of the cultural establishment. All were intimately involved, both as students and as teachers, with the culture of the higher school and the university, whose students were the primary focus of attention. In Kawai's words, "The three years of higher school life are the glory (*seika*) of student life in Japan." [19] By providing erudite guidance for self-cultivation, the contributors to the "student series" undoubtedly aspired to perpetuate that "glory," and replenish their own beleaguered ranks, well into the future. And while the authors were in agreement that each student reader should walk his own path toward the "completion of the personal self," the "series" is testimony to their anxiety about leaving the trip completely to chance.

Underlying the essays in the "series" is the assumption that cultural enrichment depends upon one's ability to transcend the immediate radius of material and political existence. As Kawai argued, the assignment of the "highest value" (*saikō kachi*) to "material objects" (*bukken*) thwarted the "growth of the personal self." [20] In the preoccupation with material existence, both capitalism and communism posed a serious threat to culture. Kawai also lashed out at education that produced narrow spe-

19. Kawai Eijirō, *Gakusei seikatsu* (Tokyo, 1935), p. 259. In his introduction to this volume Kawai states his special concern for higher school and university students. See p. i.
20. Kawai Eijirō, *Gakusei ni atau* (Gendai kyōyō bunkō 67) (Tokyo, 1971), pp. 46–75.

cialists (craftsmen, politicians, and scholars) who could not appreciate the transcending spirit of the personal self. "The flaw in capitalism" was the division of man into narrow occupational categories and the neglect of "universality" (*fuhen*).[21] During the critical period of his adolescent schooldays, the student should not be distracted by vocational studies or material circumstances, but should devote himself completely to "the study of world view" (*jinseikan no gaku*). In pursuit of this goal, he must listen carefully to his teachers, perfect deep personal friendships with his peers, and create for himself an environment of great books. To insure that the highest standards of discrimination informed the selection of suitable titles for one's "reading life" (*dokusho seikatsu*), Kawai submitted a list of 185 recommended titles.[22] Besides his own works and those of Abe Jirō, Kurata Hyakuzō, and Nishida Kitarō, the list included Theodor Lipps, *Ethische Grundfragen*; T. H. Green, *Prolegomena to Ethics*; Immanuel Kant, *Kritik der Reinen Vernunft*; Hugh Black, *Culture and Restraint*.

In an age when the intellectual curiosity of American university students rarely exceeded the *Saturday Evening Post*, Kawai's confidence that a group of eighteen- and nineteen-year-old Japanese youths would run to the library for copies of *Ethische Grundfragen* is remarkable.[23] But like his fellow contributors to the "series," Kawai postulated that reading and deliberating over the masterpieces of philosophy and literature inspired, even exhilarated, the student. Great books taught universal values that confirmed the spiritual independence of students from their parents; they also liberated young readers from animalistic impulse (*dobutsuteki hairyo kara kaihō*).[24] Elaborating on the latter, Abe Yoshishige noted that a "reading life" of abstract philosophy diverted untamed energies aroused by students' "sexual awakening" into the constructive pursuit of truth and purity. The secure and happy adolescent, Abe continued, was the young man who converted the potentially destructive physiological instincts of post-pubescence into an "opportunity" for philosophic and artistic expression. This undisguised prescrip-

21. Ibid., p. 70. For Abe Yoshishige's view, see Abe Yoshishige, *Seinen to kyōyō* (Tokyo, 1940), pp. 8–16.

22. Kawai Eijirō, *Gakusei seikatsu*, pp. 229–245.

23. For discussions of the reading tastes of American students, see Robert Angell, *The Campus: A Study of Contemporary Undergraduate Life in the American University* (New York, 1928), pp. 16–21, 236–237; Paula Fass, *The Damned and the Beautiful: American Youth in the 1920s* (New York, 1977), esp. p. 365.

24. Kawai, *Gakusei ni atau*, p. 49.

tion for sublimation won support from another contributor, who bookishly intoned the virtues of *abstinentia sexualis temporalis* and the dangers of *Selbstbefriedigung*.[25] The pursuit of pure learning was thus the key to transcending both material existence and sexual temptation.

The Vulnerability to Totalism

Is there any way to discover whether the young readers of the "student series" were actually living up to the high standards that were expected of them? The social critic Yamaji Aizan once noted, in a speech before the Ichikō Debate Club, that in order to assess the quality of the "school spirit" in any age, one must examine the graffiti in the lavatories.[26] Heeding Yamaji's advice, this writer dutifully (though not without some discomfort) inspected the lavatories around three old higher schools several years ago, where dated scribblings from the 1930s could be scrutinized.[27] The investigation uncovered school slogans interspersed with a sea of literary and philosophic references and not the faintest hint of obscenity. Photographs of graffiti appearing in alumni publications also confirm that while tending to the most prosaic of human needs, the students' thoughts could easily wander to Hermann Hesse and Romain Rolland. More scientific evidence to suggest that culture was a way of life in the higher schools before and during the war comes from a pair of reputable scholars, Kaigo Tokiomi and Yoshida Noboru. Their survey in 1943 of students in the normal schools, technical schools, youth schools, and higher schools concluded that higher school students had a "special life" (*tokubetsu na seikatsu*) marked by superior standards of cultural discrimination.[28] Essays and speeches compiled in school magazines would indicate further that students perceived themselves as custodians of high culture and even as, to quote one Ichikō student, "nobles of the spirit" (*seishinjō ni oite kizoku*).[29]

25. Abe, *Seinen to kyōyō*, pp. 81–82; Saitō Mokichi, "Seiyoku," in Kawai Eijirō, ed., *Gakusei to seikatsu* (Tokyo, 1938), pp. 377–401.
26. Kimijima Ichirō, *Daryō Ichibanshitsu*, p. 148.
27. The inspections took place within the remaining buildings from the old Second, Third, and Saga higher schools in April, August, and October of 1971. Photographs of typical graffiti can be found in Yamamoto Kazuya, p. 43.
28. Kaigo Tokiomi and Yoshida Noboru, *Gakusei seikatsu chōsa* (Tokyo, 1943), p. 76.
29. "Kinen sawakai kiji," *DIKGKZ*, no. 195 (March 30, 1910), p. 96; Miriam Beard has described the Japanese student in 1930 as "a being set apart," a member of a "holiness" caste around whose head "circles a halo of almost religious veneration"; see

Do claims to "spiritual nobility," however, mean that higher school students were also able to transcend the litanies of *koku-tai* ideology? Many alumni have argued in the affirmative, agreeing with Hayashi Kentarō that their school remained an "isolated castle of freedom" (*jiyū no kojō*) while the rest of the country fell under the sway of totalitarianism.[30] Though few would insinuate that militarism had no effect on student life, many seem inclined to believe that the "essence of the higher school" was never compromised, that educators like Abe Yoshishige, Hidaka Daishirō, Mori Gesaburō, and other "old liberals" did everything in their power to minimize the intrusion of civic rituals and to cushion the impact of external crises so that students could enjoy an unbroken continuity of life in the dormitories.[31] Finally, old-higher-school loyalists have argued, with justification, that unlike their German contemporaries, the students in the higher schools and Imperial universities were never mobilized in a fascist youth movement; that, indeed, they maintained what Maruyama Masao has called a "vague antipathy" toward right-wing politics and organizations.[32]

There are limits to this idealistic picture. The privilege to live in Ichikō's Independence Hall, Sankō's Freedom Hall, or Shikō's Transcendence Hall did not render the students immune to the appeals of political totalism or militarism. For one thing, it is impossible to overlook the importance, dating back to the foundation period, of military exercises in the training of the gentleman. In the case of Ichikō, glowing accounts of the annual marching and mock-battles in the countryside can be found in both the dormitory history and the *Society of Friends Magazine*, even during the Taishō period. "Our three days of military maneuvers," commented one student in the 1925 edition of the dormitory annals, "combined some hardship with great fun."[33] To be sure, as the war approached and the exercises became

---

Beard, *Realism in Romantic Japan* (New York, 1930), p. 290; the sense of "spiritual aristocracy" among higher school students is also expressed at Sixth Higher by Morimura Katsu, "Shisaku no ato," in *Kyūryū*, no. 37 (Feb. 28, 1937), pp. 40–41.

30. Hayashi Kentarō, *Utsuri yuku mono no kage* (Tokyo, 1960), p. 75.

31. See Takeyama Michio, "Shōwa jūkyūnen no Ichikō," in Nishizawa, pp. 102–105; Kuwabara Takeo, "Mori Gesaburō sensei no koto," in *Kuwabara Takeo zenshū*, vol. 4, esp. p. 38.

32. Maruyama Masao, *Thought and Behavior in Modern Japanese Politics* (London, 1966), p. 58; Ōmuro, *Kōkō seikatsuron*, pp. 15 and 100. Ōmuro in particular notes that the higher school students were never part of a movement like the German Wandervogel.

33. *Kōryōshi*, p. 1471.

26. In recess from military exercises. Hirosaki Higher, courtesy of Yamauchi Naosuke

more tedious, the enthusiasm of the stalwarts dampened some-what. There were even sporadic protests. But usually these took the form of lighthearted pranks, in which students appeared barefooted for exercises or with gaping holes in the seat of their pants.[34]

The tolerance for parading around the school yard with un-loaded rifles may be rooted in the traditional ethos of higher school manliness and the self-sacrificing rituals of the dormi-tory and the athletic field. Even though the students in Taishō and early Shōwa were immersed in high culture, the cult of ath-letic heroism and adolescent primitivism never disappeared. The tragic deaths of athletes in training during the 1930s in-dicate that the "no condition" attitude was still alive. Nor did the enlightened breezes of Taishō democracy and culture put a complete end to violence in the dormitory. The initiation "storm" could be as ferocious as ever in the interwar period; and although the "clenched-fist punishment" was formally disavowed at Ichikō in 1922, when a rational judicial body (shi-hōbu) replaced the Mainstream Society, ritualized beatings still

34. Interviews with Abe Hideo (Tokyo: Feb. 5, 1971), Oshikawa Atsuyuki (Ka-goshima: April 8, 1971), Sakakura Atsuyoshi (Kyoto: June 2, 1971), Inoue Kiyoshi (Kyoto: July 8, 1971).

took place when individualists abandoned their sports club or defamed the "school spirit."[35] Moreover, the traditional symbolism of the dormitory changed very little during early Shōwa. As they had before, students in the 1930s continued to wear the same unlaundered uniforms, sing the same "dormitory songs," swear allegiance to the same school flag, and recite from an ever-expanding corpus of institutional lore. Of greater significance was the persisting image of the school as a familial community without women, a utopian oasis of manliness. While it is true that direct identification of the school spirit with national spirit was less explicit than it had been during late Meiji, one wonders if it was any less real. Certainly there was much in the symbolic structure of the community that hearkened to the mystical particularism of the emperor system and the family state.

The susceptivity to totalism among higher school students was shared by campus intellectuals as well as athletic stalwarts. Since student writers embarked on a search for purity (*junsuisei*) within the self, and apart from "dormitory politics," they attempted to affect, as Tezuka Tomio recalls, a "superhuman morality" (*chōjin dōtoku*).[36] Cherishing the utopian view that they might someday inspire and lead a "personalistic society," student intellectuals had difficulty in accepting the imperfect realities of political existence. The danger in this form of idealism was that the combined quest for inner purity and social community could be surrendered to the totalistic spiritual appeals of the mystic state. Even as sober-minded an idealist as Nitobe Inazō had difficulty in his later life distinguishing between the personal self and the transcendental spirit of the nation; and for more romantic idealists, like Kurata Hyakuzō, there were no distinctions at all.

It is historical record that, during the war, a number of writers in the cultural establishment enthusiastically accommodated *kokutai* ideology. And usually this accommodation was made in the name of "transcending the modern" (*kindai no chōkoku*) or overcoming the sickness of capitalistic civilization by acknowledging the absolute purity of the utopian "family state."[37] Similar intellectual justifications for "converting" to

35. *Kōryōshi*, pp. 101–108; Sō Sakon, "Ai to . . . ," p. 100.
36. Tezuka Tomio, pp. 43–44.
37. This mentality was evidenced in a special academic symposium on "overcoming the modern" that was held in Tokyo during September and October of 1942. It was attended by such illustrious higher school alumni as Itō Sei, Kamei Katsuichirō, Naka-

kokutai ideology can be found in higher school alumni and student magazines. According to one Ichikō graduate in 1934, the way to overcome the materialistic civilization of the industrial West was to seek "the completion of the personal self within the foundation of the kokutai" (*jinkaku no kansei to yū koto o kokutai no kiso ni oite*).[38] Armed with these spiritual rationalizations, a few higher school students did go to war when their draft-exempt status was terminated in 1943; and those who did, according to Tsurumi Kazuko, were more psychically prone to battlefield sacrifice than their working-class peers, a hypothesis that adds a different perspective to Maruyama's theory of the "transfer of oppression."[39] Certainly, Ichikō sent its student soldiers off in a noble and deeply affecting style. When individuals were called to serve, the entire student body would gather for a chorus of "The Sky over the Capital" (*Miyako no sora*), a nostalgic late-Meiji "dormitory song" that blended romantic personification with hearty appeals to "the flag which protects the country." "It was," says Takeyama Michio through the narrator in the novel *Harp of Burma*, "a fine song for sending off young men, a tune with a bright, gay rhythm and yet a poignant sadness to it. . . . If the Japanese people had sung more fine songs like *Miyako no sora* during the war, instead of cheap patriotic songs, everyone might have survived with greater dig-

---

no Yoshio, and Kawakami Tetsutarō. In recollecting the conference, Kamei has written that he and the other participants saw the war as a vehicle for overcoming the "sickness" of modernization that was afflicting Japanese society. Takeuchi Yoshimi, "Kindai no chōkoku," in Yoshimoto Takaaki, ed., *Gendai Nihon shisō taikei*, vol. 4 (Tokyo, 1974), p. 400. The desire of the participants was not really to justify military conquest so much as to understand what was happening in terms of a final catharsis in industrialization. For more on this problem, see James B. Crowley, "Intellectuals as Visionaries of the New Asian Order," in James W. Morley, ed., *Dilemmas of Growth in Prewar Japan* (Princeton, 1971); Donald Keene, "Japanese Writers and the Greater East Asia War," *Journal of Asian Studies* 23, no. 2 (August 1965); Peter Duus, "Nagai Ryūtarō and the 'White Peril,'" *Journal of Asian Studies* 31, no. 1 (November 1971).

38. Aoyagi Shūsei, "Kinensai daigakusei shukuji," *Dai Ichi Kōtō Gakkō Dōsōkai kaihō* (May 1934), pp. 93–94.

39. Tsurumi Kazuko, *Social Change and the Individual*, esp. pp. 135–136; the potential for fanaticism among student soldiers is also reflected in the diaries of Ichikō students who joined suicide raids. (See Nishizawa et al., pp. 107–109.) Briefly, Maruyama's theory states that desperate acts of aggression and brutality during World War II were committed by lower-class soldiers who were overcome by the need "to transfer in a downward direction the sense of oppression that comes from above." (Maruyama, p. 18). Since students were not "oppressed from above," their participation in the war may depart from Maruyama's hypothesis. However, the fanaticism of student soldiers does not necessarily contradict Maruyama's argument, since students, according to Tsurumi, were repulsed by civilian atrocities and gave their lives in battle, not out of an urge to transfer oppression, but as an absolute resolution of a hopeless spiritual crisis.

27. On the sidewalks of Tokyo: an Ichikō student in 1941. The combination of school cap, traditional *hakama* or divided skirt, and elevated wooden clogs served as an alternative school uniform. Courtesy of Kōdansha

nity."[40] As an unflinching Ichikō loyalist, Takeyama's sentiment may be understandable but it is also disturbing.

However, to render the last judgment on the higher schools on the basis of an accommodation to militarism would be unfair. Few, if any, academic institutions can withstand the pressures of a nation going to war; and several of the higher school's staunchest defenders, notably Kawai Eijirō and Yanaihara Tadao, took courageous stands against the government in the name of liberal ideals.[41] Moreover, in certain respects, the higher schools sustained a remarkably free atmosphere. Through the late 1930s and early 1940s, Gokō's venerated "teacher of life," Yamagata Motoharu, continued to assign the works of John Stuart Mill to his classes despite grumbles from the Ministry of Education.[42] And in a 1937 article for a Sixth Higher literary magazine on "The Boarding School Principle in Britain and Japan," E. H. Hamilton expressed amazement over "the life of splendid freedom . . . which higher school boys appear to

40. Takeyama Michio, *Harp of Burma*, trans. by Howard Hibbett (Rutland, Vermont, 1975), p. 85.
41. Hashikawa Bunzō, "Antiwar Values—the Resistance in Japan," *Japan Interpreter* 9, no. 1 (Spring 1974): 88–92.
42. *Ryūnan kaiko* (Tokyo, 1967), p. 181.

28. Standing in front of the school gate: Ichikō students at the end of World War II. Courtesy of Kōdansha

lead."[43] In Hamilton's opinion, the potential for authoritarianism in the higher school dormitories was negligible when compared with the oppressive "fagging system" and blatant anti-intellectualism that was condoned in the British public schools he knew so well.

Hamilton's optimistic view of higher school students does not discount their vulnerability to spiritual totalism or an ethic of absolute ends. It does, however, force us to remember that even in the late 1930s, the students were primarily concerned with safeguarding their own untarnished and highly qualitative conception of moral freedom along with their privileged access to prestigious careers in government, business, and academia. To be left alone to cultivate the personal self and maintain the stability of personal relationships was their immediate aspiration. The students were conservative and fundamentally nationalistic, but their assiduously cultivated affectations of status, their dedication to public service, and their closed-community view of society prevented any outpouring of sentiment for the "young officers" or other groups of radical nationalists.

43. L. B. Hamilton, "The 'Boarding School' Principle in England and Japan," in *Kyōryō*, no. 37 (Feb. 28, 1937), p. 25.

The maintenance of institutional stability and international peace were very much in their self-interest; social unrest, mass mobilization, and militarism clearly were not.

A Final Assessment

Students of comparative education have been impressed by the role of academic achievement in facilitating upward mobility in Japan since the Meiji Restoration. In contrast to England, where advancement in the school system was based, until recently, on family, property, and manners acquired during childhood, Japan granted male youth of all backgrounds the opportunity to attend public primary schools and to compete as equals for admission to the secondary schools and universities. Without denying the significant distinction between "sponsored mobility" in England and "contest mobility" in Japan, one must still be careful not to draw hasty conclusions about the resulting influence of education on social structure.[44] To argue, for example, that "the unbending use of the examination merit principle" in Japan prevented social breeding or "the development of class consciousness" in the classroom would seem oversimplified in light of the higher school legacy.[45]

It has never been argued in this study that the higher school was either conceived or permitted to function as an institution whose purpose was to perpetuate the hereditary wealth and status of a feudal aristocracy. Despite the traditionalistic nostalgia of the early architects of school policy, despite the largess of the families of former feudal lords, despite the invocation of the *bun-bu* formula and the "castle-school" metaphor, there is little indication that those with hereditary ties to the old warrior class were given preferential treatment by local school administrations. Rather, the higher schools, over the long run, contributed to the gradual displacement of the former hereditary elite by middle-class achievers. At Ichikō in 1931, 87 students out of a graduating class of 320 claimed samurai descent: still a substantial number, though a marked decrease from the Meiji

44. L. Stone, "Japan and England: A Comparative Study," in P. W. Musgrave, *Sociology, History and Education* (London, 1970), p. 107. For a theoretical discussion of this problem, see Ralph H. Turner, "Modes of Social Ascent through Education: Sponsored and Contest Mobility," in A. H. Halsey, et al., eds., *Education, Economy, and Society* (New York, 1964), pp. 121–139.

45. Ronald Dore, *The Diploma Disease* (London, 1976), p. 45; Dore, "Education: Japan," p. 199.

period.[46] A rare survey conducted at Ichikō and Sankō in 1934 indicates, further, that the fathers of prewar higher school students represented a fairly broad cross section of clerks, primary school teachers, shopkeepers, wholesalers, train conductors, lawyers, prosperous farmers, and government officials.[47] Moderate tuition and examination fees virtually precluded the matriculation of working-class youth. But wealth was no guarantee for admission either. It was almost beyond the imagination of a powerful Ichikō alumnus to follow the Etonian custom of arranging for tea with the headmaster in order to chart his son's academic career. A few students entered the higher schools without taking entrance examinations, but only on the basis of outstanding achievement in middle school. Samuel Beckett's characterization of his students at Campbell College as "rich and thick" could never be applied to Ichikō.[48]

Yet, ironically, the emphasis on achievement for admission to the higher schools made the transformation of values after matriculation all the more compelling and dramatic. "The reason why the higher school experience leaves such a lasting impression," explained Hayakawa Takashi, "is that the constraining model foisted on students in the primary and middle schools was smashed, all of a sudden, on their entering the higher school."[49] The "smashing" of primary and early secondary-school models for citizenship was accompanied by a reaction against the family. "There was absolutely no atmosphere of religion or culture in the home of a middle-class merchant in Tokyo," Kawai Eijirō wrote of his own family life in the early 1900s, admitting that all he learned as a boy was the value of "getting ahead in the world." It was only when he entered Ichikō and came under the influence of Nitobe Inazō that he could "kill the vestiges of my old self" (*furuki ima made no jibun o korosu*).[50] In a similar vein, the philosopher Mashita Shin'ichi declared that the "essence" of higher school life was the sever-

46. Kokuritsu Kyōiku Kenkyūjo, ed., *Nihon kindai kyōiku hyakunenshi*, vol. 4, p. 1273.

47. Tokyo Shōka Daigaku, *Gakusei seikatsu chōsa hōkoku* (Tokyo, 1934), p. 9. A similar smattering of middle-class students were found to attend Fifth Higher, according to a survey by Takaishi Shigekatsu, "Kyōdō kumiai no hata no moto ni," *Ryūnankai zasshi*, no. 202 (July 1, 1927), pp. 78–96. A further survey by the Ministry of Education in 1938 suggests that the sons of salaried employees far outnumbered the sons of self-employed, "old-middle-class" merchants and farmers. (Kokuritsu kyōiku kenkyū-jo, *Nihon kindai . . .* , 5:585.)

48. Quoted in Gathorne-Hardy, p. 350.

49. Quoted in Asō Makoto, *Erīto to kyōiku* (Tokyo, 1969), p. 98.

50. Kawai Eijirō, "Gakusei jidai no kaiko," in Kawai Eijirō, ed., *Gakusei to kyōyō* (Tokyo, 1940), pp. 280, 292–293.

ance of self from "the vulgar society represented by family and middle school." For Mashita, the three years at Third Higher were an "epoch" in "the destruction of the old self" and the rebirth of a new man.[51] The recollections of astute intellectuals underscore the role of the higher schools in breaking social and psychological ties with the past and paving the way for a new concept of self. The extent to which this sentiment is shared among alumni is indicated by the standardized identification of the alma mater as "the birthplace of the spirit" (*kokoro no furusato*)."[52]

In remembering the higher schools as their spiritual birthplace, most alumni are quite delighted to point out that they spent their schooldays in an unhurried ambience free from the pressures of academic achievement. Students who failed their semester examinations were asked to repeat the unmastered courses the following year without any stigma attached. Since to repeat meant to extend one's stay in this generally happy moratorium from childhood dependencies and adult responsibilities, there was no shortage of "repeaters" (*rakudaisei*) in any higher school class.[53] Whether or not one joined in the notorious skulduggery involved in protracting the higher school experience to four or five years, prospects for automatically entering the university were unaffected. In this sense, the higher school students were given the ultimate freedom: to enjoy life without having to worry about "failure" as narrowly defined by their parents or some outside authority. They could even indulge in the most outlandish forms of behavior, from camping out in the library (for three days straight without eating or speaking) to strutting up and down the main street of a local town, stopping only to relieve themselves at the side of a police box or to pilfer a shopkeeper's advertising placard.[54]

The tales of pranks (*itazura*) and eccentricities (*onchi*) that

51. Mashita Shin'ichi, "*Dentō o koete: kyūsei kōtō gakkōron*," KKGK, no. 15 (January 1978), p. 6.
52. *Kōryōshi*, p. 73; Ozaki Yukiteru, "Kokoro no furusato," in Dai Shichi Kōtō Gakkō Zōshikan Dōsōkai, ed., *Shichikō omoideshū kōhen*, pp. 27–42.
53. Nakano Yoshio, "*Kyūsei kōkōteki naru mono*," *Tenbō* 72:110–117; Ogiya, *Aa gyokuhai ni . . .* , p. 271; Gotō Ryūnosuke, "Ichikō rokunen no seikatsu to Konoe Fumimaro," *Kōryō: Ichiko hyakunen kinen* 16, no. 2:32–43. See also Appendix III, Table 4, for figures on the infinitesimal rate of academic expulsion.
54. Such stories were repeated in many interviews and are immortalized in alumni storybooks such as Kobayashi Hiroyuki, *Rokkō monogatari* (Okayama, 1969); Miyajima Shin'ichi, ed., *Ryūnan monogatari*; Asahi Shinbun Matsue Shikyoku, ed., *Kyūsei Matsukō monogatari* (Matsue, 1968). Local townspeople were remarkably tolerant of student pranks. One suspects this tolerance was not extended to less-privileged youth.

have been compiled for higher school storybooks are clear testimony that schooldays in Imperial Japan were not always ordered by the "unbending" principle of academic achievement. Nevertheless, even if separated from a performance-oriented system of rewards, the antics of the students still had a serious social purpose. The more ridiculously students behaved, the more removed they became from the moral limitations of their own social background. Outlandish pranks coupled with collective rituals helped to eradicate old identities and establish a tabula rasa for a new "style of life" underscored by the values of manliness, honor, and above all, personalism. Just as important as the values per se was the capability which higher school students acquired for expressing their feelings in a highly elaborated linguistic code that structured their whole outlook on life.[55] If the higher school experience was not oriented toward achieving high scores on semester examinations, it was most certainly oriented toward the *acquisition* of personality traits, values, and linguistic affectations to which an individual student was entitled by virtue of his *membership* in the academic community.

When the fateful day of graduation finally came, students could rarely hold back the tears of recognition that their adolescence had come to an end. They did not, however, leave their "mother school" empty-handed. Along with the virtual right of automatic passage to the Imperial University, the students could anticipate promising adult careers in government, business, and academia. Even during the Depression, when higher-school-and-university graduates were having immediate difficulties securing respectable jobs, the alumni as a whole appear to have been well entrenched within the power elite. Takayama Shūgetsu's survey in 1930 of 4,859 First Higher alumni (representing nearly one-third of all Ichikō graduates at the time) makes no mention of academic unemployment, calling attention instead to an impressive breakdown of university professors, Diet members, prefectural officials, diplomats, judges, business executives, doctors, and lawyers. Fully one-quarter of those surveyed by Takayama were holding political office or serving in the bureaucracy.[56] Since the war, the fortunes of Ichikō alumni have, if anything, improved. Recent studies indicate

55. Basil Bernstein, "Social Class, Language and Socialization," in Basil Bernstein, ed., *Class, Codes and Control*, vol. 1 (London, 1971), pp. 170–189.
56. Takayama Shūgetsu, *Kōtō gakkō to sakei mondai*, p. 223.

that during the late 1950s nearly one-third of the top-level bureaucracy was composed of Ichikō graduates. Such statistics are
"extraordinary," according to Akira Kubota, since graduates of
Eton, Harrow, or Rugby have never accounted for more than 6
percent respectively of the British civil service "in any level or
year."[57] While the occupational achievements of provincial
higher school alumni fall short of the Ichikō mark, a volley of
who's who books suggests that every alumni association has a
sprinkling of notables, and very few "old boys" have failed to
attain a position of influence in their adult careers.[58]

The ease with which higher school graduates have entered
the power elite cannot be explained by the mere possession of
a degree or a certificate. When they departed the "mother
school," the graduates were already members of a "status
group" defined by the common heritage of youth in their late
teens living together, forming lasting friendships, and sharing
in the struggles of spiritual rebirth. The powerful convergence
of social and psychological identity in the higher schools, and
the continual reaffirmation of this identity in alumni organizations, had obvious advantages for the individual graduate as he
embarked on his career. There is little doubt that on questions
of recruitment and promotion alumni have been the beneficiaries of "school cliques" (gakubatsu) and friendship networks,
which have flourished in government, business, and academia.
To be able to claim "Ichikō lineage" (Ichikō keifu) or "Sankō lineage" has at the very least facilitated access to information and
persons of prominence. Also, the social mannerisms acquired
in the higher schools stood the graduate in good stead.The ability to affect a composite air of self-confidence, linguistic facility,
and noblesse oblige was important to government ministries,
which have always been elitist and were impressed as much by
writing style and "character" as by technical qualifications.[59]
The recent studies by Bradley Richardson and Lewis Austin

57. Akira Kubota, *Higher Civil Servants in Postwar Japan* (Princeton, 1969), pp. 66–67.
58. See any in the series of higher school histories published by Zaikei hyōronsha
between 1965 and 1968. Each volume devotes attention to the occupational accomplishments of the alumni of a particular school. Among the volumes used in this study are
Sakamoto Yasuyuki, ed., *Aa gyokuhai* . . . ; Nakayama Yoshio and Etō Takehito, eds.,
Ten wa Tōhoku yama takaku . . . ; Ishii Kahei and Morita Yoshiaki, eds., *Kurenai moyuru*
(Tokyo, 1965); Sakudō Yoshio and Etō Takehito, eds., *Hokushin naname ni sasu tokoro.*
Each higher school alumni organization also has a register which gives current occupational information.
59. R. M. Spaulding, *Imperial Japan's Higher Civil Service Examinations*, pp. 187–189,
216–219.

suggest that even today the essence of political power in Japan is "personalism," not performance.[60] Illustrative of this phenomenon is the continuing influence of Fukuda Takeo (the prime minister until December 1978), a supreme cultivator of personal relations, and perhaps the last in a dynasty of seven prime ministers who spent their adolescence in Independence Hall.[61]

So pervasive was resocialization in the higher schools, and so permanent was its effect on the mentality and success of alumni in their adult careers, that Ishida Takeshi, a scholar who does not underplay the role of "merit" in Japan's modernization, states flatly that graduation from First Higher "imparted a kind of status not unlike that bestowed by birth."[62] As a spiritual home and the focus of particularistic loyalties, the "twice-born" graduates of the higher schools obtained certain advantages from their experience that were, indeed, ascriptive.

However, it is inaccurate to say that because the higher schools emphasized ascription over achievement, leisure over efficiency, and the cultivation of gentlemen over the training of experts, they necessarily operated in bold defiance of modernization. On the contrary, their continuity with the past, their view of man as a moral creature, and their refusal to surrender to technological expedience made the higher schools an ideal milieu for personality growth and development. Taking full advantage of the opportunity for questioning the nature of truth and beauty, the students transformed the boarding-school experience into a philosophic adventure and a quest for personal identity. If the complete synthesis of personal identity requires a capability for "post-conventional" reasoning and self-reflection, then the higher school students were psychologically ahead of many contemporary youth who are, as Lawrence Kolberg and Carol Gilligan have argued, actively discouraged by school and family from engaging ultimate questions.[63]

60. Lewis Austin, *Saints and Samurai: The Political Culture of the American and Japanese Elites* (New Haven, 1975), pp. 22–23; Bradley M. Richardson, *The Political Culture of Japan* (Berkeley, 1974), pp. 112–116.

61. Fukuda's calligraphy has recently graced the inside cover of his alumni magazine, *Kōryō Komaba* 11, no. 2 (April 1969), and he is interviewed in no. 4 (October 1969), pp. 46–50. The other six prime ministers from Ichikō are Konoe Fumimaro, Wakatsuki Reijirō, Hirota Kōki, Ashida Hitoshi, Hatoyama Ichirō, Kishi Nobusuke. (Nishizawa, pp. 247–250.)

62. Takeshi Ishida, *Japanese Society* (New York, 1971), p. 65.

63. Lawrence Kohlberg and Carol Gilligan, "The Adolescent as a Philosopher: The Discovery of the Self in a Post-conventional World," *Daedalus* (Fall 1971), pp. 1051–1086.

The discovery of the adolescent qua philosopher allowed the higher schools to become institutional wellsprings of the Taishō and early Shōwa literary renaissance.[64] Struggling to maintain distance from the popular culture of the 1920s, with its "modern girls" singing "Darling Won't You Love Me?" (*Aishite chōdai ne*),[65] student writers developed a critical perspective on society, enabling them to react to the pathology of industrialization by scouring the depths of human consciousness for the existential meaning of life. Much that was written was experimental and sometimes garbled. But tentative probes of the inner life were a necessary step toward the self-awakening of the young artist. One is impressed by the extraordinary number of modern Japanese philosophers and literary figures whose first serious publications appeared in higher school magazines.[66]

Besides serving as a wellspring for the cultural establishment, the higher schools were a positive force for social and political stability in Japan during the most trying historical circumstances. The schools nurtured a conservative student subculture that valued its organic ties to community over social protest. The politically safe institutionalization of adolescence was complemented by the school's broader contribution to social cohesion within Japan's governing elite. For sixty years the higher schools functioned as a dependable training ground, offering future leaders a common language, a common adolescent experience, and a common locus of social identity that transcended the world of politics. Thus today, the men who control editorial policy for the Communist newspaper *Akahata* on the left and the *Nihon keizai shinbun* on the right, despite sharply differing opinions on party politics, share the same proclivity for serializing higher school memoirs.[67]

As a unique psychological and cultural experience that fostered communication and understanding within the civil elite, the higher schools stood at the forefront of modernization with-

64. In another context Niizeki Takeo makes the same assertion in *Hikari to kage: aru Abe Jirō den* (Tokyo, 1969), pp. 108–109.
65. This and other popular hits of the period are listed on the chronological chart at the end of Suzuki Tsutomu, ed., *Taishō demokurashī*, Nihon rekishi shirīzu, vol. 20 (Tokyo, 1967).
66. The list includes Tanizaki Jun'ichirō, Abe Jirō, Abe Yoshishige, Kawai Eijirō, Kawabata Yasunari, Akutagawa Ryūnosuke, Dazai Osamu, Kamei Katsuichirō, Watsuji Tetsurō, Yanaihara Tadao, Ōya Sōichi, Kume Masao, Kikuchi Kan, and Inoue Yasushi. (Yamamoto Kazuya, pp. 215–220.)
67. Nihon Keizai Shinbun has published numerous higher school memoirs in its *Watakushi no rirekisho* series. Likewise, *Akahata* printed Togawa Yukio's schoolboy romance in a series that appeared during 1971.

out revolution. Certainly Japan's impressive postwar reconstruction stems in part from the availability of a relatively ho-
mogeneous leadership driven by a strong, bureaucratic ethic of
responsibility. The high cultural standards and social stability
bequeathed by the higher schools have been accompanied,
however, by serious inequities. Like all entrenched elites, the
higher school graduates have been able to write their own rules
for who should be given access to power.[68] The intangible
qualities of character and personality, regarded as important
criteria for entry into public office, have also been the projection
of the elite's self-image. "Outsiders" could try to imitate the
character models, but by so doing they only validated their legitimacy. Furthermore, if there was one virtue conspicuously
lacking in the cultivation of the higher school gentleman, it was
tolerance. After spending several years of "ascetic dormitory
life," Kojima Nobuo reflected, the students developed an attitude that anyone deprived of philosophic anguish was an "incapable" or "lowly person" (teikyū na ningen).[69] This view, so
deeply engrained in the rituals of higher school life, could justify social exclusion and even segregation of the cultured few
from the uncultured many. The latter included narrowly focused technicians (senmonka), once described by Nitobe Inazō
as "utensils" (utsuwa),[70] along with women, whose sensibilities
were anathema to the cult of manly valor. Although the social
barriers have begun to crumble in the last decade, the higher
school alumni—in their numerous publications and reunions
extolling the glories of the past—have done very little to dispel
the illusion of a vast social and cultural chasm between themselves and everyone else. Thus the agonies and ecstasies of a
unique adolescent experience have become the foothold for a
"pseudo-class" ideology, linked to the school and the "style of
life" it inculcated as opposed to family wealth and status.

Weighing their contributions against their shortcomings, we
must, in the end, side with the opposition against any move to
restore the higher schools. Discrimination on the basis of sex or
personality, pseudo-class conceits, and the vulnerability to nationalistic appeals are too high a price for artistic creativity and
cohesion at the top of society. Yet, in bidding farewell to the last
generation of higher school graduates, we cannot hide some re-

68. Rupert Wilkinson, Governing Elites (New York, 1969).
69. Quoted in Sō Sakon, p. 103.
70. Morito Tatsuo, "Kyōikusha to shite no . . . ," pp. 332–333.

morse over the simultaneous fading of their standards for cultural excellence. It is ironic that the Japanese student left in recent years has waged its most vigorous protests against not only the intolerance of an entrenched elite but also the "repressive tolerance" for mediocrity and the neutralization of class consciousness in an industrial democracy. Significantly, the recollections of the brief "liberation" of the mammoth and impersonal Japan University by new-left activists in 1969 were published under the title, *Adolescence Wagered upon a Barricade* (*Barikēdo ni kaketa seishun*).[71] Such is the misfortune of the present era that adolescence attains its fullest expression under a crushing mountain of desks and chairs, and that mass higher education may have permanently consigned Japanese students to an undifferentiated culture of comic books, faded jeans, romance hotels, and Kentucky Fried Chicken.

71. Nichidai Zenkyōtō, ed., *Barikēdo ni kaketa seishun: dokyumento Nichidai tōsō* (Tokyo, 1970).

Appendix I

The Public School System in Imperial Japan (1908)

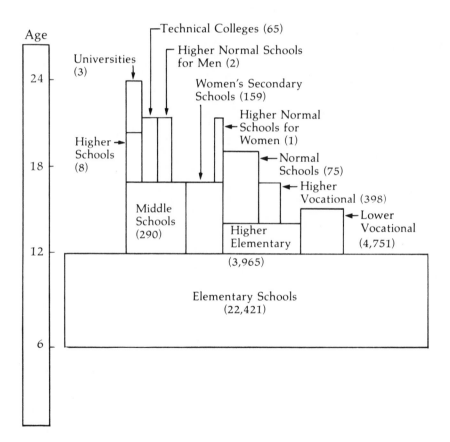

Note: Figures within parentheses represent total number of institutions. Both the lower vocational schools and technical colleges were further subdivided into separate tracks for specific trades or continuing education. *Source:* Monbushō, ed., *Gakusei hachijūnenshi*, pp. 1030–1070. The chart is adapted from p. 1030.

Appendix II

Student Enrollments in Imperial Japan (1908)

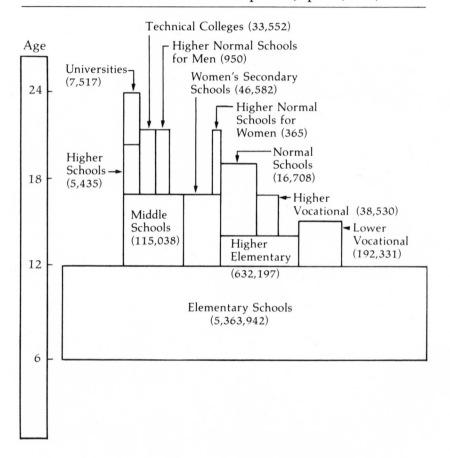

Note: Figures within parentheses represent total number of student enrollments for each sector of the school system. Chart does not include the private schools. *Source:* See Appendix I.

Appendix III

<table>
<thead>
<tr><th rowspan="3">Subjects</th><th>1888</th><th>1896</th><th>1911</th></tr>
<tr><th colspan="3" style="text-align:center">TABLE 1 First-Year
Literature Majors</th></tr>
</thead>
</table>

TABLE 1 First-Year
Literature Majors

Subjects	1888 *Class Hours Per Week*	1896 *Class Hours Per Week*	1911 *Class Hours Per Week*
English	4	7	9
German	4	7	9
Japanese & Chinese Lit.	3	6	6
Philosophy	2	0	0
History	3	4	3
Math	3	3	0
Geography	2	0	0
Geology	2	0	0
Physics	2	0	0
Economics	2	0	0
Logic	0	1 (no credit)	2
Ethics	0	0	1
Calisthenics	3	3	3
Totals	30	30	33

TABLE 1 (Continued)
First-Year Science Majors

Subjects	1888 Class Hours Per Week	1896 Class Hours Per Week	1911 Class Hours Per Week
English	4	8	7
German	4	5	7
Japanese & Chinese Lit.	0	5	2*
History	0	0	0
Math	3	5	4
Geology	2	2	0
Physics	4	0	2
Economics	2	0	0
Chemistry	2	0	2
Drawing	3	2	2
Surveying	3	0	0
Natural Hist.	0	0	3
Logic	0	1 (no credit)	0
Ethics	0	0	1
Calisthenics	3	3	3
Totals	30	30	33

Note: Figures are taken from *Rokujūnenshi*, pp. 180–182, 267–270, 330.

*The two-hour classical literature requirement for science majors was increased to four hours in 1919; *Rokujūnenshi*, p. 365.

TABLE 2 Dissolution of the Higher School Technical Courses

Year	Law	Engineering	Medicine	University Preparation
1897	42	163	1,556	2,675
1898	19	136	1,611	2,898
1899	0	113	1,806	3,171
1900	0	138	1,944	3,602
1901	x	170	x	4,191
1902	x	172	x	4,906
1903	x	184	x	4,890
1904	x	191	x	4,755
1905	x	214	x	4,690
1906	x	x	x	4,534

Note: x signifies dissolution of the course. Figures are taken from Nakajima Tarō, "Kyusei kōtō gakkō no bensen (1)," Tōhoku Daigaku nennō, vol. 11 (1963), p. 14.

TABLE 3 Matriculation Figures, 1896–1932

	1896	1904	1912	1919	1926	1932
Primary School	1,091,219	1,513,772	1,509,732	1,872,084	2,186,093	2,521,728
Middle School	18,345	31,988	37,018	44,918	77,736	73,314
Higher School	1,210	1,546	2,065	2,896	5,833	4,953
University	782	1,925	2,822	3,841	6,290	6,873

Note: Primary school figures include men and women. Figures taken from Kyōikushi Hensankai, ed., Meiji ikō kyōiku seido hattatsushi, vols. 4, 6, and 7 (Tokyo, 1964). The figures show the extremely high rate of attrition from the primary schools to the higher schools.

TABLE 4   Student Withdrawals, 1903–1934

	1903	1908	1913	1918	1924	1934
Family Problems	130	128	163	85	122	116
Sickness	72	48	49	56	121	119
Default on Tuition	7	41	50	31	22	25
Expulsion for Misbehavior	12	1	18	16	9	14
Academic Expulsion	15	4	34	38	37	20
Transfers	12	15	4	17	2	0
Deaths	21	23	28	65	72	77

Note: Total student enrollment in the national higher schools grew from 5,074 in 1903 to 18,905 in 1934. Still, the rate of academic expulsion remains infinitesimal. Except for 1913, the death rate exceeded the expulsion rate. More detailed statistics for the 1930s reveal that the most prestigious higher school, namely Ichikō, rarely expelled a single student for academic reasons. Figures are taken from *Monbushō dai sanjūgo nenpō* (p. 172); *Monbushō dai yonjū nenpō* (p. 130); *Monbushō dai yonjūgo nenpō* (p. 138); *Monbushō dai gojūni nenpō* (pp. 153–155); *Monbushō dai rokujūni nenpō* (pp. 164–165).

Glossary

Listed here are many of the Japanese terms and names used in the study.

Abe Jirō	阿部次郎
Abe Yoshishige	安倍能成
Aa gyokuhai	嗚呼玉杯
Ai to ninshiki to no shuppatsu	愛と認識との出発
Akanuma Kinzaburō	赤沼金三郎
Akase Yayoki	赤瀬八代喜
Akizuki In'ei	秋月胤永
Amano Teiyū	天野貞祐
Aoki Tokuzō	青木得三
Atoda Reizō	阿刀田令造
Awano Kenjirō	栗野健次郎
bannō kōfū	万能校風
Barikēdo ni kaketa seishun	バリケードに賭けた青春
bokō	母校
botsuga	没我
bu	武
bun	文
bunka	文科
bunmeibyō	文明病
bu-seikatsu	部生活
busshitsuteki bunmei	物質的文明
chii to sekinin	地位と責任
chigai hōken	治外法権
chishiki kaikyū	知識階級
chōja ni majiware	長者に交れ
chōjidaiteki	超時代的
chōjin dōtoku	超人道徳
Chōzenryō	超然寮
chūgakusei konjō	中学生根性
Chūkenkai	中堅会
chūkun aikoku	忠君愛国

Dai Go Kōtō Gakkō   第五高等学校
Dai Ichi Kōtō Gakkō   第一高等学校
Dai Ni Kōtō Gakkō   第二高等学校
Dai San Kōtō Gakkō   第三高等学校
Dai Yon Kōtō Gakkō   第四高等学校
daigaku yoka   大学予科
dantaiteki ishi   団体的意志
dōbutsuteki genki   動物的元気
dōsei jūkō   同性獣行

Egi Sadao   江木定男

fubun no kenpō   不文の憲法
fugen jikkō   不言実行
Fujimura Misao   藤村操
Fujiwara Tadashi   藤原正
fuka keichō   浮華軽佻
Fukui Rikichirō   福井利吉郎
Fukuzawa Yukichi   福沢諭吉
fusei na yūgi   不正な遊戯
futongan   蒲団丸
futsū jitsugyō kyōiku   普通実業教育

gakkagai no yōdō   学科外の要道
gakumon   学問
gakusei sōsho   学生叢書
Gakusuikai zasshi   嶽水会雑誌
gankotō   頑固党
gantō no kan   厳頭の感
gasshuku   合宿
genki   元気
genshiteki kōfū   原始的校風
gisei seishin   犠牲精神
go isshin   御一新
gōken   剛健
gōki bokutotsu   剛毅木訥
Gokō   五高
gokokuki   護国旗
gyōjōten   行状点

hankō   藩校
hanmon seinen   煩悶青年
Hatoyama Ichirō   鳩山一郎
Hatta Yoshiaki   八田嘉明
heifū   弊風

heishiki taisō	兵式体操
hōchishugi	法治主義
hōjin no kachi	邦人の勝ち
Ichikō	一高
Ichikō tamashii monogatari	一高魂物語
iinkai	委員会
Imamura Yūrin	今村有隣
Inoue Kowashi	井上毅
Inoue Tetsujirō	井上哲次郎
ittei no kōfū	一定の校風
Iwamoto Tei	岩元禎
Iwanami Shigeo	岩波茂雄
jichi seido	自治制度
Jichiryō	自治寮
jiga no seikatsu	自我の生活
jiko kakusei	自己覚醒
jinjō chūgakkō	尋常中学校
jinjō bon'yō no shosei	尋常凡庸の書生
jinkakushugi	人格主義
jinsei no kyōshi	人生の教師
jinseikan no gaku	人生観の学
jinzai	人材
Jisatsuron	自殺論
jisui seido	自炊制度
jitsugaku	実学
jitsurishugi	実利主義
jiyū no kojō	自由の孤城
jōjitsushugi	情実主義
junsui	純粋
kaikishuku seido	皆寄宿制度
Kaisei Gakkō	開成学校
kangei sutōmu	歓迎ストーム
kangeiko	寒稽古
kangeki	感激
Kanō Kōkichi	狩野亨吉
kanritsu gaikokugo gakkō	官立外国語学校
kansei kyōiku	完成教育
katei kyōiku	家庭教育
Kawai Eijirō	河合栄治郎
keihakushi	軽薄子
kenbu	剣舞
kindai no chōkoku	近代の超克

kinensai	記念祭
kinjō teppeki	金城鉄壁
kinken shōbu	勤倹尚武
Kinoshita Hiroji	木下広次
Kiriyama Benroku	桐山勉六
kishukusha sawakai	寄宿舎茶話会
Kitazawa Teikichi	北沢定吉
kiyaku	規約
kobushi no tenkei	古武士の典型
kōfū	校風
kōfū ronsō	校風論争
Kōfūkai	興風会
kogai yūgibu	校外遊戯部
kōha	硬派
kōhai	後輩
kokka no chūseki	国家の柱石
kokoro no furusato	心の故郷
kōkyō no kokoro	公共の心
Komachida Sanji	小町田粲爾
kōnai undō	校内運動
konpa	コンパ
Kōryōshi	向陵誌
kōshinsei	貢進生
kōtō gakkō	高等学校
kōtō gakkō bābarizumu	高等学校バーバリズム
Kōyūkai	校友会
kūyūkan seisai	校友間制裁
kunshi	君子
Kurata Hyakuzō	倉田百三
Kuwaki Genyoku	桑木厳翼
kyōdō seikatsu	共同生活
Kyōfūkai	矯風会
kyōiku	教育
kyōsaibu	共済部
kyōyō	教養
kyūsei kōkō	旧制高校
kyūsei kōkō fukkatsuron	旧制高校復活論
kyūsei kōtō gakkō	旧制高等学校
kyūshin	球神
Maeda Tamon	前田多門
makanai seibatsu	賄征伐
mannendoko	万年床
Meizenryō	明善寮
miebōshugi	外容主義

Miki Kiyoshi	三木清
Miyako no sora	都の空
mobo	モボ
moga	モガ
Mori Arinori	森有礼
Mori Ōgai	森鷗外
Mori Ritsuko	森律子
Moriyama Tsunetarō	守山恒太郎
Morito Tatsuo	森戸辰男
Motoda Eifū	元田永孚
Mukōgaoka	向ヶ岡
naibu seikatsu	内部生活
naite bōryoku o kuwae	泣て暴力を加へ
Nakagawa Gen	中川元
nanpa	軟派
Natsume Sōseki	夏目漱石
Nikō	二高
ningen keisei	人間形成
Nishida Kitarō	西田幾多郎
Nishimura Shigeki	西村茂樹
Nitobe Inazō	新渡戸稲造
nō kondishon	ノーコンデイション
Noda Heijirō	野田兵次郎
nyūryō enzetsu	入寮演説
nyūryōshiki	入寮式
Okano Yoshisaburō	岡野義三郎
Ōmuro Teiichirō	大室貞一郎
onchi	音痴
onna jiken	女事件
Orita Hikoichi	折田彦市
rakudaisei	落第生
reigi sahō	礼儀作法
risōteki kōfū	理想的校風
risshin shusse	立身出世
risshin shusse no meisō	立身出世の迷想
rōjōshugi	籠城主義
Rokumeikan	鹿鳴館
ryōka	寮歌
ryō-seikatsu	寮生活
ryōu	寮雨
Ryūnankai zasshi	龍南会雑誌

Santarō no nikki	三太郎の日記
Sankō	三高
seichi	聖地
seigi no koe	正義の声
seiji seinen	政治青年
seikō seinen	成功青年
seinen bunka	青年文化
Seiro no uta	征露の歌
seishinjō ni oite kizoku	精神上において貴族
seishun	青春
seisoku seido	正則制度
senkyō	仙境
senmon gakkō	専門学校
senpai	先輩
shakai jōryū	社会上流
shakai no chūseki	社会の柱石
shakan seido	舎監制度
shi	士
Shikō	四高
shi kōryō	四綱領
shinshichō	新思潮
shinnyū assei seisaku	新入圧制政策
shinsei naru kōfū	神聖なる校風
shishi	志士
shitsujitsu	質実
shitsuke	躾
shoseifū	書生風
shosei no honbun	書生の本分
Shōshikai	尚志会
Shūgakuryō	習学寮
shūyō	修養
sōdaikai	総代会
sōdō	騒動
soshiarichī	ソシアリチー
Suehiro Izutarō	末広厳太郎
sutōmu	ストーム
taigi meibun	大義名分
taihoshugi	退歩主義
taijin kunshi	大人君子
Takayama Chogyū	高山樗牛
Takayama Shūgetsu	高山秋月
Takeyama Michio	竹山道雄
Tanaka Tōru	田中徹
teikyū na ningen	低級な人間

tekken seisai	鉄拳制裁
tenju no hōritsu	天授の法律
tetteishugi	徹底主義
tettō tetsubi jun'itsu	徹頭徹尾純一
Tezuka Tomio	手塚富雄
tojita shakai	閉じた社会
tokuiku	徳育
Tokutomi Roka	徳富蘆花
Tokutomi Sohō	徳富蘇峰
Tōsei shosei katagi	当世書世気質
Tsubouchi Shōyō	坪内逍遙
Tsukuda Toyōo	佃土用男
Tsurumi Yūsuke	鶴見祐輔
Tsutsumi Biro	提毘盧
Uchimura Kanzō	内村鑑三
undō kōfū	運動校風
undōkai	運動会
Uozumi Kageo	魚住影雄
Uzawa Fusa'aki	鵜沢総明
Watsuji Tetsurō	和辻哲郎
Yakyūbuka	野球部歌
Yamaji Aizan	山路愛山
Yanaihara Tadao	矢内原忠雄
yaseiji	野性児
yaseiteki chiseijin	野性的知性人
Yoshida Kumaji	吉田熊次
Yoshimura Toratarō	吉村寅太郎
yowaki mono no kai	弱きものの会
yūdai gōken	雄大剛健
zenjin kyōiku	全人教育
zenkoku no mohan	全国の模範
zentorumen	ゼントルメン
zokubutsu	俗物
zokukai	俗界
Zōshikan	造士館

Bibliography

The bibliography includes the principal sources for this study. The most vivid information on student life was found in "dormitory histories," student magazines, alumni bulletins, and memoirs. Since the "dormitory histories" were collective diaries, written strictly for the private use of students in a given institution and never sold in local bookstores, there are few remaining volumes, although some are available in the National Diet Library. The student magazines that I examined include *Dai Ichi Kōtō Gakkō Kōyūkai zasshi* for First Higher, *Shōshikai zasshi* for Second Higher, *Gakusuikai zasshi* for Third Higher, and *Ryūnankai zasshi* for Fifth Higher. These are located, respectively, in the libraries of Tokyo University (Komaba campus), Tōhoku University, Kyoto University, and Kumamoto University. Most anonymous reports, and some authored ones, cited from the student and alumni magazines are not included in the bibliography.

When I embarked on this project eight years ago, the recent literature on the higher schools was characterized by a multitude of glowing reminiscences and a virtual absence of scholarly inquiry (the one notable exception being Nakajima Tarō's articles on institutional development, which are listed below). Undoubtedly, the memory of the higher school as an institution that was discredited after the war has been too vivid for scholars, who are often themselves alumni, to launch serious investigations of a portion of their own past. The situation has begun to change in the last several years, at least among specialists in educational policy and history if not among more general historians, notably with the publication of Toita Tomoyoshi's *Kyūsei kōtō gakkō kyōiku no seiritsu* (The establishment of old higher school education) and several fascinating articles by Terasaki Masao, which are listed in the bibliography. Focusing on the details of formal administration and student activities during the early years of the higher schools, Toita's book is, to date, the only full-length historical study of preparatory education in Japan. Fairly extensive treatment of the institutional development of the higher schools can also be found in the volumes of *Nihon kindai kyōiku hyakunenshi* (The one-hundred-year history of modern Japanese education) published by the National Institute for Educational Research. In addition, a group of alumni, some of whom are also educators, launched a small bulletin in 1974 entitled *Kyūsei kōtō gakkōshi kenkyū* (Studies in the history of the old higher schools). The bulletin has included a variety of essays on institutional development and student clubs, along with reminiscences and notes about sources for specific higher schools. A series of informative essays by the editor, Takahashi Samon, have been reprinted in a book listed below. Unfortunately, the bulletin suspended publication with its April 1979 issue, and there is some question as to when and if the periodical will be continued. The editorial staff is, however, working on a multi-volume collection of higher school sources that will be a welcome aid for future researchers.

BIBLIOGRAPHY

Abe Jirō. *Gōhon Santarō no nikki.* Tokyo: Kadokawa, 1962.

Abe Yoshishige. "An Address to the U.S. Education Mission." *Society* 64 (August 1946):1–3.

———. "Fujimura Misao kun o omou." *DIKGKZ*, no. 128 (June 1903), pp. 169–174.

———. *Iwanami Shigeo den.* Tokyo: Iwanami, 1970.

———, ed. *Kanō Kōkichi ibunshū.* Tokyo: Iwanami, 1958.

———. *Seinen to kyōyō.* Tokyo: Iwanami, 1940.

———, ed. *Setsuro ikō.* Tokyo: Iwanami, 1914.

———. "Waga kōfūkan." *DIKGKZ*, no. 152 (December 1905), pp. 8–23.

———. *Waga oitachi-jijoden.* Tokyo: Iwanami, 1970.

Adam, Corinna. "Duels and Jobs for the Boys." *New Statesman*, 18 June 1965, p. 952.

Akanuma Kinzaburō. "Masa ni dai ni no jichisei kishukuryō o min to suru ni tsukite shokai o nobu," part I. *DIKGKZ*, no. 6 (February 1891), pp. 9–16.

———. "Masa ni dai ni no . . . ," part II. *DIKGKZ*, no. 7 (May 1891), pp. 11–16.

———. "Masa ni dai ni no . . . ," part III. *DIKGKZ*, no. 8 (June 1891), pp. 11–15.

Akase Yayoki. "Ryūnan shisōshi," *Ryūnankai zasshi*, no. 137 (December 1910), pp. 26–46.

Amako Tamaru. *Heimin saisho Wakatsuki Reijirō.* Tokyo, 1926.

Amano Teiyū. *Gakusei ni atauru sho.* Tokyo: Iwanami, 1964.

———. "Ichikō no saiken." *Kōryō Komaba* 11 (April 1969):2–3.

———. "Ichikō to watashi." *Kōryō Komaba* 9 (April 1967):6–8.

———. *Kyōiku shiron.* Tokyo: Iwanami, 1949.

Ando Katsuichirō, ed. *Dai San Kōtō Gakkō Benronbu bushi.* Kyoto: Dai San Kōtō Gakkō, 1935.

Aoe Shunjirō. *Kanō Kōkichi no shōgai.* Tokyo: Meiji Shoin, 1974.

Aoki Tokuzō. "Kōryō seikatsu no omoide." *Kōryō Komaba* 9 (April 1967):2–5.

Aries, Philippe. *Centuries of Childhood: A Social History of Family Life.* Translated by Robert Baldick. New York: Vintage Books, 1962.

Arnold, Matthew. *Culture and Anarchy.* Cambridge: Cambridge University Press, 1961.

Asō Makoto, ed. *Erīto. Gendai no esupuri, no. 95.* Tokyo: Shibundō, 1975.

————. *Erīto to kyōiku.* Tokyo: Fukumura Shuppan, 1969.

Asukai Masamichi. "Kokuminteki bunka no keisei." In *Iwanami kōza: Nihon rekishi* 18: pp. 278–311. Tokyo: Iwanami, 1963.

Atoda Reizō. *Nikō o kataru.* Sendai: Dai Ni Kōtō Gakkō Kyōsaibu, 1937.

Austin, Lewis. *Saints and Samurai: The Political Culture of the American and Japanese Elites.* New Haven: Yale University Press, 1975.

Azuma Suehiko. "Fujimura Misao no omoide." *Kōryō Komaba* 10 (October 1964):12–17.

Azuma Toshio, ed. *Supōtsu hachijūnenshi.* Tokyo: Nihon Taiiku Kyōkai, 1958.

Bartholomew, James R. "Japanese Modernization and the Imperial Universities, 1876–1920." *Journal of Asian Studies* 37 (February 1978): 251–271.

Beard, Miriam. *Realism in Romantic Japan.* New York: MacMillan Co., 1930.

Beauchamp, Edward R. *An American Teacher in Early Meiji Japan.* Honolulu: University of Hawaii Press, 1976.

Beckman, George M. "Japanese Adaptations of Marx-Leninism." *Asia Cultural Studies* 3. Tokyo: International Christian University, 1962.

Bellah, Robert. "Japan's Cultural Identity: Some Reflections on the Work of Watsuji Tetsurō." *Journal of Asian Studies* 24 (August 1965): 573–594.

Bendix, Reinhard. "The Traditional and Modern Reconsidered." *Comparative Studies in Society and History* 9 (April 1967):292–346.

Bendix, Reinhard, and Lipset, Seymour, eds., *Class, Status and Power.* New York: Free Press, 1966.

Bernstein, Basil. "Social Class, Language and Socialization." In *Class, Codes and Control*, vol. 1, edited by Basil Bernstein. London: Routledge and Kegan Paul, 1971.

Bernstein, Gail Lee. *Japanese Marxist: A Portrait of Kawakami Hajime, 1879–1946.* Cambridge, Mass.: Harvard University Press, 1976.

Blacker, Carmen. *The Japanese Enlightenment.* Cambridge: Cambridge University Press, 1964.

Blos, Peter. *On Adolescence: A Psychoanalytic Interpretation.* New York: Free Press, 1962.

Bottomore, T. B. *Classes in Modern Society.* New York: Vintage Books, 1966.

Bungeibu. "Kyakumon," *DIKGKZ*, no. 79 (September 1898), pp. 1–7.

Camus, Albert. *The Rebel.* New York: Vintage Books, 1951.

Canby, Henry Seidel. *Alma Mater.* New York: Farrar & Rinehart, 1936.

Craig, Albert. "Kido Kōin and Ōkubo Toshimichi." In *Personality in Japanese History,* edited by Albert Craig and Donald Shively. Berkeley: University of California Press, 1970.

Crowley, James B. "Intellectuals as Visionaries of the New Asian Order." In *Dilemmas of Growth in Prewar Japan,* edited by James W. Morley. Princeton: Princeton University Press, 1971.

Dai Go Kōtō Gakkō Kaikō Gojūnen Kinenkai, ed., *Gokō gojūnenshi,* Kumamoto: Dai Go Kōtō Gakkō, 1939.

"Dai ichi gakki zenryō sawakai kiji." *DIKGKZ*, no. 151 (November 15, 1905), pp. 92–98.

Dai Ichi Kōtō Gakkō, ed., *Dai Ichi Kōtō Gakkō rokujūnenshi.* Tokyo: Dai Ichi Kōtō Gakkō, 1939.

Dai Ichi Kōtō Gakkō Kishukuryō, ed. *Kōryōshi.* Tokyo: Dai Ichi Kōtō Gakkō Kishukuryō, 1925.

"Dai jūkyūkai kishukuryō sōritsu kinensai kiji." *DIKGKZ*, no. 185 (March 1910), pp. 82–100.

Dai Roku Kōtō Gakkō Seitoryō, ed., *Rokuryō ryōshi.* Okayama: Dai Roku Kōtō Gakkō Seitoryō, 1925.

Dai San Kōtō Gakkō Dōsōkai, ed. "Kōhon Jinryōshi." Unpublished manuscript.

Dai San Kōtō Gakkō Kishukusha Ryōshi Henshūbu, ed. "Jiyūryōshi." Unpublished manuscript.

Dai Shichi Kōtō Gakkō Zōshikan Dōsōkai, ed. *Shichikō omoideshū, kōhen.* Kagoshima: Dai Shichi Kōtō Gakkō Zōshikan Dōsōkai, 1963.

Dai Yon Kōtō Gakkō Jishūryō Ryōshi Hensan Iinkai, ed. *Dai Yon Kōtō Gakkō Jishūryōshi.* Kanazawa: Dai Yon Kōtō Gakkō Jishūryō, 1948.

DeConde, Alexander, ed. *Student Activism.* New York: Scribner's, 1971.

Deguchi Kyō. *Kōtō gakkō juken hiketsu.* Tokyo: Konishi Shoten, 1919.

———. *Zenkoku kōtō gakkō hyōbanki.* Tokyo: Keibunkan, 1902.

De Vos, George A. *Socialization for Achievement.* Berkeley: University of California Press, 1973.

Dilworth, David A., and Hirano Umeyo. *Fukuzawa Yukichi's An Encouragement of Learning.* Tokyo: Sophia University, 1969.

Dixon, William G. *The Land of the Morning.* Edinburgh: J. Gemmell, 1882.

Dore, Ronald P., ed. *Aspects of Social Change in Modern Japan.* Princeton: Princeton University Press, 1967.

———. *The Diploma Disease.* London: Allen and Unwin, 1976.

———. "Education: Japan." In *Political Modernization in Japan and Tur-*

key, edited by Robert E. Ward and Dunkwart A. Rustow. Princeton: Princeton University Press, 1964.

———. *Education in Tokugawa Japan*. Berkeley: University of California Press, 1965.

———. "The Thought of Men: The Thought of Society." *Asian Cultural Studies* 3 (October 1962):73–86.

Dower, John W., ed. *Origins of the Modern Japanese State: Selected Writings of E. H. Norman*. New York: Pantheon, 1975.

Durkheim, Emile. *Moral Education: A Study in the Theory and Application of the Sociology of Education*. New York: Free Press, 1961.

Duus, Peter. "Nagai Ryūtarō and the 'White Peril,' 1905–1944." *Journal of Asian Studies* 31 (November 1971):41–48.

Eisenstadt, S. N. *From Generation to Generation: Age Groups and Social Structure*. New York: Free Press, 1964.

Eliot, T. S. *Essays Ancient and Modern*. New York: Harcourt, Brace and Co., 1932.

Elkind, David. "Egocentrism in Adolescence." In *Adolescents: Readings in Behavior and Development*, edited by Ellis D. Evans. Hinsdale, Ill.: Dryden Press, 1970.

Erikson, Erik H. *Identity, Youth and Crisis*. New York: W. W. Norton, 1968.

———. "Youth: Fidelity and Diversity." In *The Challenge of Youth*, edited by Erik H. Erikson. Garden City, N.Y.: Anchor Books, 1965.

Eto Takehito and Fujita Gōshi. *Suishō meguru-kyūsei kōtō gakkō monogatari Matsu Kōkō hen*. Tokyo: Zaikei Hyōronsha, 1967.

Feibleman, James K. "The Philosophy of Adolescence." *Adolescence* 4 (1969):477–510.

Feuer, Lewis S. *The Conflict of Generations*. New York: Basic Books, 1969.

Fishman, Sterling. "Suicide, Sex and the Discovery of the German Adolescent." *History of Education Quarterly* 10 (Summer 1970):170–188.

Fitch, Joshua. *Thomas and Matthew Arnold*. New York: Scribner's, 1897.

Fitzgerald, F. Scott. *This Side of Paradise*. New York: Scribner's, 1970.

Freud, Anna. *The Ego and the Mechanism of Defense*. New York: Free Press, 1962.

Friedenberg, Edgar Z. *The Vanishing Adolescent*. New York: Dell Pub. Co., 1959.

Fujisawa Eihiko. *Meiji fūzokushi*. Tokyo: Shunyōdō, 1929.

Fujiwara Tadashi. "Aa bōyū Fujimura Misao kun." *DIKGKZ*, no. 128 (June 1903), pp. 74–83.

Fukita Junsuke. "Sono zengo." *Ichikō Dōsōkai kaihō*. (October 1936):30–32.

Fukui Rikichirō. "Iwayuru kojinshugi no kenchi ni tachitaru kōfūkan o hyōsu." *DIKGKZ*, no. 151 (November, 1905), pp. 20–29.

Fukuzawa Yukichi. *The Autobiography of Yukichi Fukuzawa.* Translated by Eiichi Kiyooka. New York: Columbia University Press, 1966.

Futami Takeshi. "Gakusei kaikaku mondai to kōtō gakkō." *KKGK,* no. 6 (October 1975), pp. 3–18.

Gathorne-Hardy, Jonathan. *The Old School Tie.* New York: McGraw-Hill, 1977.

Geertz, Clifford. "Ideology as a Cultural System." In *Ideology and Discontent,* edited by David E. Apter. Glencoe, Ill.: Free Press, 1964.

Genkōsha, ed. *Ryōka wa ikiteiru.* Tokyo: Genkōsha, 1963.

Gerth, Hans, and Mills, C. Wright. *Character and Social Structure: The Psychology of Social Institutions.* New York: Harcourt, Brace & World, 1964.

Gillis, John R. "Conformity and Rebellion: Contrasting Styles of English and German Youth, 1900–33." *History of Education Quarterly,* Fall 1973, pp. 249–260.

———. *Youth and History.* New York: Academic Press, 1974.

Golding, William Gerald. *Lord of the Flies.* New York: Coward-McCann, 1962.

Goldmann, Lucien. "The Moral Universe of the Playwright." In *Sociology of Literature and Drama,* edited by Elizabeth and Tom Burns. Harmondsworth, England: Penguin Books, 1973.

Grew, Joseph C. *Report from Tokyo.* New York: Simon and Schuster, 1942.

Hakugansei. "Undō kōfū to tekken seisai no kachi to o ronjite Kyōfū-kai o nanzu." *Shōshikai zasshi,* no. 49 (May 1902), pp. 22–42.

Hall, G. Stanley. "Student Customs." *Proceedings of the American Antiquarian Society* 14 (1902):83–124.

Hall, Ivan Parker. *Mori Arinori.* Cambridge, Mass.: Harvard University Press, 1973.

Hall, John W., and Jansen, Marius B. eds. *Studies in the Institutional History of Early Modern Japan.* Princeton: Princeton University Press, 1968.

Hall, Robert King. *Education for a New Japan.* New Haven: Yale University Press, 1949.

Halsey, A. H. "The Sociology of Moral Education." In *Moral Education in a Changing Society,* edited by W. R. Niblett. London: Faber and Faber, 1963.

Hamilton, L. B. "The 'Boarding School' Principle in England and Japan." *Kyūryū,* no. 37 (February 1937), pp. 21–27.

Harootunian, H.D. "Between Politics and Culture: Authority and the Ambiguities of Intellectual Choice in Imperial Japan." In *Japan in Crisis,* edited by Bernard S. Silberman and H. D. Harootunian. Princeton: Princeton University Press, 1974.

———. "Introduction: A Sense of an Ending and the Problem of Taishō." In *Japan in Crisis*, edited by Bernard S. Silberman and H. D. Harootunian. Princeton: Princeton University Press, 1974.

————. *Toward Restoration: The Growth of Political Consciousness in Tokugawa Japan*. Berkeley: University of California Press, 1970.

Hasegawa Saiji, "Iwamoto Tei sensei goroku." *Kōryō* 16 (October 1974):184–185.

Hashikawa Bunzō, "Antiwar Values—the Resistance in Japan." *Japan Interpreter* 9 (Spring 1974):86–97.

Hatoyama Ichirō. *Hatoyama Ichirō kaikoroku*. Tokyo: Bungei Shunjū Shinsha, 1957.

Hayashi Kentaro. *Utsuri yuku mono no kage*. Tokyo: Bungei Shunjū Shinsha, 1960.

Hearn, Lafcadio. "The Future of the Far East." *Ryūnankai zasshi*, no. 3 (June 1894), pp. 9–10.

————. *Japan: An Attempt at an Interpretation*. New York: Grosset & Dunlap, 1904.

Hermann Hesse. *Beneath the Wheel*. Translated by Michael Roloff. New York: Bantam, 1970.

Hibbett, Howard. "Akutagawa Ryūnosuke and the Negative Ideal." In *Personality in Japanese History*, edited by Albert M. Craig and Donald H. Shively. Berkeley: University of California Press, 1970.

Hicks, W. R. *The School in English and German Fiction*. London: Soncino Press, 1933.

Hidaka Daishirō. "Kyūsei kōtō gakkō haishi no keii." *KKGK*, no. 5 (August 1975), pp. 56–60.

Higham, John. "The Reorientation of American Culture in the 1890s." In *The Origins of Modern Consciousness*, edited by John Weis. Detroit: Wayne State University Press, 1965.

Higuchi Ichiyō. "Growing Up." In *Modern Japanese Literature*, edited by Donald Keene. New York: Grove Press, 1960.

Hirose Kenzō. *Nihon no yakyūshi*. Tokyo: Nihon Yakyūshi Kankōkai, 1964.

Hirose Yutaka. *Yoshida Shōin no kenkyū*. Tokyo: Musashino Shoin, 1943.

Hsu, Francis L. K. "Prejudice and Its Intellectual Effect in American Anthropology: An Ethnographic Report," *American Anthropologist* 75 (1973):1–19.

Hughes, Thomas. *Tom Brown's Schooldays*. New York: St. Martin's Press, 1967.

Huizinga, Johan. *Homo Ludens*. Boston: Beacon, 1955.

Ide Takashi. *Tetsugaku seinen no shuki*. Ide Takashi chosaku shū, vol. 6. Tokyo: Keisō Shobō, 1969.

Ide Yoshinori and Ishida Takeshi. "The Education and Recruitment of Governing Elites in Moderｎ Japan." In *Governing Elites: Studies in*

Training and Selection, edited by Rupert Wilkinson. New York: Oxford University Press, 1969.

Ienaga Saburō. *Daigaku no jiyū no rekishi.* Tokyo: Haniwa Shobo, 1968.

Inoue Tetsujirō. "Meiji shōnen no gakusei kishitsu oyobi kongo no kibō." *Risō* 83 (March 1938):60–70.

Irokawa Daikichi. *Meiji no bunka.* Tokyo: Iwanami, 1970.

Ishida Takeshi. *Japanese Society.* New York: Random House, 1971.

Ishii Mitsuru. *Nitobe Inazō den.* Tokyo: Sekiya Shoten, 1935.

Ishisaka Kinnosuke, ed. *Meizenryō shōshi.* Sendai: Dai Ni Kōtō Gakkō Meizenryō Ryōshi Hensanbu, 1942.

"Itsuwa." *Dai Ichi Kōtō Gakkō Kōyūkai zasshi furoku,* no. 58 (June 20, 1896), pp. 13–25.

Iwai Tadakuma. "Meiji kokka no shisō kōzō." In *Kindai Nihon shakai shisōshi,* vol. 1. Tokyo: Yūhikaku, 1974.

Iwanami Shigeo, ed. *Iwanami kōza kyōiku kagaku,* vol. 17. Tokyo: Iwanami, 1933.

Izumiyama Sanroku. *Tora daijin ni naru made.* Tokyo: Tōhō Shoin, 1953.

James, William. *Memories and Studies.* New York: Longmans, Green, 1953.

Jansen, Marius B. "Changing Japanese Attitudes Toward Modernization." In *Changing Japanese Attitudes Toward Modernization,* edited by Marius B. Jansen. Princeton: Princeton University Press, 1965.

Japanese Educational Reform Council. *Education Reform in Japan.* Tokyo, 1950.

Johnson, Owen. *Stover at Yale.* Boston: Little, Brown and Co., 1937.

Jordan, David Starr. *The Voice of the Scholar.* San Francisco: Paul Elder and Co., 1903.

Kadowaki Atsushi. "Risshin shusse no shakaigaku." In *Risshin shusse,* edited by Kadowaki Atsushi. Gendai no esupuri, no. 118. Tokyo: Shibundō, 1977.

Kaigo Tokiomi, ed. *Inoue Kowashi no kyōiku seisaku.* Tokyo: Tokyo Daigaku Shuppankai, 1969.

Kaigo Tokiomi and Terasaki Masao. *Daigaku kyōiku.* Sengo Nihon no kyōiku kaikaku, vol. 9. Tokyo: Tokyo Daigaku Shuppankai, 1972.

Kaigo Tokiomi and Yoshida Noboru. *Gakusei seikatsu chōsa.* Tokyo: Nihon Hyōronsha, 1943.

Kakureishi. "Tenrai." *DIKGKZ,* no. 106 (April 1901), pp. 19–36.

Kamishima Jirō. *Kindai Nihon no seishin kōzō.* Tokyo: Iwanami, 1970.

———. "Meiji no shūen." In *Kindai Nihon seiji shisōshi,* vol. 1, edited by Hashikawa Bunzō and Matsumoto Sannosuke. Tokyo: Yūhikaku, 1971.

Kanō Kōkichi. "Tokuiku ni tsukite" II. *DIKGKZ,* no. 89 (September 30, 1899), pp. 1–4.

Karasawa Tomitarō. *Gakusei no rekishi.* Tokyo: Sōbunsha, 1969.

————. *Kōshinsei.* Tokyo: Gyōsei, 1974.

————. *Kyōshi no rekishi.* Tokyo: Sōbunsha, 1968.

Katō Hidetoshi. "Jisatsu sutairu no hensen." In *Jisatsu,* edited by Ōhara Kenshirō. Tokyo: Shinbundō, 1966.

Kawai Eijirō. "Gakusei jidai no kaiko." In *Gakusei to kyōyō,* edited by Kawai Eijirō. Tokyo: Nihon Hyōronsha, 1940.

————. *Gakusei ni atau.* Gendai kyoyo bunko, vol. 67. Tokyo: Shakai Shisōsha, 1971.

————. *Gakusei seikatsu.* Tokyo: Nihon Hyōronsha, 1936.

————, ed. *Gakusei to seikatsu.* Tokyo: Nihon Hyōronsha, 1938.

Kawakami Jōtarō. "Watakushi no rirekisho." In *Watakushi no rirekisho,* vol. 13. Tokyo: Nihon Keizai Shinbun, 1963.

Kawatake Shigetoshi and Yanagida Izumi. *Tsubouchi Shōyō.* Tokyo: Toyamabō, 1939.

Keene, Donald. "Japanese Writers and the Greater East Asia War." *Journal of Asian Studies* 23 (February 1964):209–224.

Keniston, Kenneth. "Psychological Development and Historical Change." In *The Family in History,* edited by Theodore K. Rabb and Robert I. Rotberg. New York: Harper and Row, 1973.

Kett, Joseph F. *Rites of Passage.* New York: Basic Books, 1977.

Kikukawa Tadao. *Gakusei shakai undōshi.* Tokyo: Kaiguchi, 1947.

Kimijima Ichirō. *Daryō ichibanshitsu: Tanizaki Jun'ichirō to Ichikō ryōyū tachi to.* Tokyo: Jichi Tsūshinsha, 1967.

————. *Nihon yakyū sōseiki.* Tokyo: Bēsu Bōru Magajinsha, 1972.

Kinmonth, Earl H. "Fukuzawa Reconsidered: *Gakumon no susume* and Its Audience." *Journal of Asian Studies* 37 (August 1978):677–696.

————. "The Self-made Man in Meiji Japanese Thought." Ph.D. dissertation, University of Wisconsin, Madison, 1974.

Kinoshita Masao and Kinoshita Michio. "Ko Kinoshita Hiroji no omoide." *Ichikō Dōsōkai kaihō* 30 (February 1936):23–25.

"Kishukuryō dai go kai kinensai kiji." *DIKGKZ,* no. 42 (March 1895), pp. 3–12.

Kita Morio. *Dokutoru Manbō seishunki.* Tokyo: Chūō Kōron, 1967.

Kitasawa Sukeo. *The Life of Dr. Nitobe.* Tokyo: Hokuseidō, 1953.

Kitazawa Teikichi. "Kishuku kyōikuron." *DIKGKZ,* no. 83 (January 1899), pp. 16–30.

Knauth, Lothar. "Life is Tragic." *Monumenta Nipponica* 20 (1965):335–358.

Kobayashi Hiroyuki. *Rokkō monogatari.* Okayama: Nihon Bunkyō Shuppan, 1969.

Kobayashi, Victor N. *John Dewey in Japanese Educational Thought.* Comparative Education Dissertation Series, no. 2. Ann Arbor: University of Michigan, 1964.

"Kōfū mondai enzetsukai." *DIKGKZ,* no. 153 (December 1905), pp. 74–84.

Kohlberg, Lawrence, and Gilligan, Carol. "The Adolescent as a Philosopher: The Discovery of the Self in a Post-conventional World." *Daedalus* 100 (Fall 1971): 1051–1086.

Kokubo Akihiro. "Kindai gakkō hōshiki no dōnyū." In *Kindai kyōikushi.* Kyōikugaku zenshū, vol. 3. Tokyo: Shōgakukan, 1970.

Kokuritsu Kyōiku Kenkyūjo, ed. *Nihon kindai kyōiku hyakunenshi.* Vols. 4–5. Tokyo: Kyōiku Kenkyū Shinkōkai, 1974.

Komatsu Shūkichi, "Kokumin kyōiku seido no seiritsu." In *Kindai kyōikushi.* Kyōikugaku zenshū, vol. 3. Tokyo: Shōgakukan, 1970.

Kondō Kōichirō. *Kōfū manga.* Tokyo, 1917.

Kōzu Yasuo. "Sōkan ni atatte." *Kyūsei kōtō gakkōshi kenkyū,* no. 1 (July 1974), pp. i–ii.

Kristol, Irving. "Memoirs of a Trotskyist." *New York Times Magazine* (January 23, 1977).

Kubo Masaru, ed. *Kēberu hakushi zuihitsushū.* Tokyo: Iwanami, 1970.

Kubota, Akira. *Higher Civil Servants in Postwar Japan: Their Social Origins, Educational Backgrounds and Career Patterns.* Princeton: Princeton University Press, 1969.

Kubota Shōzō. "Kōtō chūgakkō ni okeru gaikokugo kyōiku no ichi." *KKGK,* no. 7 (January 1976), pp. 6–32.

Kuda Katsuo. "Mori Arinori no kyōiku zaisei seisaku." *Kyōikushi kenkyū* 1 (October 1955): 26–31.

Kume Masao. *Gakusei jidai.* Tokyo: Shinchōsha, 1971.

Kurata Hyakuzō. *Ai to ninshiki to no shuppatsu.* In *Sekai kyōyō zenshū,* vol. 3. Tokyo: Heibonsha, 1963.

Kusajima Shigure. *Ichikō jidai.* Tokyo: Tōkai Shyppansha, 1931.

Kuwabara Takeo. "Mori Gesaburō sensei no koto." In *Kuwabara Takeo zenshū,* vol 4. Tokyo: Asahi Shinbunsha, 1968.

Kyōikushi Hensankai, ed. *Meiji ikō kyōiku seido hattatsushi.* Vols. 3–5. Tokyo: Kyōiku Shiryō Chōsakai, 1964.

Kyūchiku Zenshi. *Jichiryō seikatsu.* Tokyo: Hongō Shoin, 1907.

Lasswell, Harold D. *Psychopathology and Politics.* New York: Viking Press, 1962.

Laurenson, Diane, and Swingewood, Alan. *The Sociology of Literature.* New York: Schocken Books, 1972.

Levenson, Joseph R. *Confucian China and Its Modern Fate.* Berkeley: University of California Press, 1968.

Lipset, Seymour Martin. *Student Politics.* New York: Basic Books, 1967.

Lipset, Seymour Martin, and Altbach, Philip G. *Students in Revolt.* Boston: Houghton Mifflin, 1969.

Lipset, Seymour Martin, and Zetterberg, Hans. "A Theory of Social Mobility." In *Class, Status and Power,* edited by Reinhard Bendix and Seymour Lipset. New York: Free Press, 1966.

Lockwood, William W. *The Economic Development of Japan*. Princeton: Princeton University Press, 1968.

McCarthy, Patrick J. *Matthew Arnold and the Three Classes*. New York: Columbia University Press, 1964.

Maeda Tamon and Takagi Yasaka, eds., *Nitobe Hakushi tsuiokushū*. Tokyo: Ko Nitobe Hakushi Kinen Jigyo Iin Tajima Michiji, 1936.

Makino Gorō. *Meijiki keimō kyōiku no kenkyū*. Tokyo: Ochanomizu Shobō, 1968.

Mannheim, Karl. *Man and Society In an Age of Reconstruction*. London: Routledge and Kegan Paul, 1940.

————. *Essays on the Sociology of Culture*. London: Routledge and Kegan Paul, 1962.

Marshall, Byron K. "The Tradition of Conflict in the Governance of Japan's Imperial Universities." *History of Education Quarterly* 17 (Winter 1977): 385–406.

Martyr, Graham, ed. *Ryūnan monogatari*. Kumamoto: Inamoto Hōtokusha Shuppanbu, 1930.

Maruyama Masao. "Patterns of Individuation and the Case of Japan: A Conceptual Scheme." In *Changing Japanese Attitudes Toward Modernization*, edited by Marius B. Jansen. Princeton: Princeton University Press, 1965.

————. *Thought and Behavior in Modern Japanese Politics*. Translated by Ivan Morris. London: Oxford University Press, 1966.

Mashita Shin'ichi. "Dentō o koete: kyūsei kōtō gakkōron." *KKGK*, no. 15 (January 1978), pp. 1–19.

Matsumoto Kenji. *Zōho genten kindai kyōikushi*. Tokyo: Fukumura Shuppan, 1970.

Matsumoto Sannosuke. *Kindai Nihon no chiteki jōkyō*. Tokyo: Chūō Kōron, 1974.

Matza, David. "Subterranean Traditions of Youth." *Annals of the American Academy of Political and Social Science* 338 (November 1961): 102–118.

May, Henry Farnham. *The End of American Innocence; A Study of the First Years of Our Times, 1912–1917*. New York: Knopf, 1959.

Mayhew, Leon. "Ascription in Modern Societies." In *The Logic of Social Hierarchies*, edited by Edward O. Laumann, et al. Chicago: Markham, 1970.

Mills, C. Wright. *The Power Elite*. New York: Oxford, 1959.

Minamigumo Shōnosuke. "Hitotsubashi jidai no kaiko." *Ichikō Dōsōkai kaihō*, no. 24 (January 1934), pp. 64–83.

Mitani Takanobu. "Iwamoto Tei sensei no omoide." *Kōryō Komaba* 12 (April 1970): 25–28.

Miwa Kimitada. "Crossroads of Patriotism." Ph.D. dissertation, Princeton University, 1967.

Miyahara Seiichi and Miyasaka Kōsaku. "Seinenki kyōiku no rekishi." In *Iwanami kōza gendai kyōikugaku*, vol. 16. Tokyo: Iwanami, 1961.

Miyajima Shin'ichi, ed. *Ryūnan monogatari.* Kumamoto: Miyajima Shin'ichi, 1962.

Miyamoto Kazukichi. "Bōyū Uozumi Kageo kun." *DIKGKZ*, no. 202 (February 1911), pp. 1–15.

Miyasaka Tetsufumi. "Kagai kyōikushi." In *Kagai katsudō no rekishi*, Kyōiku bunka taikei, vol. 1. Tokyo: Kaneko Shobō, 1953.

Mizener, Arthur. *The Far Side of Paradise: A Biography of F. Scott Fitzgerald.* New York: Vintage Books, 1960.

Moiwa Toyohei. *Ichikō tamashii monogatari.* Tokyo: Hakubunkan, 1925.

Moller, Herbert. "Youth as a Force in the Modern World." *Comparative Studies in History and Society* 10 (1967–68):237–260.

Monbushō, ed. *Gakusei hachijūnenshi.* Tokyo: Ōkurashō Insatsukyoku, 1954.

Mori Ōgai. *Vita Sexualis.* Translated by Kazuji Ninomiya and Sanford Goldstein. Rutland, Vermont: Charles E. Tuttle, 1972.

Morison, Elting E., ed. *The Square Deal.* The Letters of Theodore Roosevelt, vol. 4. Cambridge, Mass.: Harvard University Press, 1951.

Morito Tatsuo. "Kyōikusha to shite no Nitobe sensei." In *Nitobe Hakushi tsuiokushū*, edited by Maeda Tamon and Takagi Yasaku. Tokyo: Ko Nitobe Hakushi Kinen Jigyo Iin Tajima Michiji, 1936.

Motoyama Yukihiko, ed. *Meiji kyōiku seron no kenkyū*, vol. 1. Tokyo: Fukumura Shuppan, 1972.

———, ed. *Meiji zenki gakkō seiritsushi.* Tokyo: Miraisha, 1965.

Musgrove, F. *Youth and the Social Order.* Bloomington: Indiana University Press, 1965.

Musil, Robert. *Young Törless.* New York: Signet, 1964.

Muus, Rolf E. *Theories of Adolescence.* New York: Random House, 1968.

Nagai Kafū. "The River Sumida." In *Kafū the Scribbler: The Life and Writings of Nagai Kafū, 1879–1959.* Stanford, Calif.: Stanford University Press, 1965.

Nagai Michio. "Chishikijin no seisan rūto." In *Kindai Nihon shisōshi kōza*, vol. 4. Tokyo: Chikuma Shobo, 1972.

———. *Higher Education in Japan: Its Take-off and Crash.* Translated by Jerry Dusenbury. Tokyo: University of Tokyo Press, 1971.

Nagai Michio and Nishijima Takeo. "Postwar Japanese Education and the United States." In *Mutual Images: Essays in American-Japanese Relations.* Cambridge, Mass.: Harvard University Press, 1975.

Nagao Tomiji. "Gendai ni okeru kyōikushi kenkyū no kadai." In *Kyōikugaku zenshū*, vol. 3. Tokyo: Shōgakukan, 1970.

Najita, Tetsuo. *Japan.* Englewood Cliffs, N.J.: Prentice-Hall, 1974.

———. "Some Reflections on Idealism in the Political Thought of

Yoshino Sakuzō." In *Japan in Crisis,* edited by Bernard S. Silberman and H. D. Harootunian. Princeton: Princeton University Press, 1974.

Naka Arata. *Meiji no kyōiku.* Tokyo: Shibundō, 1967.

Nakaizumi Tetsutoshi. *Nihon kinsei kyōiku shisō no kenkyū.* Tokyo: Yoshikawa Kōbunkan, 1966.

Nakajima Tarō. *Kindai Nihon kyōiku seidoshi.* Tokyo: Iwasaki Shoten, 1969.

————. "Kyūsei kōtō gakkō seido no hensen," part II. *Tōhoku Daigaku Kyōikugakubu kenkyū nenpo* (1964), pp. 1–50.

————. "Kyūsei kōtō gakkō seido no seiritsu." *Tōhoku Daigaku Kyōikugakubu kenkyū nenpō* (1957), pp. 1–19.

Nakane Chie. *Japanese Society.* Berkeley: University of California Press, 1970.

Nakano Yoshio. "Kyūsei kōkō teki naru mono." *Tenbō* 72: 110–117.

————. *Roka Tokutomi Kenjirō dai ni bu.* Tokyo: Chikuma Shobo, 1972.

Nakauma Kō. "Kōfū to undōka to no kankei o ronjite Kyōto ensei ni oyobu." *DIKGKZ,* no. 34 (February 1894), pp. 11–16.

Nakayama Yoshio and Etō Takehito, eds. *Ten wa Tōhoku yama takaku: Kyūsei kōtō gakkō monogatari (Nikō hen).* Tokyo: Zaikei Hyōronsha, 1966.

Naruse Mukyoku. "Dai Ichi Kōtō Gakkō hihan." *Shinchō* (June 1950), pp. 54–60.

Natsume Sōseki. "Chūgakkō kairyōsaku." *Sōseki zenshū,* vol. 22. Tokyo: Iwanami, 1957.

————. *Sanshirō.* Translated by Jay Rubin. Seattle: University of Washington Press, 1977.

Newsome, David. *Godliness and Good Learning.* London: Murray, 1961.

Niizeki Takeo. *Hikari to kage: aru Abe Jirō den.* Tokyo: Sanseido, 1969.

Nippon Daigaku Zengaku Kyōtō Kaigi. *Barikēdo ni kaketa seishun dokyumento.* Tokyo: Mikasa, 1970.

Nippon Taiiku Kyōkai, ed. *Supōtsu hachijūnenshi.* Tokyo: Nihon Taiiku Kyōkai, Azuma Toshirō, 1958.

Nishida Kitarō. *Nishida Kitarō zenshū,* vol. 12. Tokyo: Iwanami, 1966.

Nishizawa Kichi, et al., eds. *Aa gyokuhai ni hana ukete: Dai Ichi Kōtō Gakkō hachijūnenshi.* Tokyo: Kōdansha, 1972.

Nitobe Inazō. *Japan: Some Phases of Her Problems and Development.* London: Ernest Benn, 1931.

————. *The Japanese Nation.* New York: Putnam, 1912.

————. *Reminiscences of Childhood in the Early Days of Modern Japan.* Tokyo: Maruzen Co., 1934.

————. "Rōjōshugi to soshiarichī to ni tsuite." *DIKGKZ,* no. 163 (January 1907), pp. 13–16.

Noberu Shobō Henshūbu, ed. *Aa seishun dekansho.* Tokyo: Nōberu Shobo, 1969.

Noda Heijirō. "Kōfūron." *DIKGKZ*, no. 3 (January 1891), pp. 22–28.

Novak, Steven J. *The Rights of Youth*. Cambridge, Mass.: Harvard University Press, 1977.

Ōfuji Takahiko. "Orita Sensei ni tsuite." *Gakusuikai zasshi*, no. 48 (March 1911), pp. 3–4.

Ōgiya Shōzō. *Aa gyokuhai ni hana ukete*. Tokyo: Yūki Shobo, 1967.

Oguri Fuyō. *Seishun*. In *Nihon gendai bungaku zenshū*, vol. 11. Tokyo: Kōdansha, 1968.

Ōhara Kenshirō, ed. *Jisatsu*. Gendai no esupuri. Tokyo: Shibundō, 1966.

Oka Yoshitake. "Nichiro sensōgo ni okeru atarashii sedai no seichō," part 1. *Shisō*, no. 512 (1967), pp. 137–149.

———. "Nichiro sensōgo . . . ," part 2. *Shisō*, no. 513 (1967), pp. 361–376.

Okawada Tsunetada. "Seinenron to sedairon." *Shisō*, no. 514 (1967), pp. 445–465.

Ōkubo Toshiaki, ed. *Mori Arinori zenshū*, vol. 1 (Tokyo: Senbundō, 1972.

Ōmuro Teiichirō. *Daigaku oyobi daigakusei*. Tokyo: Tone Shobō, 1941.

———. *Kōkō seikatsuron*. Tokyo: Kenshinsha, 1948.

———. *Seishun no shiseki*. Tokyo: Kawade, 1955.

Ong, W. F. "Latin Language Study as a Renaissance Puberty Rite." In *Sociology, History and Education*, edited by P. W. Musgrave. London: Methuen & Co. Ltd., 1970.

Orita Hikoichi. "Nyūgaku seito e no kokuyu." *Jinshinkai zasshi*, no. 5 (October 1892), pp. 1–2.

Orwell, George I. *Such, Such Were the Joys*. New York: Harcourt, Brace, 1953.

Ōtsuka Motoe. "Jisatsu to seinen." *Taiyō* 9, no. 8 (July 1, 1903):207–213.

Ōura Hachirō, ed., *Sankō hachijūnen kaiko*. Tokyo: Seki Shoin, 1950.

Parsons, Talcott. *Toward a General Theory of Social Action*. Cambridge, Mass.: Harvard University Press, 1951.

———. "Youth in the Context of American Society." In *The Challenge of Youth*, edited by Erik H. Erikson. Garden City, N.Y.: Anchor, 1965.

Passin, Herbert. *Society and Education in Japan*. New York: Teachers College Press, 1965.

Pinner, Frank A. "Students—A Marginal Elite in Politics." In *The New Pilgrims, Youth Protest in Transition*, edited by Philip G. Altbach and Robert S. Laufer. New York: David McKay Co., 1972.

Porter, Robert P. *The Full Recognition of Japan*. London: H. Fraude, 1911.

Pyle, Kenneth B. *The New Generation in Meiji Japan: Problems of Cultural*

Identity, 1885–1895. Stanford: Stanford University Press, 1969.

————. "The Technology of Japanese Nationalism: The Local Improvement Movement, 1900–1918." *Journal of Asian Studies* 33 (November 1973):51–65.

Reed, John R. *Old School Ties: The Public Schools in British Literature.* Syracuse, N.Y.: Syracuse University Press, 1964.

Rekishigaku Kenkyūkai, ed. *Meiji ishinshi kenkyū kōza,* vol. 5. Tokyo: Heibonsha, 1969.

Report of the United States Education Mission to Japan. Washington: U.S. Government Printing Office, 1946.

Richardson, Bradley M. *The Political Culture of Japan.* Berkeley: University of California Press, 1974.

Roden, Donald T. "'Monasticism' and the Paradox of the Meiji Higher Schools." *Journal of Asian Studies* 37 (May 1978):413–425.

Rudolph, Frederick. *The American College and University: A History.* New York: Vintage Books, 1962.

————. "Neglect of Students as a Historical Tradition." In *The College and the Student,* edited by Lawrence E. Dennis and Joseph F. Kauffman. Washington, D.C.: American Council on Education, 1966.

Saitō Tokutarō. *Nijūroku daihan no hangaku to shifū.* Osaka: Zenkoku Shobō, 1944.

Saitō Yoshie. "Seisai shikō no dōki." *DIKGKZ,* no. 111 (November 1901), pp. 1–7.

————. "Seisairon." *DIKGKZ,* no. 98 (June 1900), pp. 1–20.

Sakakura Tokutarō, ed. *Jinryō shōshi.* Kyoto: Sankō Dōsōkai, 1939.

Sakamoto Yasuyuki, ed. *Aa gyokuhai: Kyūsei kōtō gakkō monogatari 1.* Tokyo: Zaikei Hyōronsha, 1967.

Sakudō Yoshio and Etō Takehito, eds. *Hokushin naname ni sasu tokoro.* Tokyo: Zaikei Hyōronsha, 1970.

Satake Kazuyo. "Kyūsei kōtō gakkō kishōron," part 1. *KKGK,* no. 2 (October 1974), pp. 1–2.

Scheiner, Irwin. *Christian Converts and Social Protest in Meiji Japan.* Berkeley: University of California Press, 1970.

Schorer, Mark. *Sinclair Lewis.* New York: McGraw-Hill, 1961.

Seidensticker, Edward. *Kafū the Scribbler: The Life and Writings of Nagai Kafū, 1879–1959.* Stanford, Calif.: Stanford University Press, 1968.

Sheldon, Henry D. *Student Life and Customs.* New York: Arno Press, 1969.

Shimamoto Hisae. *Meiji no joseitachi.* Tokyo: Misuzu Shobō, 1966.

Shimizu Yoshirō. *Shiken.* Tokyo: Iwanami, 1957.

Shively, Donald H. "Motoda Eifū: Confucian Lecturer to the Meiji Emperor." In *Confucianism in Action,* edited by David S. Nivison and Arthur F. Wright. Stanford, Calif.: Stanford University Press, 1959.

————. "Nishimura Shigeki: A Confucian View of Modernization." In *Changing Japanese Attitudes Toward Modernization,* edited by Marius Jansen. Princeton: Princeton University Press, 1965.

Shūgakuryōshi Hensanbu. *Shūgakuryōshi.* Kumamoto: Dai Go Kōtō Gakkō Shūgakuryō, 1938.

Singer, Kurt. *Mirror, Sword and Jewel.* New York: George Braziller, 1973.

Sklar, Robert. *F. Scott Fitzgerald.* New York: Oxford University Press, 1967.

Smethurst, Richard J. *A Social Basis for Prewar Japanese Militarism.* Berkeley: University of California Press, 1974.

Smith, Henry Dewitt, II. *Japan's First Student Radicals.* Cambridge, Mass.: Harvard University Press, 1972.

————. "Tokyo as an Idea: An Exploration of Japanese Urban Thought Until 1945." *Journal of Japanese Studies* 4 (Winter 1978):45–80.

Smith, Thomas C. "Landlords' Sons in the Business Elite." *Economic Development and Cultural Change,* vol. 9 no. 1, pt. 2 (1960), pp. 93–186.

Sō Sakon. "Ai to ninshiki to no shuppatsu, Dai Ichi Kōtō Gakkō IV." Seishun fudoki 80. *Shūkan Asahi* (January 27, 1978), pp. 99–103.

Sone Toranosuke. "Kōfū shūyōsaku." *Shōshikai zasshi,* no. 8 (December 1894), pp. 9–26.

Spaulding, Robert Miller. *Imperial Japan's Higher Civil Service Examinations.* Princeton: Princeton University Press, 1967.

Stone, Alan. "The Japanese Muckrakers." *Journal of Japanese Studies* 1 (Spring 1975):385–407.

Stone, Lawrence. "Japan and England: A Comparative Study." In *Sociology, History and Education,* edited by P. W. Musgrave. London: Methuen, 1970.

Sugimoto Ryō. "Watashi no sannen ni gakki." *Kōryō Komaba* 9 (October 1967):6–21.

Sumiya Mikio. "Kokuminteki buijon no tōgō to bunkai." In *Kindai Nihon shisōshi kōza,* vol. 5. Tokyo: Chikuma Shobō, 1972.

————. *Dai Nihon Teikoku no shiren.* Nihon no rekishi, vol. 22. Tokyo: Chūō Kōronsha, 1960.

Suzuki Hajime. "Jūdō to Kyōsantō." *Kōryō Komaba* 10 (July 1968):54–55.

Suzuki Tsutomu, ed. *Taishō demokurashī.* Nihon rekishi shirīzu, vol. 20. Tokyo: Sekai Bunkasha, 1967.

Tago Kazutami. "Fujimurasei no jisatsu o ronzu." *Shōshikai zasshi,* no. 57 (November 1903):1–15.

Takahashi Samon. *Kyūsei kōtō gakkō kenkyū.* Tokyo: Shōwa Shuppan, 1978.

Takami Jun. "Kaiketsu Teroren no shi." In *Kishi Michizō tsuitōroku,* edited by Hashimoto Otsuji. Tokyo: Kishi Michizō tsuitōroku Kankōkai, 1963.

Takase Naotomo, ed. *Shōshikai zenshi.* Sendai: Dai Ni Kōtō Gakkō Shōshikai, 1937.

"Takayama Hakushi yuku." *Shōshikai zasshi,* no. 53 (March 1893), pp. 52–53.

Takayama Rintarō [Chogyū]. "Gakkō sōdōron." *Taiyō* 4, no. 14 (July 1898):30–36.

Takayama Shūgetsu. *Kōtō gakkō to sakei mondai.* Tokyo: Nihon Hyōronsha, 1932.

Takeda Kiyoko. "The Christian Encounter with the Traditional Ethos of Japan: A Study of Nitobe Inazō's Ideas." *Asian Cultural Series* (October 1966), pp. 111–145.

———. *Dochaku to haikyō.* Tokyo: Shinkyo Shuppansha, 1967.

Takeuchi Yoshimi. "Kindai no chōkoku." In *Nashonarizumu.* Gendai Nihon shisō taikei, vol. 4. Tokyo: Chikuma Shobō, 1974.

Takeyama Michio. *Harp of Burma.* Translated by Howard Hibbett. Rutland, Vermont: Charles E. Tuttle, 1966.

———. *Momi no ki to bara.* Tokyo: Shinchōsha, 1951.

Takiura Bun'ya. *Kishukusha to seinen no kyōiku.* Kyoto: Tanjun Seikatsusha, 1926.

Talbott, John E. "The History of Education." *Daedalus* 100 (Winter 1971), pp. 133–150.

Tamaki Hajime. *Nihon kyōiku hattatsushi.* Tokyo: San'ichi Shobō, 1954.

Tamaki Motoi. *Nihon gakuseishi.* Tokyo: San'ichi Shobō, 1961.

Tanaka Toru. "Shinrai shokun no shimei o ronjite tokkanshugi ni oyobu." *DIKGKZ,* no. 179 (October 1907), pp. 1–11.

Tazaki Yūzō. "Watakushi no rirekisho." In *Watakushi no rirekisho,* vol. 7. Tokyo: Nihon Keizai Shinbunsha, 1970.

Terasaki Masao. "Jichiryōseido seiritsu shiron." *KKGK,* no. 15 (January 1978), pp. 20–46.

———. "Kyūsei kōkō ni okeru ningen keisei." Master's thesis, Tokyo Daigaku, 1959.

———. "Meiji Gakkōshi no ichi danmen." In *Nihon no kyōikushigaku,* no. 14 (October 1971), pp. 24–44.

———. "Tenkan o semarareru kyōikushi kenkyū." *Mainichi Shinbun,* October 4, 1973.

Tezuka Tomio. *Ichi seinen no shisō no ayumi.* Tokyo: Kōdansha, 1966.

Thayer, Nathaniel B. *How the Conservatives Rule Japan.* Princeton: Princeton University Press, 1969.

Tiger, Lionel. *Men in Groups.* New York: Random House, 1969.

Togawa Yukio. *Hikari hokuchi ni.* Tokyo: Shin Nihon Shuppansha, 1973.

Toita Tomoyoshi. *Kyūsei kōtō gakkō kyōiku no seiritsu.* Kyoto: Mineruva Shobō, 1975.

Tokutomi Iichirō [Sohō]. *Shin Nihon no seinen.* In *Nihon gendai bungaku zenshū,* vol. 2. Tokyo: Kōdansha, 1967.

Tokutomi Kenjirō [Roka]. *Footprints in the Snow.* Translated by Kenneth Strong. New York: Pegasus, 1970.

Tokyo Joshi Daigaku Nitobe Inazō Kenkyūkai. *Nitobe Inazō kenkyū.* Tokyo Shunjūsha, 1969.

Tokyo Shōka Daigaku. *Gakusei seikatsu chōsa hōkoku.* Tokyo: Tokyo Shōka Daigaku, 1934.

Tomatsu Nobuyasu. *Shikō hachijūnen.* Kanazawa: Dai Yon Kōtō Gakkō Dōsōkai, 1967.

Tsubouchi Shōyō. *Tōsei shosei katagi.* In *Nihon no bungaku,* vol. 1. Tokyo: Chūō Kōronsha, 1971.

Tsuji Jirō. "Kōryō no omoide." *Ichikō Dōsōkai kaihō,* no. 36. (January 1938), pp. 45–46.

Tsukuda Toyōo. "Aete kōyū shoshi ni uttau." *DIKGKZ,* no. 81 (1898), pp. 5–12.

Tsurumi Kazuko. *Social Change and the Individual.* Princeton: Princeton University Press, 1970.

Tsurumi Yūsuke. "Ichikō jidai no omoide." *Kōryō Komaba* 1 (October 1959), pp. 25–28.

———. *Ko.* Tokyo: Kadokawa, 1970.

———. "Yo no kōfūron." *DIKGKZ,* no. 151 (November 1905), pp. 1–20.

Tsutsumi Biro. "Jikaku." *DIKGKZ,* no. 105 (June 1901), pp. 39–45.

Turner, Ralph H. "Modes of Social Ascent through Education: Sponsored and Contest Mobility." In *Education, Economy, and Society,* edited by A. H. Halsey, et al. London: Allen and Unwin, 1964.

Uchida Yoshihiko and Shioda Shobei. "Chishiki seinen no shoruikei." In *Kindai Nihon shisōshi kōza,* vol. 4. Tokyo: Chikuma Shobō, 1972.

Uchimura Kanzō. *Uchimura Kanzō chosakushū,* vol. 18. Tokyo: Iwanami, 1954.

Ugata Junzō. "Ryōseikatsu o tsuranuite." *Dai Roku Kōtō Gakkō Kōyūkai zasshi,* no. 53 (June 1919), pp. 23–27.

Uzawa Fusa'aki. "Gakusei to seishin shūyō." *DIKGKZ,* no. 83 (January 1899), pp. 1–16.

Veysey, Lawrence R. *The Emergence of the American University.* Chicago: University of Chicago Press, 1965.

Wakeford, John. *The Cloistered Elite: A Sociological Analysis of the English Public Boarding School.* New York: Praeger, 1969.

Waller, Willard Walter. *The Sociology of Teaching.* New York: Russell & Russell, 1939.

Watsuji Tetsurō. "Seishin o ushinaitaru kōfū." *DIKGKZ,* no. 174 (February 1908), pp. 13–23.

———. *Watsuji Tetsurō zenshū,* vol. 18. Tokyo: Iwanami, 1963.

Waugh, Alec. *Public School Life.* London: W. Collins Sons and Co., 1922.

Weber, Max. *From Max Weber: Essays in Sociology.* Translated and edited by H. H. Gerth and C. Wright Mills. New York: Oxford University Press, 1958.

Weinberg, Ian. *The English Public Schools: The Sociology of Elite Education.* New York: Atherton Press, 1967.

White, James W. "Internal Migration in Prewar Japan." *Journal of Japanese Studies* 4 (Winter 1978):81–123.

Wilensky, Harold L. "Mass Society and Mass Culture: Interdependence or Independence?" *American Sociological Review* 29 (April 1964):173–197.

Wilkinson, Rupert. *Gentlemanly Power.* London: Oxford University Press, 1964.

———. *Governing Elites.* New York: Oxford University Press, 1969.

Yamagata Kōtō Gakkō Gakuryōshi Hensan Iinkai, ed. *Gakuryōshi.* Yamagata: Yamagata Kōtō Gakkō Gakuryōshi Kankōkai, 1938.

Yamamoto Kazuya, ed. *Waga seishun kyūsei kōkō.* Tokyo: Noberu Shobō, 1968.

Yamaoka Hakurō. *Kōryō sannen.* Tokyo: Hakubunkan, 1919.

Yamauchi Fuyuhiko. "Rōjōshugi o ronzu." *DIKGKZ,* no. 119 (September 1902), pp. 1–16.

Yamazaki Nobuki, "Gakufūron," *Shōshikai zasshi,* no. 18 (December 1896), pp. 1–10.

Yanaihara Tadao, ed. *Nitobe Hakushi bunshū.* Tokyo: Ko Nitobe Hakushi Kinen Jigyō Iin Tajima Michio, 1936.

———. *Yo no sonkei suru jinbutsu.* Yanaihara Tadao zenshu, vol. 24. Tokyo: Iwanami, 1965.

Yoshida Kumaji. "Jichiryō ni taisuru yo ga kenkai no kako oyobi genzai." *DIKGKZ,* no. 95 (March 1900), pp. 1–16.

———, ed. *Nihon dōtokuron.* Tokyo: Iwanami, 1935.

Index

Abe Isoo, 224
Abe Jirō, 140, 156, 174, 184, 224, 236, 237; on inner self-exploration, 212–213, 214, 215
Abe Shigetaka, 234
Abe Yoshishige, 156, 170, 171, 178, 184, 185, 186, 232, 236, 237–238, 239
Academic ladder, 4n, 5–6, 24–25, 96–98
Achievement ethic, 4, 5–6, 23–29; broken down, in higher school, 98, 107, 131, 163, 246–247; limits on, in society, 156–157. *See also* Self-improvement, ethic of; Status by achievement
Adolescence (*seishun*), 72, 215; discovery of, and suicide of Fujimura Misao, 172–173; moratorium for, in higher school, 246–248, 250–251, 252, 253; and training of leadership elite, 235
Adolescence Wagered upon a Barricade, 253
Akanuma Kinzaburō, 82–83, 85–87, 158
Akase Yayoki, 164
Akizuki In'ei, 69
Akutagawa Ryūnosuke, 208–209, 215, 217
Allied Occupation of Japan, 230–233
Alumni organizations, 8, 249
Amano Teiyū, 232
"Anguished youth" (*hanmon seinen*), 157, 165, 172–173, 193; and suicide of Fujimura Misao, 165–173

"Animalistic vitality" (*dōbutsuteki genki*), 202, 204
"Anniversary celebrations" (*kinensai*), 87, 92–93, 109–110, 224
Anti-intellectualism of higher school students, 115–116
Aoki Tokuzō, 168, 175, 182
Aoyama Shioya, 175
Arai Tsuneo, 175
Ariès, Philippe, 42
Arnold, Matthew, 123, 192, 208
Arnold, Thomas, 13, 72, 151, 207
Asceticism, 130–131, 153; in school rituals, 113–122, 130–131; of student leftists, 225–226, 229. *See also* Primitivism
Ascription. *See* Status by ascription
Asukai Masamichi, 161
Athletics in higher schools, 113–122; and appeal of totalism, 240, 241; and bureaucratic "team" ethos, 131–132; and conflict with intellectualism, 155, 157, 192–193; heroes of, 119–120; at Ichikō, 122–126; inter-school rivalries in, 118–119; and Kinoshita, 59; leftist interest in, 226; martyrdom theme in, 120; at Osaka Middle School, 36; prestige of, 122–123; relation of, to national prestige, 122–126; and shaping of status and identity, 128–132; shifting role of, 154–156; social tensions reflected in, 123–126; student intellectuals on, 158–159, 164, 165, 173–174; Uozumi Kageo's critique of, 180–182

Austin, Lewis, 249–250
Awano Kenjirō, 162, 164

"Barbarism," 98–99, 165, 201–203. *See also* Primitivism
Bartholomew, James, 4
Baseball, 119, 123–126, 165, 174
Beard, Miriam, 238–239n
Beckett, Samuel, 246
"Bedroll crunch" (*futongan*), 150, 152
Bentham, Jeremy, 20
Black, Hugh, 237
Blos, Peter, 130
Bolshevik Revolution, 222
Bureaucratic civil service, 248–249

Cafeteria riots (*makanai seibatsu*), 88, 144
Camus, Albert, 173
Canby, Henry Seidel, 71, 159
Carlyle, Thomas, 204
Censorship by government, 199–200
Character building (*shūyō*), 162; athletics in, 116–117; defense of self-cultivation and, in 1930s, 234–238; as distinguished from self-cultivation, 162; and exigencies of industrialization, 233–235; in higher school program, 44–53, 157–159; reemphasis on, after 1870s, 30–38; in secondary schools, 34–35
Christianity, 160, 161, 163, 175–176
"Civilization sickness" (*bunmeibyō*), 157, 195
"Cleanliness edicts" (*seiketsuhō*), 202–203
"Clenched-fist punishment" (*tekken seisai*), 26, 147–150, 152, 153, 183–184, 185; disavowed at Ichikō, 240; faculty view of, 151–152; student intellectuals on, 158
"Club-life" (*bu-seikatsu*), 113–122; diversification of, in Taishō, 211, 216–217, 219; leftist student interest in, 224–226
College, American: student rituals of, 127–128; types of students in, 154–155
Compulsory schooling, 4, 5, 22, 195

Comte, Auguste, 20
Conformism in student culture, 136; debates as check on, 193; reinforcement of, 145–147; Uozumi Kageo's critique of, 176–177
Confucianism, 53; in domain schools, 15–16; in higher school pedagogy, 56–57, 58, 68, 69, 72, 79, 81
Connolly, Cyril, 155, 230
Contest mobility, 245
Contract (*kiyaku*) for self-governing dormitories, 79, 83–87, 92, 99–100; negative injunctions to bolster, 137–147; student punishment within, 145–147
Corporal punishment. *See* Punishment, student-initiated
"Costume parades" (*kasō-gyōretsu*), 109–110
Cruelty. *See* Punishment, student-initiated; Rituals, school
Cultivated gentleman ideal, 2, 9, 45–53, 68–70, 151, 153; as ascriptive status, 51–52, 55–56; and inseparability of private and public life, 48, 60, 78; Kinoshita on, 55–57; Meiji reformers critical of, 20–21, 22–23; Nitobe Inazō on, 200–210; pedagogical assumptions about, 47–53; reemphasis on, after 1870s, 30–31; as Samurai ideal in domain school, 15–19; versus training of specialized expert, 2, 16, 29–31, 43, 48–50, 73–75, 196–198, 234–235, 252. *See also* Moral education
Culturalism (*kyōyōshugi*), Taishō, 196
Curriculum in higher schools, 48–50, 68, 72, 73–75, 157–158; Nitobe Inazō's reform of, 203–206; student intellectuals on, 159–160; Taishō reform of, 196–200; Taishō student tastes in, 215–221. *See also* Foreign language instruction

"Dangerous thoughts" (*kiken shisō*), 195, 197, 199–200
Debate Club at Ichikō, 115, 211, 222–223

"Democracy movement," 222, 224
"Deportment point system" (*gyō-jōten seido*), 59
Descartes, Rene, 216
Dewey, John, 16
"Diehard faction" (*gankotō*), 27
"Dinner assemblies" (*bansankai*), 109
Doi Bansui, 160
Domain schools, 14–19, 30–31, 41, 47; compared to higher schools, 68–70, 150; criticized by Meiji reformers, 18, 21
Dore, Ronald, 16, 17, 245
Dormitories, 36–37, 58–59
Dormitories, self-governing, 75, 76–94; alumni recollections of, 93–94; and athletics, 120–122; autocratic features of, 150–153; and constitutional nation-state, 81–82; contract for, 79, 83–87, 92, 99–100; disciplinary jurisdiction for, 140–147; as educational policy, 79–82; leftist use of ideology of, 225; moderate students' defense of, 185–186; Nitobe Inazō's reforms of, 202–203; persistence of, 241; polarization of sexual characteristics in, 152–153; in provincial higher schools, 88–89; significance of, 93–94; social education in, 131–132, 134–135; and student culture, 92–93, 94, 99; student response to, 77, 82–94; Taishō modifications of, 217–221; traditionalistic aspects of, 79–80; Uozumi Kageo on, 177–178, 179–180, 181–182
Dormitory entrance ceremony (*nyūryōshiki*), 102–103
Dormitory entrance speeches (*nyūryō enzetsu*), 102–103
"Dormitory histories" (*ryōshi*), 93
Dormitory inspectors (*shakan*), 59, 78–79, 82
"Dormitory life" (*ryō-seikatsu*), 100–113
"Dormitory rain" (*ryōu*), 111, 112, 126–127, 137, 219
"Dormitory songs" (*ryōka*), 87, 93,

110, 112, 137, 241; softening melodies of, in Taishō, 218

Earthquake of 1923, 193n
Eccentricities (*onchi*) of students, 247–248
Educational Code of 1872, 21, 22–23, 24, 32
Educational furor (*kyōikukyō*), 4–5
Educational Reform Council (Kyōiku Sasshin Iinkai), 231–232
Egi Sadao, 178–179, 184
Eliot, Charles W., 197
Eliot, T.S., 42
Emile, 86
Enomoto Takeaki, 80
Entrance examinations, 4, 22, 69, 246; at Ichikō, 51, 52; literature to prepare for, 97–98
Erickson, Erik, 153
Ethics, teaching of: in early Meiji schools, 20, 23; at Ichikō, 58, 203–204; Nitobe Inazō's method of, 203–204
Eton, 71–73, 77, 249
Executive Committee (Iinkai) in self-governing dormitories, 83–85, 94, 102–103

Family model for higher schools, 47–48, 57–58, 68, 71, 204–205, 241
Farewell parties (*sōbetsukai*), 109
"Female incidents" (*onna jiken*), 139–140
Femininity. *See* Masculinity
Fifth Higher School, 49n, 64, 65, 66, 67, 68, 69–70; clenched-fist punishment at, 150; debate on school spirit at, 187; Hearn on atmosphere at, 150; mythology at, 137; self-governing dormitories at, 88–89
"Fire storm," 110–111
First Higher School. *See* Ichikō
Fitch, Joshua, 127
Fitzgerald, F. Scott, 155
Flag, school, 48; at freshman initiation, 101, 241; at Ichikō, 61–64; persistence of, as symbol, 241; stu-

dent intellectuals on, 158
Foreign language instruction, 32–38; as symbol of status, 36, 50
Forster, E. M., 155
"Four tenets" (shi kōryō), 78, 81, 83, 103, 181; punishments for violation of, 140–141; student intellectuals on, 158
Fourth Higher School, 64, 65, 66, 67, 68; debate on school spirit at, 187; mythology at, 137; study groups at, 161; taboos at, 140
Fraternal associations in domain schools, 17–18
Freud, Anna, 130
Froebel, Friedrich, 86
Fujimura Misao, suicide of, 165–173, 174, 175–176, 178, 193, 196
Fukuda Takeo, 250
Fukui Rikichirō, 182–183
Fukuzawa Yukichi, 15, 18n, 20, 21, 23, 24

Gathorne-Hardy, Jonathan, 155
General Assembly (Sōdaikai) of self-governing dormitories, 83–85, 94
Gentleman ideal. See Cultivated gentleman ideal
Giddings, Franklin, 205
Gilligan, Carol, 250
"Glorious Manifesto," 77–79, 82, 103
Goethe, J. W., 170, 204
Goffman, Erving, 48
Golding, William, 153
Government foreign language schools (kanritsu gaikokugo gakkō), 32–38
Graffiti, 238
Green, T. H., 237
Gymnasium, German, 6, 9, 75n, 188, 198, 210

Halévy, Elie, 71
Hall, G. Stanley, 127
Hall, Ivan, 17n, 35
Hamilton, E. H., 243–244
Harootunian, H. D., 18–19, 190
Harrow, 77, 249
Haruyama Sakuki, 235

Hatoyama Haruko, 133–135, 145
Hatoyama Ichirō, 133–134
Hatta Yoshiake, 132
Hausknecht, Emil, 74–75
Hayakawa Takashi, 246
Hayashi Hisao, 170
Hayashi Kentarō, 239
Headmasters, 9; as defenders of higher schools in public debates, 200, 235–236; pedagogy of, 45–64; posture of, toward self-governing dormitories, 76–82, 87–93, 133–134, 144–145; posture of, toward student rituals, 128, 144, 151–152, 202
Hearn, Lafcadio, 150
Hegel, G. W. F., 165
Herbart, J. F., 47
Hesse, Hermann, 71, 157, 238
Hidaka Daishirō, 239
Higher middle schools (kōtō chūgakkō), 39–40. See also Higher schools
"Higher school barbarism" (kōtō gakkō bābarizumu), 98–99, 201–203. See also Primitivism
Higher school gentleman ideal. See Cultivated gentleman ideal; Warrior gentleman ideal
Higher School Ordinance of 1894, 74–75, 92, 159
Higher schools: alumni loyalty to, 8–9, 232–233, 252–253; and Anglo-American boarding schools, 71–73, 197–198; as arena for adolescent moratorium, 72, 246–248; attendance statistics for, 7, 97, 199, 256, 259; contemporary campaign to revive, 232–233, 252–253; creativity fostered in, 250–251; curriculum of, 48–50, 68, 72, 73–75, 157–158, 159–160, 203–206; defense of, in 1930s, 234–238; and domain schools, 14, 17–18, 68–70, 150; and exigencies of industrialization, 233–235; as family surrogate, 47–48, 57–58, 68, 71, 204–205, 241; founding of, 38–41; and German Gymnasium, 75n; government re-

form proposals in Taishō, 196–200; as institutional barrier for women, 231n, 252; liquidation of, during Allied Occupation, 230–233; manliness versus precocity as goals in, 72–75; nostalgia for, 7–9, 232–233, 252–253; number of, 6–7, 64n, 198–199; political stability fostered by, 131–132, 251; and "pseudo-class" ideology, 252; remedial courses in, 49–50; as sacred cosmos, 136–147; seclusion of, 47, 53–60, 64–70, 71–75; social background of students in, 68–69, 245–246; socialization in, 5–11, 245–253; symbols in, 48, 60–64; as traditionalistic institutions, 45–47, 66–72, 79–80

Higher schools, provincial: careers of alumni of, 249; athletic clubs at, 115, 116; debates on school spirit at, 187–191; expansion of number of, 198–199; foundation of, 64–70; freshmen ritual ordeals at, 104–105; natural setting of, 65–67, 199; self-governing dormitories at, 88–89

Hirai Nobuo, 26

Hirose Yutaka, 18n

Holmes, Lulu H., 231n

Homosexuality, 37, 141, 142, 178–179, 188, 206, 214, 219

Honor, 5, 6, 9, 45, 62, 153

Hosei University, 22

Hozumi Yatsuka, 197

Hughes, Thomas, 133

Hugo, Victor, 152

Huizinga, Johan, 120

Huss, John, 180

Ichikō: ascriptive entrance requirements at, 51–52; architecture and setting of, 76–77; athletics at, 122–126; careers of alumni of, 248–249; class backgrounds of students at, 245–246; establishment of, 51–53; fees and tuition of, 51–52; leftism at, 222–229; military exercises at, 59, 239–240; and nationalism, 60–64; new location for, 76–77; and "new thought wave," 164–165;

Nitobe Inazō's reforms at, 202–210; and pedagogy of seclusion, 53–60; self-governing dormitory system of, 75, 76–94; symbolism of school spirit of, 60–64; Uozumi Kageo on, 173–182; uprisings at, 89, 90, 91–92; watchdog committees at, 142–147; World War II service of students from, 242–243

Ichikō Christian Youth Society, 161, 190–191

Imamura Yūrin, 101, 175

Imbrie Incident, 138–139

Imperial University, 6, 8, 248

"Incidents" (jiken), 138–140

Individualism: incorporated into school spirit, 186–191; limits on, in society, 156–157; Uozumi Kageo on, 176–177. See also Personal self; Self-cultivation

Industrialization, 233–235. See also Modernization

Inoue Kowashi, 73–74, 75, 92, 196

Inoue Tetsujirō, 6, 26, 31, 97, 148, 152, 170n, 197

Intellectuals, student, 141, 153, 154–155, 251; accommodation of, to student culture and outside social order, 189–191; appeal of totalism to, 241–242; versus athletes, 158–159, 192–193; and campus primitivism in Taishō, 219–220; censorship of, 199–200; curricular aims of, 159–160; on Fujimura Misao's suicide, 168–173; as leftists, 224–225, 228–229; moderate faction of, 184–187, 189–190, 206; and "new thought wave," 163–165; position of, improved after school spirit debates, 189–191; on school spirit, 158–159; and seclusion, 158; tensions between private claims and public demands among, 190–192; Uozumi Kageo as, 173–182

Irokawa Daikichi, 24

Ishida Takeshi, 250

Ishimoto Eikichi, 206, 207

Itō Sei, 241n

Iwamoto Tei, 162, 163, 164, 203, 204
Iwanami Shigeo, 170

James, William, 230
Japan: economic growth in, 194–195; international stature of, after Russo-Japanese War, 156–157
Japan University, 253
Jishūkan, 66, 69
Johnson, Owen, 154
Jordan, David S., 13

Kaigo Tokiomi, 238
Kaisei Gakkō, 22, 25–26, 80, 81. See also Tokyo University
Kamei Katsuichirō, 241–242n
Kamishima Jirō, 5, 18–19, 56n, 79–80, 157
Kanō Jigorō, 50
Kanō Kōkichi, 133–135, 176, 228; on communal aspects of dormitory life, 151; compared to Nitobe Inazō, 200–201; educational philosophy of, 143–144; and watchdog committees, 143–147
Kant, Immanuel, 160, 164, 165, 215, 216, 237
Karasawa Tomitarō, 17n, 126n
Katō Hidetoshi, 167n
Kawabata Yasunari, 220
Kawai Eijirō, 156, 206, 224, 236–239, 243, 246
Kawakami Hajime, 223
Kawakami Tetsutarō, 242n
Keiō University, 22, 23
Kett, Joseph, 94
Kido Kōin, 20, 38
Kikuchi Dairoku, 196
Kikuchi Kan, 209
Kinmonth, Earl, 167
Kinoshita Hiroji, 53–60, 200; on adolescence, 72; on nation-school bond, 60–64; and self-governing dormitory system, 75, 76–82, 83, 86, 92; on student-initiated discipline, 151, 152; taboos defended by, 139
Kiriyama Benroku, 27–29
Kitamura Tōkoku, 160, 164

Kitazawa Teikichi, 158
Koeber, Raphael, 160, 161
Koganei Ryosei, 25
Kohlberg, Lawrence, 250
Kojima Nobuo, 252
Kokutai ideology in higher school culture, 238–245
Komatsubara Eitarō, 196n
Komatsu Shūichi, 38
Komishima Jirō, 209
Kristol, Irving, 221–222
Kubota, Akira, 249
Kuhara Kyūgen, 61–62, 90, 92
Kume Masao, 209
Kurata Hyakuzō, 209, 236, 237; on exploration of inner self, 212–215; totalism of, 241
Kuriyagawa Hakuson, 160
Kuwaki Genyoku, 160, 203, 236
Kyoto University, 222

Lasswell, Harold, 95
Law on Public Meetings, 29
Levenson, Joseph, 9, 68
Lewis, Sinclair, 155
Lipps, Theodor, 237
Literary studies (bun), 60, 68
Longfellow, H. W., 204
Lowell, A. Lawrence, 57
Loyalty to school, 5, 48, 59–64; changes in meaning of, 9; Orita's reforms for, 35, 36–37; rituals as reinforcement of, 131–132. See also School spirit
Lycée, French, 198

Maeda Tamon, 184, 185, 186
Magazines, school, 87–88, 92, 115, 116; intellectuals grouped around, 158–159; "new thought wave" in, 164–165; Taishō student interest in, 216–217
Mainstream Society (Chūkenkai), 143, 144, 145, 240; and "clenched-fist punishment," 147–150
"Mandatory residence system" (kaikishuku seido), 77–79. See also Dormitories, self-governing
Mann, Thomas, 157

Mannheim, Karl, 57
Marshall, Byron, 74n
Martial arts (*bu*), 16, 68
Martyr, Graham, 132
Maruyama Masao, 94n, 239, 242n
Marxism, 196, 222, 228–229, 234
Masculinity, 6, 17–18, 93; Kinoshita
    Hiroji on, 56, 151; versus femi-
    ninity, 27–28, 116, 138–140, 152–153,
    241; versus precocity, 72–75; rites
    of, 99–112; and sports, 116–117
Mashita Shin'ichi, 246–247
Materialism, 45, 156–157, 195–196
Matriculation ceremony
    (*nyugakushiki*), 101–102
Matsue Higher School, 227
Matsuoka Yuzuru, 209
Matsuyama Higher School, 227
Matsuzaki Kuranosuke, 197
May Fourth Movement, 10
Mazaki Sorō, 18
Meiji Gakuin, 138–139
Meiji Restoration: educational re-
    form in, 4–6, 18–23, 29–38; and
    modernization, 2–6; students dur-
    ing, 23–29
Meiji University, 22
Men of noble purpose (*shishi*), 18–19
Middle School Ordinance of 1886,
    39–40, 48–49
Middle schools, 22; attendance sta-
    tistics for, 96–97; and Mori
    Arinori, 38–41; and new middle
    class, 96–98; reforms in, 32–41; up-
    risings at, 90–91
Militarism, 231, 232; and higher
    school students, 239–245
Mill, John Stuart, 20, 243
Mills, C. Wright, 7
Mitani Takanobu, 162
Miwa Kimitada, 209
Miyake Setsurei, 31, 33–34, 193
Miyasaka Tetsufumi, 79
Miyoshi Aikichi, 151
"Modern boys" (*mobo*), 194, 196, 221
"Modern girls" (*moga*), 194, 251
Modernization: and education, 2–6,
    245–253; higher school's contribu-
    tion to, 233–235, 250–253; re-

sistance to, in higher school cul-
    ture, 241–242; and socialization,
    249–253
"Monasticism" (*rōjōshugi*), 180, 181,
    185–186, 205–206. *See also* Seclu-
    sion, theory of
Moral education, 43–45, 250; de-
    fended by student intellectuals,
    159; in early Meiji schools, 20, 23;
    Nitobe Inazō on, 205–206; re-
    emphasized after 1870s, 30–38; in
    Tokugawa domain school, 15–17.
    See also Cultivated gentleman ideal
Mori Arinori, 38–41, 43, 44, 46, 49,
    53, 55, 56, 66, 73
Mori Gesaburō, 239
Mori Ōgai, 27, 28, 37
Mori Ritsuko, 139
Morito Tatsuo, 206, 211, 212
Moriyama Tsunetarō, 119, 130, 155
Motoda Eifū, 30, 31
Musil, Robert, 154, 157

Nagai Kafū, 96
Najita, Tetsuo, 4
Nakagawa Gen, 52, 67, 200
Nakagawa Zennosuke, 233n
Nakajima Takanao, 210–211
Nakamura Kōhei, 158
Nakamura Sannosuke, 214
Nakano Yoshio, 167, 241–242n
Nambara Shigeru, 5
"Name schools," 199
Naruse Mukyoku, 149, 171–172
National service: as aim of educa-
    tion, 38–41, 43–45, 241; and Ichikō
    spirit, 60–64; Nitobe Inazō on,
    209–210; and school loyalty, 48
Natsume Sōseki, 58–59, 116, 160, 161,
    162, 175
Neoromanticism, 160, 163, 202
New middle class, 96–98, 194–195,
    245–246
"New self," 228–229
"New thought wave" (*shinshichō*),
    160, 163–165; and reaction to sui-
    cide of Fujimura Misao, 168–173
Nietzsche, Friedrich, 11, 170, 177
Nishi Amane, 20

Nishida Kitarō, 160, 161, 212–213, 214, 237
Nishimura Shigeki, 30, 31, 75n
Nitobe Inazō, 22–23, 29–30, 146, 151–152, 224–225, 228; compared to Kanō Kōkichi, 200–201; educational philosophy of, 200–210; student response to, 206–209; on technicians, 252; and totalism, 241
Noda Heijirō, 59–60, 139, 158
Nogi Maresuke, 203
Normal schools, 44, 52, 157; behavioral norms in, 5; uprisings in, 90–91
Norman, E. H., 3
"Number schools," 199

Obara Kuniyoshi, 235
"Off-campus recreational clubs" (kōgai yūgibu), 114
Ogata School, 18n
Okakura Tenshin, 61
Okano Yoshisaburō, 227, 228
Ōkawa Shūmei, 187
"Old bushi types" (kobushi no tenkei), 50, 68, 69, 174–175, 204; ceremonial role of, 159–160; compared to "teachers of life," 162
Ōmuro Teiichirō, 172, 216, 220
Ordinary middle schools (jinjō chūgakkō), 39, 40
Orita Hikoichi, 35–37, 41, 48, 50, 65, 151–152, 228
Orwell, George, 155
Osaka English Academy, 33
Osaka Middle School, 33, 35–37, 65
Ōtsuka Motoe, 193
Ōtsuyama Kinnosuke, 117
Ōyama Ikuo, 224

Palmer, R. R., 2
Passin, Herbert, 134
Peer group solidarity: and club-life rituals, 113–114, 117–119; and dormitory rituals, 92–93, 98–99, 101, 107, 108–112, 128–132; and punishment, 151; student revolt against, 153, 154–158, 164–166, 168–182

Personalism (jinkakushugi), 248, 250, 252
Personal self: as antithesis of egoism, 186; as apotheosis of status, 221; and breaking down of old bourgeois identity, 246–248; defense of, in 1930s, 235–238; and "new self," 228–229; in Taishō, 208, 209, 210–221, 223
Pestalozzi, J. H., 86
Philosophy in higher schools: student interest in, 215–216; teachers influenced by, in late 1890s, 160–163
"Political youth" (seiji seinen), 55
Porter, Noah, 151
Power elite: higher school alumni in, 248–250
Practical learning (jitsugaku), 15
Pranks (itazura), 247–248
Precocity, 39, 72
Primary schools, 22, 38, 39, 195; behavioral norms in, 5; socialization in, 43–44
Primitivism, 99, 126, 127–128, 153, 158; as cross-cultural phenomenon, 127–128, 153; Nitobe Inazō's campaign against, 202–203; persistence of, 219–220, 240; in school rituals, 111–112, 128, 129; Uozumi Kageo's critique of, 177, 180–181
Private academies, 18, 19–20, 22
Privatization: disdain of, in higher school student culture, 131, 141–142, 145–147; and self-cultivation, 211–221
"Public opinion" (yoron), as control on student behavior, 140–141, 145–146
Public school, British, 6, 8, 9, 17, 54, 94, 132, 152n, 188, 198, 210, 244; compared to higher school, 71–73, 128n, 132; relative deprivation in, 111; rituals in, 127–128; student types in, 154–155
Punishment, student-initiated: criticized by intellectuals, 189; faculty approval of, 151–152; persistence of, 240–241; reasons for, 150–153;

as students' jurisdiction, 140–150; as totalistic response, 153. *See also* "Clenched-fist punishment"
Pyle, Kenneth, 195

Rebellion, student: in domain schools, 17n, 18–19; in higher school subculture, 135–136; Uozumi Kageo's, 173–182
"Repeaters" (*rakudaisei*), 247
Rice Riots, 222
Richardson, Bradley, 249–250
Rites of initiation, 100–107; significance of, 127–132; toughening of, 142
Rites of intensification, 100, 108–112; in day-to-day customs, 108, 110–112; periodic observances as, 108–110; significance of, 126–132; and "uncivilized" lifestyle, 111–112
Rituals, school: as antithesis of competitive ethos of outside society, 98–99; asceticism in, 113–122; as career preparation, 131–132; as cross-cultural phenomena, 127–128, 132, 152; "clenched-fist punishment" as, 147–150; lack of study of, 126–127; and leftist students, 225; of masculinity, 99–112; sexual polarizations in, 152–153; and shaping of status and identity, 128–132; significance of, 126–132; student intellectuals on, 164–165; Taishō modifications of, 217–218; as totalistic, 153; and transformation of school setting into sacred cosmos, 136–147; Uozumi Kageo's critique of, 177–182
Rolland, Romain, 238
Room parties (*konpa*), 110–111, 217
Roosevelt, Theodore, 156
"Rough faction" (*kōha*), 27–29
Rousseau, J. J., 86
Rugby, 249
Russell, Bertrand, 133
Russo-Japanese War, 155, 156, 174–175

Saint Paul's, 71–73
Saitō Tokutarō, 17n

Saitō Yoshie, 145–146, 149
Sakanoue no Tamuramaro, 61, 101
Samurai class: domain school socialization of, 14–19; and higher school student backgrounds, 68–69, 245–246; higher school student identification with, 67, 110; university students drawn from, 6; values of, 6
Santarō's Diary (*Santarō no nikki*), 7–8, 212–213, 214, 215, 216
Sawayanagi Masatarō, 193
School spirit (*kōfū*), 48, 60–64, 68; and athletics, 115–116; change in meaning of, in Taishō, 220–221; debates about, 192–193, 210–211; and Fujimura Misao's suicide, 171–173; graffiti as evidence of, 238; individualism incorporated into, 186–191; intellectual justifications of, 158–159; nationalism and, 48, 51, 60–64, 68, 182–183, 241; negative injunctions to reinforce, 137–147; new synthesis of, 182–187, 208–209; persistence of, 241; revitalization of, 141–147; and school rituals, 108–112, 131–132; students as defenders of, 75, 85–87, 92–93; Uozumi Kageo's critique of, 179–182
School system: changes in, during Allied Occupation, 230–233; in early Meiji period, 19–23; as ladder, 4n, 5–6, 24–25, 96–98; impact on social structure, 245–253; modernizing and traditionalistic counter-currents in, 4–6; reforms of 1880s, 32–33, 43–45; Taishō government reform proposals for, 196–200; tracks in, 44–45
Schopenhauer, Arthur, 160, 216
Seclusion, theory of (*rōjōshugi*): and dormitory contract, 83; in higher school pedagogy, 47, 53–60, 64–70, 71–75; and initiation of freshmen, 101; intellectualism fostered by, 158; Kanō Kōkichi on, 143–144; Nitobe Inazō on, 205–206; and self-governing dormitories, 80–81, 83; sociality as balance for, 205–

206; and student rituals, 99, 101; Tokugawa feudal aspects of, 56–57

Secondary education, 32–38

Second Higher School, 64, 65, 66–67, 68; "clenched-fist punishment" in, 150; debate on school spirit at, 187–188; study groups in, 161; up-risings at, 89–90, 91, 92, 227

"Self-cultivation" (*kyōyō*): defense of, in 1930s, 235–238; and exigencies of industrialization, 233–235; as pedagogical ideal of "teachers of life," 162; and susceptibility to totalism, 238–245; as Taishō cultural norm, 211–221, 223. *See also* Personal self

Self-government (*jichi*). *See* Dormitories, self-governing

Self-improvement, ethic of (*risshin shusse*), 14; and academic competition, 96–98; criticized by intellectuals, 159; Meiji reformers on, 21–22, 23–29

Seto Toraki, 81–82

Setting out with Love and Understanding, 212–215, 216

Seventh Higher School, 14n, 97

Shakespeare, William, 169–170

Sheldon, Robert, 128–129

Shimazaki Tōson, 160

Shinobu Seisaburō, 223n

Shioya Yutaka, 91–92

Shōka Village School, 18n

Sinclair, Upton, 155

Singer, Kurt, 104

Sixth Higher School, 97, 187, 227

Smith, Henry D., 24, 222, 226, 228–229

Social Darwinism, 9, 97, 129, 154–155

Social education, 131–132, 134–135

"Sociality" (*soshiarichī*), 205–206, 207–208, 209, 210

Socialization, 9–10; as aim of educational reform, 34, 43–44; higher schools' role in, 5–11, 246–253; and mechanisms of cultivation, 45–53; and modernization, 249–251; in Taishō, 193–196; teachers' role in, 9–10; in Tokugawa domain schools, 14–19. *See also* Dormitories, self-governing; Peer group solidarity; Rituals, school; Seclusion, theory of

Social mobility, 14; academic achievement as aid to, 245–247, 248–250; and early Meiji school reforms, 4–5, 20–21, 22–29; fees and tuition as barrier to, 52; limits on, 52, 156–157; after Russo-Japanese War, 156–157; sponsored versus contest, 245

Social structure, impact of education on, 2–6, 245–253

Social Studies Research Club, 224–226, 228–229

Society for Moral Reform, 142, 150

Society for Moral Restoration, 142–143

Society of Friends (*Kōyūkai*), 114–116

"Soft faction" (*nanpa*), 27–29

Special Council on Education, 197–200, 210

Spencer, Herbert, 31, 86

Sponsored mobility, 245

Status, affirmation of, 221, 249–250; as aim of higher schools, 41; at Ichikō, 51–53

Status by achievement: in early private academies, 19; as goal of Meiji reforms, 21–22; and higher schools, 68–69, 245–246, 248–250; and Mori Arinori, 38–39, 41; and school admissions, 4, 5, 245–246; and socialization, 5–6, 246–250

Status by ascription, 4–6, 6n, 41; criticized by Meiji reformers, 21; and gentleman ideal, 55–56; and higher school entrance exams, 69; and higher school experience, 131–132, 245, 248–250, 252; at Ichikō, 51–52; personal self as apotheosis of, 221; reinforced in domain schools, 15–17, 19, 21; and school admissions, 4, 5, 51–52, 245–246; and school rituals, 131–132

"Storms," 151, 193; destructiveness of, 141, 150; persistence of, 219; student efforts to contain, 141; stu-

dent intellectuals on, 158. *See also*
"Welcome storms"
Storry, Richard, 8
Stover at Yale, 154, 155
Students, higher school: as "anguished youth," 157, 165–173; appeal of totalism to, 238–245; careers after graduation, 248–250; class backgrounds of, 68–69, 245–246; dedication to self-cultivation, 238–245; lack of identification with masses, 10, 246–253; leftist, 222–229; physical bearing and style, 1–2, 6, 7–8; pranks and eccentricities, 247–248
"Student series" (*gakusei sōsho*), 236–238
Study groups, 160–161
Study of Goodness, 212–213, 214
"Success youth" (*seikō seinen*), 156–157
Suehiro Izutarō, 206–207
Sugawara Michizane, 61, 101
Suge Torao, 162
Suicide, 165–173, 175–176
Suita Junsuke, 168
Suzuki Hajime, 226
Suzuki Yasuzō, 216
Sword dances (*kenbu*), 109, 110, 136, 139

Taboos, 138–147
Taishō, higher schools in, 192–229
Takami Jun, 117
Takayama Chogyū, 90, 92, 116, 160, 161, 164, 170, 172
Takayama Shūgetsu, 228, 248
Takeyama Michio, 242–243
Tales of the Ichikō Soul, The, 119–120, 154
Tanaka Tōru, 206
Taniyama Shohichirō, 81, 209
Taoka Reiun, 193
Tea assemblies (*sawakai*), 109–110, 118, 136
Teachers, 50; changes in types of, in late 1890s, 160–163; in domain schools, 16; and dormitory life, 151–152; as dormitory inspectors,

59; in early Meiji schools, 23, 25; foreign, 23, 25, 32, 33–34, 36; role of, in student socialization, 9–10. *See also* "Old *bushi* types"; "Teachers of life"
"Teachers of life" (*jinsei no kyōshi*), 161–163, 164, 174, 200, 203, 204
"Technical course" (*senmon gakka*), 49, 74, 75, 92
Technical schools (*senmon gakko*), 44
Temperament of Present-Day Students, The, 26–29
Tennyson, Alfred Lord, 204
Terasaki Masao, 79–80
Tezuka Tomio, 1–2, 241
Third Higher School, 35n, 64, 65, 67, 68; debate on school spirit at, 187; self-governing dormitories in, 88; vocational curriculum at, 74
Thoreau, Henry David, 177
Thring, Edward, 95
Tocqueville, Alexis de, 57
Tokugawa Bakufu, 3, 19
Tokugawa period, 3–4; domain schools in, 14–19
Tokutomi Roka, 24–25, 28, 135, 193, 222–223
Tokutomi Sohō, 18n, 31, 46–47, 68, 193–194
Tokyo, 95–96
Tokyo English Academy, 33, 37
Tokyo School of Commerce, 123
Tokyo University, 22, 23, 53, 160, 222
Tokyo University Preparatory School, 33, 37, 51, 80. *See also* Ichikō
Tom Brown's Schooldays, 154, 155
Total institution, higher school as, 48, 100, 172
Totalism, appeal of, to higher school students, 153, 238–245
Toyama Shōichi, 75n
Tsubouchi Shōyō, 26–29, 114
Tsukamoto Ryūgai, 164
Tsukuda Toyōo, 158
Tsuneto Kiyoshi, 209
Tsurumi Kazuko, 242

Tsurumi Yūsuke, 183, 184, 186, 189–190, 236
Tsutsumi Biro, 190

Uchida Masao, 20
Uchimura Kanzō, 63–64, 160–161
Uniforms, school, 60–61, 83, 241
United States Education Mission Report, 230–231, 232
University, 22, 38–39, 40; attendance statistics, 97; centered in Tokyo in 1870s, 24–25; higher school as preparation for, 197–199
"Unwritten constitution" (fubun no kenpō), 137–138, 146, 147
Uozumi Kageo, 173–182, 189, 213; student attacks on, 182–187
Uprisings (sōdō), 138; and limits of student self-government, 87–93; by student leftists, 226–228
Utilitarianism (jitsurishugi): criticized after 1870s, 29–38; headmasters on, 45; intellectuals on, 159–160; in schools in Meiji period, 20–23
Uzawa Fusa'aki, 165

"Victory storm," 118
Vocational schools, 44, 97
Vocational training in higher schools, 49–50; calls for, in 1930s, 234–235; debated after Mori's assassination, 73–75; student disdain for, 67, 75, 89–92; in Taishō government reform proposals, 196–200

Wada Heishirō, 17n
Wada Ichirō, 165
Wagashuguan, 155, 156
Wakatsuki Reijirō, 63
Warrior gentleman ideal, 14–19, 46, 67
Warrior prowess (bu), 60, 68
Waseda University, 22
Washington, George, 149

Watchdog committees, 142–147, 150
Watsuji Tetsurō, 100, 111, 206
Waugh, Alec, 192
Weber, Max, 16, 132, 136
"Welcome storm" (kangei sutōmu), 105–107, 110, 136; and hazing, 128; in interwar period, 240
White, James W., 96
"Winter exercises" (kangeiko), 117, 120, 127
Women: barred from academic ladder, 5; taboos about, in student subculture, 139–140, 146, 147–148, 152–153, 220, 241, 252. See also Masculinity
Women's secondary schools, 44
Wordsworth, William, 169

Yamagata Motoharu, 162, 243
Yamaji Aizan, 31, 46–47, 238
Yamakawa Kenjirō, 197
Yamamoto Yūzō, 209
Yamazaki Kyōsuke, 232
Yamazaki Nobuki, 68
Yanaihara Tadao, 115, 156, 206, 243
Yokoyama Taikan, 169
Yoshida Kumaji, 234–235
Yoshida Noboru, 238
Yoshida Osao, 164
Yoshida Shōin, 18
Yoshimura Toratarō, 46, 89–90, 91
Yoshino Sakuzō, 222, 223, 224
Youth: crisis of, after Russo-Japanese War, 156–157; in late Meiji Japan, 193–196
Youth culture: diversification of, in Taishō, 194–196; in domain school, 17–19; in early Meiji Japan, 23–29; and self-governing dormitories, 92–93, 94. See also Students, higher school
"Youth groups" (seinendan), 195

Zōshikan, 17–18

Designer:	Barbara Llewellyn
Compositor:	G&S Typesetters
Printer:	Thomson-Shore, Inc.
Binder:	Thomson-Shore, Inc.
Text:	VIP Palatino
Display:	VIP Palatino
Cloth:	Holliston Roxite B 53544
Paper:	55 lb P&S regular